When Sorry Isn't Enough

Critical America
General Editors: RICHARD DELGADO and JEAN STEFANCIC

The Empire Strikes Back:
Outsiders and the Struggle over Legal Education
Arthur Austin

Interracial Justice:
Conflict and Reconciliation in Post–Civil Rights America
Eric K. Yamamoto

Black Men on Race, Gender, and Sexuality:
A Critical Reader
Edited by Devon Carbado

When Sorry Isn't Enough:
The Controversy over Apologies and Reparations for Human Injustice
Edited by Roy L. Brooks

When Sorry Isn't Enough

The Controversy over Apologies and
Reparations for Human Injustice

Edited by
Roy L. Brooks

NEW YORK UNIVERSITY PRESS · New York & London

NEW YORK UNIVERSITY PRESS
New York and London

Library of Congress Cataloging-in-Publication Data
When sorry isn't enough : the controversy over apologies and
reparations for human injustice / edited by Roy L. Brooks.
p.   cm.
"This anthology is a collection of essays, written by both
internationally renowned and emerging scholars, and of public
documents that concern claims from around the world that seek
redress for human injustice."—Preface.
Includes bibliographical references and index.
ISBN 0-8147-1331-9 (cloth : alk. paper)
ISBN 0-8147-1332-7 (pbk. : alk. paper)
1. Social justice. 2. Claims. I. Brooks, Roy L. (Roy Lavon),
1950–
HM671 .W48 1999
303.3'72—dc21   99-6248
                            CIP

New York University Press books are printed on acid-free paper,
and their binding materials are chosen for strength and durability.

Manufactured in the United States of America

10 9 8 7 6 5 4 3 2 1

To Joe Feagin

and in memory of A. Leon Higginbotham, Jr.

Contents

Preface

This anthology brings together essays, written by both internationally renowned and emerging scholars, and public documents concerning claims from around the world that seek redress for human injustice. My ambition is to provide readers with an intellectual and informational foundation to understand the controversy over redressing human injustice and to pursue on their own further investigation into the ugly side of human nature.

Part 1 of the book sketches some larger themes surrounding the issue of redress (e.g., why nations apologize, women as special targets of injustice, "blood money" versus "atonement money," the meaning of "human injustice," a theory of redress, and the forms of redress) and provides a template for raising deeper questions. Parts 2–8 focus on individual redress claims asserted during the nineteenth and twentieth centuries. These are among the most important claims ever made: victims of Nazi persecution, American racism, and South African Apartheid, to name a few. Each part begins with an introduction that summarizes the essays around a thematic issue. The essays provide factual information about the injustice committed (including victim narratives) and the claims asserted. Arguments concerning the propriety or fairness of redress are presented on both sides. An appendix lists many other significant acts of injustice that could not be included in the collection because of space limitations.

Some of the terminology (in particular the term "reparations") is more precisely developed in Part 1 and the introductory essays than in other chapters. Reading Part 1 and the introductory essays is, therefore, important for a thoughtful reading of the rest of the book. Finally, I would like to bring to the reader's attention, most of the reprinted documents are reprinted in part.

I owe a debt of gratitude to several people. Hugh Kim, Abby Snyder, and Mary E. Smith, each of whom has contributed an essay, provided excellent research assistance and helpful suggestions. Kim and Snyder were particularly instrumental in the initial conceptualization of the project. Richard Delgado and Jean Stefancic of the University of Colorado Law School brought the project to my attention along with many useful suggestions. Niko Pfund of New York University Press has been an enthusiastic supporter of the project from the beginning. Thanks also to Despina Papazoglou Gimbel, managing editor, and Andrew Katz, desktop publishing manager, for their superb work on the manuscript. My secretary, Roanne Shamsky, as always, produced draft after draft without complaint.

Roy L. Brooks
San Diego, California,
1999

1 | Introduction

1 | The Age of Apology

Roy L. Brooks

"Man's inhumanity to man makes countless thousands mourn." So wrote the poet Robert Burns two centuries ago. Burns was looking back over centuries of human injustices. But even now, long after the Enlightenment, we have not been able to reverse our proclivity to commit acts of injustice. Emotion still triumphs over reason, anger over restraint, and hate over love. Perhaps the only thing that has significantly changed through the centuries is the human capacity to say "I'm sorry."

Mea culpa is not a post-Enlightenment sentiment, of course. Forever etched in Western culture as the symbol of remorse is the image of Henry IV standing barefoot and repentant at the castle of Pope Gregory VII in 1077. The excommunicated Holy Roman Emperor sought forgiveness from his papal adversary for having bickered with him over the question of lay investiture. But with apologies coming from all corners of the world—Britain's Queen Elizabeth apologizing to the Maori people; Australia to the stolen aboriginal children; the Canadian government to the Canadian Ukrainians; President Bill Clinton to many groups, including native Hawaiians and African American survivors of the Tuskegee, Alabama, syphilis experiment; South Africa's former president F. W. de Klerk to victims of Apartheid; and Polish, French, and Czech notables for human injustices perpetrated during World War II—we have clearly entered what can be called the "Age of Apology."

What is happening is more complex than "contrition chic," or the canonization of sentimentality. The apologies offered today can be described as "a matrix of guilt and mourning, atonement and national revival." Remorse improves the national spirit and health. It raises the moral threshold of a society. German society is a much better place today because Germans have been forced, and have forced themselves, to face their guilt with deep humility and penitence. So painful and enduring is the moral stain on the German soul that it may lend some truth to

3

Socrates' argument that it is better to be the victim than the perpetrator of an injustice.

Heartfelt contrition just might signify a nation's capacity to suppress its next impulse to harm others. The significance of this point cannot be overstated. Before working on this book, I was not conscious of the undercurrent of fear that exists among survivors of human injustices that the very same atrocity might be revisited upon them. Jews fear that the Holocaust could be repeated, if not in Germany then in some other nation in the "civilized world," and Japanese Americans worry that relocation and internment could happen again on American soil, given the right set of circumstances. Head-bowed apologies from the leaders of Germany and the United States have only quieted the survivors' apprehension. But without such apologies, there would be greater concern, perhaps not just among the survivors, that those shameful acts might be repeated.

One of the questions that arises from this book is whether some societies have a natural proclivity to do evil. There is enough information in this book to conclude, comfortably, that *all* societies have the capacity to do evil. No society holds a monopoly on the commission of human injustices, nor is any society exempted. To Max Frankel's question—"Is there a beast in each of us waiting to be unleashed by extraordinary fear, greed or fury?"—I would have to answer, yes.

Many of the most heinous acts can be attributed to the military gone amok during times of war. Examples include Japanese soldiers raping and torturing three hundred thousand civilians within a three-month period in Nanking, China, during World War II; American GIs slaughtering 504 women, children, and old men in four hours at the Vietnamese village of My Lai during the Vietnam War; and Argentine Navy officials throwing as many as fifteen hundred suspected leftist dissidents into the ocean from airplanes (the so-called "death flights") during Argentina's "Dirty War" (1976–1983).

Most human injustices, however, can be tied directly to conscious political choice. Millions of Jews, Gypsies, and others were murdered as a result of Nazi policy before and during World War II. Millions of blacks were killed and millions more enslaved under three centuries of American domestic policy. Thousands of Native Americans were killed and mistreated under similar policies. And millions of blacks were killed and subjugated by a ruling white minority through Apartheid policies in South Africa.[1]

Women seem to occupy an especially precarious position during times of war. Not only are women victims of the same injustices as men (e.g., slavery, assault, torture, looting, burning), but they are often singled out for additional sexual and reproductive brutalities (rape, sexual mutilation, and forced prostitution, sterilization, impregnation, and maternity). Throughout history, men have sexually abused women during times of war (and to an alarming extent during times of peace). Seen as an inevitability of war—a sort of "boys will be boys" extreme—rape is a historically well-documented war strategy that is highly effective for terrorizing the enemy.

In medieval times, unpaid soldiers' only "compensation" was the opportunity to rape and pillage. As George Hicks notes in his contribution to this anthology, during the Crusades the king conscripted women to follow behind the troops to provide sexual services on demand. Some reports estimate that Allied soldiers raped more than one hundred thousand women in Berlin during the last two weeks of World War II. Also during World War II, approximately two hundred thousand Korean, Chinese, Filipino, Indonesian, and other women were forced into sexual slavery as "comfort women" for the Japanese military.

Catharine A. MacKinnon argues that rape during war is not just a harm that one enemy army does to another; it is also one gender enforcing domination over another. Rape occurs "among and between sides" and "the fact that these rapes are part of [a war] . . . means that . . . women are facing twice as many rapists with twice as many excuses, two layers of men on top of them rather than one, and two layers of impunity serving to justify the rapes: just war and just life."[2] Perhaps this argument sheds some light on the otherwise unexplainable estimate by Joan Furey, director of the Center for Women's Affairs at the Veterans Administration, that approximately half of American nurses were raped by *American GIs* while serving in Vietnam.

Making matters worse, the international human rights community has largely ignored women's issues. "What happens to women is either too particular to be universal or too universal to be particular, meaning either too human to be female or too female to be human," MacKinnon contends.[3] Mass rapes and other sexual assaults, long ago established as war crimes, are not prosecuted in war tribunals as often as other war crimes. The cultural barriers to prosecuting rape in the United States exist in other countries as well. Silence about sexual atrocities is the norm, and shame is routinely placed on the victims of rape rather than the perpetrators. For example, Muslim victims of recent mass rapes in Bosnia are considered soiled and unmarriageable in Muslim culture. Some traditional Muslims believe that killing or exiling rape victims is the only way for husbands and families to cleanse themselves of their family shame.

Genocidal rape—mass rape for the purpose of eliminating unwanted ethnic groups from a territory—is a particularly egregious war crime that targets women. The Serbian rape of Bosnian women was implemented for this ghastly purpose. Serbians believe that a father's sperm carries the genetic make-up of his baby, which means that all babies conceived from the mass rapes are Serbian. Hence, Serbian rapes were designed to remove Bosnian Muslims from disputed territory and populate remaining Muslim areas with Serbians.

In 1997, Bosnian Serb leader Radovan Karadzic was convicted in absentia in an American court for masterminding a genocidal rape strategy that involved approximately twenty thousand victims. This verdict has only symbolic significance because it can be enforced only if Karadzic enters the United States. One could not construct a more powerful argument in favor of an international criminal court with extensive jurisdictional reach.

Rather than relying on the community of nation-states to bring criminal proceedings against perpetrators of human injustices, the victims can take matters into their own hands by seeking civil redress—money or other forms of relief—from the perpetrators under certain conditions. Civil redress is a central focus of this book. However, some victims of human injustices find such redress morally objectionable. They see it as little more than "blood money." While one must, of course, be sensitive to the concerns of the victims, I do not equate redress with "blood money," nor do the many victims who seek monetary redress. True, a price cannot and should not be placed on suffering exacted by the Holocaust, Japanese American internment, African American slavery, and the like. But when rights are ripped away, the victim or his family is entitled to compensation and much more.

The essays in this book discuss various conditions that are necessary for successful redress of human injustices. These conditions can be woven into a *theory of redress*, which has four elements. First, the demands or claims for redress must be placed in the hands of legislators rather than judges. Legislators, quite simply, can do more than judges. In every nation of the world, the judiciary has the least lawmaking authority of any branch of government. "If it be true that the Cherokee Nation have rights," Chief Justice John Marshall of the United States Supreme Court said in *The Cherokee Nation v. Georgia*, "this is not the tribunal in which these rights are to be asserted. If it be true that wrongs have been inflicted, and still greater are to be apprehended, this is not the tribunal which can redress the past or prevent the future."[4] This message is particularly instructive because it comes from a judicial tribunal that probably has more lawmaking power than any other judiciary in the world.

Courts do, however, play a useful role in the redress process. They can and have been used to interpret and enforce extant rights and laws handed down by the legislature. Sometimes the legislature will create a court or quasijudicial body for the specific purpose of resolving redress claims. This happened in the United States with the creation of the now-defunct Indian Claims Commission. But most of the time, the highest court in the land can only apply existing rights and remedies; it cannot create new ones.

Within the legislative realm, successful redress movements have been able to reach the hearts and minds of lawmakers and citizens alike. But the success of any redress movement has depended largely on the degree of pressure (public and private) brought to bear upon the legislators—that is, politics—than with matters of logic, justice, or culture. Political pressure, then, is the second condition necessary for successful redress. This is a clear acknowledgment of the fact that not all meritorious claims succeed. Intuitions of public policy, the prejudices that legislators share with their constituencies, the willingness of political leaders to step forward and take political risks, and the simple exchange of favors have had a good deal more to do with the fate of redress than have the merits of the claims.

Strong internal support is a third element of successful redress. The victims themselves must exhibit unquestioned support for the claims being pressed. Redress must be a top priority within the group. Indeed, it is the absence of this element from the African American redress movement that, in my judgment, is most responsible for the refusal of American political leaders (including President Clinton, who has been more attentive to African American concerns than any other American president) to offer even an apology for slavery or Jim Crow. The redress movement is growing, as scholars Joe R. Feagin and Eileen O'Brien correctly note in chapter 53 below. But it has yet to reach the level of passion and necessity displayed in the successful Japanese American redress movement (discussed in Part 4).

Although the politics of redress claims overshadow their merits, such claims still must be meritorious. There must be something of substance for lawmakers to promote. This is the fourth and final element of my theory of redress. The critical question, of course, is what constitutes a meritorious claim.

Mari Matsuda has identified several prerequisites for a meritorious redress claim.[5] These requirements find support in this book, if modified into the following factors: (1) a human injustice must have been committed; (2) it must be well-documented; (3) the victims must be identifiable as a distinct group; (4) the current members of the group must continue to suffer harm; and (5) such harm must be causally connected to a past injustice. The first and last prerequisites warrant further discussion.

The definition of "human injustice" can be formulated from the concept of "human rights." The place to begin is international law, the United Nations Charter in particular. Article 55(c) of the Charter reads in relevant part: "The United Nations shall promote . . . universal respect for, and observance of, human rights and fundamental freedoms for all without distinction as to race, sex, language, or religion." Various multilateral and bilateral conventions, covenants, resolutions, and treaties more sharply define the rights of all humans and provide for their enforcement in domestic courts. Also, although a specific list of rights legitimized and enforceable under customary international law is elusive, there are many clearly prohibited acts contained therein, the violation of which constitutes a human injustice.

Based upon a synthesis of these instruments of international law, we can say that a human injustice is the violation or suppression of human rights or fundamental freedoms recognized by international law, including but not limited to genocide; slavery; extrajudicial killings; torture and other cruel or degrading treatment; arbitrary detention; rape; the denial of due process of law; forced refugee movements; the deprivation of a means of subsistence; the denial of universal suffrage; and discrimination, distinction, exclusion, or preference based on race, sex, descent, religion, or other identifying factor with the purpose or effect of impairing the recognition, enjoyment, or exercise, on an equal footing, of human rights and fundamental freedoms in the political, social, economic, cultural, or any other field of public life. In sum, a human injustice is simply the violation or suppression of human rights or fundamental freedoms recognized by international law.

This definition does not cover war crimes, which are adequately codified in the Geneva Conventions. But to the extent that any of the acts specified in the detailed definition above are committed during times of war, they would be subject to civil redress, provided that the chosen court accepts jurisdiction over the claim. This definition also does not limit human injustices to the violation of "sacred rights"—rights that cannot be compromised during times of war or other national emergencies. Such rights are specified in instruments such as the International Covenant on Civil and Political Rights of December 16, 1966, and include the right to be free from arbitrary deprivation of life (Article 6); torture, cruel, inhuman or degrading treatment or punishment (Article 7); and slavery, servitude, or compulsory labor (Article 8). Finally, the definition of human injustice proffered here is not intended to be conclusive. Any such definition must be a living or evolving one. Furthermore, it should be informed not only by international standards, but also by "contemporary national" standards found in "liberal national constitutions," to borrow from international law scholar Louis Henkin.[6]

The last prerequisite for a meritorious redress claim—that the harm must be causally connected to a past human injustice—raises the important question of privity: how does a claimant (or alleged victim) establish privity between himself (or his group) and the perpetrator when the latter belongs to a different era? The privity prerequisite is usually cited as the major technical reason for denying African Americans redress for slavery. Boris I. Bittker and I discuss the legal aspects of this problem under American law in chapter 65. In addition, Ruth Levor (chapter 6) and Jennifer Fleischner (chapter 51) argue that a causal link spanning generations can be established through emotional ties and identities. Alan Dershowitz maintains that all Jews are victims of the Holocaust. Camille Paglia, however, finds fault with "identity politics" (chapter 57). Joe R. Feagin and Eileen O'Brien argue that a causal connection between the past injustice of Jim Crow as well as slavery and the current suffering of African Americans can be established by socioeconomic factors (chapter 70).

Once a meritorious claim for redress is presented, how should a government respond? What is the proper *form of redress*? The essays in this collection offer important lessons regarding these questions. They discuss and critique the various ways in which governments have responded to human injustice claims. The list of responses is dizzying. Some governments have issued sincere apologies; others have not. Some have followed up their apologies with payments to victims or their families; others have paid money to victims without issuing an apology. And still others have invested money, services, or both in the victims' community in lieu of compensating victims individually.

Although the forms of redress are diverse, they can be subsumed under conceptual categories for deeper understanding. First, we can distinguish between responses that are remorseful (some more so than others) and those that are not. Responses that seek atonement for the commission of an injustice are properly called *reparations*. Responses in which the government does not express atonement are more suitably called *settlements*. The latter can be analogized to their use in American law. Often a defendant corporation will settle a dispute by signing a consent decree in which it agrees to pay the plaintiff(s) a certain sum of money, but does not concede any wrongdoing. In fact, both parties stipulate to the fact that the defendant has *not* violated any law. A settlement is less a victory than a compromise. It gives the victim a monetary award (not necessarily enough to cover actual losses) and gives the perpetrator a chance to end the dispute without a finding of liability. Usually, a reparation is easily distinguishable from a settlement by the presence or absence of an accompanying statement of apology.

Reparations and settlements can be subdivided into *monetary* and *nonmonetary* responses. Examples of the latter include amnesty, affirmative action, and municipal services such as the construction of new medical facilities or the creation of new educational programs. Nonmonetary reparations or settlements can be more effective than cash in responding to the victims' individual or collective current needs.

Monetary or nonmonetary reparations and settlements can be directed toward the victims individually or collectively. A reparation or settlement directed toward the individual is intended to be *compensatory*—in other words, to return the victim to the status quo ante. One directed toward the group is designed to be *rehabilitative* of the community—in other words, to nurture the group's self-empowerment or the community's cultural transformation, or at least to improve the conditions under which the victims live. "You could . . . try to help clean up the mess your grandpa made—like help me fix up my place, or help my cousin find a job."[7] That is rehabilitation.

This conceptual template fits perfectly well over the forms of redress discussed in the chapters that follow. It can also help us recognize and analyze important issues regarding the victim's or government's particular choice of redress. These issues are explored in the introductory essays that open each part of the book. A few illustrations may be useful.

Germany (see part 2) has paid reparations (i.e., atonement) in the forms of individual compensation and community rehabilitation, the latter mostly to Israel. In total, it has paid more reparations (currently about 80 billion deutsche marks) than perhaps any other government in world history. Germany would seem to have created a successful program of redress. But has it? Are payments to Jewish survivors sufficiently compensatory? What about atonement money for the Gypsies? Does community rehabilitation make sense in their case? Also, is the compensation fund Switzerland has set up in response to its World War II injustices an admission of guilt or simply a settlement?

Japan (see Part 3) was forced to pay a settlement (i.e., nonatonement money) to compensate several women exploited as sex slaves during World War II. This relatively small settlement came by way of a judicial decree, an unusual source of redress. However, Japan's parliament, the Diet, has provided for community rehabilitation through the "Asian Women's Fund." Because the Diet has not issued an apology (though several prime ministers have), the question arises as to whether the Asian Women's Fund constitutes a reparation or a settlement. Another question concerns the propriety and effectiveness of community rehabilitation versus individual compensation. What form of reparation is appropriate? That is the central issue running through Part 3.

Japanese Americans and Aleuts (see Part 4) have received a variety of reparations from the United States for forcible relocation and internment during World War II. Reparations were made monetarily and in-kind to both the individuals and the groups involved pursuant to the Civil Liberties Act of 1988. For example, twenty thousand dollars in compensation was allocated to each Japanese American victim. Nonmonetary individual compensation was given in the forms of a presidential pardon and restitution of status and entitlements lost due to discrimination. Nonmonetary rehabilitation was offered in the form of certain educational programs. Was such a generous reparations package a unique achievement within the American political process? Should other American groups pressing similar claims (e.g., German Americans, Italian Americans, and African Americans) expect similar political success?

Native Americans (see Part 5) have received no dearth of governmental responses to their various claims for redress. Most of these appear to be settlements rather than reparations, and rehabilitative rather than compensatory. But the central question is whether the government's responses have been result-oriented, nonresponsive to Indian demands and culture (e.g., the American tendency to equate justice with money, and to separate sovereignty from land), and erratic—i.e., "wild"—in other respects as well?

African American claims for suffering under slavery and Jim Crow have not even merited an apology from the United States, although Thomas Geoghegan (chapter 60) argues that Lincoln did in fact issue an apology for slavery. Whether a clear apology or reparations should be given to African Americans is the major issue running through Parts 6 and 7 of the book. A subsidiary issue is whether African Americans should rethink their redress strategy in light of the Rosewood Compensation Act. In 1994, the Florida legislature enacted the legislation to settle certain claims arising out of white violence that demolished the all-black town of Rosewood during the Jim Crow era. The settlement is both compensatory (actual proven losses are repaid) and rehabilitative (e.g., a scholarship fund is established for minority students who are not direct descendants of the Rosewood families), but no apology has been made. Can African Americans live with a settlement rather than atonement, given how emotional the issues of slavery and Jim Crow are among some vocal individuals and organizations? Is a state and local strategy more feasible than the failed national approach taken thus far? Is community rehabilitation more fruitful than individual compensation, especially in light of the privity problems? But, in the end, the most important question is whether the average African American citizen cares enough about redress to make it a political issue, even at the state and local levels.

South Africa (see Part 8) has opted for reparations rather than settlement. A great deal of remorse exists in South Africa (perhaps more so among its political and intellectual leaders than its average citizens) over the injustices of Apartheid. The government's Truth and Reconciliation Commission (TRC), which on July 31, 1998, ended two and a half years of investigations into Apartheid-related injustices, has provided reparations in the form of individual compensation and community rehabilitation. Similar forms of redress (e.g., affirmative action in employment) are being considered by other government entities. How effective these reparations will be in moving the country from a regime of racial oppression to one of racial justice and democratic process—what the South Africans call "reconciliation"—is difficult to discern at this time. But what is clear about South Africa is that reconciliation is the overriding political imperative that has shaped the forms of redress. It is what has made amnesty for the oppressors an acceptable, if highly unusual, form of reparations. But amnesty is not just for the oppressors. Indeed, just prior to ending its public hearings, the TRC, headed by Bishop Desmond Tutu, granted amnesty to four black Africans who beat and stabbed Amy Biehl, a twenty-six-year-old white American who was in South Africa to work on voter education, as she pleaded for mercy. Like so many whites who came before the TRC claiming they had killed, tortured, maimed, and raped as a means of exerting political pressure, and who expressed remorse for their injustices, these men walked out of the hearing immune from criminal or civil prosecution. The deal in South Africa is that the oppressors get amnesty and the victims get compensation and rehabilitation as well as amnesty. This is designed to lead to reconciliation. But what price reconciliation? That is the thematic question that ties together the essays in part 8.

NOTES

1. This is not to say that one should attempt to compare human injustices. Trying to compare one human injustice against another is tasteless. It is also divisive in that it undermines an international movement toward universal human rights.

2. Catharine A. MacKinnon, "Crimes of War, Crimes of Peace," *UCLA Women's Law Journal* 4 (1993): 59, 65.

3. Ibid., 60.

4. *The Cherokee Nation v. Georgia*, 30 U.S. 1, 20 (1831).

5. Mari J. Matsuda, "Looking to the Bottom: Critical Legal Studies and Reparations," *Harvard Civil Liberties–Civil Rights Law Review* 22 (1987): 323, 362–97.

6. Louis Henkin, "Human Rights and State 'Sovereignty,'" *Georgia Journal of International & Comparative Law* 25 (1995–1996): 31, 40.

7. William Raspberry, "Don't Bother Saying You're Sorry," *San Diego Union-Tribune*, July 8, 1997, B-6 (quoting an African American cab driver).

Suggested Readings

Askin, Kelly Dawn. *War Crimes against Women*. Cambridge, Mass.: Kluwer Law International, 1997.

Banco Nacional de Cuba v. Sabbatino, 376 U.S. 398 (1964).

Brownmiller, Susan. *Against Our Will: Men, Women and Rape*. New York: Simon and Schuster, 1975. (A chronicle of wartime rape dating back hundreds of years.)

D'Amato, Anthony. "Human Rights as Part of Customary International Law: A Plea for Change of Paradigms." *Georgia Journal of International and Comparative Law* 25 (1994): 47.

Ermacora, Felix, Manfred Nowak, and Hannes Tretter, eds. *International Human Rights*. Vienna: Law Books in Europe, 1993.

Hersh, Seymour M. *Cover-up: The Army's Secret Investigation of the Massacre at My Lai 4*. New York: Random House, 1972.

Jamison, Sandra L. "A Permanent International Criminal Court: A Proposal That Overcomes Past Objections." *Denver Journal of International Law and Policy* 23 (1995): 419.

Kadic v. Radovan Karadzic 70 F.3d 232 (1995).

MacKinnon, Catharine A. "Crimes of War, Crimes of Peace." *UCLA Women's Law Journal* 4 (1993): 59.

Magee, Rhonda V. "The Master's Tools, from the Bottom up: Responses to African-American Reparations Theory in Mainstream and Outsider Remedies Discourse." *Virginia Law Review* 79 (1993): 863.

Matsuda, Mari J. "Looking to the Bottom: Critical Legal Studies and Reparations." *Harvard Civil Liberties–Civil Rights Law Review* 22 (1987): 323, 362–97.

Minow, Martha L. *Between Vengeance and Forgiveness: Facing History after Genocide and Mass Violence*. Boston: Beacon Press, 1998.

Pietila, Hilkka, and Jeanne Vickers. *Making Women Matter: The Role of the United Nations*. Atlantic Highlands, N.J.: Zed Books, 1990.

Shandley, Robert R., ed. *Unwilling Germans? The Goldhagen Debate*. Minneapolis: University of Minnesota Press, 1998.

"The Unsung Heroes of War: Combat Nurses Who Saved American Lives, But Had Their Own Lives Ruined in the Process." *Public Eye*, CBS, March 24, 1998.

Verdum, Vincene. "If the Shoe Fits, Wear It: An Analysis of Reparations to African Americans." *Tulane Law Review* 67 (1993): 597.

2 | Nazi Persecution

Introduction

2 | A Reparations Success Story?

Roy L. Brooks

In the closing days of fighting in the European theater, Nazi Germany lay in ruins, exposed to international condemnation as the grim details of Hitler's murderous reign began to surface. The years immediately following Germany's unconditional surrender were marked by the Nürnberg (Nuremberg) war crimes trials and the unprecedented German redress plan for the victims of Nazi atrocities. These episodes transformed Germany's social and geopolitical landscape, providing some measure of closure for a most shameful period of history.

By most accounts, the postwar German redress program has been a success, if only as an exemplar of meaningful national atonement for past wrongdoing. Billions of deutsche marks have been paid out in various forms of reparations, and Germany has taken great pains to eliminate anti-Semitism within its borders. Jewish Holocaust scholars such as Harvard's Daniel Jonah Goldhagen, author of *Hitler's Willing Executioners: Ordinary Germans and the Holocaust*, have hailed the German reparation plan as indicative of Germany's good-faith effort to make amends with victims of Nazi persecution. Moreover, observers are quick to praise the economic, social, and political metamorphosis Germany has undergone in the postwar era as a model for the international community, attributing a significant portion of Germany's postwar success to its unabashed willingness to deal with the darker chapters of its past. Yet, despite outward vestiges of success, questions of adequacy still plague the redress process.

Part 2 begins with an examination of the scope of Nazi persecution. Alan Davies, world-renowned Holocaust scholar, points to Hitler's long-held ideological foundations as the likely rationale behind the sweeping genocidal policies of the Nazi regime. At the core of Hitler's social policies were racial and anti-Semitic theories, exemplified by his pseudoscientific "racial hygiene" campaign. These policies set the stage for what was later to become the "Final Solution of the Jewish Question," resulting in the death of millions of European Jews. In turn, Hitler's geopolitical aspirations and romanticization of the "people's community" (united by common German blood and devoid of Jews, political parties, religious groups, and homosexuals) propelled Germany on a perilous quest to secure more *Lebensraum* (living space) for Hitler's self-proclaimed master race. German territorial expansion, in conjunction with Hitler's racial hygiene and social policies, subjected millions of people to persecution. Hence, the displacement and persecution of Jews, Slavs, Poles, Gypsies, and other so-called "undesirables" were integral components of Hitler's grand design.

Within the broad scope of Nazi persecution, countless individual tragedies took place, many of which are documented. In her powerful narrative, "Memories of My Childhood in the Holocaust," Judith Jaegermann provides an eyewitness account of the numerous atrocities committed against millions of Jews in Nazi concentration camps. Next, Wanda Poltawska, a Polish Christian arrested for aiding the resistance, describes in gruesome detail her personal experiences as a "guinea pig" for Nazi medical experimentation. Stories like these impel one to question whether any formulation of reparations could sufficiently redress such suffering. But, then again, without an apology or reparations, how is atonement to be made?

The effects of Nazi persecution have not been confined to those who were its direct victims. As prominent Jewish advocate Alan Dershowitz argues, all Jews are victims of the Holocaust. Ruth Levor gives a personal account of the lingering effects the Holocaust has had on survivors and subsequent generations. Levor, whose parents and grandparents escaped Nazi Germany and emigrated to the United States, shares the experience of Jews who maintain a sense of heightened vigilance against the possibility of another Holocaust. Levor's essay is also a heartfelt protest against the current German reparations scheme, which limits payments to direct victims or, in some cases, their spouses.

Otto Ohlendorf's frightening testimony before the International Military Tribunal at Nürnberg not only underscores the moral bankruptcy of the Nazi regime, but also lends credence to Dershowitz, Levor, and other Jews who fear a possible recurrence of the Holocaust. During his testimony, Ohlendorf, an SS officer responsible for the deaths of thousands of Jews, Gypsies, and Slavs, asserted a "national security defense" to mitigate his moral culpability. Ohlendorf maintained that these mass executions were justified because the victims constituted a threat to German national security. In addition, Ohlendorf repeatedly refused to assess the morality of the Führer Order (a command from Hitler directing German troops to exterminate all threats to the regime) or his own actions, instead stating that he had "surrendered [his] moral conscience to the fact that [he] was a soldier." Testimony concerning Ohlendorf's background is particularly alarming. It reveals a well-educated, intelligent, and highly sophisticated family man who nevertheless willingly surrendered his moral judgment to Hitler in the commission of acts that shock the conscience. This seeming inconsistency underscores the extent of the Nazis' stranglehold on the moral reasoning of the German people—a cultural phenomenon that transformed average citizens, even the educated and presumably "civilized," into murderers. Revelations such as these evoke or reinforce fears that another Holocaust could occur in the future.

Chapter 8 provides an outline of the German Compensation Plan, as prepared by the United States Department of Justice. The numerous redress measures implemented since 1949 clearly demonstrate Germany's desire to atone for its past wrongdoing on a scale not seen before. As of 1996, the German government had disbursed more than 72 billion deutsche marks to the state of Israel and individual survivors of the Holocaust through programs negotiated among Israel, the United States, Germany, and Jewish groups. The German government has also made significant payments into funds created to assist non-Jewish victims of the Nazis, though the funding for these programs is relatively small in comparison.

However successful Germany's redress program appears to be, significant numbers of victims have been excluded from receiving substantive reparations. The essay by Ian Hancock openly challenges the adequacy of Germany's record of redress. Shortcomings reveal themselves upon examination of the Gypsies' ongoing efforts to gain reparations for persecution inflicted by the Nazis. Although the wartime experiences of the Gypsies and the Jews were similar, Gypsy claims for reparations have not been similarly treated. Historically, Gypsies have been marginalized from the mainstream reparations movement as well as the political process, leaving them with very few avenues of redress. Although Nazi persecution of ethnic Gypsies was comparable in degree and scale to that of the Jews, Gypsies have been woefully underrepresented in formal reparations negotiations, which have been dominated by Jewish reparations claims. Consequently, Gypsies have not enjoyed the robust reparations provisions provided to Jewish Holocaust survivors.

Hancock's essay also takes us through recent developments that expose the complicity of the Swiss and other "neutral" countries in helping Nazi Germany finance its war machine by handling assets confiscated from Jews and Gypsies. Swiss authorities have begun to investigate the return of confiscated assets still held by Swiss banks, but, once again, Hancock argues, Gypsy interests in this matter appear to have been subordinated to Jewish claims.

In the final essay in Part 2, Hubert Kim expands on the critique of the German redress program offered by Hancock. Kim questions the adequacy of German redress on several grounds, including the small amounts of monetary reparations paid to Jewish survivors and the failure to compensate homosexuals, forced laborers, and other victims of Nazi injustices.

The Scope of Persecution

3 The German Third Reich and Its Victims

Nazi Ideology

Alan Davies

The third German empire, inaugurated in 1933, bore scant resemblance to the second German empire of the Kaisers, which Bismarck established in 1871, and no resemblance whatever to the supposed first German empire of the Middle Ages. It was *sui generis,* the creation of Adolf Hitler, and, as such, a revolutionary rather than a conservative regime, with a dark and murderous essence distilled from the mind of its creator. To understand its policies, therefore, we must understand their genesis and rationale in the self-styled "leader" (Führer) of the revolution, whose title itself reflects the novelty of the new order.

Revolutions, unlike coups d'état, are rooted in ideas, and in this respect the National Socialist revolution was no different from other revolutions. The ideas behind the Nazi revolution emerge, as Hugh Trevor-Roper has insisted, with startling clarity and consistency in Hitler's writings and declamations, both private and public, notably his prison tract *Mein Kampf* (1924), his political conversations as recorded by Hermann Rauschning in *Gespräche mit Hitler* (1932–1934), and the various editions of his "table-talk" during the war years.[1] At their core lies a racial ideology with its antecedents in the nineteenth century, when the language of race was on everyone's lips and biological determinism was a potent intellectual fashion. At their core also lies a virulent and fanatical anti-Semitism with independent origins in the European psyche, although the term itself, from the German *Anti-semitismus*, was a racial concoction. Finally, at their core lies an extraordinary geopolitical dream, the conquest of the east in order to carve out extra living space (*Lebensraum*) for Germans, at the expense of the Slavic peoples, in a vast new Germanic colonial state stretching in a single undifferentiated land mass to the Urals. In this greater Germany-to-be, the mystique of race and the mystique of soil acquire paramount value, since every member of the master race (*Herrenvolk*) is deemed to possess an innate racial right to his own proper "sacred" territory.[2] Hitler's war aims were defined with this goal in mind.

With such ideas in his head, and with the apparatus of a modern state increasingly at his disposal, the German tyrant began the task of reshaping the character of the nation as soon as the dust had settled on his ascent to power. An important component of contemporary racial theory, which had pre-Nazi antecedents, was the notion of racial hygiene, promoted by the eugenics movement, which originated in Great Britain and had infiltrated German science and medicine. In its Nazi expression, racial hygiene sought to refine the German racial stock both by promoting "Aryan" marriages and by preventing Aryan/non-Aryan or otherwise unhygienic sexual unions, notably among the so-called defective and degenerate members of society. Compulsory sterilization served the latter purpose; so did euthanasia.

Interestingly, the first Nazi sterilization law (1933) contained no racial provisions as such, concentrating instead on the "genetically diseased," or Germans with inherited conditions such as mental retardation, schizophrenia, manic-depressive psychosis, and epilepsy.[3] These early victims of the Third Reich were destined for a fate worse than sterilization; once designated as a useless burden on society, it was only a matter of time before an inexorable Nazi logic dictated their elimination, as happened in 1939.[4] The mass euthanasia program began with children. Malformed or otherwise unsatisfactory children were cajoled away from their parents and shipped to special "pediatric" clinics to suffer either starvation or lethal injections.[5] Many were used to supply Nazi scientists with subjects for experimentation. Adults soon followed. On state orders, asylums were forced to tabulate and classify their inmates according to condition and race for assessment by a central committee of experts, with life or death hanging in the balance. For the condemned, gassing with carbon monoxide was the chosen means of execution. Although this liquidation technique was abruptly halted on August 24, 1941, on Hitler's command, following a rising tide of public protest, particularly from the German churches,[6] in fact the murders continued in other insidious forms throughout the war years, especially by starvation. Death, after all, has many faces.

The Jews, however, were Hitler's prime victims. Anti-Semitism was no stranger to German culture in pre-Nazi times. Even in the nineteenth century, certain German intellectuals had recommended extreme measures against the Jewish presence in Germany, including extermination.[7] Whether their rhetoric was intended in a literal or only in a metaphorical sense, the fact remains that modern political language had taken a sinister turn. Many debates continue to rage about the genesis and exact character of what the Nazis called the Final Solution (*Endlösung*) and Jews the Holocaust, or Shoah.[8] Did it have extra-German European derivations, for example, in the Russian Revolution?[9] Was it conceived and enacted without deviation as a Hitlerian dictate with prewar origins, or did it emerge in a more piecemeal fashion, after other proposed solutions to the "Jewish problem" were abandoned?[10] However, except for pro-Hitler apologists,[11] no one seriously doubts that its authorization came from the "artist-politician" who wrote *Mein Kampf*; it bears the peculiar stamp of Hitler's soul. Not only did the Nazi leader openly predict the annihilation (*Vernichtung*) of the Jews in the event of a new world war,[12] but he was intelligent enough to realize that an enterprise on such a scale would require a highly organized bureaucracy, as well as total military and political control; it could not have been perpetrated in a premodern state.[13] What transpired was consistent with this insight.

The persecution began in the form of racial legislation to "reform" the German civil service (April 7, 1933), by excluding non-Aryans (i.e., Jews) from public office. These Aryan provisions were soon extended into the professions, including the state-related Protestant ministry. *Kristallnacht*, the night of broken glass, which was not one night but several nights (November 9–12, 1938) during which synagogues and other Jewish institutions were destroyed, revealed the ugliness of the regime beneath its public mask, provoking both angry reactions abroad and a new flight of refugees from Germany. The Nazis' wartime program of destruction, from the mobile killing squads (*Einsatzgruppen*) that slaughtered Jews in the wake of Hitler's victorious legions to the establishment of death camps in Poland following the Wannsee Conference (January 20, 1942), has been amply described and documented, as have its attendant horrors.[14] What remains controversial is whether or not the attempted annihilation of the Jews was truly unique in some fundamental sense in comparison with the other mass murders of World War II, as well as the other genocides of the twentieth century. Were Jews alone the objects of a "unique intentionality" in the annals of human infamy?[15] Or did any of Hitler's other victims, for example, the Gypsies (Romani), perish for the same biological and metaphysical reasons?

The persecution of the Gypsies, who, like the Jews, were regarded as non-Aryans (in spite of the "Aryan affiliation of the Romani language"),[16] began in 1934. Viewed as "asocials," they were rounded up for internment and eugenic sterilization. Gypsies, like Jews, were affected by the racial laws forbidding intermarriage with Germans and were deported during the early war years to the newly conquered territories in eastern Europe, where they also died cruelly at Nazi hands, either in mass shootings or in gas chambers. Because few have bothered to commemorate the traditionally despised Gypsies, in that respect at least, as an eminent Jewish scholar has declared,[17] their destruction was even more tragic than that of the Jews. However, the claim, advanced by some historians, that Gypsies were trapped in exactly the same ideological mesh as the Jews and murdered for essentially the same set of Nazi race principles has not been widely accepted, although the issue remains unsettled.[18] Certainly, the racial parallels are close.

Since the larger purpose of Hitler's great sweep eastward after the manner of the thirteenth-century Teutonic knights was to create a greater Germany, a dark fate lay in store for the broad array of Poles, Ukrainians, Russians, and other "native" peoples who already inhabited these coveted regions.

> The folkish state . . . must under no conditions annex Poles with the intention of
> wanting to make Germans out of them some day. On the contrary it must muster the

determination either to seal off these alien racial elements, so that the blood of its own people will not be corrupted again, or it must without further ado remove them and hand over the vacated territory to its own national comrades.[19]

This was Hitler's geopolitical vision: a "nightmare, barbarian empire" to be established in the subjugated east, an empire in which those Slavs not liquidated would live as a "depressed Helot class, hewing wood and drawing water for a privileged aristocracy of German colonists . . . in fortified cities connected by strategic autobahns, glorying in their nationality and listening to *The Merry Widow* for ever and ever."[20] Bizarre though it seems, the Nazi tyrant was serious; by 1943, approximately a million Nordic settlers from both within and outside of Germany proper had been assigned expropriated farmlands on Polish soil (Hitler, like all bad romantics, idealized rural life), having been screened first by Nazi experts in order to determine their racial eligibility.[21] As for the unfortunate Slavs, it scarcely mattered whether they lived or died.

Because of the strange sexual puritanism of official (as opposed to unofficial) National Socialism, homosexuals, who had long dwelt in the shadows of both German society and European society at large, became early victims of the Nazi moral code and its stringent notions of "degeneracy." Homosexuality was already a crime, so persecution was easy. The sentence imposed on the "men with the pink triangle" was grim indeed. According to available accounts, they were treated with a peculiar sadism and either killed outright or worked to death, although little has been written about the subject and exact numbers are difficult to estimate.[22] Paradoxically, a strong covert strain of homosexuality was allowed to exist in Nazi ranks, notably the brownshirt leader Ernst Röhm, who was murdered on Hitler's orders in 1934 when his usefulness had passed. Such inconsistencies are not rare in the annals of history.

Apart from the Jews, who were murdered more for racial than religious reasons, the religious community to feel the deepest fury of the neo-pagan state was the tiny and socially insignificant sect of Jehovah's Witnesses, a third of whom eventually suffered martyrdom for their convictions.[23] Not unlike the early Christians in Roman times, they were simply intransigent in their refusal to accommodate themselves to the political order of their day, and were swiftly proscribed as a consequence. (The same was not true of most members of the mainstream German churches.) In Nazi eyes, the Jehovah's Witnesses represented a peculiar danger, not only because of their attachment to the Hebrew Bible and Jewish apocalyptic themes, but also because of their fanatical zeal and organizational talents, which reminded the German rulers too much of their own origins. Was the little religious sect bent on the conquest of Germany in much the same manner and with the same tactics as the little political sect spawned in Munich and adopted by Hitler had once been bent?[24] Were the religious beliefs so energetically propagated by its devotees a mask for more nefarious political goals?[25] Something apparently made the Nazi high command think so. Thus, the Witnesses fell into condemnation and death. Numerous other small sects and cults whose ideas were deemed uncongenial for one reason or another also suffered various forms of oppression.

Open persecution of the larger Christian churches of Germany, both Protestant and Catholic, was more difficult, partly because of their size and historical importance in an old Christian country, and partly because public opinion was not prepared for such an assault. That Hitler despised Christianity and intended to destroy the churches as soon as he had finished with the Jews is indisputable; Christianity, in his Nietzschean view, was nothing more than the last remnant of Judaism on German soil—an "utterly destructive Bolshevism."[26] But the churches were too powerful to break "over one's knee"; like gangrenous limbs, it was better to help them "rot away."[27] In the meantime, they could be made to serve the regime by subjecting them to direct state authority, thereby crushing their capacity to resist its decrees. A covert campaign of terrorism and intimidation was conducted against recalcitrant churchmen who believed that Christianity could not, and should not, be reconciled with National Socialism.[28] Among those finally arrested and incarcerated was Martin Niemöller, a famous Lutheran pastor who became a symbol of the anti-Nazi Christian resistance. Of course, the pro-Nazi and neutral factions within German Christianity greatly outnumbered the voices of conscience that spoke against Hitler on Christian grounds, sometimes at the cost of life itself.

Such were the main victims of the German Third Reich, designated in order to serve a fantastic and evil dream, the Nazi *novus ordo saeclorum*. The National Socialist revolution in Germany was a genuine revolution, but a revolution, as Klaus Fischer has written, "bereft of a single humane principle of conduct," indeed, of a single humane idea, consisting only of murderous ones.[29] Had Hitler prevailed, a perpetual reign of terror would have ensued.

NOTES

1. H. R. Trevor-Roper, "Hitler's War Aims," in *Aspects of the Third Reich*, ed. H. W. Koch (London: Macmillan, 1985), 235f.

2. "Never regard the Reich as secure unless for centuries to come it can give every scion of our people his own parcel of soil. Never forget that the most sacred right on this earth is a man's right to have earth to till with his own hands, and the most sacred sacrifice the blood that a man sheds for this earth." Adolph Hitler, *Mein Kampf*, trans. Ralph Manheim (Boston: Houghton Mifflin, 1943), 664.

3. See Pauline M. H. Mazumdar, "Two Models for Human Genetics: Blood Grouping and Psychiatry in Germany between the World Wars," *Bulletin of the History of Medicine*, no. 70 (1996): 653.

4. See "The 'Euthanasia' Programme," in *Nazism 1919–1945*, ed. J. Noakes and G. Pridham, vol. 3, *Foreign Policy, War and Racial Etermination* (Exeter: University of Exeter Press, 1988), 1002f.

5. Ibid., 1007.

6. Most notable was a sermon preached by the Roman Catholic bishop of Münster, Graf August von Galen, on August 3, 1941.

7. For example, Paul de Lagarde and Eugen Dühring.

8. The term "Final Solution" seems to have been of Nazi bureaucratic origin. The term "Holocaust," from the Greek *holokaustos* and the Latin *holocaustum*, is derived from the ancient Greek translation of the Hebrew Scriptures known as the Septuagint and signifies the Hebrew *olah* or burnt offering. In its modern setting, it seems to have originated in wartime France. The Hebrew term *Shoah* signifies a catastrophic destruction.

9. As argued, for example, by Ernst Nolte, "Between Myth and Revisionism? The Third Reich in the Perspective of the 1980s," in *Aspects of The Third Reich*, ed. Koch, 17–38.

10. For a good discussion of the debate between the "intentionalists" and the "functionalists," see Michael R. Marrus, *The Holocaust in History* (Toronto: Lester and Orphen Dennys, 1987), chap. 3.

11. Notoriously, the English writer David Irving.

12. Before the Reichstag on January 30, 1939.

13. See George L. Mosse, *Nazism: A Historical and Comparative Analysis of National Socialism* (New Brunswick, N.J.: Transaction Books, 1978), 72.

14. Notably by Raul Hilberg in his massive work *The Destruction of the European Jews* (Chicago: Quadrangle Books, 1961).

15. See Stephen T. Katz, *Post-Holocaust Dialogues: Critical Issues in Modern Jewish Thought* (New York: New York University Press, 1985), 287f. See also Katz's larger comparative study, *The Holocaust in Historical Context*, vol. 1 (New York: Oxford University Press, 1994).

16. Ian Hancock, "Uniqueness, Gypsies and Jews," in *Remembering for the Future: Working Papers and Addenda*, ed. Yehuda Bauer et al. (Oxford: Pergamon Press, 1988), 2:2020.

17. Emil L. Fackenheim, *The Jewish Return into History: Reflections in the Age of Auschwitz and a New Jerusalem* (New York: Schocken Books, 1978), 93 n. 11.

18. See, for example, Yehuda Bauer, *The Holocaust in Historical Perspective* (Seattle: University of Washington Press, 1978), 36; Steven T. Katz, "Quantity and Interpretation: Issues in the Comparative Historical Analysis of the Holocaust," in *Remembering for the Future*, ed. Bauer et al., supp., 210f. Hancock argues in favor of the opposite view in "Uniqueness, Gypsies and Jews," 2017f. Alan Bullock states the SS pursued the extermination of the Gypsies "with almost the same determination as that of the Jews." *Hitler and Stalin: Parallel Lives* (Toronto: McClelland and Stewart, 1993), 805.

19. *Hitler's Secret Book*, trans. Salvator Attanasio (New York: Grove Press, 1961), 47–48.

20. Trevor-Roper, "Hitler's War Aims," 246.

21. See Klaus P. Fischer, *Nazi Germany: A New History* (New York: Continuum, 1995), 493.

22. See the harrowing account of an anonymous Austrian homosexual survivor in Heinz Heger, *The Men with the Pink Triangle*, trans. David Fernbach (London: Gay Men's Press, 1980). The various concentration camp colors were: yellow for Jews, red for political prisoners, green for criminals, pink for homosexuals, black for antisocials, purple for Jehovah's Witnesses, blue for emigrants, brown for Gypsies.

23. See J. S. Conway, *The Nazi Persecution of the Churches 1933–45* (London: Weidenfeld and Nicolson, 1968), 196.

24. Ibid., 197.

25. Ibid.

26. See Klaus Scholder, "Judaism and Christianity in the Ideology and Politics of National

Socialism," in *Judaism and Christianity under the Impact of National Socialism*, ed. Otto Dov Kulka and Paul R. Mendes-Flohr (Jerusalem: Historical Society of Israel and Zalman Shazar Center for Jewish History, 1987), 194.

27. Ibid., 195.
28. Conway, *Nazi Persecution of the Churches*, 96.
29. Fischer, *Nazi Germany*, 496.

Holocaust Narratives

4 | Memories of My Childhood in the Holocaust

Judith Jaegermann (née Pinczovsky)

Judith Jaegermann was sixteen years old at the time of her liberation from the concentration camp.

At the age of seven I knew already that we were different from our neighbours. We lived in Karlsbad, where I was also born. It was Sukkoth (Feast of Tabernacles) and my Papa had just been busy making a "Sukka" (a small house celebrating the harvest) in the yard of the house where we lived and where my parents had a big kosher restaurant when, all of a sudden, stones were thrown from the neighbours' windows. I was terribly scared and asked Papa why they did this to us. He said only softly, "Because we are Jews." That was in the year 1937.

We stayed for another two years in Karlsbad, after which we had to flee from the Germans to Prague. Once in Prague, we had to wear the yellow Star of David and we were not allowed to leave our homes after 8 P.M. We could ride only in the last carriage of the tramway, since the first ones were "Not allowed for Jews."

Many houses bore captions in large letters: "Do not buy in Jewish shops" or "Jews get out." Instinctively I didn't want to know anything about it and that's why my teddy bear was my best friend. . . .

One day, when I was eleven and a half years old, Mama received a printed summons, instructing us to appear at Prague's Exhibition Halls, in order to join a "transport" (i.e., the actual deportation convoy of human beings to the concentration camps) which would drag us into the unknown.

■　■　■

Reprinted by permission of the author.

After a couple of days we were sent from Prague to Theresienstadt. It was an enormous confusion. Men, women, and children, all were separated; my sister Ruth and I were transferred to a children's home. From the very first day I reached Theresienstadt, I was crying there all the time. I simply couldn't get used to this situation of being without my parents and I even isolated myself from the other children. This continued for a couple of weeks, until one day I simply escaped from the children's home and ran straight to Mama. She somehow could give me shelter and that is why I stayed with her in the same room, together with many adult women. Mostly they were Czech women, but also some Viennese and a few German Jews, who knew nothing whatsoever about Jewishness and who wouldn't believe that something could happen to them. They were German and felt themselves as such. And so we started to live together with total strangers.

■   ■   ■

Meanwhile my father was employed as a cook at the Hanover barracks and though he had to work hard, I believe that he didn't go hungry at least. We could see him only very seldom because he was very busy. All the young men who got to know him and who worked with him liked him very much and called him "Pincza," derived from his name, Pinczovsky. In Theresienstadt I came down with a very bad case of scarlet fever and had to be put in quarantine. All around me children died of meningitis, which came as a result of the scarlet fever. At the time I figured that I would end up in the same way.

We were sixteen months in Theresienstadt, when one day we heard that people were being sent to Auschwitz, where they were going to be gassed. Of course nobody wanted to believe this and everybody said that this is impossible and that these were only rumours. Unfortunately Papa, Mama, Ruth and I were also amongst those to be sent to Auschwitz. Our fear grew by the hour since we didn't know what to expect. The unknown is something dreadful, which is even impossible to describe. As long as we were all together, even though we didn't live together in the same place, it was somehow bearable, but how would this go on? Where would they send us next? Would they tear us all apart? Would we continue to live? It was an enormous chaos.

We were pushed into the cattle cars of the train, in the presence of Eichmann, in his flawless uniform, his booted legs spread wide apart. With his famous slanted smile he was looking on, how these unhappy, nothing-anticipating people were treated like animals. Struck with dismay and terrified, nobody would think of refusing or resisting to board the train cars. Everything went so unbelievably fast, with shouts of "Now come on, you miserable Jews!" . . . The dogs were barking from all directions.

■   ■   ■

In the cattle cars one could hear nothing but moaning and crying, as well as whispers that this "transport" was going to Auschwitz. Of course, absolutely nobody knew anything definite, but everyone had bad forebodings. At present I cannot recall how long the trip from Theresienstadt to Auschwitz took, but one of my most dreadful memories, which I even cannot forget until this day, was the fact that they had set up a "shit bucket" in the middle of the car, which was placed there to serve as a toilet for all: men, women and children. It was inhuman and degrading.

As we were pretty near to this murderous death machine called Auschwitz, Papa spoke through a tiny opening and asked a railway employee whether from here "transports" would go on to some other destination. The employee replied—thumb up—and said, "Sure, to up there, through the chimney, which is burning twenty-four hours a day, that's where the 'transports' go." I had overheard this conversation by chance and my poor Papa, upon hearing this, immediately got stomach cramps and diarrhea. I had to watch how my big, strong Papa, who to me seemed the most daring and strongest in the whole world, had to let down his trousers and without shame, had to sit down on the shit bucket in front of all these people. The fact that he had to go to the toilet in such a degrading fashion made me feel that my entire world collapsed. I immediately understood that we would be gassed. But how? How would they torture us until we die? I started shivering and so did Papa. He was very depressed from that moment on, when he got the reply with the thumb up.

Finally the cross bars were taken off the doors outside and the doors opened. Though it was dark, searchlights were focused on us from all directions and again the barking dogs and the shouts, "Out, out, faster, faster, come on, come on." Nobody knew what was happening. The men and women were kept separated. Everything happened very fast and again we were without Papa. I saw lots of barbed wire and searchlights and felt a strong smell of smoke. We were herded into a huge hall and we had to undress completely. I was thirteen years old and I felt probably more ashamed at this age than the adult women, who couldn't care less.

We were standing in rows in order to be shaved everywhere. Our clothes and personal belongings had immediately been taken away from us and it was evident that the people who had to execute this action were already so callous and dulled by their long imprisonment in Auschwitz that they lacked all human likeness. These were the early settlers of the place. When it was my turn to be shaved, I discovered that the person who did the shaving was a man. But then, in fact, he wasn't a man. He was just a poor prisoner in a striped suit with hollow eyes and gaunt cheeks. He did his job without caring and without strength. Once we girls had been shaved everywhere—heads, underarms, pubic area—we all looked like monkeys. None of us dared to look at the others. Some had cried, while others started to laugh hysterically. It was definitely grotesque.

Then we . . . stood for hours naked until we were given old rags and, again, as if on purpose to degrade and to debase the people, they would give tiny rags to the big women, while the smaller women were given oversized things. Some girls had only received a coat, without anything underneath, while others got torn thin dresses without anything over it. And no underwear whatsoever. Everything went quickly; we were totally at the mercy of destiny without being able to complain to anyone.

. . . After we were given the clothes to wear, we had to stand in line again to be tattooed. To stand around for hours was not unusual in Auschwitz. Mama was standing in front of me, then I, behind me my sister Ruth. Mama was given number 71501, I was 71502, and Ruth got 71503. It was very painful and when I wanted to take my hand away because it hurt, I was given a slap in the face. It was a big, ugly Polish woman who did the tattooing.

In short, it took only a couple of hours after our arrival to Auschwitz and we were no human beings anymore, but only numbers and none of us could do or say anything about it. I was only thinking, "How is it possible that grownups are capable to do these things to others?" Where is Justice and why do we deserve this? In my unhappiness [I] became more and more silent and reserved.

After the tattooing, we were driven into barracks without mattresses. From now on the women had to live squeezed together, on three levels of bunk beds. It was terrible and cold, and we didn't know what the next minute would have in store for us. The only thing one could do was to swallow hard and to suffer in silence.

The food was some kind of feed, called soup: a dark, watery liquid for which one had again to stand in line in order to get some of it into a small tin bowl—not even full. Within a couple of weeks we all became thin, numb and listless, just as those who had been before us in Auschwitz. Our camp was called Birkenau. B 2 B. Block 12.

We saw Papa again after a couple of days and my heart was crying out when I saw him. He was wearing a very short and narrow coat and looked terribly wretched and degraded in it. He was totally depressed, because we too must have looked terrible to him. After some time he reported as a cook and had to work for the SS. If they didn't like the food, they would keep his head immersed under water, until he almost suffocated. I overheard this by chance when he told it to Mama. Sometimes he would bring us, under mortal danger, some boiled potatoes and then he ran immediately back to his barrack, where he would rack his brains what to cook for the SS so that they would like it and he wouldn't be tortured as a result.

■　■　■

One day Ruth was looking when another "transport" arrived at Birkenau's railway station. These were Hungarian Jews, who were taken straight away to be gassed. . . .

The roll-calls in Birkenau were horrible. They drove us already at half past four in the morning from the barracks and would let us stand for hours at a time at attention, either in the freezing cold or during a heat wave. Many women could not take it and fainted, being already extremely weak due to the lack of food, while the cold also bothered us a lot. My feet were totally frostbitten. I had only wooden house-shoes which were constantly falling off my feet, because Birkenau had during winter heavy mud in which my house-shoes got stuck.

■　■　■

Also appalling were Birkenau's latrines. Made as deep pits, they were separated in the middle by a narrow board and divided by a transparent canvas fabric, so that men and women could see each other through the material. This was so degrading and inhuman, because all one could see were the naked and skinny behinds of the men. Since everyone was suffering from a watery diarrhea as a result of the long period of undernourishment, this was the sight we were seeing when we had to go to the latrines.

I will never forget a woman, I believe her name was Kleinova, who always used to carry her bread ration around with her, so that she would not die of hunger. One day her bread ration fell into the dirty latrine and out of sheer despair she crept into the pit, or it seems that she had let herself fall into it, to recover her bread ration. Though she, as the bread, were disgustingly filthy, this was of no importance to her. The animal instinct to survive, by keeping food at hand, had triumphed.

I saw this same Kleinova woman die next to me a couple of months later in Bergen-Belsen. It is a miracle that she even stayed alive that long, because she had literally eaten nothing at all, while only hoarding and storing rations. I will never ever forget this incident with the latrine. People simply became animals.

The daily roll-calls, which took hours, were totally senseless. Occasionally two to three times daily and only in order to annoy us. More and more people collapsed. They just were shot and taken away. The eternal barbed wire was our only view and all the camps were divided by high-tension wires. Many people committed suicide in this way; they simply would crawl up to the barbed wires and would die immediately, glued to the wires. I still can clearly recall a young girl who did this. I had seen her still alive and the very next moment she had chosen death by reaching out and clutching the barbed wire. There we had hell in its purest form, impossible to describe.

One day Mengele appeared in person and asked the barrack's responsible whether there were any twins amongst the girls. Since nobody ever knew whether these questions meant life or death, she didn't want to take the responsibility upon herself and asked loudly: "Are there any twins amongst you?" By chance I had become the best friend of two of the girls who were twins. They slept opposite me on the bunk beds on the third level and we had become very friendly, since we all were of the same age. . . . These two girls said, "Yes, we are twins." Mengele came closer. He looked at them very carefully. They were almost identical with their freckled faces. All Mengele said was, "O.K., so come with me. Anyhow, by night you'll be back here." My instincts told me that I would never see my friends again and, indeed, I never saw them again and I even couldn't inquire about them since I have forgotten their names. I have been thinking a lot about these two. Who knows what experiments this brute carried out on them and how they had to die.

■ ■ ■

I believe it was spring when my dear Mama said, "Look Laluschka, look over there, a little bird is flying there and I tell you, that this is a sign of life or a sign to live and with the Lord's help we'll get yet out of here." I marvelled at her for being able to be so optimistic, because I didn't believe anymore in such miracles and I said only very softly and without strength, "Do you really believe this, Mama?" "Oh yes, I definitely believe that G. will help us." This is what she answered me, this poor, starving, yet admirably devout and dear little Mama. How terribly must she have felt to see her children so miserable and hungry.

. . . Again we were standing in line, four rows deep and had of course not the faintest idea what was going to happen to us next. Anyhow, we always stayed together and rubbed each others cheeks, so that we would look healthier and more capable to work. . . .

■ ■ ■

Amongst us was a Viennese girl, called Martha. Since the girl made the impression that she was smiling, the barrack's responsible became so upset that she had Martha fall on her knees with both hands stretched up. She had to stay in this position—without moving—for quite a while and again it seemed to her that Martha was smiling. The beast became even more furious and gave Martha a brick, which she was to hold up with stretched out arms, while being on her knees. I was standing facing her and until this day am unable to describe the pity and heartache I felt for her. I could see very clearly that one can humiliate and degrade a human being to a degree lower than that of a worm. By this time I had totally lost my confidence in adults, even before I started trusting them. For me, it was again a shocking experience. I will never ever, for as long as I'll live, forget it. I have been told today that Martha has survived and is living somewhere abroad.

I don't even remember how long we had been standing there, but after a very long time of standing, we were driven into the cattle cars. That's when Mama said to me, "You see, Laluschka, I told you that the little bird brought us the good news to get out of this hell. This is the most beautiful birthday present in my life." Neither had she lost faith to see Papa again some day.

We were travelling into uncertainty. Though nobody knew where to, everyone said that it couldn't be anywhere worse than Auschwitz. Today I cannot remember anymore how long we were riding in these cattle cars, all squeezed together like sardines. We also had lost all sense of time. Unfortunately, many girls suffocated and when the railroad cars were opened their dead bodies fell out.

We arrived in Hamburg, where they accommodated us next to the port, where we had to engage immediately in the cleaning up after bombardments. . . . Hamburg had more water and all of us were quite happy that after a long time we finally could somehow wash and drink. In the beginning we even got a little more food, but then winter came. Again it was snowing heavily and we had to shovel the snow from under a bridge in the icy cold. I can remember that one day during work, I blacked out and kind of started to sleep. Suddenly I felt as if someone [was waking] me and I saw the faces of many women over me. I overheard them saying, "The little one almost froze to death." They let me lie down for a little while longer and then many girls started massaging me and rubbing me, so that I started to feel my body, hands and feet again.

I felt miserable, totally depressed and without strength. I got up and continued to shovel snow and was thinking how one can go on living like this. Everything was so inhuman, always connected with fear, and one had to take the utmost care that the SS people should not notice that one of us women would feel bad, so that they would not—G. forbid—declare her as unfit to work. Because there was always the danger of being sent back to Birkenau, which would of course mean death by gas. With this the Germans used to threaten us all the time. That's why we used to work over and beyond our strength. . . .

Sometimes we also saw political prisoners, who had of course much better conditions; seeing us wretched, hungry and in rags, they would sometimes throw us a cigarette or a piece of bread. I personally never dared to pick up something, since everything was linked to the greatest danger. Girls who were lucky enough to pick something up would usually share it with a neighbour or a friend. As a matter of fact, there was never any scuffling. Only at night, when we used to come back to the camp, it was terrible. Then they used to check us, even gynecologically, to verify whether we hadn't smuggled anything into the camp from the outside. The name of the camp's responsible was Trude. She, together with camp commander Spiess, would search us very thoroughly and G. forbid if a piece of potato peel or something else would be found. Then the person in question would be treated to fifty whippings on his naked behind in front of all and administered with the greatest pleasure by Spiess himself. This would sadden me so much that for days on end I couldn't speak a word. Once a friend of Mama was beaten like this; she fainted, couldn't sit for weeks and all swollen, she only moaned in pain.

■　　■　　■

This same Spiess had almost once beaten Mama to death with a revolver, because Mama had found a potato peel. She said that he wanted to shoot her, but possibly the revolver hadn't been loaded and therefore he had beaten her with it on her head like a madman, until foam appeared at his mouth. For many weeks Mama couldn't go to work and her head was terribly swollen.

We had many rats in our barrack, which at night would crawl over us. We had to get used to that too and learned to live with it.

And then, the number of lice we had! We of course couldn't control them, because no sanitation whatsoever was possible. On the pillar in our barrack there was written, "One louse, your death" and that's why we couldn't show that we were full of lice; furtively we used to delouse one another and crush the lice.

One night, when we returned dead tired from work, the camp had disappeared. It had been bombed by the British and totally wiped out; we had nowhere to put our head. Some girls, who for some reason had stayed in the camp that day, had been killed or injured. Our doctor had also been hit and injured. And one of our guards was lying there stretched out and dead. I still can see the picture before my eyes. And that's how we [were] once more sent on; again into uncertainty, without anything tangible, only fear in our souls, hungry and uprooted, not knowing what else [was] in store for us. And always in a herd. The only thing I kept thinking about, the only important thing, was to stay together, because that was the one thing that kept us alive. Many women who had been alone just didn't care any more, they didn't want to live any more and finally died due to emotional exhaustion.

So they accommodated us in another camp in Hamburg and straight away we had begun working again.

■   ■   ■

Then came the day when the front drew nearer and once more we [were] evacuated. Partly again squeezed into cattle cars, where I felt like [I was] being choked. The bang of the bolt being shut still remains until this day in my ears. After a couple of days, I cannot recall how many, the door was opened. Most of us were already half dead when we saw also other trains with emaciated—to us totally unknown—people. These must have been people from other concentration camps, being evacuated to another place. Once out of the trains, we were standing again in rows of four and that's how the death march started on foot. Again, we had not the faintest idea where they would drag us.

In the beginning it was somehow still all right, mostly because we very happy to be in the fresh air and not like cattle in the cattle carriages. But slowly, every now and then, one of us would sit down by the road, feet all swollen, not being able to continue to walk any more. Those who couldn't go any further were simply shot down, without much ado. Further and further we went, with the strength of an iron will. And again I must stress that hadn't it been for my beloved Mama, who was next to me, I'm sure I wouldn't have survived this. She gave me courage, she comforted me in my desperation; she, who was desperate herself. She was my guardian angel. She also was mother to all the girls who were alone and she always found a word of comfort for them. All the girls tried to stay near to her and felt sheltered with her.

After many days of walking and after the house-shoes fell off from some swollen feet, we arrived in Bergen-Belsen. Though we had absolutely no notion where we were, we learned it afterwards. The very first sight of this ghastly camp was a huge hill of naked, dead people, who were practically only skeletons. Such a terrible and frightening sight I even hadn't seen in Auschwitz and right away I was thinking that within a few short days we would be looking the same, stacked like these ones. Because we wouldn't be able to take it much longer. Since we had lost a number of women from exhaustion on our way, I felt that we too were nearing the end.

■   ■   ■

There was absolutely nothing to eat. There was no water whatsoever. It was a total chaos, because the Germans had all run away, while the front was drawing closer and closer. We could hear cannon shots, but nobody could estimate the distance from which they were shot. There was nobody to supervise us, or to ask any questions.

Suddenly we saw Hungarian soldiers, or maybe they were Ukrainians, who had taken over the sentry boxes. They were shooting quite brutally all around and it seemed as if they would have liked to hit someone for fun. That's how they kept themselves happy and amused themselves. A couple of days later I personally witnessed when one of these soldiers shot at two sisters who could hardly creep anymore. One of them died on the spot. The wailing of the living sister was heart-rending. The only thing she was yet capable of was to whine and to moan. And that's how we all became "Mussulmen." Emaciated, lifeless, thrown together in dirty barracks.

Destiny brought me again together with the woman whose bread ration had fallen into the latrine in Auschwitz. She died on the floor one morning in my presence. Her daughter sat next to her, indifferent and numb. We had been for approximately two weeks in this snakepit, without eating or drinking. People died like flies; they simply collapsed. Death was everywhere and everywhere death was anticipated.

One morning we heard tanks and someone came into our barrack and said, "Kids, we are free!!!" But nobody moved, because nobody had any strength left over to be happy. All of us were already so apathetic that even with the best of intentions, this is almost indescribable.

Now we had a typhoid fever epidemic, because the British, when entering the camp with their tanks, threw canned food and bread to the people. Those who could still crawl ate some of it and the results were terrible. These people simply died like flies, not used any more to food. Mama, my guardian angel, had immediately warned us in a soft voice, "Children, do not touch this. After being hungry for so many years, the stomach is not able to process this food. Wait and eat slowly. Eat only tiny portions."

∎　∎　∎

The British soldiers taught us to walk again, just as one would teach a small child. So we stayed on for some more time, until they organized the repatriation, for each one to go back to his homeland.

∎　∎　∎

On our way from Bergen-Belsen to Prague, after the liberation, we made several stops. When the train would stop, we could even leave the train for a few minutes. One of these stops was Pilsen in Czechoslovakia. When the people saw us, they asked us from where we were coming and about the meaning of the tattooed numbers on our arms. We told them that we had spent three and a half years in concentration camps and that we had gone through hell. Upon which these people asked us, "And why didn't you stay where you were? Who needs you here?" We went back to the train, emotionally totally worn out. This was the welcome reception to freedom, for which we had so desperately been waiting.

Back in Prague, we didn't know what to do. Transportation was being arranged to Palestine and thus Mama had registered me with the Youth Aliya. According to her, at least one of us should take this step to freedom, after we hadn't been able to find Papa again. My eldest sister, Esther, had been living in Palestine for the last seven years already. She lived in Netanya and I went to stay with her.

■   ■   ■

My terrible traumatic memories will never leave me. Everything is still very much alive in me. My dearest Mama will always stay sacred to me. G. bless her memory. She was my guardian angel during the most horrible times.

December, 1985

5

The Human "Guinea Pigs" of Ravensbrück

Wanda Poltawska

Wanda Poltawska was nineteen when she was arrested by the Gestapo for aiding the Polish resistance. She spent four years in the women's concentration camp at Ravensbrück. Her narrative describes "medical" experiments that she and other Polish Christian women at Ravensbrück had to endure.

The same six women, the same beds, the same dressing-gowns we'd left behind, the same injections—except that this time it was Wanda who returned unconscious on the trolley, with her leg in plaster up to the knee and a Roman "I" painted on the plaster.

One at a time we were wheeled away on that trolley, weak and unresisting.

In the corridor outside the operating theatre, Dr. Schidlausky anaesthetized us with an intravenous injection. Before I lost consciousness, a single thought chased round my mind: "But we're not guinea-pigs, for heaven's sake." I think I must have kept repeating this sentence throughout the operation, and afterwards Dziunia and some of the others took it up. No, a thousand times no, we were not guinea-pigs. We were human beings.

But the term stuck. We used it of ourselves, and soon the whole camp came to know us as "the guinea pigs." The name was so apt that everyone, even the camp doctors, used it. To have spoken of "the women whose legs were operated on" might have left room for doubt as to identity, but "the guinea-pigs" left none at all.

When I came round, it was already late afternoon. The perimeter wall of the camp was casting a long shadow which reached the window of our room. I looked round at the others. Marysia Gnas was sitting up, with a feverish flush on her

This excerpt is reprinted from Wanda Poltawska's memoirs, *And I Am Afraid of My Dreams* (New York: Hippocrene Books, 1989).

round freckled face, while Wanda was gesticulating wildly. Only Zielonkowa lay immobile, for she was still unconscious.

I was desperately thirsty. The Sister passed me a white mug. I held out my hand to take it and was amazed that something so small could feel so appallingly heavy. I couldn't hold the mug and it fell with a crash and broke, scattering white fragments over the floor.

Consciousness began to flood back. I remembered my leg, and drew back the blanket. On the plaster were the letters III TK. I asked the others what was written on their cast: Wanda had I; Aniela I TK; Rozia II; Gnas II TK; Zielonkowa III; and me III TK. The mystery deepened.

I wasn't in any pain, but my leg was totally numb and my head ached with an unbearable heaviness.

I longed for sleep. The hot, August night had already fallen. And that was when it all began! Suddenly the girls were no longer sitting up, they were lying in a semi-stupor, tossing and turning in all directions, trying to find a less painful position for their poor legs. But it was impossible: the slightest movement intensified that monstrous, intolerable pain.

Sleep abandoned us. Wanda was screaming. Rozia moaning quietly; and every so often Zielonkowa cried out: "O, Jesus." Wanda's screams pierced my ear-drums and drilled into my brain until I thought I should go mad. "Shut up!" I shouted. She looked at me in an unfocused sort of way, and went on screaming. "Shut up!" I shouted again. "Shut up or I'll squash you to a pulp."

A glimmer of understanding came into her fever-bright eyes. . . . "I can't stop myself screaming," she said suddenly, quite calmly.

But she didn't go on screaming, just lay there groaning through clenched teeth. Aniela bit her pillow and uttered the occasional long-drawn-out groan. Marysia Gnas cursed quietly and colorfully. Me? I wanted to swear, scream, cry out, everything. I was terrifyingly clear-headed. Sister looked in at us from time to time, and went away without a word. (Only our group, the first of the "guinea-pigs," were fortunate enough to have a night-sister on duty. Our successors were simply locked in for the night, completely unattended.)

Outside the window I could see the black walls covered with hideously grinning barbed-wire. Here, not long ago, they had hung the charred body of a young gypsy girl who had tried to escape.

Wires, high-tension wires. I spoke the words aloud, as my heart leapt with a sudden resolve. *If I can only touch those wires, I can be at peace. I shall not have to go on enduring this atrocious pain. . . .*

It was morning again. Sunday mornings were different from other days in that a radio loudspeaker was put up on the camp's main street. In a show camp like Ravensbrück, care was taken to provide "cultural entertainment" for the prisoners. What a joke! The loudspeaker blared forth, blasting our ear-drums and dragging us out of sleep. The nauseating tones of Träumerei jangled our nerves. Sister came in to collect samples of blood and urine, samples which from now on she would take every second day. She put a thermometer into our mouths, and when she took out mine again I got a look at the silvery column of mercury and read out, "Just over 40 degrees Centigrade (104°F). Good heavens, I must be dreaming!"

Zielonkowa had a temperature of 40°C, and so did the others. Wanda's was the lowest, 39.7°C. So now I knew where Aniela's pretty rosy cheeks had come from.

Our legs swelled up, scarlet and angry. Mine was so swollen that the plaster cut into my flesh. A red streak ran up my right thigh all the way to the groin, where it ended in a painful lump. Dr. Oberheuser came in with a notebook. She bent over each leg and sniffed, before making a careful entry in her book.

On Monday, 3 August, we had another visit from Dr. Fischer, assistant to Professor Gebhardt, who had performed the operations on us. He was a man in the prime of life, greying at the temples, with a surgeon's skillful hands. I surveyed him with interest, trying to discern some trace of feeling in his expressionless gaze. So that's what a man who has committed a cold-blooded crime looks like! Why? For what motive had he done it? . . .

On the day that Fischer first came to see us, they applied the first dressings. God knows what it actually was, but they called it a dressing. They removed the plaster and did something or other to the wounds. We weren't able to see, because they put sheets over our heads, but whatever it was, it certainly hurt. I felt as though there were two gaping holes in my leg: one on the ankle bone, the other higher up; and that they were extracting something from these holes, something which was responsible for this atrocious pain.

They bandaged our legs and replaced the plaster. And they did not remove either plaster or bandages till a week later—and then only in the case of the first two numbers. Zielonkowa and I had to wait for two weeks.

The days succeeded each other in unchanging monotony. Our temperatures stayed in the region of 39 to 40°C. Every time we tried to move our mutilated legs, an evil-smelling yellowish brown fluid would seep from under the plaster sheath. Zielonkowa always had a pool on her bed, with swarms of flies buzzing round it.

They no longer had to bend down to sniff our legs. Dr. Oberheuser would wrinkle her nose whenever she came in: "It smells revolting in here." We stank with the sickly-sweet odor of pus and rotting flesh. Pus oozed out of a deep groove in Zielonkowa's leg. Quite apart from the wound itself, our muscles were wasting away from the effect of the discharge. We had pain in our legs and in our heads; and the morphine which they gave us, at first three times and then twice a day, had scarcely any effect on the terrible pain.

They did strange things to us. . . . I think that those who came after us also suffered as we did, though not in precisely the same way. It was not just a question of pain, but of the gnawing anxiety which tormented us in those first post-operative days. New unexpected problems suddenly faced us. We were undergoing a totally new experience and life had acquired a new and bitter taste. Uncertainty about the future, the fear of being crippled for life, and the monstrous unmerited pain thrust in front of us a host of new and unanswerable questions. . . .

One by one we were taken on the trolley to the theatre and laid on tables.

They removed the bandages and for the first time I could see the wounds they had inflicted on our legs. They were all in the same place, along the right tibia, 4–6 cm above the ankle—a cut about 11.5 cms long, its width increasing according to the number written on the plaster. I touched my own wound with my hand: it was very wide, yellowish-green and putrid. But Zielonkowa's was the worst.

We lay there for several hours. The tables were hard, and, in spite of the August heat, cold (we were clad only in thin night-dresses). Zielonkowa, who had been given a purgative in the morning, was writhing in agony. There were no bedpans and no one paid any attention to our shouts, though we could hear footsteps nearby and the sound of people talking.

When at last someone came, there were eleven of them. Eleven men. Eleven healthy men looking down at six defenseless women. They put our temperature charts and the results of our blood and urine tests on the sheets beside us.

All eleven of them leaned over me, sniffing excitedly at my putrid wound. I glared at them with what I hoped was defiance and boundless contempt.

6 Stranger in Exile

Ruth Levor

It haunted me, not so much that they had left everything behind that day when they turned the key in the lock of their comfortable Frankfurt apartment for the last time, but mostly that my immaculate housekeeper grandmother had left unwashed dishes in the sink to make it appear that she, my grandfather, my mother, and my uncles were planning to return shortly, so that they would not be turned back as they left to flee Nazi Germany for a new life in the United States. In the midst of stories of the unimaginable horrors of the concentration camps, it is this poignant image of the total and abrupt disruption of the upper-middle-class life my mother, her parents, and her brothers had enjoyed in their homeland that preoccupied me, that I could identify with most closely from the safety of my life in suburban America.

Although I was born and raised in the United States, far in distance and time from the savage events in Europe that doubtless shaped my own psychological and emotional development, I always felt somehow that I was a stranger in the "New World," that I was alienated from my surroundings. According to psychologist Yael Danieli in her article "Differing Adaptational Styles in Families of Survivors of the Nazi Holocaust," this alienation was more than just a sense shared by survivor families; it became a characteristic and even a coping mechanism for dealing with the need for eternal vigilance, for if the horror that had so terribly disrupted our parents' lives could happen in Germany, it could most certainly recur in our own lives.

My playmates and classmates, Jewish as well as non-Jewish, whose parents were American-born did not live under the same cloud that I did. Their mothers had not set out for school in Frankfurt as my mother did one morning only to find that the friends who walked to school with her every day were now wearing brown shirts and walking on the opposite side of the street to avoid contact with her. . . . *You are my friend today, but will you be my persecutor tomorrow?* . . . Their fathers had not left a widowed mother behind to come study at an American rabbinical seminary as my father did and then failed to secure her passage to America before the Nazis took her off to die in a concentration camp. . . . *If I go away, will you be here when I return?* . . .

My father was a Hillel rabbi, providing Jewish activities and leadership for students on college campuses. In the early sixties, a time when free speech was valued far above the then unknown virtue of political correctness, a group of students invited George Lincoln Rockwell of the American Nazi Party to speak on the campus where my father served. When he was unable to prevent Rockwell's appearance, Dad reacted with dreadful fear, rage, and depression that far exceeded any of the other uncontrollable tirades that periodically consumed him. In his view, based upon his own experience, the only way to control the awful results of hate speech was to suppress it.

I couldn't understand why none of my friends shared Dad's and my fears (we were college freshmen then). I thought that they were foolishly blinding themselves to the dangers of prejudice. It was only nearly twenty years later, when I studied the Supreme Court decision allowing the American Nazis to parade through Skokie, Illinois, an area heavily populated by Holocaust survivors, in Constitutional Law class, that I appreciated that the protection of free speech was more likely to prevent the empowerment of oppressive regimes than was the suppression of hateful ideas. However, I am still unable to distinguish in my heart between the supposedly benign ethnic and racial characterizations that shock the soul in the course of casual conversations and the vilest acts of violence and persecution produced by hatred and bigotry. Perhaps I never will.

The National Security Defense

7 Putative National Security Defense

Extracts from the Testimony of Nazi SS Group Leader Otto Ohlendorf at the Nuremberg War Crimes Trials

DIRECT EXAMINATION

DR. ASCHENAUER (Counsel for defendant Ohlendorf): What is your name?

DEFENDANT OHLENDORF: Otto Ohlendorf.

Q. When and where were you born?

A. On 4 February 1907, in Hoheneggelsen, District of Hanover.

Q. What was the profession of your father?

A. My father was an owner of a farm.

Q. Do you have any brothers or sisters?

A. I am the youngest of four.

Q. What is the profession of your brothers and sisters?

A. My oldest brother is a scientist; my second brother owns a farm; my sister has a business.

Q. What was the political opinion in your parents' house?

A. My father was an old National Liberal, and later he was at times a liaison official of the German People's Party.

Q. What was the religious attitude in your parents' home?

A. My parents were both practicing protestants.

Q. Where did you spend your childhood and adolescence?

A. Up to the last school year, I lived in my home town and worked on the farm in my leisure hours.

From *Trials of War Criminals before the Nuremberg Military Tribunals under Control Council Law No. 10*, vol. 4 (Washington, D.C.: U.S. Government Printing Office, 1950), 223–25, 283–87, 304–6, October 8–15, 1947.

Q. You emphasize the fact that you worked on your father's farm. Does that have any special significance in your development?

A. Unconsciously, I got to know the conditions and ways of handling a farm and got to know the human conditions in a farm district, that is, the cooperation and living together of farmers, industrial workers, peasants, merchants, tradesmen, and people of other trades. The rest of the time my professional development proceeded along with my political development. These conditions of administration, culture, religion, and education, as I got to know them in that village, always remained with me, and they became the leading motives for my own philosophy.

Q. What kind of education did you have?

A. After a few years of public school and high school, I graduated from the Gymnasium.

Q. Where and what did you study?

A. I studied in Leipzig, in Goettingen, and my fields were law and economics. Later, after my graduation, I spent one year in Italy studying the Fascist system and the Fascist philosophy of international law.

Q. Are you married?

A. Yes.

Q. Since when?

A. Since 1934.

Q. Do you have any children?

A. Yes. I have 5 children from 2 to 11 years of age.

Q. When did you become a member of the Nazi Party?

A. In 1925.

Q. How did you come to enter the Nazi Party?

A. I have been interested in politics from my earliest days on. When I was 16 years old, I was director of a youth group of the German National People's Party; but I was not sufficiently bourgeois and involved in the class system not to turn my back very quickly on this bourgeois party, since its special interests and political methods could not appeal to me. However, on the other hand, I was too closely connected with the moral, religious, and social philosophy of the traditional bourgeoisie to become a Marxist for instance. But at that time I recognized that the social demands were a truly national problem, a problem, that is to say, concerning the whole people, and I recognized that the national demands were also a truly social problem. These two points of view seemed likely to find the best solution in National Socialism in my opinion. In addition, I was attracted very much by the principle of achievement and the fact that active people were taken as criterion for building up the social organism, which was symbolically expressed in the term "Worker's Party." The doctrine of the national idea was also attractive to me, that is, the doctrine that peoples are independent organisms which by themselves and in themselves have to solve their own problems.

■   ■   ■

CROSS-EXAMINATION

MR. HEATH (Counsel for the Prosecution): You don't mean to say that the persons you killed had to endanger security in order to be killed, do you?

DEFENDANT OHLENDORF: In the sense of the Fuehrer Order, yes.

Q. Well, let's not say about the sense of the Fuehrer Order. Let's talk about reality. Did the people you killed in fact endanger security in any conceivable way?

A. Even if you don't want to discuss the Fuehrer Order it cannot be explained in any other way. There were two different categories; one, where those people who, through the Fuehrer Order, were considered to endanger the security were concerned and, therefore, had to be killed. The others, namely, the active Communists or other people were people whose endangering of security was established by us and they were only killed if they actually seemed to endanger the security.

Q. Very well. I repeat my question. Apart from the Fuehrer Order, and not because the Fuehrer Order assumed that every man of Jewish blood endangered the security of the Wehrmacht [armed forces], but from your own experience in Russia, from your own objective witnessing of the situation in Russia, did every Jew in Russia that you killed in fact endanger security, in your judgment?

A. I cannot talk about this without mentioning the Fuehrer Order because this Fuehrer Order did not only try to fight temporary danger, but also danger which might arise in the future.

Q. Well, let us get back to it immediately, and let us see if we can't talk about it without the Fuehrer Order. I ask you the simple question. . . . From your own objective view of the situation in Russia, did the Jews whom you killed, and the gypsies, endanger the security of the German army in any way?

A. I did not examine that in detail. I only know that many of the Jews who were killed actually endangered the security by their conduct, because they were members of the partisan groups for example, or supported the partisans in some way, or sheltered agents, etc.

Q. Let's put the partisans or those who were aiding the partisans completely aside.

A. I will assist you, Mr. Prosecutor. Of course, at a certain time there were persons of whom one could not have said at that moment that they were an immediate danger, but that does not change the fact that for us it meant a danger insofar as they were determined to be a danger, and none of us examined whether these persons at the moment, or in the future, would actually constitute danger, because this was outside our knowledge, and not part of our task.

Q. Very well. You did not do it then because it was outside of your task. I want you to do it today for this Tribunal. Will you tell us then whether in your objective judgment, apart from the Fuehrer's Decree, all of the Jews that you killed constituted any conceivable threat to the German Wehrmacht.

A. For me, during my time in Russia there is no condition which is not connected with the Fuehrer Order. Therefore, I cannot give you this answer which you would like to have.

Q. You refuse to make the distinction, which any person can easily make—you need not answer that. Let me make it clear then, in the Crimea—no, I believe near Niko-laev, Himmler came to see you in the spring of 1942, did he not, or fall of 1941?

A. Beginning of October 1941.

Q. You had then been working in that area a considerable number of Jewish farmers, is that right, and you had determined not to put them to death?

A. Yes.

Q. You made a determination then that those men did not then constitute any security threat whatever to the German armed forces?

A. No; I did not make such a determination but, in the interest of the general situation, and of the army, I considered it more correct not to kill these Jews because the contrary would be achieved by this, namely, in the economic system of this country everything would be upset, which would have its effect on the operation of the Wehrmacht as well.

Q. Then, I ask you the question again. Because these people were farmers, you concluded that it was wiser to get the grain they produced, than to put them to death?

A. Also because of the danger that they might shelter partisans, yes; I was conscious of this danger.

Q. What danger, that they might shelter partisans in their houses?

A. That these Jews might have contact with the partisans.

Q. So the only threat you saw to security was the possibility that the Jews would conceal partisans in their houses?

A. No; I only named this as an example. There might have been agents against us who could endanger us in every way. I only mentioned this as an example.

Q. The same situation would exist in the case of the Krimchaks, wouldn't it, or what do you call them, Karaims.

A. Karaims.

PRESIDING JUDGE MUSMANNO: Mr. Heath, I must confess a confusion here. I understand the witness to say, or perhaps you said it, that the reason the Jewish farmers were not executed is that they were used to bring in the harvest. Then a discussion ensued as to the possible threat that these Jews could bring to the security because they could house partisans. There must be a contradiction there; in one instance, they were a threat and, therefore, were subject to executions. Were they saved, or were they not saved? If they were saved, why, and if they were killed, why?

MR. HEATH: As I understood the witness, your Honor, he said he was balancing the desirability of getting in the harvest as against a potential threat.

PRESIDING JUDGE MUSMANNO: I see.

MR. HEATH: He exercised discretion.

PRESIDING JUDGE MUSMANNO: And came to the conclusion that there was more to be gained by not liquidating.

MR. HEATH: Precisely, so I understand it.

PRESIDING JUDGE MUSMANNO: Is that correct?

DEFENDANT OHLENDORF: I think it is even simpler. They were not farmers, they were craftsmen, who when there would be no longer work for them to do would endanger considerably the interests of the Wehrmacht. I never considered this problem in discussion but now Himmler came to me and ordered that these Jews were to be treated according to the Fuehrer Order, without any further discussion, and without any further consideration of circumstances.

MR. HEATH: What about the gypsies? I believe you have no idea whatever as to how many gypsies your Kommando killed, have you?

A. No. I don't know.

Q. On what basis did you kill gypsies, just because they were gypsies? Why were they a threat to the security of the Wehrmacht?

A. It is the same as for the Jews.

Q. Blood?

A. I think I can add up from my own knowledge of European history that the Jews actually during wars regularly carried on espionage service on both sides.

PRESIDING JUDGE MUSMANNO: You were asked about gypsies.

MR. HEATH: I was asking you about gypsies, as the Court points out, and not Jews. . . . I would like to ask you now on what basis you determined that every gypsy found in Russia should be executed, because of the danger to the German Wehrmacht?

A. There was no difference between gypsies and Jews. At the time the same order existed for the Jews. I added the explanation that it is known from European history that the Jews actually during all wars carried out espionage service on both sides.

PRESIDING JUDGE MUSMANNO: Well, now, what we are trying to do is to find out what you are going to say about the gypsies, but you still insist on going back to the Jews, and Mr. Heath is questioning about gypsies. Is it also in European history that gypsies always participated in political strategy and campaigns?

DEFENDANT OHLENDORF: Espionage organizations during campaigns.

PRESIDING JUDGE MUSMANNO: The gypsies did?

A. The gypsies in particular. I want to draw your recollection to extensive descriptions of the Thirty Year War by Ricarda Huch and Schiller—

Q. That is going back pretty far in order to justify the killing of gypsies in 1941, isn't it?

A. I added that as an explanation, as such motive might have played a part in this, to get at this decision.

Q. Could you give us an illustration of any activity of a band of gypsies on behalf of Russia against Germany during this late war?

A. Only the same claim that can be maintained as with regard to Jews, that they actually played a part in the partisan war.

Q. You, yourself cannot give us any illustration of any gypsies being engaged in espionage or in any way sabotaging the German war effort?

A. That is what I tried to say just now. I don't know whether it came out correctly in the translation. For example, in the Yaila Mountains, such activity of gypsies has also been found.

Q. Do you know that of your own personal knowledge?

A. From my personal knowledge, of course, that is to say always from the reports which came up from the Yaila Mountains.

Q. In an instance in which gypsies were included among those who were liquidated, could you find an objective reason for their liquidation?

A. From Russia I only knew of the gypsy problem from Simferopol. I do not know any other actions against gypsies, except from the one in Simferopol.

PRESIDING JUDGE MUSMANNO: Very well.

MR. HEATH: May I proceed, your Honor?

PRESIDING JUDGE MUSMANNO: Yes, please.

MR. HEATH: Mr. Ohlendorf, you say the gypsies are notorious bearers of intelligence? Isn't it a fact that the nationals of any invaded state are notorious bearers of intelligence. Didn't the Americans bear intelligence, and the Germans bear intelligence, and the Russians bear intelligence for their countries when they were at war?

A. But the difference is here that these populations, for example, the German population, or the American population have permanent homes, whereas gypsies being unsettled as people without permanent homes are more prepared to change their residence for a more favorable economic situation, which another place might promise them. I believe that a German, for example, is very unsuited for espionage.

■ ■ ■

MR. HEATH: . . . Was the [Fuehrer Order] a moral one; was it morally right, or was it morally wrong?

DEFENDANT OHLENDORF: I have just said that I do not think that I am in a position to decide on the moral issue, but I considered it to be wrong because such factors are able to bring such results which may have and, in my opinion, are bound to have immoral effects. But I do not think I am in a position to judge the responsibility of a statesman who, as is shown in history, rightly saw his people before the question of existence or nonexistence, or to judge whether a measure in such a fight against fate, for which this leader is responsible, is moral or immoral.

PRESIDING JUDGE MUSMANNO: Do we extract from all that you have said, this thought that you are not prepared to pass upon whether the order was morally right or morally wrong, but you do say that the order could only lead to very bad circumstances which would be injurious to Germany itself.

DEFENDANT OHLENDORF: Not only to Germany itself, your Honor. I consider this to be much more serious even. I see the order which Hitler gave, not as a first cause for this order, but I already consider it as a result of logical developments which may have started—or at least became very obvious—when in 1935, in our opinion, Germany was encircled. Such measures must further such developments, for example, to the effect that instead of an understanding, hatred, revenge, and an exaggerated effort to gain security will become very strong and, therefore, the general insecurity of the world will be increased. For example, causing effects, as can be described with the name "Morgenthau Plan" or requests, such as that Germany is being weakened in its greatness and strength so that this people will no longer endanger the security of anyone. That is what I meant by "effect" which might result from such factors, because they are intended for this, while I believe that throughout historical development at some time a chain of hatred or mistrust has to be broken in order to start anew somewhere, and that, for example, I hoped would be achieved through National Socialism which owing to its national basis, must be respected by each individual people, but here the chain is continued, a sequence is continued, which instead of reconciliation breeds more hatred, and increases the craving for security. That is my opinion on this.

MR. HEATH: May I put the question once more, if your Honor please?

PRESIDING JUDGE MUSMANNO: Yes, you may put the question and then the witness may answer it directly, or, if he feels he has already answered it, he may so indicate, or he may refuse to answer it. We will see what happens.

MR. HEATH: I do not ask you for a judgment of Hitler's morals; I ask you for an expression of your own moral conception. The question is not whether Hitler was moral; but what, in your moral judgment, was the character of this order—was it a moral order, or an immoral order?

DEFENDANT OHLENDORF: The question concludes itself, because you are not asking abstractly for a moral estimate of nothing—but a moral estimate and judgment about a deed of Hitler. And for that reason the judgment which I may make is a judgment on the deed of Hitler.

Q. Then may I ask one more question, and this is the last one, your Honor. You surrendered your moral conscience to Adolf Hitler, did you not?

A. No. But I surrendered my moral conscience to the fact that I was a soldier, and, therefore, a wheel in a low position, relatively, of a great machinery; and what I did there is the same as is done in any other army, and I am convinced that in spite of facts and comparisons which I do not want to mention again, the persons receiving the orders—and all armies are in the same position—until today, until this very day.

Q. It was not the coercion of the Hitler Order which overcame your moral scruple. It was the fact that you had surrendered to Hitler the power to decide moral questions for you—is that right?

A. That is an argumentation on your part which I never said. No, it is not correct. But as a soldier I got an order, and I obeyed this order as a soldier.

Q. Well, as a soldier you still had a moral conscience—I suppose you did—which required, if you had a moral conscience, you had to judge the orders that came to you. You got an order from Adolf Hitler, and you tell us you accepted his moral judgment absolutely, whether right or wrong—is that right?

A. That I accepted a moral judgment I certainly did not say. I think my answer will not be changed by the fact that you want me to make a certain reply.

Q. Let us put it in the negative, then. You refused to make any moral judgment then, and you refuse now to make any moral judgment?

A. The reason is—

Q. I am not asking you the reason. I am asking whether you refuse to express a moral judgment as to that time, or as of today.

A. Yes.

■   ■   ■

German Reparations

8 German Compensation for National Socialist Crimes

March 6, 1996

United States Department of Justice
Foreign Claims Settlement Commission

Since the Second World War, Germany has enacted a number of laws providing compensation for people who suffered persecution at the hands of the Nazis. Over the course of its forty year–plus compensation program, these laws have resulted in billions of dollars being paid to hundreds of thousands of individuals.

Compensation for crimes committed by the Nazi regime began soon after the Second World War when the occupation powers, with the exception of the Soviet Union, enacted laws in their individual zones restoring property confiscated by the Nazis to the original owners. The first such law was American: U.S. Military Government Law 59, which went into effect in November, 1947.

The Federal Republic of Germany (FRG) undertook its first compensation initiatives soon after its founding in 1949. Compensation was a high priority for Konrad Adenauer, the FRG's first Chancellor, who stated on September 27, 1951: "In our name, unspeakable crimes have been committed and demand compensation and restitution, both moral and material, for the persons and properties of the Jews who have been so seriously harmed."

I. HISTORY AND LEGISLATIVE ROOTS OF GERMAN COMPENSATION

THE BEGINNINGS

Konrad Adenauer began the process leading to the institution of a compensation and restitution program by inviting the State of Israel and a representative of world Jewry to enter into negotiations for the provision of material redress to Nazi crimes.

In response to his invitation, representatives of 23 Jewish organizations, which had a major interest in Jewish refugee problems on a worldwide or national scale, organized a representative body called the Conference on Jewish Material Claims against Germany, otherwise known as the "Claims Conference" or simply "CJMC."[1]

Simultaneous and parallel negotiations occurred between the FRG and Israel and the FRG and the Claims Conference. In September, 1952, two sets of agreements were signed at the Hague. One, between the FRG and Israel, required the FRG to provide goods and services to the newly born State of Israel. The second, between the FRG and the CJMC, required the FRG to (i) enact laws that would compensate Jewish victims of Nazi persecution directly, called Protocol No. 1, and (ii) provide funds for the relief, rehabilitation and resettlement of Jewish victims of Nazi persecution, called Protocol No. 2.

II. COMPENSATION PROGRAMS

A. BEG

The German laws regulating the implementation of Protocol No. 1 are known by the acronym of their German title, "Bundesentschaedigungsgesetz," or BEG. In English, the formal name for the BEG is "Federal Law for the Compensation of the Victims of National Socialist Persecution." Programs derived from BEG laws compensate individuals persecuted for political, racial, religious, or ideological reasons, and provide compensation to those who suffered physical injury or loss of freedom, property, income, professional or financial advancement as a result of that persecution.

The German compensation efforts were codified in three laws of the 1950's and 1960's. The first law, entitled the "Supplementary Law for the Compensation of the Victims of National Socialist Persecution," enacted October 1, 1953, implemented the initial German compensation program. It, in turn, was followed by the "Federal Law for the Compensation of the Victims of National Socialist Persecution" of June 29, 1956, which substantially expanded the first law's scope in favor of those receiving compensation. The "Final Federal Compensation Law," enacted on September 14, 1965, then increased the number of persons eligible for compensation as well as the assistance offered. The final deadline for application under the BEG was December 31, 1969.

A large number of people have benefitted from German compensation. Although German authorities did not document the exact number of people who applied for BEG and other compensation, more than four million claims were submitted between 1953 and 1987. It is important to note this is just a very general indication of the numbers of claimants as individuals submitted multiple claims under different categories, e.g., loss of property, loss of freedom, damage to health, etc. In terms of amounts of compensation paid, the German government provided a total of more than DM 72 billion for claims settled over this time. The German government continues to pay money for pensions awarded under the BEG. The deadlines for filing claims under the BEG laws of the 1950's and 1960's have expired. Thus, it is no longer possible to apply for compensation under these laws.

B. HARDSHIP FUND

During the period of detente, a large number of Jews were allowed to emigrate from the Soviet Union and from behind the Iron Curtain. These people had not been eligible to apply under the BEG and found that, by the time of their emigration to the West, the filing period for the BEG had expired. In order to make compensation available to eligible members of this group, the FRG created the Hardship Fund which is administered by the Claims Conference.

Applications for compensation under the Hardship Fund are still being accepted. Compensation is available to Jewish victims of Nazi persecution who (i) have received no previous compensation and (ii) currently live under difficult financial conditions. Compensation under the Hardship Fund consists of a one-time payment of DM 5000.

■   ■   ■

C. ARTICLE 2 FUND

Unification forced the German government to evaluate how the country would continue, or change, the compensation efforts of its two predecessor states, East and West Germany. During the 1990 negotiations on German unification, the decision was taken to confirm, and partially extend, West Germany's existing provisions on compensation. This decision was formalized in Article 2 of the "Agreement on the Enactment and Interpretation of the Unification Treaty" of September 18, 1990, that unified Germany.

The Article 2 Fund was established and, like the Hardship Fund, is administered by the Claims Conference.

Applications for compensation under the Article 2 Fund are still being accepted. Jewish victims of Nazi persecution are eligible if they were:

i. six months or longer in a concentration camp or eighteen months or longer in a ghetto or eighteen months or longer in hiding; and
ii. received no more than DM 10,000 in previous compensation;
iii. currently live under difficult financial circumstances.

If eligible, compensation is a lifetime pension in the amount of DM 500 per month.[2]

■   ■   ■

D. COMPENSATION FOR NON-JEWISH VICTIMS

In 1981, the Bundestag decided to make up to DM 100 million available for payments to non-Jewish victims of the Nazi regime who had previously been unable to receive compensation.

Applications are still being accepted for this fund, which is managed by the Regierungspraesident in Cologne (Koeln). Based on the German Federal Government's guidelines of August 26, 1981, one-time aid can be granted if the recipient is a non-Jewish victim of persecution who resides in a Western country, who suffered injury to health as a result of injustices perpetrated by the Nazis and who is in a state of particular (financial) need.

A further prerequisite is that the victim has received no or very little compensation for the injustices committed against them by the Nazis.

■   ■   ■

E. THE U.S.-GERMAN NAZI PERSECUTION (PRINCZ) AGREEMENT

In early 1995, Germany offered to negotiate an agreement with the United States to compensate victims who were U.S. nationals at the time they suffered persecution, including the well-known claimant, Hugo Princz. The U.S. and Germany concluded the agreement in September, 1995. A first tranche of money was paid that month to a number of individuals known to qualify under the agreement.

Article 2(2) of the Agreement provides for negotiation of an additional lump sum payment by Germany to compensate claimants who satisfy the Agreement's criteria, but who did not share in the first tranche. Negotiation of the additional compensation amount will take place two years after entry into force of the Agreement, assuming the United States identifies further eligible claimants.

To be eligible for compensation under the Agreement, claimants must satisfy several criteria. These require that the claimant:

- was a victim of Nazi measures of persecution (this generally requires incarceration in a concentration camp, and does not include persons detained as civilian internees);
- was a U.S. citizen at the time he or she suffered Nazi persecution;
- suffered loss of liberty or damage to body or health as a result of the persecution;
- was a direct victim of persecution (i.e., heirs are not covered); and
- has to date received no compensation from the FRG.

In January, 1996 Congress enacted legislation authorizing the Foreign Claims Settlement Commission (FCSC), an agency with the Department of Justice, to receive and adjudicate claims for any additional eligible claimants under the Agreement. . . . This will permit negotiation between the U.S. and Germany within the time frame contemplated in the Agreement.[3]

■ ■ ■

Persons who were subjected to forced labor alone while not also being detained in a concentration camp are not eligible for compensation under this Agreement. Please see the section on forced labor which follows.

III. SOCIAL SECURITY SUPPLEMENTARY AGREEMENT

The United States and Germany have concluded a new Social Security supplementary agreement that will pay German benefits to German Jews from Eastern Europe who settled in the U.S. after fleeing their Nazi-occupied homelands. The agreement should take effect in the first half of 1996 and result in German benefit payments to an estimated several thousand U.S. residents.

The Agreement amends a bilateral Social Security Agreement between the U.S. and Germany that dates back to 1979. It includes a new provision that grants benefits to people who previously lived in parts of Eastern Europe that were taken over by the Nazis during World War II and the pre-War era. Those who qualify may be able to receive monthly Social Security benefits from Germany based on the time they spent working in their former homelands, even though they may never have worked in Germany. Benefits can also be paid to the surviving spouses and children of these workers.

To be eligible for benefits, which can be paid as far back as July 1, 1990, claimants must pay contributions to the German Social Security system. There will be no actual cost for most people, however, since the contributions may be deducted from back benefits. In almost all cases, the back benefits will exceed the required contributions.

People who wish to receive the new benefits must meet a number of requirements, including:

   i. They must be U.S. or German citizens (or refugees or stateless persons); and
  ii. They must have established residence in the U.S. before July 1, 1990; and
 iii. They must be Jewish; and
  iv. Their mother tongue must have been German; and
   v. They must have reached the age of 16 before the Nazis took control of their former homeland. This date varies depending on the region, but anyone who reached age 16 after September 1, 1941, will generally not be eligible.

■ ■ ■

IV. WHAT CAN THE U.S. GOVERNMENT DO TO HELP?

The United States Government is very concerned with the question of securing compensation for suffering caused by the Nazi oppression of the 1930's and 1940's. It has engaged the German government intensively over the years since the Second World War to press for the resolution of these claims as a whole.

It is important to note that the ability of our Government to pursue individual claims is determined under principles of international law. One of these principles limits the United States to pressing claims against foreign governments only on behalf of citizens who were U.S. nationals at the time that the claim or loss occurred and who continuously maintained their citizenship to the present. Other American citizens need to resolve their claims under the domestic procedures of the country of which they were a national at the time of their persecution.

Those Americans who were citizens of Germany at the time the persecution occurred must therefore resolve their claims under German domestic procedures. The State Department can provide the names of German attorneys who can assist in such cases.

APPENDIX I: COMPENSATION FOR FORCED LABOR

Germany considers forced labor cases to be reparation claims arising from the actions of the German military forces during the Second World War. Reparations claims are to be addressed at the state-to-state level, and again depend on the nationality of the individual at the time of persecution. Forced laborers were brought to Germany mainly from Poland and the former Soviet Union, both of which waived reparation claims in the early years after the war. However, in October 1991, Germany agreed with Poland to establish the German-Polish Reconciliation Foundation to provide financial assistance to Polish citizens who suffered mistreatment at the hands of the Nazis during World War II. By agreement between the two governments, payments under this German-funded program were limited to current residents of Poland. We have, however, received conflicting reports of whether the Polish residency requirement still applies.

Forced laborers who suffered other forms of Nazi persecution may still file for compensation as described above.

APPENDIX II: NON-BEG, BILATERAL AGREEMENTS

Between 1959 and 1964, the FRG worked out bilateral agreements with twelve western European nations. As a result of these agreements, the FRG provided a total of nearly DM 900 million to those nations to enable them to compensate citizens not eligible under the BEG for damages incurred as victims of Nazi policies. This was just a portion, however, of the total compensation provided by these countries to their citizens. Under these lump sum agreements, the government receiving the payment is responsible for distribution of compensation to its nationals. Distribution is governed by the claims procedures of these nations' legal systems. The victims' survivors are sometimes eligible for compensation under these agreements.

This approach has been continued since unification. As noted above, in 1991 Germany agreed to pay DM 500 million to the "Foundation for German-Polish Reconciliation." The money will be used to compensate Polish citizens who had been victims of Nazi persecution. Germany has established a similar arrangement with three of the successor states to the Soviet Union: Belarus, the Russian Federation, and Ukraine. Under this agreement, Germany will contribute DM 1 billion to a "Foundation for Understanding and Reconciliation." The U.S.-German Nazi Persecution Agreement is the latest in this series of bilateral agreements.

NOTES

1. The Claims Conference is a non-profit organization, headquartered in New York City, which continues to negotiate with Germany for compensation programs on behalf of Jewish victims of Nazi persecution. Currently the Claims Conference also administers two active compensation programs: the Hardship Fund and Article 2 Fund, both of which are described [in the text]. . . .

2. The Conference has received many more applications than anticipated under the program, and has a substantial back-log of claims to be processed.

3. See 22 U.S.C. § 1621 et seq.

9 | Romani Victims of the Holocaust and Swiss Complicity

Ian Hancock

The Holocaust has been established in the historical tradition as something separate from both the Second World War and—for the overwhelming majority of its historians—from the targeting of *all* populations regarded as undesirable in the Third Reich's new world order. While the latter distinction has been challenged on a number of grounds, the factor of genocide—the intent systematically to exterminate—justifiably sets just two ethnically or "racially" defined peoples apart: the Jews and the Roma. From this perspective, the Holocaust becomes synonymous with the Final Solution, and while Romani and Jewish scholars may argue that the treatment of their own individual populations by the Nazis was quantitatively or qualitatively unique,[1] Reinhardt Heydrich's directive of July 31, 1941, which set the machinery of the Holocaust in motion, ordered the Einsatzkommandos to begin the eradication of "all Jews, Gypsies and mental patients"; no other groups were included in that order. Heydrich, who was the chief architect of the Final Solution, included mental patients because, like Jews and Roma, they too were regarded as genetic contaminants in the body of the master race. Roma were included "with no regard to the degree of their racial impurity" in the transport order issued by Heinrich Himmler, acting upon a direct order from Adolf Hitler, following the Wannsee Conference in 1942.[2]

BACKGROUND

Indications of the racist rationale for singling out Roma (called Sinti in German-speaking countries) parallel the emergence of Germans' sense of their own racial exclusiveness and date from the very time of the Roma's arrival in Germany.[3] Martin Luther's anti-Semitic and anti-Roma proclamations in the sixteenth century have prompted statements of apology and regret from the Lutheran Church today. In 1721, 220 years before Hitler, Emperor Karl VI ordered the extermination of all Roma everywhere; in 1725 his successor, Friedrich Wilhelm I, condemned all Roma of eighteen years and older to be hanged. In 1793, the Lutheran minister Martin Zippel compared Roma in a "well-ordered state" to vermin on an animal's body. In 1808, Johann Fichte wrote in his *Addresses to the German Nation* that the "German race" had been chosen by God to lead humanity. Two years later, the German nationalist Friedrich Jahn wrote that a people without a homeland is "nothing—a bodiless, airless phantom, like the Gypsies and the Jews." In 1835, Theodor Tetzner wrote that Roma in Germany were the "excrement of humanity," wording repeated by Robert Knox in his *Races of Men* (1850). The German sense of racial superiority was greatly fueled by Joseph Gobineau's statement in his *Essay on the Inequality of the Human Races*, published in 1855, that the Aryan peoples constituted "the cream of mankind," and that "the Germans [were] the cream of the cream: A race of princes."

A significant phrase coined by Richard Liebich appeared in an anti-Roma treatise he wrote in 1863: "lives unworthy of life" (*Lebensunwertesleben*). Again with reference to Roma, it was picked up and used by Richard Kulemann in 1869. It became part of the title of an influential book by Karl Binding and Alfred Hoche that appeared in 1920, and was the name of one of Hitler's first laws, introduced July 14, 1933, not long after he became chancellor.[4] In 1871, Charles Darwin described the behavior of "Jews and Gypsies . . . which contrasted sharply with the culturally advanced Nordic Aryan race," influencing Cesare Lombroso (1876), whose work appeared in German, and who typified Roma as "a whole *race* of criminals." In 1886, Otto von Bismarck called for the "especially severe" treatment of Roma and introduced legislation to control their movement. This led in 1890 to a national conference on "the Gypsy Scum" at which the military was empowered to expel Roma from any area. In 1899, the Gypsy Information Agency was established in Munich to monitor the movements of the Roma throughout Germany and to begin their complete registration. This was also the year that Houston Stewart Chamberlain's *Foundations of the Nineteenth Century* appeared, in which he credited the German people with the greatest scientific and cultural accomplishments and called for them to lead a "newly-shaped" and "especially-deserving Aryan race."

In 1905, Alfred Dillman's *Gypsy Book* appeared, the product of the 1899 resolution, which listed names and personal data for all Roma throughout Germany. The first part of the book called upon the German people "unflaggingly to defend itself" against Roma, which it referred to as "pests" and a "plague." This academically sanctioned dehumanization, and the likening of Roma to infestation and disease, steadily gained momentum and was a major tool in generating public disdain in Nazi Germany. Binding and Hoche's 1920 book argued for the disposal of certain categories of people through euthanasia; their second category—people with incurable hereditarily transmitted defects—was considered to apply to Roma, since their supposed criminality was interpreted as a genetic disease. This "criminality," it should be pointed out, included lighting fires in public areas, stealing food, and

trespassing—all social responses to centuries-old discriminatory legislative measures.

During the 1920s, laws were introduced that forbade Roma throughout Germany to enter public facilities such as parks, fairgrounds, or baths; required their
wholesale photographing and fingerprinting; and incarcerated those without employment or fixed abode in specially created camps. When Hitler came to power,
tight legislative control of Roma was already firmly in place, and public sentiment
against them needed no prompting.

NAZI GERMANY

The July 1933 law against "lives not worthy of life" was directed "specifically [at]
Gypsies and most of the Germans of black color"—that is, mainly the Afro-Euro-
pean children resulting from unions between Senegalese troops (brought in by the
French during World War I) and local German women. From 1934 on, Roma were
selected for sterilization by injection or castration to prevent any "hereditarily-dis-
eased offspring" and sent to camps at Dachau, Dieselstrasse, Sachsenhausen,
Marzahn, and Vennhausen. In 1935, Roma became subject to the restrictions of the
Nuremberg Law for the Protection of German Blood and Honor, which forbade
marriage or sexual unions between non-Aryan and Aryan people. The National
Citizenship Law that same year deprived both Roma and Jews of their civil rights.
In June 1938, "Gypsy Clean-Up Week" saw the beating and arrest of hundreds of
Roma throught Germany and Austria. The first mention of "The Final Solution of
the Gypsy Question" appears in a statement issued by Himmler on December 8,
1938. In January 1940, the first mass genocidal action of the Holocaust took place
at Buchenwald, where 250 Romani children were used as guinea pigs to test the
Zyklon-B crystals later used in the gas chambers at Auschwitz-Birkenau. Deportation orders followed Himmler's directive of December 16, 1942, and by 1945 between half a million and 1.5 million Roma, perhaps half of all Roma in Nazi-con-
trolled Europe, had perished in the *Porrajmos* ("the Devouring"), as the Holocaust
is called in Romani.[5]

SWITZERLAND

The arrival of Roma in Switzerland was first documented in 1428; "Gypsy hunts"
were encouraged among its citizens from 1514 on, as a means of clearing Roma out
of the country. A twentieth-century Swiss attempt to destroy its Romani population
came to light in 1986, when it was revealed that "proto-Nazi ideas of race hygiene"
motivated Pro Juventute's "Operation Children of the Road," which since 1926
had been forcibly removing the children of Romani and non-Romani traveling families for permanent placement in state institutions.[6] The Swiss provision of refuge to
the Jews fleeing from Nazi Germany, who until 1938 were arriving "in extraordi-

nary proportions,"[7] was never extended to Roma.[8] Instead, and despite the general understanding to the contrary, the Swiss government was handing its Romani citizens over to the Nazis and certain death.[9] It has also been revealed that during the Nazi period, a "high number" of forced sterilizations were carried out upon Roma in Switzerland. When the news broke in 1977, "a health ministry spokesman declined to comment, saying the issue was a thing of the past."[10] Since 1945, Roma in Switzerland have continued to suffer ongoing, systematic incarceration and abuse in police custody.[11]

The Roma, like the Jews prior to 1948, have lived in Europe as a nonterritorial population since their arrival in the West from Asia at the beginning of the fourteenth century. Because of this distinctive history, Roma have lacked political, economic, national, and military strength, a situation which remains unchanged today. For this reason, they have been easy prey to discriminatory legislation, and have been powerless to defend themselves against it. The most pervasive form of legalized anti-Gypsyism over the centuries has been the countless edicts forbidding Roma to stay in an area—keeping them on the move in a constant search for an income, food, and shelter.[12] Because of this, the Romani presence in Western Europe has been characterized by constant movement, and the subsequent lack of access to establishment institutions, including banks.

Because most Roma carried their wealth on their person—in the form of gold teeth, necklaces, rings, bracelets, coins serving as buttons on clothing, earrings, and so on—rather than protecting it in safety-deposit vaults or converting it to paper assets, little documentation exists for property stolen by the Nazis from the Romani people. Carrying coins and other small items of value is an established Romani practice; they were useful for buying one's way out of trouble when such situations presented themselves. However, it was illegal in Nazi Germany for private citizens to own gold, and this was a premise for its confiscation by the police. Receipts were generally not provided, and the documentation available to us today is scant for the precious metals, gems, jewelry, furniture, conveyances, farm animals and implements, and musical instruments that were taken from them. Thus the greater part of the assets confiscated from Roma were not in the form of appropriated bank accounts, but rather were personal valuables only later converted into bankable property by the Nazis, and categorized as "non-monetary gold."

At the end of 1996, when the news broke that money confiscated by the Nazis was being held in Swiss banks, compounded by the discovery the following January by a security guard of Nazi-related bank records about to be destroyed—in violation of a federal ban—charges were made that the central bank had routinely laundered plundered gold for the Nazis throughout the Second World War. The response from the Swiss government was swift: It announced that restitution would be forthcoming to those who could present valid claims. The amount first mentioned was 5 billion Swiss francs, or 4.7 billion U.S. dollars. But in all of the ensuing international media coverage, Roma were not mentioned.

On February 12, 1997, the Swiss government agreed to explore with Jewish groups, but not with Romani groups, how to compensate Holocaust survivors.

After meeting with representatives of the State of Israel and of the World Jewish Congress, Swiss Minister of Foreign Affairs Flavio Cotti announced that as of March 1, 1997, a fund of $70 million would be put in place, donated by the Union Bank of Switzerland, the Swiss Bank Corporation, and Credit Suisse, Switzerland's three largest banks. On March 5, the Associated Press reported Swiss President Arnold Koller as saying that his government would set up an additional fund of $5 billion to aid victims of the Holocaust and of any other genocide or disaster, and would finance it by selling off tons of gold over the next few decades.

This is not the first such deal involving Swiss banks. Some thirty-five years earlier in 1962, after having consistently denied holding any victims' assets, a number of Swiss banks announced that they had "discovered" $7 million belonging to Jews killed in the Holocaust, which were then turned over to various Jewish charities. Responding to ongoing pressure from attorneys representing Jewish groups, they unearthed a further $28 million in 1995, although those attorneys claim that as much as $7 *billion* still remains unaccounted for. Whether this money was demonstrably only of Jewish origin, or had in part been converted from property also taken from Roma, was not addressed at that time, though there is no reason to believe that the situation thirty-five years ago was any different from today's. Nor is Switzerland alone in its complicity, since some of the gold in its banks was then sent on by the Nazis to pay neutral countries, such as Sweden, Spain, Portugal, and Argentina, for war materials and supplies.[13]

On April 16, 1997, the Swiss Federal Council announced that it had appointed a prominent Swiss businessman, Rolf Bloch, to head a new committee to oversee the disbursement of the stolen funds. In consultation with the World Jewish Restitution Organization, an umbrella group of major Jewish organizations together with Israeli state representatives, three prominent Jews were selected for membership on the same board to serve alongside the four members appointed by the Swiss government. All of the media coverage, without exception, focused on the property confiscated from the Jewish victims of the Nazis, prompting the representative of one Swiss Romani association to complain that they were treating the situation as though it were "purely a Swiss-Jewish concern";[14] indeed, a year later *USA Today* could still refer to the "$300 million in gold stolen from Jews."[15] The Roma representative, not even named in the article, despaired that arguments over who was to serve on the board "have eliminated a role for the Nazis' number two victims [since] . . . no Gypsies were named to the seven-member board."[16]

An eighteen-member advisory council was also created by Swiss and non-Swiss organizations, which was to include representatives of various groups victimized in the Holocaust. "European Gypsies" were included in this proposal, and two were appointed: Dr. Rajko Djurić, president of the International Romani Union and now residing in Berlin; and Robert Huber, president of Radgenossenschaft der Landstrasse, the main Swiss organization of Roma and non-Roma travelers. Not appointed, but working closely with the various parties, is Jan Czory, of the Kris Rom International, and Dr. Jan Cibula, past president of the International Romani Union, both of whom reside in Switzerland.

THE UNITED STATES

In the United States, the national bureau of the International Romani Union, led by UN Praesidium Head Dr. Ian Hancock and National Representative John Nickels, appointed Philadelphia attorneys Sebastian Rainone and Joseph Nicola to file claims for reparations on behalf of that organization. This required locating survivors and relatives of survivors who could prove their case. The ancestors of the overwhelming majority of Romani Americans, who number about one million, arrived in this country several decades before the Nazi period and consequently have no direct link to the Holocaust. Only five survivors have been located in the United States, and because of cultural restrictions on speaking of the dead, only a couple of those are willing to become involved in the campaign for reparations. There are more eligible individuals among the post-1990 influx of Roma from central and eastern Europe, but their sometimes illegal status makes them reluctant to come forward. The national bureau is gathering the names of survivors in Europe, particularly in Poland and Romania, but Romani organizations in those countries have first access to them. In December 1997, an official statement by Dr. Hancock was circulated at the London Conference on Nazi Gold, and Dr. Donald Kenrick of the Romani Institute in London was deputized to present the Romani case. He gave an overview of the plight of Roma in the Holocaust and reported that the International Romani Union was asking for a fund of $115 million to be created to help European Roma. The request received no response. A very small number of Romani individuals reportedly have been given insignificant amounts of money (as little as $1,500) by way of compensation, and concerns have been raised that this will be seen as sufficient compensation and acknowledgment on the part of the Swiss. Those individuals were likely pleased to receive any money at all and were not in a position to decline it in the hopes of a more equitable settlement, which may or may not be forthcoming.

It may be that greater recognition of the Roma will come from the United States than from Europe; the U.S.-based Executive Monitoring Committee, an informal network of more than eight hundred public finance officers, was instrumental in getting a joint U.S.-Swiss statement issued by the State Department reaffirming the commitment of both governments to "address openly all issues related to the Holocaust, and to its victims."[17]

In 1998, Senate Bill 1900 created a federal Commission on the Swiss Gold. In addition to two U.S. congressmen, four senators, and the chairperson of the U.S. Holocaust Memorial Council, the bill provides for the appointment of individuals from the private sector, and an effort is being made to have John Nickels placed on this committee. If this effort is successful, a Romani voice will find a place.

Generally, however, efforts to become a part of the process have not been particularly successful. This is to a large extent because as a people Roma are fragmented and have no funded, international organizational base. Roma are divided not only geographically, but economically, for it takes money to meet together in person, engage legal representation, and even to maintain ongoing telephone and fax communication. Furthermore, anti-Gypsyism is at an all-time high and, sadly, finds its way upward to the administrative levels. Roma are simply not given the acknowledgment they are rightfully due, first as people, and second as central participants in the matter of the confiscated assets.[18]

The fate of the Romani people in the Holocaust is slowly gaining recognition. Organizations such as the Romani Union Holocaust Archives in Texas and the Sinti and Roma Documentation Centre in Heidelberg are able to provide documented evidence of the Nazi appropriation of Romani assets; to give just two examples, all belongings were confiscated from Roma being transported from Germany into Poland, and at Klincy in Russia, where the mass execution of Roma was taking place, all of their possessions were collected and sent to Germany. The Romani Union is also gathering evidence that personal property stolen from Roma in Serbia, in particular at the extermination camp at Jasenovac, was sent to the Vatican by the Ustashi, handed over to them by the Catholic monks who ran that camp. It was claimed at the London Conference that nearly $2 million in gold coins and personal jewelry was confiscated from the more than 28,000 Roma murdered there. The Vatican refused to respond to this and other charges leveled at it during that conference.[19]

Even if only 100,000 Roma holding their family savings in the form of jewelry and money had been arrested—a considerable underestimation—and even if these assets were worth only $1,000 per family by today's standards, this would amount to $100 million. Romani organizations agree that if restitution is forthcoming, only part of it should go in the form of pensions to the survivors, while the rest should be used to improve the situation of Roma in Europe today, particularly in the areas of human rights, health, and education.

NOTES

1. Some Jewish Holocaust scholars, such as Selma Steinmetz (*Oesterreichs Zigeuner im NS-Staat: Monographien zur Zeitgeschichte* [Frankfurt: Europa Verlag, 1966], p. 5), have argued that "numbers decide" in the ranking of victimhood; others point to the pathologically obsessive and ruthless targeting of Jews not matched by any other victimized group. Some Romani scholars argue that oppressive anti-Roma laws were already in place before 1933, and that the criteria for determining who was Romani were exactly twice as strict as those determining who was Jewish. Neither position is productive; they both create aspects of a "suffering olympics," as well as tensions between Roma and Jews that serve only to delight the common enemies of both peoples. See Ward Churchill, "Assaults on Truth and Memory: Holocaust Denial in Context," in his *A Little Matter of Genocide* (San Francisco: City Lights Books, 1997), pp. 19–62; David Young, "The Trial of Remembrance: Monuments and Memories of the Porrajmos," in *Genocide Perspectives I: Essays in Comparative Genocide*, ed. Colin Tatz (Sydney: Centre for Comparative Genocide Studies, Macquarie University, 1997); Ian Hancock, "'Uniqueness' of the Victims: Gypsies, Jews and the Holocaust," *Without Prejudice: International Review of Racial Discrimination* 1, no. 2 (1988): 45–67.

2. Ian Hancock, "Responses to the Porrajmos: The Romani Holocaust," in *Is the Holocaust Unique?* ed. Alan Rosenbaum (Boulder, Colo.: Westview Press, 1996), pp. 39–64.

3. Ian Hancock, "Gypsy History in Germany and Neighboring Lands: A Chronology Leading to the Holocaust," in *The Gypsies of Eastern Europe*, ed. David Crowe and John Kolsti (Armonk, N.Y.: M. E. Sharpe, 1989), pp. 24–25.

4. This is also the title of a recent book on the Holocaust. See James M. Glass, *Life Unworthy of Life: Racial Phobia and Mass Murder in Hitler's Germany* (New York: Basic Books, 1997).

5. Estimates of Romani losses vary enormously. Those given here are from Sybil Milton, former senior historian at the U.S. Holocaust Memorial Research Institute, who estimates that "something between a half-million and a million-and-a-half Roma and Sinti were murdered in Nazi Germany and Occupied Europe between 1939 and 1945." Judith Latham, *First U.S. Conference on Gypsies in the Holocaust* (Washington, D.C.: Voice of America Transcript, 1995), No. 3-23928.

6. See Frances Williams, "Swiss Shame over Stolen Children," *Sunday Times* (London), June 8, 1986, p. 10; Reto Pieth, "Switzerland's Secret Crusade against the Gypsies," *In These Times*, January 27–February 2, 1988, p. 4.

7. Raul Hilberg, *The Destruction of the European Jews* (New York and London: Holmes and Meier, 1985), p. 55.

8. Swiss immigration officials refused to admit the Romani refugees seeking asylum who had marched to Geneva from Germany in 1993, led by Rudko Kawczynski, following the German government's declaration—subsequently carried out—to return them to eastern Europe.

9. Hans Caprez, "Zigeuner an die Nazis ausgeliefert" ["Roma Handed over to the Nazis"], *Brennpunkt* 17 (1997): 10–13.

10. Jacqueline Fihr, "Swiss Women's Groups React with Outrage over Gypsy Sterilizations," RNN News Bulletin, Geneva and Westeros, August 27, 1997.

11. The best source documenting this over the years is the periodical *Scharotl*, published by the Genossenshaft der Landstrasse Interessengemeinschaft des Fahrendes Volkes in der Schweitz, available from the Secretariat, Postfach 1647, 8048 Zurich, Switzerland.

12. This has given rise to the romanticized image of the "wandering Gypsy" in Western literature, reinterpreted as an innate urge to be free to travel. Even during the period of the Third Reich, this so-called *Zigeunerromantik* flourished; a number of German films were made reflecting this theme, even as Roma were being sent to the extermination camps.

13. Maria Puente, "Report Says Nazis Paid Neutral Nations with Stolen Gold," *USA Today*, June 2, 1998, p. 6-A.

14. "Gypsies Aggravated at Being Left Off Holocaust Fund Board: Omission by the Swiss Government Is Called an Insult to the Memory of Nameless Victims," *Fort Worth Star-Telegram*, April 20, 1997, p. 2.

15. Puente, "Report says Nazis Paid Neutral Nations with Stolen Gold," p. 6-A.

16. Ibid.

17. *Swiss Monitor: An Update on Switzerland's Progress in Making Restitution to Holocaust Survivors* (June 1998): 1.

18. This extends to due acknowledgment of the status of Roma in the Holocaust generally. See Hancock, "Responses to the Porrajmos"; Ian Hancock, "The Roots of Antigypsyism: To the Holocaust and After," in *Confronting the Holocaust*, ed. Jan Colijn and Marcia Sachs Littell (Lanham, Md.: University Press of America, 1997), pp. 19–49. By way of a

contemporary example, the ongoing opposition to the erection of non-Jewish memorials at Auschwitz does not take into account that Auschwitz-Birkenau was the main killing center for Europe's Roma, too, most of whom were Christian.

19. Maureen Johnson, "Gypsy Gold in the Vatican?" Associated Press news feature on America Online, December 4, 1997, p. 1.

10 | German Reparations

Institutionalized Insufficiency

Hubert Kim

More than forty years after Germany enacted its redress program to compensate victims of Nazi atrocities, questions continue to surface regarding the success of the German plan. Unprecedented in its scale, the German plan has been extolled as a model redress scheme, with few doubting Germany's willingness to accept its moral responsibility for the dark chapters of its Nazi past, or its genuine desire to compensate those it victimized. Nevertheless, time has demonstrated that the German effort has not been adequate to fully compensate the hundreds of thousands of current survivors of Nazi persecution.

From the outset, Konrad Adenauer, West Germany's first chancellor, offered his nation's apologies for Nazi atrocities and committed Germany's resources to make amends with survivors and the international community. Although the German government has disbursed over $60 billion (U.S.) in reparations over the past forty years, scores of survivors who endured Nazi persecution have not received any share of reparations payments for their suffering, while many more have only received a mere pittance. It has been estimated that more than fifty thousand Holocaust survivors have received nothing or next to nothing for their suffering.[1] Moreover, Gypsies (Roma), homosexuals, and forced laborers, among others, have historically been overlooked by the redress establishment on both sides of the negotiating table and have suffered in relative silence.

Bonn's response to these concerns has been rather lukewarm. Even for European Jews, the intended primary beneficiaries of the redress programs, the process has not been without its pitfalls. Only recently has Germany allocated funds to eastern European Jews, who had gone uncompensated for more than forty years, and even then, only at a fraction of the level of funding allocated to western Jews under earlier phases of the redress programs. Until 1998, these "double victims" of both the Nazis and subsequent Soviet bloc regimes, many of whom currently live in abject poverty, had no method of redress due to their location behind the Iron Curtain and structural limitations in previous redress agreements. Spurred by the efforts of Senator Chris Dodd and others, the German government finally agreed to pay $110 million in reparations to eighteen thousand eastern European Holocaust survivors.[2] These new provisions are a welcome development, financially assisting survivors as they live out their final years. For many eastern European Jews, however, relief has come too late as the average age of Holocaust survivors approaches eighty.

For those fortunate enough to have collected some form of monetary compensation, the amount received has often been inadequate. More than one hundred thousand Holocaust survivors currently receive pensions from the German government, but this number is steadily shrinking due to the advanced age of the recipients. Reparations checks average only $550 per month—arguably enough to sustain a meager existence, but a pitiful amount if it is intended to atone for the recipients' tremendous suffering. Frequently, reparations checks fail to cover even medical expenses for ailments directly linked to Nazi persecution.[3] Some receive checks as little as three hundred dollars per month despite spending years working hard labor at Auschwitz and losing family members to the Nazis.[4] To the extent that the objective of reparations payments is to substantially compensate or rehabilitate victims, it is obvious that there are serious flaws in the German redress program.

In an effort to address these deficiencies, the Article II Fund was established in 1992, promising to compensate Jewish victims who had received little or nothing under earlier reparations programs. In 1997, Germany and the Conference on Jewish Material Claims Against Germany, the principal international negotiator on behalf of Jewish Holocaust victims and the administrator of the fund, agreed to liberalize the Article II Fund. Even under Article II, claimants must overcome substantial obstacles to qualify for payments. Jewish survivors seeking reparations under Article II have been frustrated and outraged by the strict rules and eligibility requirements the German government has set up to administer reparations funds. For example, in order to be eligible, claimants must prove that they have spent at least six months in a concentration camp, eighteen months confined to a ghetto, or eighteen months living in hiding—conditions that are strictly defined by Germany. Moreover, potential claimants must be currently suffering financial hardship. Those who do not meet this relatively high "persecution threshold" are effectively precluded from asserting further claims for reparations under the existing reparations process. As Bill Marks, a Washington-based attorney who represents Holocaust survivors in claims against Germany, observes, "You're dealing with a lot of fine-print rules and regulations in several books bigger than the Manhattan phone book."[5]

Aware of the limitations of the German plan, the United States has recently taken action to facilitate reparations payments on behalf of Holocaust survivors who are U.S. citizens. In 1995, the United States and Germany reached the Princz Agreement, under which Germany agreed to compensate several survivors who were U.S. citizens at the time of their incarceration in concentration camps. Following the agreement, roughly 1,300 claims for possible reparations have been filed by U.S. citizens who were slave laborers in German concentration camps.[6] While certainly a step forward, this agreement came only after forty years of attempts to obtain reparations and affects only a small segment of victims, illustrating the relative deficiency of the redress plan.

Germany has also played a negligible role in resolving the recent Swiss banking scandals, calling into question its goal of expiation for Nazi wrongdoing. It has been disclosed that Swiss banks refused to hand over to survivors of death camps or their heirs assets deposited in accounts before World War II. Jewish organizations estimate Swiss bank vaults still hold prewar deposits that could be worth $3 billion to $7 billion today.[7] The "neutral" Swiss have also been implicated as financiers of the Nazi war machine as well as participants in the Nazis' conversion of stolen gold, a portion of which was derived from the dental fillings and jewelry of Jews sent to death camps. Recent scholarship, such as Jean Ziegler's *The Swiss, the Gold, and the Dead*, describes Swiss complicity with the Axis powers; some even suggest that Switzerland's participation prolonged the war by as much as several months.

In August 1998, reacting to mounting international pressure and the threat of American sanctions, several prominent Swiss banking institutions capitulated and entered into a landmark settlement with Jewish Holocaust survivors who had filed a class action suit against the banks in American courts. According to the terms of the settlement, $1.25 billion in reparations will be paid to thousands of Jewish survivors whose families lost assets during World War II.[8] The funds will be distributed over a three-year period, most likely beginning in late 1999, though the details of the settlement have not been finalized. It is notable that the German government has not taken a leading role in restoring these plundered assets, the seizure of which is directly linked to Nazi policies and atrocities. Atonement is an integral facet of the redress process. Thus, Germany should have maintained its commitment to righting past wrongs by taking the initiative in resolving this matter—to do otherwise calls into question the sincerity of German atonement.

The Swiss also announced in August 1998 that a fund created to help needy Jewish Holocaust survivors will make individual payments of $1,350 to some two thousand Roma living in Germany, in a compensation package totaling $2.7 million.[9] The fund, created in 1997 with $190 million in financing from Swiss banks, was a response to the criticism surrounding the Swiss banking scandal.[10] The bulk of the fund is intended to aid destitute Jewish Holocaust victims, with the remaining amount to be allocated among non-Jewish survivors, including homosexuals and former political opponents of the Nazi regime.[11] Though these indigent "outsider" survivors will receive *something* for their immeasurable hardship and personal loss, is the amount being offered enough to atone for and adequately compensate these victims? Moreover, why has redress taken so long?

Adding insult to injury, it has been reported that SS and Gestapo veterans have been receiving lifetime pensions courtesy of the German government. According to the Simon Wiesenthal Center, roughly fifty thousand former SS members, some of whom are suspected war criminals, are receiving pensions from the German government—the same government that has created substantial administrative and legal hurdles for survivors seeking compensation.

In the end, one wonders whether meaningful redress for all deserving victims will ever be made, or if Germany has truly atoned for its past sins. Perhaps full redress for atrocities such as those committed by the Nazis is an impossible task. In the words of Sam Solnik, a survivor of the concentration camps, "They can never in a lifetime pay off 6 million [people]. They will never pay off what we lost. I lost my father. I lost my mother. I worked for them [the Nazis] for nothing."[12]

NOTES

1. Neal M. Sher, "Germany Still Has a Debt to Holocaust Survivors," *MetroWest Jewish News*, May 1, 1997.

2. "Dodd Effort Brings Reparations to Holocaust Survivors: Government to Pay $110 Million," U.S. Government Press Release, January 14, 1998.

3. Menachem Z. Rosensaft, "Dignity for Holocaust Victims," *New York Times*, May 5, 1997, A2.

4. John de Groot, "What's the Fair Price for Pain and Suffering? German Checks Average $2,000 for Holocaust Horror," *Ft. Lauderdale Sun-Sentinel*, February 16, 1997, 1G.

5. Ibid.

6. Jeff Donn, "Aging Survivors of Nazi Camps Still Awaiting Reparations," *San Diego Union-Tribune*, January 19, 1998, A7.

7. Bruce W. Nelan, "The Goods of Evil: At Last, Swiss Banks May Loosen Their Hold on the Deposits—and the Gold—of Holocaust Victims," *Time*, October 28, 1996.

8. Joseph P. Fried, "Swiss Banks Reach Holocaust Accord," *New York Times*, August 13, 1998, A1.

9. "Holocaust Fund Will Benefit Gypsies," *San Diego Union-Tribune*, August 12, 1998, A12.

10. "Swiss Holocaust Fund Makes Payments," *Associated Press*, August 11, 1998.

11. Ibid.

12. Lisa J. Huriash, "A Rocky Path: Holocaust Survivors Pursue Reparations," *Ft. Lauderdale Sun-Sentinel*, April 17, 1996, 4B.

Suggested Readings

Conway, John S. *The Nazi Persecution of the Churches, 1933–45.* New York: Basic Books, 1968.

Danieli, Yael. "Differing Adaptational Styles in Families of Survivors of the Nazi Holocaust." *Children Today* 10 (1981): 6.

Finkelstein, Norman G., and Ruth Bettina Birn. *The Goldhagen Thesis and Historical Truth.* New York: Henry Holland and Company, 1998.

Friedlander, Henry. *The Origins of Nazi Genocide: From Euthanasia to the Final Solution.* Chapel Hill: University of North Carolina Press, 1995.

Gimbel, John. *Science, Technology and Reparations: Exploitation and Plunder in Postwar Germany.* Stanford: Stanford University Press, 1990.

Goldhagen, Daniel Jonah. *Hitler's Willing Executioners.* New York: Vintage Books, 1996.

Hertzberg, Arthur, and Aron Hirt-Maheimer. *Jews: The Essence and Character of a People.* San Francisco: Harper, 1998.

Ofer, Dalia, and Lenore J. Weitzman, eds. *Women in the Holocaust.* New Haven: Yale University Press, 1998.

Plant, Richard. *The Pink Triangle: The Nazi War against Homosexuals.* New York: Henry Holt, 1986.

Trials of War Criminals before the Nuremberg Military Tribunals under Control Council Law No. 10. 15 vols. Washington, D.C.: U.S. Government Printing Office, 1950.

Trunk, Isaiah. *Jewish Responses to Nazi Persecution: Collective and Individual Behavior in Extremis.* New York: Stein and Day, 1979.

Wiesel, Elie. *Night.* New York: Hill and Wang, 1960.

Ziegler, Jean. *The Swiss, the Gold, and the Dead.* New York: Harcourt Brace, 1997.

3 | Comfort Women

Introduction

11 | What Form Redress?

Roy L. Brooks

The most heinous acts have often occurred under the cloak of war. World War II provided the setting for numerous well-documented acts of atrocity by the Japanese Imperial Army, including the *jugun ianfu* (comfort women) system and the decimation of Nanking. Although the existence of the comfort women operation was first exposed in 1948 when Batavia (now Jakarta) hosted public trials concerning the sexual internment of Dutch women, no other war crimes trials were brought against Japan for these inhumane acts. The world looked to the future at the expense of the victims of the past. It was not until 1990, forty-five years after the end of World War II, that a Japanese official, in the person of Prime Minister Miyazawa Kiichi, offered an apology for the acts perpetrated by the military against the comfort women. More recently, the Japanese Diet, although refusing to issue an apology, has allocated money to administer a fund for Asian women. The form and source of such redress has, however, raised important questions that are explored in Part 3.

We begin with an overview of the *jugun ianfu* system by noted human rights scholar Karen Parker and law student Jennifer Chew. Under the comfort women system, an estimated two hundred thousand women were held as sex slaves for the Japanese Imperial Army. Through abduction, coercion, and false promises, women and girls as young as twelve were taken from their homes in Korea, China, the Dutch East Indies, Malaysia, Burma, and the Philippines to serve in facilities controlled, directly or indirectly, by the military. Each was then raped by soldiers and officers some fifteen to thirty times a day.

Several narratives presented to the United Nations Commission on Human Rights by former comfort women are included here. They vividly illustrate the military's depravity in perpetrating not only rape, but also other atrocities—acts of torture, starvation, mutilation, and even murder. Chong Ok Sun, Hwang So Gyun, and Kum Ju Hwang describe the fear of living with the knowledge that any spark of defiance or protest could lead to death.

Approximately three out of four comfort women did not survive the war. Disease, suicide, fatal beatings, and murder claimed most of these lives. Those who did survive were often left barren and scarred by physical and psychological problems. Comfort women continue to die from conditions attributable to their sexual enslavement.

Ironically, the comfort women system originated as the military's attempt to curb the rising number of rapes committed by Japanese soldiers and the spread of venereal diseases throughout Japanese society. Iris Chang's chapter on the Nanking massacre describes the infamous event that precipitated Japan's comfort women policy. Within a three-month period, Japanese soldiers raped eighty thousand women and killed three hundred thousand civilians in Nanking, which was at that time the capital of China. Japan's official apology for the incident at Nanking follows Chang's essay. Chang argues, however, that an apology is not enough; reparations are an "official gesture of remorse" and must be part of any meaningful redress program.

In many respects, the atrocities perpetrated in Nanking and the lack of satisfactory redress parallel the plight of the comfort women. The long and arduous path of the comfort women redress movement is chronicled by George Hicks. Despite the Japanese military's actions, apologies and reparations did not follow Japan's surrender. Hicks argues that a complicated system of political relationships and cultural norms have militated against atonement by the Japanese. Western Allies quickly terminated war crimes trials to forge a Cold War strategy, including the formation of alliances with former enemies such as Japan. The Japanese government denied all involvement in sexual slavery and insisted that the comfort women "had just been taken around with the Forces by private operators," a position maintained until documents surfaced in the early 1990s that directly implicated military officials.

Public opinion in Japan supported the government's stance. Many Japanese citizens opposed redress, especially involving money, on the grounds that injustices are an unavoidable cost of war and that the past is best left alone. The denial of redress was further reinforced by the lack of action from the victims' countries. Hicks reminds us that "historically, women throughout Asia were accorded a low ranking de jure." Rape and sexual abuse were viewed as an inevitable part of the wartime experience. In addition, the women who had suffered were mostly from poor families with little influence over the ruling elites. Perhaps more significantly, few women were willing to come forward because of the cultural shame attached to their sexual experiences in a society that prized chastity. For all these reasons, the comfort women issue was ignored in postwar treaty negotiations.

Japan was finally forced to take notice of the issue as attitudes toward women's rights began to change worldwide in the 1980s. Public awareness in Japan was further heightened when the first lawsuit was filed by Korean comfort women in

1991. Other lawsuits followed. In April 1998, a decision was rendered in one of the cases in favor of three Korean comfort women, awarding each $2,300 (U.S.).

The lawsuits also prompted the appointment of a Japanese committee to study the comfort women issue. This led to several official expressions of remorse, some of which are included here. For example, Prime Minister Tomiichi Murayama acknowledges Japan's "mistaken national policy" and offers his "feelings of deep remorse" and "heartfelt apology." He also recognizes that the situation in Nanking did not justify the creation of comfort women stations. Continuing this tone, the chief cabinet secretary promises that Japan will "face squarely the historical facts . . . instead of evading them, and take them to heart as lessons of history." Although these statements mark a turning point in the official position of the Japanese government, some opponents argue that they are not apologies at all; they are merely individual responses that do not represent the people of Japan, as long as the Diet, Japan's parliament, refuses to issue an apology.

More controversial than the apology is Japan's approach to monetary redress. The final report issued by the Japanese investigative committee proposed the establishment of what is called the "Asian Women's Fund." Money contributed to the fund is used to aid comfort women in need and support projects addressing contemporary women's issues. The fund purports to represent the Japanese people's "feelings of apology and remorse" by allowing them to contribute directly to the fund. In fact, the fund is financed by donations from private individuals and organizations in Japan. The government pays the administrative cost of the fund and as of March 1996 has contributed some 211 million yen (approximately $4.8 million) for that purpose. Japan's response is an example of redress in the form of community rehabilitation. Rather than paying compensation to individual victims, redress money is used to improve conditions for all women (i.e., the victims' class).

Japan's attempt to provide a rehabilitative form of redress through the Asian Women's Fund has met with considerable criticism. Comfort women and advocacy organizations argue that this is not redress in the form of reparations; atonement can only be achieved through money paid by the government in the form of personal compensation, along with a formal apology from the Diet. They maintain that the Asian Women's Fund is a welfare-type system because individual payments are based on socioeconomic need rather than moral restitution. Such payments add to the overall sense that Japan is failing to take responsibility for its actions.

Japan's approach to redress raises at least three important questions: Should redress be in the form of rehabilitation or compensation? Regardless of form, who should provide for such redress? And who should apologize? These questions do not lend themselves to easy answers. It could be argued, on the one hand, that payments to the individual can never be fully compensatory. No amount of money will fully restore the human spirit and loss of dignity suffered by these victims. One cannot place a price tag on such suffering. Accordingly, rehabilitation might be a more acceptable, constructive, and targeted response to the violation of the comfort women's human rights. Arguably, the Asian Women's Fund seeks to address vestiges of Asia's outdated attitudes toward women that were the source of the comfort women problem. Indeed, addressing the cultural forces that led to sexual slavery might be the only way to ensure that the situation does not recur in a future war. But this argument only raises another question. Even if redress in the form of rehabilitation is a better solution to the comfort women problem, can the Japanese government still reject the victims' demands for redress in the form of personal compensation? Does ignoring the wishes of the comfort women add insult to an injury that for too long has been denied?

The obvious answer to the preceding question is that both forms of redress should be provided, but the questions concerning who should pay and who should apologize remain. Compelling arguments exist on both sides of this issue. For example, it could be argued that the Japanese people should pay and apologize because the comfort women system precluded the raping of Japanese women by the military during World War II and benefited Japanese society as a whole by limiting the spread of venereal disease. Others might argue that it is unfair and inappropriate to make the Japanese people pay or apologize when the government not only sanctioned the atrocity but also maintained a policy of collective amnesia for so long after the atrocity ended. Given this context, true atonement can only come from the government. And yet, with respect to payment, it can be argued that even when the government pays, the people are actually paying because all government funds come from citizens.

Although, as previously noted, several Korean women have received favorable judgments from a Japanese court, the legal status of such claims is far from clear under international law. This complex issue remains important due to both pending comfort women cases and more recent human rights violations, such as those committed in Bosnia. Two chapters in Part 3 focus on the legal arguments raised concerning Japan's responsibility to provide monetary redress to the comfort women. Tetsuo Ito, former director of the Legal Affairs Division at the Ministry of Foreign Affairs of Japan, advances the proposition that tackling the legal issues has little meaning when policy issues regarding the practicality of monetary redress have not been considered. While his legal analysis ultimately finds that the plaintiffs in recent comfort women cases have the legal "status" to sue—as opposed to his conclusion that foreign nations cannot sue on the victims' behalf because of their waiver of diplomatic protection in postwar treaties—he argues that their past claims cannot be judged on present-day legal standards of human injustice. Ito maintains, however, that any redress program is likely to be problematic because it requires choosing the victims to be compensated and then structuring, financing, and implementing the payments.

In contrast, Karen Parker and Jennifer Chew, while ultimately agreeing with Ito on the question of the legal status of comfort women claims, dismiss the significance of the difficulties Ito raises. They assert that *jus cogens* rights, or international customary law, require compensation for human rights violations and that governments do not have the authority to avoid liability for crimes against humanity by signing treaties that waive the private rights of victims. Furthermore, such issues as the passage of time and financial difficulties should not by themselves bar lawsuits for war violations of this nature, which, they observe, are distinguishable from the inevitable casualties of war. Parker and Chew urge that regardless of the victims' rights to sue, Japan should take the initiative to redress these wrongs by instituting a comprehensive compensation plan.

Part 3 concludes with a 1997 congressional bill introduced by Rep. William Lipinski seeking from the Japanese government both a formal, unambiguous apology and the payment of compensation to victims of the comfort women system and the massacre at Nanking.

The Comfort Women System

12 | The *Jugun Ianfu* System

Karen Parker and Jennifer F. Chew

"I could speak no Japanese and I was a virgin. Every day my body was soiled by [fifteen] Japanese soldiers. I was so tired I wanted to die. It lasted four years. After it was over, I could not have children."[1]

They were *jugun ianfu*—"comfort women."[2] As many as two hundred thousand women were tricked or abducted into slavery for sexual services for the Japanese Imperial Army during World War II.[3] Women and girls as young as twelve were taken from their homes in Korea, China, the Dutch East Indies, Taiwan, Malaysia, Burma, and the Philippines.[4] They were sent to locations throughout Japanese-occupied Asia where they were imprisoned in facilities known as "comfort houses,"[5] raped daily by soldiers, and forced to endure torture and abuse. Only about 25 percent survived this treatment.[6] Of these postwar survivors, possibly only two thousand, now about sixty-five to eighty-five years old, are still alive.[7] Never compensated, they continue to suffer from their brutal treatment.

■   ■   ■

. . . [T]he primary purpose for the *jugun ianfu* scheme was to reduce the large number of rapes committed by Japanese soldiers. The scheme is thought to have arisen especially because of the Nanking massacre [see chapter 14].[8] The rapes fueled anti-Japanese sentiment among the civilian populations and led to attacks against army patrols.[9] They also led to the widespread occurrence of venereal disease among Japanese soldiers, which then spread to the civilian population of Japan upon the return of the soldiers.[10] General Okabe Naosaburo issued an order

From Karen Parker and Jennifer F. Chew, "Compensation for Japan's World War II War-Rape Victims," *Hastings International and Comparative Law Review* 17 (1994): 498–510.

to establish "comfort houses" in China on a mass scale as soon as possible to prevent Japanese soldiers from continuing to rape.[11]

■ ■ ■

After establishing the program in China, the Japanese government duplicated it in other locations under its occupation, which by 1942 included large parts of the Asia/Pacific region. The Japanese Imperial Army established facilities for sex slaves in the following places: China, Korea, Hong Kong, French Indochina, Philippines, Malaysia, Singapore, British Borneo, Dutch East Indies, Burma, a number of Pacific Islands (New Britain, Trobriand), and Okinawa.[12]

Documents reveal three types of facilities for sex slaves: (1) those directly run by Japanese military authorities; (2) those run by civilians, but essentially set up and controlled by Japanese military authorities; and (3) those that were mainly private facilities but with some priority for military use.[13] Despite these differences, there are characteristics common to at least the first two types of facilities or "comfort houses." These include: (1) the facilities were used exclusively by Japanese soldiers and army civilian employees; (2) the facilities were under strict control of the Japanese Army, which helped to establish and to manage these facilities and helped to recruit sex slaves; (3) the facilities had to obtain a permit from the army and accept its support and control in all procedures; and (4) all facilities followed written regulations created by the Japanese Army.[14]

The Japanese Army set out regulations for all facilities for the sex slaves, though compliance varied widely.[15] For example, while each facility's working hours varied somewhat on paper, generally, working hours were to begin at nine or ten in the morning and end at six or seven in the evening for enlisted men and later for officers. The rank of the soldier would determine the length of time allowed for a visit, ranging from thirty minutes to one hour. Even after regular working hours, the facilities could be used throughout the night, mostly by officers. In many cases, even where a time schedule did exist, it was rarely adhered to, especially on weekends when many soldiers would arrive.[16]

These facilities varied in the fees they charged, with some having strict control on the ticketing process.[17] Usually, the amount of fees varied according to the soldier's rank and the ethnicity of the sex slave, with higher fees charged for Korean women. These regulations did not provide for payments to the women themselves, and many war-rape victims report that they were never paid at all.[18] Some were provided with cosmetics and clothing while others were given occasional tips. . . . [*Editor's Note: The* jugun ianfu *system began with "professional prostitutes continuing their existing way of life, moving on to different degrees of deception or pressure and, finally, forcible seizure."*[19] *Those brought into the system by deception or force were "sex slaves," properly speaking.*]

■ ■ ■

The harshness of their conditions is perhaps best illustrated by the fact that thousands of sex slaves died in captivity.[20] Although many sex slaves were murdered in cold blood, some of these deaths may be attributed to wartime conditions. For example, some facilities were sometimes located near front lines and consequently many women were killed during military operations.[21] Others died during distant travels under wartime conditions. Deaths also occurred due to lack of or inappropriate medical care. For example, some died from ill-performed abortions,[22] while others died from malaria and a variety of other diseases, especially since many victims were weakened by near-starvation diets.[23] Injuries from beatings were rarely treated, and many women died from broken bones or internal injuries.[24] A fairly large number committed suicide because of their physical and psychological anguish.[25]

Daily existence was degrading. For example, the majority of the sex slaves were regularly examined by army doctors for venereal diseases. Many of these women were forced to clean used condoms.[26] Some were ordered to clean their vaginas with an antiseptic solution every time they served a soldier. Some report receiving injections called "number 606." Despite these regulations, many soldiers did not use condoms, and many former sex slaves were infected with venereal diseases.[27]

Survivors who have come forward almost uniformly report serious continuing medical and psychological problems due to being treated as sex slaves.[28] Most have been unable or unwilling to marry or have children, and many have no family to support them. As these victims age, their medical problems are becoming more acute and their financial needs ever higher.[29] Today, former sex slaves are dying as a direct result of their treatment at the hands of the Japanese military.

■ ■ ■

NOTES

1. Statement of a sixty-nine-year-old Korean survivor during a Japanese television broadcast. Mark O'Neill, "Koreans Forced into Prostitution by Japan Army Demand Payment," *Reuter Library Report*, December 2, 1991 (available in LEXIS, World Library, Lbyrpt File).

2. "Comfort women" is a direct translation of the Japanese phrase *jugun ianfu* and is a widely used term for these victims. The authors prefer the terms "women and girls forced into sexual slavery," "war-rape victims," or "sex slaves." "War-rape victims" is a term used also by many claimants. See, e.g., Letter to Prime Minister K. Miyazawa, in *War Victimization and Japan: International Public Hearing Report*, ed. Executive Committee International Public Hearing (1993), p. 148 (copy on file with Parker).

3. While no figure can probably be proven now, investigators now generally indicate about two hundred thousand women were war-rape victims of Japan. Then Japanese Prime Minister Kiichi Miyazawa admitted this figure. See "Japan Should Compensate Canadian POWs, Expert Says," *Toronto Globe and Mail*, August 17, 1993, p. 3D; *U.N. Sub-Commission on Prevention of Discrimination and Protection of Minorities; Statement of Democratic People's Republic of Korea*, U.N. Doc. E/CN.4/Sub.2/SR.10, pp. 14, 15 (1993) (noting that investigation carried out by the Committee for the Investigation of Damage Caused by

Japanese Imperialists during Their Occupation of Korea placed the figure at two hundred thousand). Sources that indicate fewer victims discuss the difficulties in verifying any number. See, e.g., George Hicks, "They Won't Allow Japan to Push the 'Comfort Women' Aside," *International Herald Tribune*, February 10, 1993, p. 2.

4. See "Letter to Prime Minister Miyazawa" (discussing historical and personal testimony of sex slaves from North Korea, South Korea, Philippines, China, the Dutch East Indies, including both Indonesian and Dutch nationals, and Taiwan). In February 1993, a number of Malaysian women publicly admitted that they had been sex slaves. See Gwen Benjamin, "Two Malaysian 'Comfort Women' Seek Japanese Compensation," *Japan Economic Newswire*, February 19, 1993 (available in LEXIS, Asiapc Library, JEN file) (citing evidence that about two hundred women were abducted from Kelantan State alone). Some sources verify sex slaves from Burma. Interview with See Sein, World War II survivor from Burma (Karenni State), in New York (November 18, 1993) (stating that many Karen, Karenni, and Mon women and girls were taken to "sex camps"); see also George Hicks, "Ghosts Gathering," *Far East Economic Review*, February 18, 1993, p. 32 (indicating sex slaves from Burma). A report of the Celebes Civil Administration (Indonesia) contained in a Japanese Military Report of June 20, 1942, lists "Toradjas, Javanese, Makassars, Karossas, Enrekangese, Mandalese" women. "Army Regulations Governed Care of Forced Prostitutes," *Japan Times*, August 8, 1992, p. 3. A 1945 Australian document contains testimony of Australian nurses who resisted attempts to force them into being sex slaves and discusses the presence of civilian internees at "pleasure houses." Letter from Major-General Lloyd to General Headquarters in Melbourne (September 28, 1945) (document from Australian National Archives, marked "Secret and Confidential") (copy on file with author).

5. Yoshiaki Yoshimi, "Historical Understandings on the 'Military Comfort Women' Issue," in *War Victimization and Japan*, pp. 81, 82 (verifying documents showing facilities for sex slaves in China, Hong Kong, French-occupied Indochina, the Philippines, Malaysia, Singapore, British-occupied Borneo, the Dutch East Indies, Burma, New Britain, Trobriand, Okinawa, and Ogasawara).

6. Representative Seijuro Arahune, late of the Japanese Diet (Liberal Democratic Party), made public statements as early as 1975 that 145,000 Korean sex slaves died during World War II. Interview with Senator Tamako Nakanishi, in Tokyo (December 8, 1992). Representative Arahune's remarks were recently raised in Diet debates. See "Japan Should Compensate Canadian POWS." This statement also contains a quote from a November 20, 1975, campaign speech of Representative Arahune: "142,000 Korean comfort women died. The Japanese soldiers killed them." Ibid.

7. This figure is the authors' speculation based on interviews and review of documents.

8. Yoshimi, "Historical Understandings on the 'Military Comfort Women' Issue," 85 (citing Diary of Iinuma Mamoru, Chief of Staff, Japanese Expeditionary Force in Shanghai, entry on December 11, 1937); see also "Nankin Senshi Shiryoshu," in *Jugun Ianfu Shiryo Shu* [Documents on Military Comfort Women], ed. Yoshiaki Yoshimi (1992), p. 211 (Japanese only). According to Yoshimi, Japan feared reaction from the United States, Europe, and China because of extensive rapes during the sieges of Nanking and Shanghai. The chief of staff for the Japanese Expeditionary Force in Shanghai conjectured that the first "comfort houses" were established in Shanghai in 1932. Okabe Naosaburo Taisho No Nikki [General Okabe Naosaburo's Diary], cited in Yoshimi, "Historical Understandings on the 'Military Comfort Women' Issue," p. 81.

9. *Jugun Ianfu Shiryo Shu* [Documents on Military Comfort Women], p. 209.

Recently sabotage of transportation networks in Shandong Province has been frequently reported. . . . [I]t is . . . also true that illegal conduct by soldiers and officers towards local residents has stirred up their hatred and resistance. . . . Reported rapes involving Japanese officers and men in various places have spread over the whole area, fermenting unexpectedly serious anti-Japanese sentiment. Local residents are in the habit of uniting in retaliation, making it a rule to kill a person who has committed rape.

Order of June 27, 1938, by Okabe Naosaburo, Chief of Staff, Japanese Expeditionary Force in North China, reprinted in "Rapes Sparked Call for Facilities," *Japan Times*, August 5, 1992, p. 3. See also *Jugun Ianfu Shiryo Shu*, p. 209; Colin Nickerson, "Japan Admits Forcing Koreans into Wartime Prostitution," *Boston Globe*, January 14, 1992 (National/Foreign), p. 1.

10. See Naomi Hirakawa and Rieko Tenaka, "Secret Service Monitored Brothels," *Japan Times*, August 6, 1992, p. 3.

11. "Rapes Sparked Call for Facilities," p. 3 ("It is vital to strictly control the conduct of individual officers and men and also to establish facilities for providing sexual comfort as soon as possible."). See also *Jugun Ianfu Shiryo Shu*, p. 209.

12. Yoshimi, "Historical Understandings on the 'Military Comfort Women' Issue," p. 82. The authors refer to the places where the sex slaves were detained as "facilities for sex slaves" rather than "comfort houses" or "brothels" because the sex slaves were detained involuntarily. The terms "brothels" or "comfort houses" imply that the presence of these sex slaves was voluntary. There were in fact brothels with voluntary prostitutes, but this chapter is not about them.

13. Interview with Yoshiaki Yoshimi, in Tokyo (December 9, 1992). Documents thus far discovered describe four types of comfort houses. The fourth type were ordinary brothels, where most of the women were presumed to be "voluntary" prostitutes and not sex slaves. See Yoshimi, "Historical Understandings on the 'Military Comfort Women' Issue," p. 84.

14. Lee Mi-Gyeong, "Realities of the 'Comfort Women' in South Korea," in *War Victimization and Japan*, pp. 9–10. See also *Jugun Ianfu Shiryo Shu*, pp. 105–6, 324–26, 367.

15. Lee, "Realities of the 'Comfort Women' in South Korea," pp. 13–15.

16. Kim Hak-Soon, a former sex slave, recounts, "[Japanese soldiers] visited us day and night. We had to received [sic] some twenty soldiers on normal days and more than thirty soldiers when the troops returned from field operations." Karen Parker, *Research on War Crimes and Crimes against Humanity* (December 10, 1992) (unpublished manuscript on file with Parker).

17. According to two reports by Americans who interrogated twenty Korean woman forced into becoming sex slaves in Burma, the Japanese facility owners operated on detailed instructions from the army. The women provided sex daily for up to ninety noncommissioned officers and soldiers and fifteen officers. They were paid up to sixteen cents per man depending on rank. The facility owner subsequently took up to 60 percent of the women's gross earnings. "Wartime Army Directly Involved in Brothels, Report Says," *UPI*, January 27, 1992 (available in LEXIS, World Library, UPI File).

18. When asked if she was ever paid, Kim Hak-Soon, a former comfort woman, stated, "The Japanese treated us like slaves, and gave us nothing but food, just enough to survive." Parker, *Research on War Crimes and Crimes against Humanity*. Another woman, allowed also to work in a grocery store, saved more than 10,000 Japanese yen. After the war, this was worth very little, and she never took it, claiming, "I did not withdraw it because I could

not stand the fact that the money which I got for the rapes I suffered, for my abused youth and for my miserable life became nothing. I lost my bankbook, but my friend, who went with me to Timor Island with me, still keeps hers." A Taiwanese Woman, "Like an Animal on Timor Island," in *War Victimization and Japan*, p. 80.

19. George Hicks, *The Comfort Women: Japan's Brutal Regime of Enforced Prostitution in the Second World War* (New York: W. W. Norton, 1995), p. 168.

20. See generally note 6.

21. Interview with Yoshiaki Yoshimi, in Tokyo (December 8, 1992) (commenting on number of facilities in combat zones and testimonies of war-rape victims regarding military attacks on them).

22. Some commentators also report on crudely performed hysterectomies. See Hicks, "They Won't Allow Japan to Push the 'Comfort Women' Aside," p. 33.

23. Medical care that existed generally was for venereal disease and was provided primarily so that Japanese soldiers would not return home infected. Interview with Yoshiaki Yoshimi, in Tokyo (December 8, 1992) (discussing prevention of rape and venereal disease as primary motive for having facilities, as illustrated by large number of documents containing regulations expressing concern about spread of venereal diseases to returning soldiers). See also "Daitoa Senso Kankei Shohei No Seibyo Shoshi Ni Kansuru Ken" [Sex Disease Treatment for Officers and Men Dispatched Overseas for the Great East-Asia War], in *Jugun Ianfu Shiryo Shu*, pp. 171–72.

24. See, e.g., Wan Ai-Hua, "I Hate Japanese Soldiers," in *War Victimization and Japan*, pp. 68, 70 (victim left to die with ribs and pelvic bones broken).

25. "Very few of the Koreans returned after the war. They were killed by the soldiers because they were a nuisance, or they died of illness or starvation. Some committed suicide because of the shame of what they had done." Fumiko Kawada, "The House with the Red Tiles," cited in O'Neill, "Koreans Forced into Prostitution by Japan Army Demand Payment." See also Wang Ching-Feng, "Japanese Military Sexual Slavery of the Taiwanese during World War II," in *War Victimization and Japan*, p. 73.

26. Lee, "Realities of the 'Comfort Women' in South Korea," 14 (commenting that sex slaves were "disgusted" at cleaning condoms, each used up to five times). See also Naomi Hirakawa and Maya Maruko, "Doctors Recall Steps to Curb VD at Brothels," *Japan Times*, August 7, 1992, p. 3. The soldiers were ordered to use condoms provided by the Army, but they were usually in short supply. See, e.g., "Rules for Hygiene," *Japan Times*, August 7, 1992, p. 3 (excerpts from wartime documents of the Japanese Army).

27. See Lee, "Realities of the 'Comfort Women' in South Korea."

28. See generally *War Victimization and Japan*.

29. Ibid.

13 Comfort Women Narratives

Report of the Special Rapporteur on Violence against Women, Its Causes and Consequences, Ms. Radhika Coomaraswamy, in Accordance with Commission on Human Rights Resolution 1994/45

The testimony of Chong Ok Sun, who is now seventy-four years old, reflects in particular the brutal and harsh treatment that these women had to endure in addition to sexual assault and daily rape by soldiers of the Japanese Imperial Army:

I was born on 28 December 1920, in Phabal-Ri, Pungsan County, South Hamgyong Province, in the north of the Korean peninsula.

One day in June, at the age of 13, I had to prepare lunch for my parents who were working in the field and so I went to the village well to fetch water. A Japanese garrison soldier surprised me there and took me away, so that my parents never knew what had happened to their daughter. I was taken to the police station in a truck, where I was raped by several policemen.

When I shouted, they put socks in my mouth and continued to rape me. The head of the police station hit me in my left eye because I was crying. That day I lost my eyesight in the left eye.

After ten days or so, I was taken to the Japanese army garrison barracks in Heysan City. There were around four hundred other Korean young girls with me and we had to serve over five thousand Japanese soldiers as sex slaves every day—up to forty men per day. Each time I protested, they hit me or stuffed rags in my mouth. One held a matchstick to my private parts until I obeyed him. My private parts were oozing with blood.

One Korean girl who was with us once demanded why we had to serve so many, up to forty, men per day. To punish her for her questioning, the Japanese company commander Yamamoto ordered her to be beaten with a sword. While we were

From United Nations Economic and Social Council, Commission on Human Rights, *Report of the Special Rapporteur on Violence against Women*, E/CN.4/1996/53/Add.1 (1996).

watching, they took off her clothes, tied her legs and hands and rolled her over a board with nails until the nails were covered with blood and pieces of her flesh. In the end, they cut off her head. Another Japanese, Yamamoto, told us that "it's easy to kill you all, easier than killing dogs." He also said "since those Korean girls are crying because they have not eaten, boil the human flesh and make them eat it."

One Korean girl caught a venereal disease from being raped so often and, as a result, over fifty Japanese soldiers were infected. In order to stop the disease from spreading and to "sterilize" the Korean girl, they stuck a hot iron bar in her private parts.

Once they took forty of us on a truck far away to a pool filled with water and snakes. The soldiers beat several of the girls, shoved them into the water, heaped earth into the pool and buried them alive.

I think over half of the girls who were at the garrison barracks were killed. Twice I tried to run away, but both times we were caught after a few days. We were tortured even more and I was hit on my head so many times that all the scars still remain. They also tattooed me on the inside of my lips, my chest, my stomach and my body. I fainted. When I woke up, I was on a mountainside, presumably left for dead. Of the two girls with me, only Kuk Hae and I survived. A fifty-year-old man who lived in the mountains found us, gave us clothes and something to eat. He also helped us to travel back to Korea, where I returned, scarred, barren and with difficulties in speaking, at the age of eighteen, after five years of serving as a sex slave for the Japanese.

Seventy-seven-year-old Hwang So Gyun's testimony bears witness to the deceptive way of recruitment, which lured so many young women into being military sexual slaves:

I was born on 28 November 1918 as the second daughter of a day laborer. We lived in the Taeri Workers' District, Kangdong County, Pyongyang City.

When I was seventeen years old, in 1936, the head of our village came to our house and promised me to help me find a job in a factory. Because my family was so poor, I gladly accepted this offer of a well-paid job. I was taken to the railway station in a Japanese truck where twenty or so other Korean girls were already waiting. We were put on the train, then onto a truck and after a few days' travel we reached a big house at the River Mudinjian in China. I thought it was the factory, but I realized that there was no factory. Each girl was assigned one small room with a straw bag to sleep on, with a number on each door. After two days of waiting, without knowing what was happening to me, a Japanese soldier in army uniform, wearing a sword, came to my room. He asked me "will you obey my words or not?" then pulled my hair, put me on the floor and asked me to open my legs. He raped me. When he left, I saw there were twenty or thirty more men waiting outside. They all raped me that day. From then on, every night I was assaulted by fifteen to twenty men.

We had to undergo medical examinations regularly. Those who were found disease-stricken were killed and buried in unknown places. One day, a new girl was put in the compartment next to me. She tried to resist the men and bit one of them in his arm. She was then taken to the courtyard and in front of all of us, her head was cut off with a sword and her body was cut into small pieces.

The testimony by Kum Ju Hwang, now seventy-three years old, of Dungchong-dong, Youngdungpoku, Republic of Korea, illustrates [yet another method of forcible seizure and some of] the regulations under which comfort stations . . . operated . . . :

I thought I was drafted as a labor worker when, at the age of seventeen, the Japanese village leader's wife ordered all unmarried Korean girls to go to work at a Japanese military factory. I worked there for three years, until the day that I was asked to follow a Japanese soldier into his tent. He told me to take my clothes off. I resisted because I was so scared, I was still a virgin. But he just ripped my skirt and cut my underwear from my body with a gun which had a knife attached to it. At that point I fainted. And when I woke up again, I was covered with a blanket but there was blood everywhere.

From then on, I realized that during the first year I, like all the other Korean girls with me, was ordered to service high-ranking officials, and as time passed, and as we were more and more "used," we served lower-ranking officers. If a woman got a disease, she usually vanished. We were also given "606-shots" so that we would not get pregnant or that any pregnancies would result in miscarriage.

We only received clothes two times per year and not enough food, only rice cakes and water. I was never paid for my "services." I worked for five years as a "comfort woman," but all my life I suffered from it. My intestines are mostly removed because they were infected so many times, I have not been able to have intercourse because of the painful and shameful experiences. I cannot drink milk or fruit juices without feeling sick because it reminds me too much of those dirty things they made me do.

14 | The Nanking Massacre

Iris Chang

In the 1920s, Japan was struggling with an economic depression and the pressures of overpopulation. Japan set its sights on expanding its territory into eastern Asia in pursuit of renewed prosperity and power. The invasion of Manchuria in 1931 marked the beginning of Japan's efforts to seize control of China. By 1937, Japan was engaged in a full-scale war with China. Japan's expectations of a quick victory over China were shattered when the battle for Shanghai stretched on for several months before that city finally fell in November 1937. The imperial troops advanced toward Nanking, the capital city of Chiang Kai-shek's Nationalist government, with heightened aggression, raiding small villages and razing entire cities to the ground.[1]

In December 1937, the Japanese army swept into the city of Nanking, then the capital of China, and within six to eight weeks massacred more than threen hundred thousand civilians and raped eighty thousand women.[2] The death toll in Nanking was higher than those of Hiroshima and Nagasaki combined.[3] In fact, it is higher than the total number of civilians who died in England, France, and Belgium for the *entire* World War II period.[4]

More than the number of people murdered, the manner in which they were killed is what sets Nanking apart from other World War II atrocities. Even Nazi officials working in Nanking at the time were shocked by the orgy of violence they witnessed.[5] The Japanese turned murder into sport. They rounded up tens of thousands of men and used them for bayonet practice or decapitation contests.[6] Sometimes they simply sprayed gasoline on them and burned them alive.[7] Some men were skinned alive, tortured to death with needles, or buried up to the waist in the soil, where they were ripped apart by German shepherds.[8] The Chinese women suffered far worse. Many of them were mutilated horribly after being raped.[9] The Japanese even forced fathers to rape their own daughters, or sons their mothers, or

104

brothers their sisters, all in an attempt to further degrade the victims.[10] The Japanese were equally brutal to the small children. Babies were tossed into the air and bayoneted as they came down. Some were thrown into vats of oil and water.[11]

Especially chilling is the fact that many of these atrocities were committed not by people who were diabolical by nature, but by very ordinary citizens. Many were model citizens from Japan who returned after the war to become respectable members of the community. For example, one doctor who committed horrible crimes against humanity in Nanking is now a respectable family practitioner in Japan. His is a true-life Dr. Jekyll/Mr. Hyde story.[12]

It is difficult to explain the psychology behind the orgy of violence in Nanking. Perhaps the greatest factor is the concentration of power. Scholars argue that the more concentrated the power in the hands of a few, such as in a totalitarian regime or a dictatorship, the more likely it is that the power elites will commit atrocities both at home and abroad. Almost all people have the potential for evil, which can be unleashed under the right set of dangerous social circumstances. In short, the unfettered exercise of power (regardless of nationality, political affiliation, race, or religion) seems to be the greatest source for the kind of atrocities committed by the Japanese in Nanking.[13]

Although more people were killed in Nanking than in Hiroshima and Nagasaki combined, until recently the world has known far less about Nanking. The Cold War is the primary factor that accounts for the world's amnesia regarding Nanking. After 1949, neither the People's Republic of China nor the Republic of China in Taiwan wanted to push the Japanese for reparations or an apology because each needed Japan as an ally against the other. They needed Japan's economic support as well. To this day, both governments are reluctant to broach the subject with Japan.[14]

The United States failed to pursue the Nanking issue after the war because it saw Japan as a stable base from which to counter communist forces in the Soviet Union and Asia. Deep-seated guilt over the atomic bombings of Hiroshima and Nagasaki may also have made American criticism of Japanese wartime behavior difficult, leaving the Chinese victims of Nanking without an advocate for justice.[15]

In the years since World War II, Germany has paid reparations to Holocaust victims, apologized to them, and even sent its leaders into the Warsaw Ghetto to apologize.[16] We have not seen comparable actions by the Japanese government. This is, in part, because the United States permitted the Japanese wartime bureaucracy to remain virtually intact after the war. Unlike Germany, whose top officials were thrown in prison, executed, or at the very least had to live as fugitives in other countries, many of Japan's leading wartime officials were permitted to stay in power or to flourish in academia or business. By 1957, Japan had elected as its prime minister a Class A war criminal.[17]

Japan has also argued that all matters related to reparations were settled in the 1952 San Francisco Peace Treaty, which officially ended World War II. But a close reading of the treaty shows that the reparations issue was merely postponed until the Japanese economy, still devastated by war, could make good on any restitution assigned to Japan. Such an excuse for delay is laughable today. Japan ranks as one of the world's wealthiest countries, despite its occasional economic problems.[18]

In February 1997, ten Chinese survivors of the Nanking massacre filed a lawsuit against Japan in Tokyo District Court. The lawsuit sought a public apology from the Japanese government and compensation totaling 100 million yen ($806,000 U.S.). Approximately two hundred Japanese citizens, mainly lawyers and academics, have joined together to pay the legal costs of the lawsuit. A judgment has not yet been rendered. The testimony of one plaintiff, seventy-eight-year-old Liu Xiuying, is typical of the other plaintiffs. She was "wounded 37 times with a sword for resisting a soldier who wanted to rape her."[19]

The issue raised in the lawsuit is not just money, but the sanctity of human life. It is impossible to right the Nanking wrongs fully with reparations. But reparations, at the very least, will help some of the surviving victims live out their remaining days with some semblance of dignity. In essence, reparations will be seen by all as an official gesture of remorse, a national acknowledgment of past wrongdoing.

In 1997, Rep. William Lipinski (D-Ill.) introduced a bill in Congress denouncing Japan for its crimes and demanding both a formal apology and reparations for the victims [see chapter 20]. The "Rape of Nanking" is only one event in a long list of atrocities mentioned in the bill; other victims include those who were subjected to the Bataan death march, the Korean comfort women, and the subjects of the diabolical medical experimentation inflicted on live American and Chinese prisoners by Japanese doctors in the notorious Unit 731 laboratory in Manchuria.[20]

If the Lipinski bill passes, it will not only help Asians who endured outrages such as the Nanking massacre, but also American veterans who survived conditions in Japan far worse than those in Nazi camps. (One out of twenty-five Americans died under Nazi captivity; one out of three in Japanese captivity.[21]) Yet American veterans received on average only fourteen dollars each in reparations from the Japanese—much less than Japanese Americans, who received twenty thousand dollars each from the U.S. government for their internment in relocation camps during the war.[22]

Action must be taken quickly. The survivors are dying, and the world has a short memory. There is still a chance for vindication before the last voices from the Nanking massacre are extinguished forever.

NOTES

1. Iris Chang, *The Rape of Nanking* (New York: Basic Books, 1997), pp. 25–29, 33–38.

2. For one of the most thorough studies of the number of people killed during the Rape of Nanking, see Sun Zhawei, "Nanjing datusha yu nanjing renkou" [The Nanking Massacre and the Nanking population], *Nanjing shehuai kexue* [Nanking social science journal] 37, no. 3 (1990): 75–80; Sun Zhawei, "Guanyu nanjing datusha siti chunide yenjou" [On the subject of body disposal during the Nanking Massacre], *Nanjing shehui kexue* 44, no. 4

(1991): 72–78. Sun Zhawei's estimate of 377,400 killed is supported by other authorities, e.g., Li En-han, "Questions of How Many Chinese Were Killed by the Japanese Army in the Great Nanking Massacre," *Journal of Studies of Japanese Aggression Against China* (August 1990) (430,000 killed); Wu Tienwei, "Let the Whole World Know the Nanking Massacre: A Review of Three Recent Pictorial Books on the Massacre and Its Studies," report distributed by Society for Studies of Japanese Aggression Against China, 1977 (340,000 killed); Foreign Minister Hirota Koki, "Red Machine" Japanese diplomatic messages, translated 1 February 1938, no. 1263, record group 457, National Archives (minimum 300,000 killed). The International Military Tribunal for the Far East (IMTFE) concluded that at least 260,000 people were killed; see "Table, Estimated Number of Victims of Japanese Massacre in Nanking," IMTFE records, court exhibits, 1948, no. 1702, box 134, entry 14, record group 238, World War II War Crimes Records Collection, National Archives. However, estimates put forward by some Japanese authorities stand in stark contrast to the preceding figures. See, e.g., estimates cited in Haruko Taya Cook and Theodore F. Cook, *Japan at War: An Oral History* (New York: New Press, 1992), p. 39 (3,000–42,000 killed). The estimate of the number of women raped is supported by Li En-han, "'The Great Nanking Massacre' Committed by the Japanese Army as Related to International Law on War Crimes," *Journal of Studies of Japanese Aggression Against China* (May 1991): 74. Other estimates put the number of rape victims as low as twenty thousand. See Catherine Rosair, "For One Veteran, Emperor Visit Should Be Atonement," *Reuters* (October 15, 1992); George Fitch, "Nanking Outrages," 10 January 1938, George Fitch Collection, Yale Divinity School Library.

3. Richard Rhodes, *The Making of the Atomic Bomb* (New York: Simon & Schuster, 1996), pp. 734, 740.

4. R. J. Rummel, *China's Bloody Century: Genocide and Mass Murder since 1900* (New Brunswick, N.J.: Transaction Publishers, 1991), p. 138.

5. See, e.g., John Rabe, "Enemy Planes over Nanking," on file at Yale Divinity School Library; Christian Kröger, "Days of Fate in Nanking," unpublished diary in the collection of Peter Kröger. Rabe and Kröger were Nazi officials stationed in Nanking during the massacre. Rabe's paper is his official report to Adolf Hitler.

6. Zhu Chengshan, *Qinghua rijun Nanjing datusha xincunshe* [The testimony of the survivors of the Nanking Massacre committed by the invading Japanese] (Nanking: University of Nanking Press, 1994), p. 53; "Jingdi shouxing muji ji" [Witnessing the beastly action of the Japanese in Nanking], *Hankou Dagongbao*, 7 February 1938, reprinted in *Nanjing datusha shiliao bianji weiyuanhei* [Source materials relating to the horrible massacre committed by the Japanese troops in Nanking in December 1937], ed. Committee for the Historical Materials of the Nanking Massacre and the Nanjing Tushuguan (Nanking Library) (Nanking: Jiangsu Ancient Books Publishing, 1985), pp. 129, 142–44.

7. Gao Xingzu, Wu Shimin, Hu Yungong, and Zha Ruishen (History Department of Nanjing University), "Japanese Imperialism and the Massacre in Nanjing—An English Translation of a Classified Chinese Document on the Nanjing Massacre," translated from Chinese to English by Robert P. Gray (pgray@pro.net); Nanking Massacre Historical Editorial Committee, ed., *Zhongguo dier lishe dang an gan guan, Nanjing shi dang an guan* [Archival documents relating to the horrible massacre committed by the Japanese troops in Nanking in December 1937] no. 2 (Nanking: Jiansu Ancient Books Publishing, 1987), p. 46.

8. *Archival Documents Relating to the Horrible Massacre* (1987), pp. 68–77; *Source Materials Relating to the Horrible Massacre* (1985), p. 129.

9. Military Commission of the Kuomingtang, Political Department, "A True Record of the

Atrocities Committed by the Invading Japanese Army," July 1938, reprinted in Xingzu et al., "Japanese Imperialism and the Massacre in Nanjing"; Hu Hua-ling, "Chinese Women under the Rape of Nanking," *Journal of Studies of Japanese Aggression Against China* (November 1991): 70.

10. Hua-ling, "Chinese Women under the Rape of Nanking," 68; IMTFE records, court exhibits, 1948, box 134, entry 14, record group 238, 1706, World War II War Crimes Records Collection, National Archives; "Deutshe Botshaft China," report no. 21, starting on p. 114, German diplomatic reports, National History Archives, Republic of China.

11. Nagatomi Hakudo, quoted in Joanne Pitman, "Repentance," *New Republic*, February 10, 1992, 14.

12. Hakudo, quoted in Pitman, "Repentance," p. 14.

13. See, e.g., R. J. Rummel, *Death by Government* (New Brunswick, N.J.: Transaction Publishers, 1995), pp. 1–2.

14. Chang, *The Rape of Nanking,* p. 11; Iris Chang, "Japan Must Pay for Its War Crimes," *Newsday*, February 19, 1998, p. A37.

15. Chang, "Japan Must Pay," p. A37.

16. Information on German postwar restitution comes from the German Information Center, New York City.

17. Chang, *The Rape of Nanking*, pp. 11, 55, 181–82.

18. Ibid., p. 222; Chang, "Japan Must Pay," p. A37.

19. Pierre-Antoine Donnet, "Nanjing Massacre Court Trial Opens," *Agence France Presse*, February 12, 1997.

20. House Congressional Resolution 126, 105th Congress, 1st Session, introduced on 25 July 1997 and referred to the Committee on International Relations.

21. Gavin Daws, *Prisoners of the Japanese: POWs of World War II in the Pacific* (New York: William Morrow, 1994), pp. 360–61, 437.

22. Civil Liberties Act of 1988, 50 App. U.S.C.A. § 1989b-4; Chang, "Japan Must Pay," p. A37.

15 | Japan's Official Responses to Nanking

Japan's responses to the Nanking incident are presented in the following two documents: a letter and a joint communiqué.

LETTER FROM THE CONSUL GENERAL OF JAPAN, AKIO EGAWA, DEPUTY COUNSEL GENERAL, TO PROFESSOR BROOKS, JUNE 8, 1998

With respect to the "Nan-Jing Incident," the murdering of civilians and acts of plunder following the entry of Japanese troops into Nan-Jing are undeniable facts. The Government hopes to establish a relationship with China, squarely facing the problem of the past, but at the same time, looking toward the future. The Government will do so under the recognition manifested in the "Joint Communiqué of the Government of Japan and the Government of the People's Republic of China" of 1972 [see below], that "[t]he Japanese side is keenly conscious of the responsibility for the serious damage that Japan caused in the past to the Chinese people through war, and deeply reproaches itself," and more generally, on the basis of the notions expressed in Prime Minister Murayama's . . . statement [see the introduction to Part 3].

JOINT COMMUNIQUÉ OF THE GOVERNMENT OF JAPAN AND THE GOVERNMENT OF THE PEOPLE'S REPUBLIC OF CHINA

Prime Minister Kakuei Tanaka of Japan visited the People's Republic of China at the invitation of Premier of the State Council Chou En-lai of the People's Republic

109

of China from September 25 to September 30, 1972. Accompanying Prime Minister Tanaka were Minister for Foreign Affairs Masayoshi Ohira, Chief Cabinet Secretary Susumu Nikaido and other government officials.

Chairman Mao Tse-tung met Prime Minister Kakuei Tanaka on September 27. They had an earnest and friendly conversation.

Japan and China . . . agreed to issue the following Joint Communiqué of the two Governments:

■   ■   ■

The Japanese side is keenly conscious of the responsibility for the serious damage that Japan caused in the past to the Chinese people through war, and deeply reproaches itself. Further the Japanese side reaffirms its position that it intends to realize the normalization of relations between the two countries from the stand of fully understanding "the three principles for the restoration of relations" put forward by the Government of the People's Republic of China. The Chinese side expresses its welcome for this.

■   ■   ■

Done at Peking, September 29, 1972
Prime Minister of Japan [signature]

Minister of Foreign Affairs of Japan [signature]

Premier of the State Council
of the People's Republic of China [signature]

Minister for Foreign Affairs
of the People's Republic of China [signature]

The Redress Movement

16 | The Comfort Women Redress Movement

George Hicks

THE EXPOSURE AND CONSCIOUSNESS-RAISING PHASE

The initial exposure of Japan's sex-slave operations came in 1948 in Dutch Indonesia. Batavia (now Jakarta) played host to public trials concerning the sexual internment of Dutch women. The Indonesian trials resulted in the conviction of high-ranking Japanese officers and operators of the comfort system. Punishment of varying degrees was meted out, including short and long prison sentences and one execution. Some officers carried out ritual suicide rather than face prolonged incarceration.

The Indonesian trials, which ended in 1949 and received little attention outside Dutch circles, were the only war crimes trials brought against Japan for atrocities involving the comfort women. The Western Allies made a geopolitical judgment to terminate the war crimes trials in all venues as quickly as possible and to concentrate their energies on forging a Cold War strategy. Such a strategy included alliance with former enemies. As Winston Churchill stated, "Our policy should henceforth be to draw the sponge across the crimes and horrors of the past—hard as that may be—and look, for the sake of all our salvation, toward the future."[1]

In Korea, which was more affected than any other country by the comfort system (some scholars estimate that over 70 percent of all comfort women were from Korea, Japan's colony from 1910 to 1945), the issues of Japanese rape and forced prostitution received little public attention. Korean comfort women simply melted into Korean society after the war.

In 1965, South Korea and Japan entered into "the Japanese–South Korean Treaty of 1965." Korea was not a party to the 1952 San Francisco Peace Treaty, which officially ended the war between the Allies and Japan, because it was deemed to be a Japanese colony rather than a sovereign belligerent on either side. The 1952 peace

113

treaty did, however, restore sovereignty to Korea and provided the basis for a nego-tiated settlement of Korean wartime claims against Japan. The 1965 treaty was a product of this process.

Under the terms of the 1965 treaty, the South Korean government received vari-ous forms of monetary relief from Japan. Claims were made for debts owed, unpaid wages, savings held in Japan, and other specific damages. Millions of dollars were paid to South Korea, primarily in the form of grants and loans. By its own terms, the treaty released Japan from further claims. Whether this waiver of liability en-compassed the individual claims of the comfort women, which were not mentioned in the treaty negotiations, would be left to the courts in Japan to resolve years later.

South Korea's subordination of women is the primary reason the Korean govern-ment, a repressive regime even outside matters of gender, did not seek redress on behalf of Korean comfort women in the 1965 treaty. True, South Korea was preoc-cupied during the 1950s and 1960s with a hostile communist regime to its north. But, historically, women throughout Asia were accorded a low ranking de jure. Japan and its colonies were male-dominated societies that viewed rape and sexual abuse as part of the wartime experience. These social attitudes, coupled with the fact that many Korean comfort women came from poor families, made redress a nonissue for the male elites who negotiated the treaty.

It took changing attitudes toward women's rights, as well as campaigns by women on both sides of the Sea of Japan, to turn the comfort women issue into a larger one over women's rights. The strategy was to make the comfort women issue part of a larger indictment of sexual exploitation of women. The first significant opportunity for such consciousness-raising came in the 1970s.

During the 1970s, the main concern of many Korean women's groups was the prevalence of sex tourism, mainly from Japan, and of prostitution around United States bases. The authorities tolerated and even cooperated in these activities, ap-parently seeing them as sources of foreign exchange.

Acting in concert with Japanese women's organizations, the South Korean Church Women's Alliance, a prominent women's group, held demonstrations against sex tourism at airports in both countries. The response of the Japanese and South Korean governments was restrained—particularly as 1975 was International Women's Year. Most of the women's organizations in South Korea, however, re-mained for some years dominated by the officially sponsored leadership carried over from Japanese colonial days.

Tens of thousands of non-Japanese women were being exploited in clubs in Japan, sometimes violently. One case that received wide publicity was that of Filip-ina Maricris Siosin, an entertainer in Fukuoka prefecture, whose body was returned to the Philippines with head injuries and stabbed genitals and covered with other knife wounds. Despite clear evidence of sexual torture and murder, and photo-graphs of her battered and bloodied body notwithstanding, the official Japanese pathology report said she had died from hepatitis. In response to the outcry, Presi-dent Corazon Aquino banned Filipinas under twenty-three from "entertaining" in

Japan. Male Filipino recruiters objected on the grounds that "the Japanese prefer teenage girls."[2]

In 1988, the year the Olympic Games were held in Seoul, a group of women led by Professor Yun Chung Ok of Ehwa Women's University was formed within the South Korean Church Women's Alliance. This became the center of action on the comfort women issue.

Influenced by feminist thought, the group abandoned the traditional condemnation of prostitution as an offense against chastity—an essentially patriarchal concept. It favored instead an emphasis on women's sexual freedom and self-determination. The distinction between "respectable" and "disreputable" women was meaningless, they argued, if neither had sexual freedom under patriarchy:

> So long as there is no change in the sexual consciousness both of men, who do not realize that they are being controlled by using women's sex, or of women, who have internalized the "ideal of chastity" imposed upon them, there will be no end to the danger of sex being used again as an expedient means of control.[3]

Yun's group came to adopt the view that the comfort women issue, simultaneously shocking from the standpoints of morality, feminism, and patriotism, could be linked to current practices of sexual exploitation of women and used to arouse feelings against such practices. The two issues could be closely linked by portraying sex tourists as "industrial warriors," today's equivalent of the wartime Japanese soldier, now working at the industrial frontline to contribute to Japan's wealth as an economic great power, while taking comfort from the oppressed women of foreign lands. Sometimes, of course, the very same procurers who had once served the Japanese military continued as sex tour operators.

Yun's sense of the link between comfort women and postwar Allied base prostitution had been stimulated by Yamatani Tetsuo's 1979 film, *An Old Lady in Okinawa: Testimony of a Military Comfort Woman*, based on the experiences of a Korean comfort woman, Pae Pong Gi. She was the first Korean comfort woman to be publicly identified. Like so many other comfort women, Pae remained in the same role with the American occupation forces.

In 1989, Yun and two other feminists undertook some investigative travels throughout Southeast Asia for a series of articles on the Korean comfort women. These articles, which were published under the title "In the Footsteps of the Voluntary Service Corps," were somewhat hampered by the lack of sufficient firsthand accounts that could bear witness to the sexual atrocities.

Nonetheless, Yun's reports, published in early 1990, had a considerable impact in South Korea, where they heightened awareness of the comfort women issue. Following up on this, the South Korean Women's and Church Women's Alliances, together with the Seoul District Female Students' Representative Council, took the opportunity offered by the announcement of President Roh Tae Wu's visit to Japan. In May 1990, they issued a joint statement addressed to him. The issue was not taken up by the government, but using Roh's impending visit as a pretext, the South

Korean Foreign Ministry requested Japanese cooperation in compiling a list of all wartime labor draftees, some of whom were comfort women.

During Roh's visit, Japan's new emperor, Akihito, expressed "intense sorrow" at the wrongs inflicted on Korea. Korean activists, however, did not regard this as atonement for the lack of an adequate apology from his late father, under whom the crimes occurred.

About a month after Roh's May 1990 visit, the comfort women issue was raised in the Japanese Diet by Social Democratic member Motooka Shoji. In the course of a House of Councillors Budget Committee session in June, Motooka asked Director-General Shimizu Tadao of the Employment Security Office (where relevant documentation was likely to be available) whether comfort women were included in Korean forced drafts. Motooka had fairly strong evidence of official involvement in the control of comfort women. The following exchange took place between Motooka and Shimizu:

> MOTOOKA: Is it a fact that matters like the Naval Operations Patriotic Corps, the Southern Expeditionary National Service Corps, and military comfort women are in the process of being buried in complete obscurity? I insist that they be clarified in the course of investigations. Surely that would be possible if the attempt is made?
> SHIMIZU: From what I understand, including what is said by senior people, the situation is that as regards comfort women, they had just been taken around with the Forces by private operators so, frankly speaking, I do not believe it is possible to obtain any results by investigation as to the true facts of the matter.[4]

Shimizu's words were later to be constantly thrown back in the faces of government officials by activists.

Some months later, when the South Korean women's groups learned of this June 1990 exchange through the Diet minutes, it spurred them to create the Voluntary Service Corps Study Association. This group combined seven affiliates of the Church Women's Alliance, twenty-four affiliates belonging to the Alliance of South Korean Women's Organizations, and some regional groups, including the YWCA and student bodies, for a total of thirty-seven organizations.

The association drafted an open letter to the Japanese government, addressed to Prime Minister Kaifu Toshiki, that contained six demands:

1. That the Japanese government admit the forced draft of Korean women as comfort women;
2. That a public apology be made for this;
3. That all barbarities be fully disclosed;
4. That a memorial be raised for the victims;
5. That the survivors or their bereaved families be compensated;
6. That these facts be continuously related in historical education so that such misdeeds are not repeated.[5]

Copies of this letter, dated October 17, 1990, and signed by the thirty-seven organizations, were delivered to the Japanese Embassy in Seoul and to the South Korean government, though at this stage the latter displayed little sign of official interest in the issue. Echoing the position taken by Director-General Shimizu in the Diet in June 1990, the Japanese Foreign Ministry denied any government responsibility for the sexual slavery of Korean women. No public apology, disclosure, memorial, or compensation was forthcoming.

In May 1991, Yun attended a symposium in Japan titled "Peace in Asia and the Role of Women," sponsored by Japanese, North Korean, and South Korean women's groups. The symposium played an important role in raising awareness and furthering cooperation between Japanese and Korean women's groups. Public awareness was further raised by the release in the second half of 1991 of a film on comfort women called *Song of Arirang*.

The efforts of the women's groups reached a turning point on August 14, 1991, when former comfort woman Kim Hak Sun announced her willingness to testify publicly about her wartime experiences and raise the issue to the level of formal legal action. Kim Hak Sun's decision to testify was motivated in large part by anger at the Japanese government's denial of responsibility. Her lack of immediate family to suffer shame or aftereffects also facilitated her decision to testify. Kim Hak Sun was also acquainted with an atomic bomb victim who was being helped by the women's organizations.

Not long after Kim Hak Sun agreed to go public, two other former comfort women were found who were prepared to join her in her legal action, though not under their true names. They are referred to as Plaintiffs A and B. They claim not to have been paid for their services. Plaintiff A had been taken to Rabaul after being offered a spinning mill job in Japan. Plaintiff B had been taken to Shanghai after what seemed a tempting advance payment of thirty yen.

THE LITIGATION PHASE

The first lawsuit by Korean comfort women was filed in Japan in 1991. Kim Hak Sun's suit with two other anonymous comfort women was later joined by Mun Ok Ju and five others. In addition, it carried the claims of thirty-three ex-military and paramilitary plaintiffs. The case, formally described as the Asia-Pacific War Korean Victims Compensation Claim Case, opened on December 6, 1991, practically coinciding with the fiftieth anniversary of the December 7 attack on Pearl Harbor.

The most dramatic, immediate, and unexpected result of the launch of the lawsuit was the surfacing of original wartime Defense Agency documents. The Japanese authorities had long claimed that these did not exist. In the absence of official documents on the comfort system, their stance had been that it was run by private operators and that the women were volunteers or paid prostitutes. These new documents demonstrated the extent of direct Japanese military coercion and involvement with comfort facilities.

Early in January 1992, Professor Yoshimi Yoshiaki of Chuo University, hearing of the lawsuit, recalled the original wartime documents relating to comfort women in the Library of the National Institute for Defense Studies attached to the Defense Agency. Professor Yoshimi promptly retrieved five of these documents. His speed showed up the official unwillingness to find relevant documents.

On January 11, the *Asahi Shimbun*, a Japanese newspaper, published key extracts from these "nonexistent" documents. The afternoon edition carried the admission from government sources that "the deep involvement by the Forces of the time cannot be denied. . . . The truth of the matter is rapidly being revealed by the efforts of scholars and citizen groups. The facts will continue to be investigated through both official and private channels."[6]

Over the weeks following publication of Professor Yoshimi's documents, scores of similar documents were discovered and reported. These included some wartime American studies, stimulating lively debate in the media that both added to the data available and revealed the variety of attitudes toward the comfort women issue. Professor Yoshimi published the complete text of his documents in the magazine *Sekai* in March 1992, with references to earlier anecdotal accounts to demonstrate their agreement with the "new sources."

On January 20, 1992, the Comfort Women Problem Resolution Council demanded that the South Korean government provide urgent livelihood support for the affected victims. It also demanded that the government erect a memorial to them in the Independence Commemoration Hall.

The accumulation of public disclosures, Professor Yoshimi's work in particular, finally forced the Japanese government to issue an apology. Prime Minister Miyazawa Kiichi expressed his regret in terms so strong that an attempt at an English translation sounds too exaggerated to be convincing. During his visit to Seoul on January 16, 1992, the prime minister repeated this apology to the South Korean president at the National Assembly. The South Korean and North Korean governments and the activists do not consider this to be an official government apology. Additionally, Prime Minister Miyazawa was condemned by activists for not also promising compensation, which he maintained was ruled out by the 1965 Basic Treaty. But he and his spokespeople accepted the right of the litigants to pursue legal recourse. He added that the issue involved a "wound to the spirit" that merited some "visible redress."[7] The possibility of some measure "in lieu of compensation" would be considered after receiving the report of fact-finding committees being set up in South Korea and Japan.

At the same time, the North Korean government also issued a statement to the effect that the comfort women issue had also affected its people. The issue, the government stated, had to be settled as part of the normalization of relations with Japan, which was in the process of tortuous negotiation. North Korea had, of course, not been part of the 1965 Basic Treaty.

Cases involving Dutch, Filipina, Malaysian, and other comfort women were filed in the Tokyo District Court in subsequent years, joining the original case. In all, some thirty reparation cases were eventually filed against Japan by various victims' groups in addition to comfort women advocacy organizations. These include various POWs, internees, and others who suffered at the hands of Japan during the war.[8]

In April 1998, one of the comfort women trials came to a decision. The court condemned government policy and ruled that Japan must compensate three South Korean women the equivalent of $2,300 (U.S.) each. This ruling is expected to profoundly affect pending cases and may encourage others to file similar lawsuits.[9] But for Kim Hak Sun, the first former comfort woman to go public with her story and one of the original plaintiffs in the lawsuits, reparations came too late. She died on December 16, 1997, from chronic problems stemming from her sexual slavery.[10]

THE LEGISLATIVE PHASE AND PUBLIC OPINION

The comfort women issue was further pursued in the Diet shortly after the Korean comfort women lawsuit was filed. In a House of Representatives Budget Committee session in February 1992, the matter was raised by Social Democratic member Ito Hideko, who had personally investigated the Defense Studies Library and obtained fifty-six new documents. She expressed appreciation for Prime Minister Miyazawa's apology to South Korea, but also expressed her regret for the lack of compensation to give it substance. She described the apology as having had a negative character in that it was based on "inability to deny military involvement."[11] She then recalled a government statement on the renunciation of claims under the Japanese-Soviet Joint Declaration, to the effect that this constituted a waiver of state claims and of the right of diplomatic protection for individual cases, but not of individual claims on either state or individuals. She went on to raise the question of whether the same applied to the 1965 Basic Treaty with South Korea as it affected comfort women.

The head of the Economic Cooperation Bureau of the Foreign Ministry replied in some detail on the coverage of the 1965 Basic Treaty, as well as on an internal law passed at the same time, terminating South Korean property rights with a statutory basis. It was concluded that no bar existed to action in a Japanese court by individual claimants.

Similar discussion kept the comfort women issue before the Diet pending the government's promised investigation into the issue and release of its findings by July 1992. Activist groups and the media in Japan and South Korea also kept the issue in the public's eye during this waiting period.

PUBLIC OPINION AGAINST REPARATIONS

Despite mounting evidence of heavy Japanese involvement in the comfort women system, many Japanese citizens, mainly on the political right, opposed compensation. Critics of compensation did not hesitate to voice their opinions in the months leading up to the government's July report.

Opposition to compensating comfort women ranged from arguments that they had been compensated by payment at the time to the position that it was much too late to revive such an outdated issue. Some opposed the raising of the issue by Japanese activists on the grounds that all countries have shameful secrets it would be unseemly to expose, much like the pudenda of the human body. The influential economic newspaper *Sankei* carried arguments that it was proper, as in the proverb, to "keep a lid on something smelly." One feature article argued that a subject such as comfort women was something to be spoken of in whispers, not paraded in public or taught in schools: "The management of troops and sex is a conundrum that causes headaches in any country." Not all Korean comfort women were forced to comply, as alleged, any more than the women who served the U.S. Navy in the Amusement House at the Yokosuka base, it argued. A history of Napoleon's career related that every company in his army had six "camp followers" attached to provide this service. During the Crusades, the king conscripted women to follow behind the troops, providing sexual services on demand—hence the term "fornication under command of the king" and its more commonly known acronym. These explanations were offered not to excuse the Japanese armed forces, but rather to say that "this is the reality of a country's lower organs and human history."[12]

One letter expressed concerns that probably reflected the true attitude that most government officials held in secret. A seventy-year-old retiree wrote:

> If a haphazard investigation is made, it will produce new injustices and there will be a limitless torrent of claims for compensation. It will not stop at China and Korea but doubtless claims will be made from far-flung countries in Southeast Asia and the South Pacific. If settlement is made in amounts acceptable to war compensation claimants, the present Japanese nation would probably have to shoulder a tax burden several times the current level.[13]

He concluded that Japan should reflect on past mistakes and guard against their repetition. Individual compensation for victims was not practicable, but Japan should give as much economic aid as possible.

A letter from a sixty-five-year-old Korean businessman living in Japan represents the attitude of those of his countrymen hoping for a mutually beneficial *modus vivendi*. He concluded that Japan deprived Korea of sovereignty and property, but also recalled that Japan invested a great amount in Korea's modernization, and that the leaders who had established the basis for the South Korean state had benefited from the modern education introduced. The expansionism of the Japanese leadership had brought "comparable suffering to both peoples." The comfort women problem was not one that had arisen suddenly. It went back half a century. The fact that only at this stage had the call for apology and compensation been raised exposed the negligence of the South Korean government. These "unfortunate women," he went on, have little life left to them.

> The South Korean government should now lend them a helping hand. . . . No courage or endurance is required to blame an offender, but courage, tolerance and

endurance are required to forgive one. As one of their countrymen living in Japan, I believe that the South Korean nation is one that has such endurance. What about it?[14]

A letter from a thirty-five-year-old company employee represented the fairly widespread attitude of preferring simply to bury the past. "The comfort women problem, although a matter of past events which cannot directly involve us of the post-war generation, is a serious issue in that we and our country are being accused." After enlarging on the new world situation where so many barriers between peoples are breaking down, he continued:

> The comfort women problem from the past, which seems to have been abruptly thrust upon us by South Korea, with demands for compensation from the national level, imparts a sense among us, as we are putting forth our best efforts for the present and future society, of being subject to "psychological aggression." There can be no need to drag the younger generation back into a relationship like that of the past. I constantly hope that, rather than be bound by history, we can devote our effort to the creation of a future history.[15]

This argument was rejected a few days later in a letter written by a student, who argued that the true "psychological aggression" was Japan's failure to right the wrongs of the past, arising from failure to come to terms with it.

Not all women have espoused the cause of the comfort women. The more systematic arguments against their cause have come from a small group of women who perhaps feel their sex saves them from charges of male chauvinism. The most prominent is Uesaka Fuyuko, a freelance journalist and critic with South Korean contacts. In February 1992, she wrote an article that appeared in the *Shukan Post* weekly, under the headline "As No One Will Speak Out, I Venture to Write." She began by asking why there had been no serious debate on the comfort women issue. "Do not superficial sympathy and facile apologies amount to a slight on these women who were forced to suffer in the past?" After noting the emotional tension created by the images of fighting men with heroic qualities on the one hand, and needing "comfort" on the other, she listed some of the "false premises" that she felt had dominated the discussion. For example, she questioned the sudden prominence of the issue, when as early as 1962 writers such as Senda Kako had made considerable studies of comfort women with no political repercussions. She speculated that the present stir might be economically motivated, as a way of putting pressure on Japan, or helping improve relations between North and South Korea.

Uesaka considered Prime Minister Miyazawa's apologies to be ill-conceived, whether he hoped that they would settle the matter or was simply playing for time. She preferred President George Bush's refusal to apologize for the American use of nuclear weapons on Japanese cities, even though she herself had written a book on the victims. She contended that Miyazawa should have had the courage to say, "I am not prepared to apologize at this stage for what the then Japanese Forces judged was a necessary evil to be adopted in war zones to avoid harm to local women."

She did not believe that the present Japanese government, forty-seven years after the country's complete reconstruction, could be made responsible for the deeds of the long-vanished armed forces. She did admit, however, the right of individuals to sue for damages and to receive due compensation.[16]

The arguments against the comfort women's case have been summarized by the women's groups as falling into the following categories:

- Enormities of all kinds are inevitable in war;
- Comfort women were a "necessary evil" to maintain order and health;
- Apart from possible coercion, which is asserted and not proved, recruitment was on a contractual basis in accordance with then-legal procedures;
- Compensation was settled by the 1965 Basic Treaty;
- The whole issue is Japanese media hype to gain public interest and sell newspapers;
- The past is past, which most people prefer to forget like a bad dream;
- Why only Koreans? (This, however, can be applied in the positive sense of expanding the scope of the issue);
- Korean brothel keepers were involved;
- There is no way of determining the total number of women involved;
- The issue is best ignored for the sake of future good relations, since it can only be a source of friction.

THE JAPANESE REPORT

The Japanese committee investigating the comfort women issue published a report on July 6, 1992, titled *Results of Investigation into the Question of "Military Comfort Women" Originating from the Korean Peninsula*. Despite the title, it also included material on comfort women of other nationalities. The report proposed the establishment of a relief fund in lieu of individual compensation for the former Korean comfort women, provided the basis of a general statement of apology to all countries concerned, and contributed significantly to the information available on comfort women. The Japanese government also appeared for the first time to be taking the subject seriously. However, it did not escape notice that there were no relevant documents released from the Police Agency or the Labor Ministry, the two agencies most implicated in the forced recruitment of women.

The absence of documents on the recruitment of comfort women provoked a torrent of criticism on the shortcomings of the scope of the committee's investigations. Professor Yoshimi, the various women's groups, and, a little later, the South Korean government's report on its own investigations were especially critical. The lack of police documents, particularly from regional sources, was described as remarkable, since Foreign Ministry documents indicated widespread police activity on such matters as identity cards. The Labor Ministry's failure to produce documents was similarly seen as a shortcoming. The Justice Ministry was not even involved in the investigation, although it was known to have the full records of all war crime trials, including the Dutch cases.

The Comfort Women Problem Resolution Council of South Korea recorded its reaction to the Japanese report in an open letter to Prime Minister Miyazawa, dated October 13, 1992:

> Even among the war crimes committed by Japan, the comfort women issue involves the most inhuman, atrocious national crimes, unparalleled in the world. We have consistently demanded that the concealed truth of the matter be brought to light and that apology and compensation be made to the victims. This is a movement to restore the human rights denied the comfort women. It also aims to correct the distortions in the history of Korean and Japanese relations and to sound an alarm bell to the world so that such war crimes are not repeated.[17]

It described the report as "no more than an enumeration of data, something extremely insincere which does not mention the concrete content of injuries or the locus of command and responsibility." The Council had placed the issue on the agenda of the United Nations Subcommission on Human Rights:

> We feel deep disquiet and indignation on receiving reports that your government has recently been considering the establishment of a relief fund for former comfort women as "a measure in lieu of compensation." It is clear to anyone that such a move by your government arises from a wish to find a hurried monetary solution to its own shameful crimes which have surfaced as a matter of worldwide concern.
>
> We realize that your government takes the position that the question of compensation was settled by the South Korea–Japan agreement of 1965. We repeat, however, that the comfort woman question was not discussed at that time. You and your government must well realize that under the *jus cogens* [enforcing norm, or fundamental law overriding any inconsistent national law or international agreement] individual rights are not extinguished even by agreements between states. We therefore declare that a "livelihood fund" as a "measure in lieu of compensation" is a deceitful conception incompatible with reason.[18]

The Council argued that the former comfort women were unable to accept welfare money, for it would only signal renewed humiliation for them.[19] Moreover, the Council regarded relief measures as properly the duty of the Koreans' own people, and noted that a national fundraising movement for former comfort women was being developed.[20]

CONCLUSION

To this day, the Diet has not issued an official apology to the former comfort women. The latter do not consider Emperor Akihito's or Prime Minister Miyazawa's apologies, issued in 1990, official government apologies—statements that speak for the people of Japan. Rather, they are viewed as personal expressions of remorse, however deeply felt, that do not countermand the Diet's long-standing position that postwar treaties, including the 1965 Basic Treaty with South Korea, released Japan from all World War II claims. The governments of South Korea and North Korea also do not see Japan as having issued an official apology to the former comfort women.[21]

The Diet's reparations scheme adds further support to the sense that Tokyo has yet to own up to atrocities committed against the comfort women. Japan has pursued two methods of paying monetary reparations to the former comfort women. Both have the appearance of an attempt to sidestep responsibility.

The first method of payment is through the administration of a fund that receives donations from private individuals and organizations. This fund, called the "Asian Women's Fund," was initiated in July 1995 and offers financial assistance to former comfort women. Each woman who is able to fully document her case receives 2 million yen (approximately $18,000 to $20,000 U.S., depending upon the exchange rate) and a letter from the Japanese prime minister expressing his "sincere apologies and remorse" and stating that Japan is "painfully aware of its moral responsibility."[22]

Although some former comfort women have accepted money from the fund, many have refused to even apply. These women oppose money coming from private sources. They argue that the Japanese government must shoulder the full cost of the payments; otherwise, the money is not a form of reparations or compensation for grievous wrongs, but rather a form of charity or welfare—a government largesse. What these women seek is "atonement money," not "consolation money," which can only come directly from the perpetrator, the Japanese government.[23]

Some former comfort women have accepted financial assistance from their own government when offered. For example, in December 1997, each of Taiwan's surviving comfort women received NT$500,000 (approximately $15,000 U.S.) in assistance from the Republic of China government. "The move became necessary because the Japanese government is still reluctant to compensate the women."[24] The Republic of China is expected to be reimbursed should Japan compensate the former comfort women.[25] The South Korean government has announced the establishment of a similar fund in which it will pay the equivalent of $25,000 U.S. to each of the 152 surviving South Korean comfort women.[26]

In addition to operating the private fund, Japan has set up a government-funded reparations plan. This fund pays each surviving Filipina comfort woman 1.2 million yen (approximately $9,302 U.S.). This plan has been criticized not only for the unrealistically low amount of money it pays, but also because it excludes former comfort women from South Korea and Taiwan. Also problematic is the fact that funds are paid through government welfare agencies, such as the Philippine Department of Social Welfare and Development, which makes the money seem more like welfare than reparations.[27]

NOTES

1. George Hicks, *The Comfort Women* (New York: W. W. Norton, 1995), p. 168.

2. Ibid., p. 175.

3. Ibid., p. 174.

4. Ibid., p. 182

5. Ibid., p. 185.

6. Ibid., p. 206.

7. Ibid., p. 198.

8. See, e.g., "Time to Pay for Crimes against Humanity," *The Lawyer*, March 2, 1998 (Lexis/Nexis); "Filipino Ex-'Comfort Women' Urge Tokyo Court to Find Japan Liable," *Deutsche Presse-Agentur*, January 22, 1998 (Lexis/Nexis).

9. Yuri Kageyama, "One-Time Sex Slaves Win Fight in Court," *San Diego Union-Tribune*, April 28, 1998, p. A2.

10. See, e.g., "Strained Relations," *Business Korea*, January 1998 (Lexis/Nexis); "Former Comfort Woman Dies at 73," *Korea Herald*, December 17, 1997 (Lexis/Nexis); "Japanese Lawyers for Sex Slaves Vow to Speed Up Case," *Japan Economic Newswire*, August 23, 1997 (Lexis/Nexis); "Japan Urged to Pay Compensation to 'Comfort Women,'" *Japanese Economic Newswire*, August 20, 1997 (Lexis/Nexis).

11. Hicks, *The Comfort Women*, p. 208.

12. Ibid., p. 214.

13. Ibid., p. 215.

14. Ibid.

15. Ibid.

16. Ibid., p. 218.

17. Ibid., p. 231.

18. Ibid., p. 232.

19. Ibid., p. 229.

20. Ibid., p. 233.

21. See, e.g., "Japanese NGO in Letter to Kim Urge Action on Sex Slaves," *Japanese Economic Newswire*, February 25, 1998 (Lexis/Nexis); "Yoo Says Japan Responsible for Sex Slave Compensation," *Asian Political News*, February 2, 1998 (Lexis/Nexis).

22. "Former Sex Slave Testifies in Last Tokyo Hearing," *Asian Political News*, September 22 and August 25, 1997 (Lexis/Nexis); Juliet Mindell, "Japanese Are Just Waiting for British POWs to Die," *Daily Telegraph*, June 24, 1997 (Lexis/Nexis).

23. See, e.g., "Foreign Ministry Protests over Japanese 'Comfort Women,'" BBC Summary of World Broadcasts, January 7, 1998 (Lexis/Nexis); "Asian Comfort Women Recount Japanese Atrocities in World War II," *Central News Agency*, August 10, 1997.

24. Sofia Wu, "ROC Government Compensates 42 Comfort Women," *Central News Agency*, December 5, 1997 (Lexis/Nexis).

25. Ibid.

26. See, e.g., "South Korea to Directly Compensate Former Sex Slaves," *Associated Press*, April 21, 1998; "South Korea Considers Paying Comfort Women, Then Seeking Japan Repayment," *Agence France Presse*, February 24, 1998 (Lexis/Nexis).

27. "Former Filipino 'Comfort Women' Reject Hashimoto's Apology," *Deutsche Presse-Agentur*, January 20, 1998 (Lexis/Nexis).

17 | Japan's Official Responses to Reparations

Japan's responses to the reparations question are presented in statements by the prime minister and the chief cabinet secretary and a document from the Asian Women's Fund.

STATEMENT BY PRIME MINISTER TOMIICHI MURAYAMA, AUGUST 15, 1995

The world has seen fifty years elapse since the war came to an end. Now, when I remember the many people both at home and abroad who fell victim to war, my heart is overwhelmed by a flood of emotions.

The peace and prosperity of today were built as Japan overcame great difficulty to arise from a devastated land after defeat in the war. That achievement is something of which we are proud, and let me herein express my heartfelt admiration for the wisdom and untiring effort of each and every one of our citizens. Let me also express once again my profound gratitude for the indispensable support and assistance extended to Japan by the countries of the world, beginning with the United States of America. I am also delighted that we have been able to build the friendly relations which we enjoy today with the neighboring countries of the Asia-Pacific region, the United States and the countries of Europe.

Now that Japan has come to enjoy peace and abundance, we tend to overlook the pricelessness and blessings of peace. Our task is to convey to younger generations the horrors of war, so that we never repeat the errors in our history. I believe that, as we join hands, especially with the people of neighboring countries, to ensure true peace in the Asia-Pacific region—indeed, in the entire world—it is necessary, more than anything else, that we foster relations with all countries based on deep understanding and trust. Guided by this conviction, the Government has launched the Peace, Friendship and Exchange Initiative, which consists of two parts promoting: support for historical research into relations in the modern era between Japan and the neighboring countries of Asia and elsewhere; and rapid expansion of exchanges with those countries. Furthermore, I will continue in all sincerity to do my utmost in efforts being made on the issues arisen from the war, in order to further strengthen the relations of trust between Japan and those countries.

Now, upon this historic occasion of the 50th anniversary of the war's end, we should bear in mind that we must look into the past to learn from the lessons of history, and ensure that we do not stray from the path to the peace and prosperity of human society in the future.

During a certain period in the not too distant past, Japan, following a mistaken national policy, advanced along the road to war, only to ensnare the Japanese people in a fateful crisis, and, through its colonial rule and aggression, caused tremendous damage and suffering to the people of many countries, particularly to those of Asian nations. In the hope that no such mistake be made in the future, I regard, in a spirit of humility, these irrefutable facts of history, and express here once again my feelings of deep remorse and state my heartfelt apology. Allow me also to express my feelings of profound mourning for all victims, both at home and abroad, of that history.

Building from our deep remorse on this occasion of the 50th anniversary of the end of the war, Japan must eliminate self-righteous nationalism, promote international coordination as a responsible member of the international community and, thereby, advance the principles of peace and democracy. At the same time, as the only country to have experienced the devastation of atomic bombing, Japan, with a view to the ultimate elimination of nuclear weapons, must actively strive to further global disarmament in areas such as the strengthening of the nuclear non-proliferation regime. It is my conviction that in this way alone can Japan atone for its past and lay to rest the spirits of those who perished.

It is said that one can rely on good faith. And so, at this time of remembrance, I declare to the people of Japan and abroad my intention to make good faith the foundation of our Government policy, and this is my view.

STATEMENT BY THE CHIEF CABINET SECRETARY, AUGUST 4, 1993

The Government of Japan has been conducting a study on the issue of wartime "comfort women" since December 1991. I wish to announce the findings as a result of that study.

As a result of the study which indicates that comfort stations were operated in extensive areas for long periods, it is apparent that there existed a great number of comfort women. Comfort stations were operated in response to the request of the military authorities of the day. The then Japanese military was, directly or indirectly, involved in the establishment and management of the comfort stations and the transfer of comfort women. The recruitment of the comfort women was conducted mainly by private recruiters who acted in response to the request of the military. The Government study has revealed that in many cases they were recruited against their own will, through coaxing, coercion, etc., and that, at the time, administrative/military personnel directly took part in the recruitment. They lived in misery at comfort stations under a coercive atmosphere.

As to the origin of those comfort women who were transferred to the war areas, excluding those from Japan, those from the Korean Peninsula accounted for a large part. The Korean Peninsula was under Japanese rule in those days, and their recruitment, transfer, control, etc., were conducted generally against their will, through coaxing, coercion, etc.

Undeniably, this was an act, with the involvement of the military authorities of the day, that severely injured the honor and dignity of many women. The Government of Japan would like to take this opportunity once again to extend its sincerest apologies and remorse to all those, irrespective of place of origin, who suffered immeasurable pain and incurable physical and psychological wounds as comfort women. It is incumbent upon us, the Government of Japan, to continue to consider seriously, while listening to the views of learned circles, how best we can express this sentiment.

We shall face squarely the historical facts as described above instead of evading them, and take them to heart as lessons of history. We hereby reiterate our firm determination never to repeat the same mistake by forever engraving such issues in our memories through the study and teaching of history.

As actions have been brought to court in Japan and interests have been shown in this issue outside Japan, the Government of Japan shall continue to pay full attention to this matter, including private researches related thereto.

ASIAN WOMEN'S FUND*

1. Development Toward the Inauguration of Asian Women's Fund
   (1) In the Statement by the Prime Minister (August 1994) . . . , the Government expressed the idea that in order for the Japanese people to share the feelings of apology and remorse for the issue of "comfort women," the Government, together with the people, seeks for ways of their wide participation.
   (2) Following this statement, Japan's Ruling Parties seriously considered how Japan should address the issue of "comfort women," and made the following report.

*Excerpt from "Japan's Policy on the Issues of Violence Against Women and 'Comfort Women,'" submitted to the Commission on Human Rights, United Nations document E/CN.4/1996/137.

- An expression of the Japanese people's atonement toward former "comfort women," based on the people's sentiment of apology and remorse, will be a significant act not only in restoring the stained dignity of former "comfort women," but also in demonstrating at home and abroad the strong resolution of Japan to respect women;
- Problems concerning the dignity and honor of women still exist throughout the modern world. It is important that we, the Japanese people, take a strong interest in these problems and make efforts to eliminate them from the entire world;
- Establishment of a Fund with the participation of the Japanese people should be studied from the above consideration;
- The Fund will take appropriate measures for former "comfort women," who suffered unbearable hardship;
- In addition, the Fund will conduct such projects as support for activities to address contemporary issues related to the dignity and honor of women;
- The Government should provide all possible assistance, including financial contributions, to the Fund.

(3) Receiving the above report by the Ruling Parties, the Government of Japan intensified its study for the materialization of the proposal concerning the Fund, including consultations with those groups interested in the issue. In June 1995, the incumbent Chief Cabinet Secretary Kozo Igarashi made the result of the study public announcing that, in the remorse for the past, on the occasion of the fiftieth anniversary of the end of the War, the Asian Women's Fund would conduct the following projects.

- The projects below will be conducted for former "comfort women," through the cooperation of the Japanese people and the Government:

(i) The Fund will raise funds from the private sector as a means to enact *the Japanese people's atonement for former "comfort women."*

(ii) The Fund will support those who conduct *medical and/or welfare projects and other similar projects which are of service to former "comfort women,"* through the use of government funds and others.

(iii) When these projects are implemented, the Government will express once again the nation's sentiment of sincere remorse and apology to the former "comfort women."

(iv) The Government will *collate historical documents on "comfort women," a source of the lesson of history.*

- In addition to the support for the projects mentioned in (ii) above, the Fund will, using government funds and others, support those who undertake projects that *address such contemporary problems as violence against women,* as part of its projects addressing issues concerning the honor and dignity of women.

2. The Activities of Asian Women's Fund

   (1) Asian Women's Fund was formally inaugurated in response to an appeal drafted by proponents in July 1995. These proponents consist of men and women representing academic circles, lawyers, labor unions, the press and other groups in Japanese society. The appeal addressed by the proponents to the Japanese people received nation-wide reverberation.

   (2) Currently, Asian Women's Fund is inviting donations for enacting the people's atonement for "comfort women." As of March 14, 1996, *211 million yen (increasing daily) has been contributed to the Fund by a wide range of people* who support this initiative. This spread of people's participation is now promoting contributions from private companies, trade unions and other various private groups which agree with the purpose of the Fund.

   (3) Further, the Asian Women's Fund, with the active assistance of the Government of Japan, is working hard to *raise public awareness on the issue of "comfort women"* through such means as advertisement on all major and local newspapers, magazines and TV programs, seminars held around the country, and distribution of brochures and pamphlets to the young and the elderly. Many people around the country have responded by sending heart-warming messages to the Asian Women's Fund with their personal contribution.

   (4) In addition, Asian Women's Fund is engaged in *dialogues with former "comfort women"* and those at home and abroad who will be involved in the Fund's projects, so that they will accept the Japanese people's atonement money and other related projects which are to be undertaken through the Fund. In January 1996, the Fund dispatched dialogue teams for following purposes to the Philippines and Chinese-Taipei. The Fund sent a preliminary mission for the same purposes to the Republic of Korea as well:

   - To explain aims of the Asian Women's Fund to the former "comfort women" and the related organizations for their better understanding of the Fund.
   - To obtain support for the Fund and cooperation with the Fund by related organizations.
   - To share information with former "comfort women" on their past experiences and current living conditions.

   (5) The Asian Women's Fund, through such dialogues, is making efforts so that the views and opinions of former "comfort women" and related organizations be reflected in its projects as far as possible. The Fund intends to continue the dialogues.

(6) In addition, Asian Women's Fund is currently preparing for the initiation in April 1996 of the projects addressing such contemporary women's issues as violence against women, which are another pillar of the Fund's projects. Specifically, the Fund plans to hold *an international conference* this Autumn in cooperation with ESCAP on such issues as violence against women and to conduct researches on them, as *"preventive projects,"* and to assist the activities of rescue institutions for women who face the urgent problems such as violence and prostitution, as *"rescue-victims projects."*

3. The Government of Japan's Cooperation and Assistance to Asian Women's Fund

   (1) Following the inauguration of the Asian Women's Fund, the Government of Japan, at the Cabinet meeting in August 1995, confirmed its policy to provide needed cooperation for the activities of the Fund, and has been making its utmost efforts for the Fund to attain its aims.

   (2) For instance, based on the resolution of the Diet, the Government contributed *480 million yen (approximately U.S. $4.8 million)* to the Fund for its administrative expense in the fiscal year of 1995. Furthermore, to FY 1996 budget, the Government appropriated the same amount as a subsidy for the Fund's administrative expense and the expense to address the issues such as violence against women, and, in addition to it, *U.S. $1.5 million* to support medical and welfare projects which will be of service to former "comfort women."

   (3) Further, the Government has provided various forms of cooperation to the Fund, such as authorizing it as a non-profit foundation and exempting the contribution to it from taxation, to facilitate its activities.

   (4) In December 1995, 40 (currently 46) members of the National Diet who belong to the Ruling Parties, have organized "Diet Members' Association for Asian Women," the purpose of which is to support the overall projects of Asian Women's Fund including enlightenment activities. The association is to provide cooperation to the Fund from the standpoint of lawmakers.

   (5) The above cooperation and assistance by the Government of Japan, which the Special Rapporteur's document does not describe, deserves proper attention.

A Legal Analysis of Reparations

18 | Japan's Settlement of the Post–World War II Reparations and Claims

Tetsuo Ito

CLAIMS OF INDIVIDUALS IN TREATIES OF THE POST-WAR SETTLEMENT

(1) THE RIGHT OF AN INDIVIDUAL TO DEMAND COMPENSATION UNDER INTERNATIONAL LAW

The term "claims of individuals" or "claims of its nationals," provided for in treaties of the post-war settlement, poses some questions in international law. The first question is whether it can be said from this term that an individual has the right to make claims or demand compensation against a state in international law. According to a conventional theory of international law, an individual can not be a subject of rights or duties in international law, as international law regulates, in principle, the relations between states. Accordingly, even when the rights or duties of an individual are specifically mentioned in treaty provisions, in most cases, the individual is still an object, not a subject, of the treaty, legally possessing the rights or duties prescribed in the treaty only through domestic legislation of his national state which is a party to the treaty. The generally accepted theory of international law assumes that, in order for an individual to be recognized as a subject of international law, such procedural capacity of the individual has to be ensured so as to: (i) assert and realize his own claims without the exercising of the right of diplomatic protection by his national state, in the sphere of rights, and (ii) be prosecuted

From Tetsuo Ito, "Japan's Settlement of the Post–World War II Reparations and Claims," *Japanese Annual of International Law* 37 (1994): 65–71. Former Director of the Legal Affairs Division, Treaties Bureau, Ministry of Foreign Affairs of Japan. Currently Counselor, Embassy of Japan in London. The views expressed in this paper are the author's own and should not be taken to represent those of the Ministry.

directly by international law for a violation of the obligation prescribed in the treaty, in the case of obligations.[1]

With regard to the concept of criminal responsibility of an individual under international law, at the International Military Tribunals held in Nuremberg and Tokyo after the Second World War, which were conducted in accordance with their respective Charters, the new concepts of crimes against peace and crimes against humanity under international law were introduced. Those crimes were directly applied to punish individuals in the German and Japanese Forces. By the establishment of international instruments such as the Military Tribunals in both Nuremberg and Tokyo, the procedural capacity of the individual criminals to be prosecuted directly by international law was secured. This made it possible to assert that, in both cases, an individual was acknowledged as a subject of duties under international law, though there were criticisms against the legitimacy of the Charters, of both the Tribunals, which punished military personnel by applying new crimes in international law introduced after the acts had been committed. The tradition of prosecuting individuals who violated the regulations of a criminal nature in international law was succeeded by the recent establishment of the Criminal Court of the Former Yugoslavia by Security Council Resolution 827 on May 1993.[2] However, these international instruments to punish crimes of individuals directly by international law have been rarely established, and it can not be said that an individual has been generally recognized as a subject of international law from these few examples.

Meanwhile, concerning the right of an individual to demand compensation for damage in international law, which is analogous to civil liability in municipal law, we can also observe some cases where the right was recognized. One noteworthy example acknowledging the independent procedural capacity of an individual was seen in the provisions of the Versailles Peace Treaty (1919). Article 304 of the treaty established the international instrument of a Mixed Arbitral Tribunal, where any individual of the Allied Powers can directly exercise his right to demand compensation against Germany, on the basis of Article 297(e) of the Versailles Treaty, for damage or injury inflicted upon his property in the German territory during the war. Though a few other cases where such independent status of an individual as a claimant for compensation under international law can be found in treaties concluded in the period between the two World Wars, these should be taken as exceptions.

Article 3 of the Hague Convention of 1907 concerning the Laws and Customs of Land Warfare provided that the party of belligerence who had violated the provisions of the Convention must compensate for the loss caused by the violation. This article was understood to regulate the relations between states in demanding and paying reparations related to the violations of the Convention, and it did not mean to give to each individual victim a right to directly demand compensation for the loss he suffered against the state whose military personnel had violated the convention and caused the damage. There was no international instrument to assert or realize the claim of an individual in international law except for the right of diplomatic protection exercised by his home government.[3]

As we have already noted, the right of an individual to demand compensation in international law can not be acknowledged unless the procedural capacity of the individual to assert and realize the right is ensured in international law. This leads us to the answer of the first question. The term "claims of its nationals" in the provisions of the San Francisco Peace Treaty can not be taken as the rights of individuals to make claims under international law, but should be interpreted as either the rights of the individuals based on municipal laws of the territory where the cause of the claim had occurred or, at least, those rights, the legitimacy of which could be discussed in the light of such municipal legislation.[4]

(2) WAIVER OF THE RIGHT OF DIPLOMATIC PROTECTION

The second question concerning the term "claims of its nationals" in peace treaties is related to the waiver of such claims by their national state. As we have seen, it has often been provided for in peace treaties that claims of a state and its nationals against the other state at war were waived by the state in the treaties. The question is what is the legal meaning of the waiver of "claims of its nationals" by the state. Can the state waive such claims in treaties though its nationals are different legal persons? In order to find the answer to this question, it is necessary to begin with a brief review of the theory of the right of diplomatic protection in international law.

The right of diplomatic protection is generally defined as "the right under international law given to a state to protect its national who suffered damage as a result of the act of another state, which is in violation of international law."[5] As seen in the previous section, unless a certain international instrument exists through which an individual can directly insist on his claims, claims of an individual for damages caused by an unlawful act in international law, committed by a foreign state, can be presented for settlement only by the government of his national state through the exercise of the right of diplomatic protection. This general rule is also applicable to the claims of individuals for damages caused by acts of a belligerent state during the war, as well as those caused by acts of a suzerain state in the colonial period.[6] A national state exercises the right of diplomatic protection in its own capacity by interpreting theoretically that the national state itself was injured by the damages caused to its national. The claim by means of diplomatic protection is that of the state; the subject-matter of the claim is the individual and his property which were actually subjected to damage. One noteworthy aspect of the theory of diplomatic protection is that after the compensation is paid, a foreign state liable for damages is relieved completely from its international responsibility related to the damage, but a national state which was successful in collecting the compensation has no legal duty to distribute it to the individual. It is left to the discretion of the state how to deal with its national with regard to the compensation acquired.[7] Unfortunately, there were few countries who took such measures to directly compensate their nationals by using the resources obtained through reparations or other post-war settlement-related economic cooperation from Japan.[8]

Returning to the second question, with regard to the claims of the nationals of the Allied Powers or those of the "detached territories" such as Korea, the Japanese Government has maintained the view that the problem of the claims not only of states, but also of individuals stemming from the Second World War has been completely settled, between states, by the post-war settlement treaties. This view is based on the concrete existence of the waiver provisions for each national state regarding "claims of its nationals" in these treaties, as we have seen in Section 1. However, the waiver of "claims of its nationals" can not mean the renunciation of such claims by a state in rigid legal terms, firstly because such claims of individuals provided for in the treaties concerned are not included in those acknowledged in international law, as the answer to the first question has indicated, and, secondly because a state can not theoretically waive the right of a third person, without its consent, who is not a party to the treaty concerned, regardless of whether it is a state or an individual. Thus, it seems the following view of the Japanese Government is persuasive: "the waiver by a state of claims of its nationals," provided for in treaties concerned, does not mean the renunciation of the right to claims themselves, which its nationals possess, or, at least, can claim to possess, on the basis of its municipal laws, but means the renunciation of the right of diplomatic protection, which the state possesses, in respect to the claims of its nationals, under international law. Therefore, after waiving the claims of its nationals in treaties, the state can not take up the issue of such claims on an intergovernmental basis, even if its individuals request to do so. This interpretation of international law seems to be reinforced by recent state practices; though there have been several lawsuits filed by foreign individuals demanding compensation for damages caused by the acts of Japan during the war, there has been no such case where their national governments expressed their intention to exercise the right of diplomatic protection, if necessary, with respect to these claims against the Japanese Government.

(3) CLAIMS IN ARTICLE 2 OF THE AGREEMENT WITH SOUTH KOREA

It would be useful to examine the problem of the waiver of claims of individuals in relation to South Korea, in the light of the analyses made in the preceding section, as most of the lawsuits now pending in Japanese courts are related to claims from Korean nationals. The examination is related to the argument on whether or not the Japanese Government has a legal obligation to compensate for the mistreatment of wartime "comfort women." . . . Article 2(1) of the Agreement between Japan and the Republic of Korea for the Settlement of the Problem Concerning Property and Claims and for Economic Cooperation confirmed the final and complete settlement of the problem of "property, rights and interests" as well as that of claims, between the states and their peoples. Article 2(3) stipulates that each party to the treaty can not make any claim against the measures taken by the other party regarding the "property, rights and interests" as well as regarding the claims of the party or its people under the jurisdiction of the other party. In interpreting these paragraphs, we have to note that Clause 2 of the Agreed Minutes annexed to the agreement defines the term "property, rights and interests."[9] The Japanese Government, in accordance with the above article, enacted domestic legislation . . . to extinguish the "property, rights and interests" of the Republic of Korea and its nationals under Japan's jurisdiction. In Parliamentary deliberations, the question whether claims of the Korean people still remain has been raised occasionally, as the above legislation only extinguished "property, rights and interests," leaving claims alive. However, according to the definition given in the Agreed Minutes, all substantial legal rights were included in the term "property, rights and interests" and the term "claims" in the treaty is interpreted as the "status" of being able to raise claims. Such a status can not be included in the category of substantial legal rights. As long as the "claims" were not recognized as existing rights, there was no need to extinguish them by domestic legislation. However, although the Korean Government can not resort to the right of diplomatic protection, the people who have "claims" can file a lawsuit seeking the compensation for their claims which allegedly have legal substance to be compensated. Accordingly, the related lawsuits recently filed by Korean people in Japanese courts can be regarded as legally based upon this "status" of each plaintiff.

■ ■ ■

[An] example suggesting the importance of distinguishing between legal and policy aspects can be seen in the arguments concerning Japanese wartime violations of human rights. It seems that lawyers supporting the victims in lawsuits tend to emphasize such violations under international law as a legal basis for demanding compensation against the Japanese Government. In this regard, we should note that since the end of the Second World War human rights standards have been remarkably enhanced in international law by the adoption of various global and regional human rights treaties, and that we can not give proper judgment to past wartime acts on the basis of present standards of respect for human rights, as an argument in international law. However, such consideration of the evolution of international humanitarian law in the past 50 years can be reflected in the discussion of possible policy measures.

Therefore, it seems that the core of the problem of how to deal with various claims can not be reached by trying to unearth the Japanese Government's legal obligations, but lies in policy arguments. If one insists on additional measures, one can not avoid the argument concerning a wider range of practical issues, including how to choose categories of victims which should be taken care of, in what form measures should be implemented, and how to finance such measures. By indulging oneself only in legal arguments without tackling squarely such issues, one can not find a final solution to the problems concerning post-war settlement.

NOTES

1. See Shigejiro Tabara, *Kokusaiho Shinko* (New Lectures on International Law), Vol. 1 (1994), pp. 65–70.

2. See Tetsuo Ito, "Kyu Yugo Kokusai Saibansho no Horeki Wakugumi to Mondaiten" (The International Criminal Tribunal for the Former Yugoslavia—Its Legal Framework and Problems), *Ribbyo Huguba* (St. Paul's Review of Law and Politics) 40 (1994): 270–74. The Tribunal entrusts the treatment of the possible civil liability of a criminal to domestic legislation and courts of the former Republics of Yugoslavia, as seen in Rule 106(b) of the Rules of Procedure and Evidence of the Tribunal developed in February (1994): "Pursuant to the relevant national legislation, a victim . . . may bring an action in a national court . . . to obtain compensation."

3. Keishiro Irie, *Nihon . . . Tuyaku no Krukyn* (Study of the Peace Treaty with Japan) (1951), p. 249.

4. Yasuo Yamashita, "Seikyuken Oyobi Zaisan" (Claims and Property), *Heiwa Joyaku no Sogo Kenkyu* (Comprehensive Study of the Peace Treaty), 2 (1952): 27.

5. Soji Yamamoto, *Kokusaiho* (International Law) (1993), p. 654.

6. The principle of the continuity of nationality generally applied to the exercise of the right of diplomatic protection can be modified in the case of involuntary changes of nationality by operation of law, including cession of territory. See Ian Brownlie, *Principles of Public International Law,* 4th ed. (1990), pp. 480–82.

7. Also, in the case when a state waived the claims of its nationals (the renunciation of the rights of diplomatic protection) from political considerations, it is a matter of domestic concern whether the nationals concerned are paid some remedy or left without it by its government. See Irie, *Nihon*, p. 248.

8. In accordance with "Law on Compensation for Private Claims against Japan" of December 1974, the Korean Government took certain compensation measures for the claims of its people reported from May 1971 to March 1972 on a basis of "Law on Reports of Private Claims against Japan" of January 1971.

9. Paragraph 2 of the Agreed Minutes relating to the agreement prescribed: "property, rights and interests" mean "all kinds of substantive rights which are recognized to have a property value on a legal basis."

19 | Reparations
A Legal Analysis

Karen Parker and Jennifer F. Chew

Despite [its] admissions and apologies, when pressed for monetary compensation, Japan asserts it settled all claims arising from World War II in its treaties with the Allied Powers and the Republic of Korea.[1] In addition, one Japanese representative has stated that these acts took place too long ago, that wars are always bad, and that with so many victims, the process of compensation would be endless and the amounts necessary to pay all the victims would be too high.[2] None of these explanations [is] compelling.

ALLIED AND KOREAN TREATIES WITH JAPAN

The Democratic People's Republic of Korea, China, the Philippines and Taiwan are not parties to [the Allied Treaty[3] or the Korean Treaty],[4] so claimants from these and other countries not a party to the treaties are unaffected by any treaty-based argument for denying compensation. A number of claimants who reside in Japan are similarly unaffected by the treaties.[5] Regarding the treaties themselves, . . . both address reparations. The Allied Treaty states "[i]t is recognized that Japan should pay reparations to the Allied Powers for the damage and suffering caused by it during the war,"[6] and it sets out specific provisions for the return of property, rights, and interests by Japan.[7] In the section presumably relied on by Japan to show settlement of all claims, the treaty states:

> Except as otherwise provided in the present Treaty, the Allied Powers waive all reparation claims of the Allied Powers, other claims of the Allied Powers and their

From Karen Parker and Jennifer F. Chew, "Compensation for Japanese World War II War-Rape Victims," *Hastings International and Comparative Law Review* 17 (1994): 536–41.

nationals arising out of any actions taken by Japan and its nationals in the course of the prosecution of the war, and claims of the Allied Powers for direct military cost of occupation.[8]

The Korean Treaty resolves claims "concerning property of the two countries and their nationals and claims between the two countries and their nation,"[9] and specifies products and services of the Japanese people and loans to be given to the Republic of Korea.[10] The Korean Treaty provides:

> The Contracting Parties confirm that [the] problem concerning property, rights and interests of the two Contracting Parties and their nationals (including juridical persons) and concerning claims between the Contracting Parties and their nationals, including those provided for in Article IV, paragraph (a) of the Treaty of Peace with Japan signed at the city of San Francisco on September 8, 1951, is settled completely and finally.[11]

Japan presumably relies on this provision to show settlement of all claims.

Neither treaty provides for or mentions war-rape victims.[12] Neither treaty addresses private claims but only claims in which states are the parties. According to these treaties, the parties have agreed not to take up additional state claims against the other parties. In the cases raised by the war-rape victims, no party to the treaty has brought a legal action on its behalf—these victims seek private remedies on their own.

Even if language in the treaties could be found that purported to extinguish private claims, the parties to these treaties had no legal authority to do so. First of all, the underlying claims arise from violations of *jus cogens* norms and *erga omnes* obligations which require an appropriate remedy—compensation. The right to seek that remedy is itself a *jus cogens* right. If any provision of either the Allied Treaty or the Korean Treaty effectively nullifies these *jus cogens* rights or allows violations of *jus cogens* to go uncompensated, then that provision would be void.[13] As Oppenheim stated in his 1905 treatise:

> It is a unanimously recognized customary rule of International Law that obligations which are at variance with universally recognized principles of International Law cannot be the object of a treaty. If, for instance, a State entered into a convention with another State not to interfere in case the latter should appropriate a certain part of the Open Sea, or should command its vessels to commit piratical acts on the Open Sea, such treaty would be null and void, because it is a principle of International Law that no part of the Open Sea may be appropriated, and that it is the duty of every State to interdict to its vessels the commission of piracy on the High Seas.[14]

Other leading scholars of the prewar period concur with Oppenheim's finding that recognition of this rule is unanimous. For example, Hall states: "A treaty becomes [void] . . . [b]y incompatibility with the general obligations of states, when a change has taken place in undisputed law or in views universally held with respect to morals."[15] This principle is also incorporated into the postwar codification of treaty law.[16] Accordingly, Japan may not rely on its treaties with the allied powers or the Republic of Korea to circumvent its liability or its duty to remedy individual claimants for acts governed by *jus cogens*.

This result is the only possible one given the nature of violations of *jus cogens*; the result of governments entering into treaties purporting to terminate private claims of victims to avoid liability for war crimes and crimes against humanity would be a legal catastrophe. Because of the gravity of these violations, if all the other signatories to these treaties failed to seek adequate remedy for their own citizens, neither they nor Japan could prevent individuals and groups of victims from obtaining remedies on their own.

TIME BARS

Time should not be a bar to recovery for the war-rape victims. The policy reasons supporting a time bar such as a statute of limitations or laches are absent. The victims seeking remedy are still alive. The evidence is not stale, but compelling, and Japan has admitted to the existence of the overall scheme. The evidence has only come forth recently, and the victims have not unduly delayed in seeking compensation. Japan itself has been in custody of most of the documentary evidence. It would be unfair to allow Japan to claim a time bar when it controlled much of the evidence. Moreover, the violations the war-rape victims suffered are serious, and redress should not be limited because of time.[17]

A strong reason for precluding a time bar is that soon after the war, Japan was not in a financial position to provide compensation. While other forms of compensation may be possible, adequate monetary compensation may not be possible immediately after a war of this magnitude. In these circumstances, a recovery period is needed before a state may have sufficient resources to settle claims.[18] When the state is in a financial position to provide meaningful financial compensation, the state should pay. However, even in these circumstances emergency funds should be provided the victims before full compensation is awarded.

NUMBER OF VICTIMS AND CLAIMS

No government can excuse *jus cogens* violations and their monetary consequences by claiming difficulties, especially financial ones, arising from too many victims. It is unreasonable for Japan to claim that because it injured too many victims it cannot compensate anyone. The German compensation scheme for Holocaust survivors exemplifies an attempt to provide remedy for multitudes of people injured by a particular event. No less can be expected of the Japanese government. Although wars cause many deaths, international law distinguishes casualties resulting from legitimate military activities and those arising from senseless brutality. The atrocities the Japanese government inflicted on the war-rape victims fall under the latter category.

Japan should undertake immediate action to redress all serious wrongs committed in the course of Japan's military operations in the World War II period. While individual and group judicial actions undertaken in Japanese courts are needed, many claimants will be unable to avail themselves of such judicial action. The government of Japan should institute a comprehensive compensation plan.[19]

NOTES

1. *Sub-Commission on Prevention of Discrimination; Statement of Japan (Right of Reply)*, U.N. Doc. E/CN.4/Sub.21SR.23 (1993). Regarding this apology, the government of the Democratic People's Republic of Korea stated: "Such an 'apology'. . . 'is too little too late' and far from bringing to light the true facts about the issue of the 'comfort women' for the army. . . . After all the Japanese government has not put forward a final solution to the issue of 'comfort women for the army' including a convincing apology acceptable to all, a full investigation and its publication and due compensation." *Sub-Commission on Prevention of Discrimination; Statement of the Democratic People's Republic of Korea,* U.N. Doc. E/CN 4/sub.2/sr.10 (1993).

2. Interview with Masataka Okano, Japanese Ministry of Foreign Affairs, Asian Affairs Bureau, in Tokyo (December 8, 1992). Japan has also claimed that prostitution was legal in Japan until 1957 and so the wartime program did not violate its own laws. See, e.g., Shinji Ito, "Wartime Brothels Called 'Natural,'" *Japan Times,* August 5, 1992, p. 3. Presumably Japan will no longer present this argument, as the government has clearly conceded that the *jugun ianfu* scheme was involuntary and condemned in Japanese law at that time. Then Prime Minister Kiichi Miyazawa also claimed that compensation should be decided by the courts. "Kim Tells Japan to Apologize for and Fully Reveal War Abuse," *Agence France Presse,* September 2, 1993 (available in LEXIS, World Library, AFP File).

3. *Treaty of Peace with Japan,* September 8, 1951, 3 U.S.T. 3169, 136 U.N.T.S. 45 (hereinafter Allied Treaty).

4. *Agreement on the Settlement Problems Concerning Property and Claims and on Economic Cooperation, June 22, 1965, Japan-Korea,* 583 U.N.T.S. 173 (hereinafter Korean Treaty).

5. Some war-rape victims belong to the Korean minority in Japan who, although denied full citizenship rights, cannot claim citizenship from either North or South Korea.

6. *Allied Treaty* art. 14(a), 136 U.N.T.S. at p. 60.

7. Ibid., p. 62.

8. Ibid. art. 14(V)(b), 136 U.N.T.S. at p. 64.

9. *Korean Treaty,* pmbl., 583 U.N.T.S. at p. 258.

10. Ibid. art. I, 583 U.N.T.S. at p. 258.

11. Ibid. art. II(1), 583 U.N.T.S. at p. 260.

12. According to Professor Yoshimi, the issue of war-rape victims was not even discussed in any reparation or treaty negotiations, including those leading to the Korean Treaty. Yoshiaki Yoshimi, "Historical Understanding on the 'Military Comfort Women' Issue," in *War Victimization and Japan: International Public Hearing Report,* ed. Executive Committee International Public Hearing (1993), p. 148.

13. S.S. Wimbledon (Kiel Canal), 1923 P.C.I.J. (ser. A) No. 15, pp. 43, 47 (August 17) (Schucking, J. dissenting).

14. Lassa Oppenheim, *International Law: A Treatise* 528 (1905).

15. William E. Hall, *A Treatise in International Law* 1 (7th ed. 1917), p. 319; in accord Alfred von Verdross, "Forbidden Treaties in International Law," *American Journal of International Law* 31 (1937): 571; see also Oscar Chinn Case (Belg. v. U.K.), 1934 P.C.I.J. (ser. A/B) No. 63, pp. 149-150 (December 12) (separate opinion by Judge Schucking) (Court not applying treaty contrary to *jus cogens*). In *United States v. Krupp*, the Nuremberg Tribunal claimed any agreement between Germany and the Vichy government to employ prisoners of war in war operations was "void under the law of nations . . . it was manifestly *contra bones mores.*" *United States v. Krupp*, International Military Tribunal (July 31, 1948), reprinted in *Trials of War Criminals Before the Nuremberg Military Tribunals*, vol. 9 (Washington, D.C.: U.S. Government Printing Office, 1952).

16. *Vienna Convention on the Law of Treaties*, January 27, 1980, 1155 U.N.T.S. 331. Article 53 sets out the rule that treaties are void if they conflict with *jus cogens* norms. Article 64 provides: "If a new peremptory norm of general international law emerges, any existing treaty which is in conflict with that norm becomes void and terminates." Ibid. art. 64, 1155 U.N.T.S. at p. 347. Although the Vienna Convention only applies to subsequent treaties, ibid. art. 4, 1155 U.N.T.S. at p. 334, the *jus cogens* provisions must be considered retroactive because under no circumstances may governments enforce acts violating *jus cogens*.

17. See, e.g., *Convention on the Non-Applicability of Statutory Limitations to War Crimes and Crimes Against Humanity*, November 11, 1970, 754 U.N.T.S. 73; see *U.N. Commission on Human Rights; Rape and Abuse of Women in the Territory of the Former Yugoslavia*, U.N. Doc. E/CN.4/199415, p. 6 (1993). "Rape constitutes an extremely grave violation of international humanitarian law as recognized by Article 27(2) of the Fourth Geneva Convention . . . and defined as a war crime according to Article 147; of the same Convention. The definition covers not only rape, but any attack on a woman's honour." Ibid.

18. The Allied Treaty recognizes that Japan had insufficient resources to pay reparations and sets out a scheme for long-term payment. *Allied Treaty* art. 14, 136 U.N.T.S. at p. 50. Ferencz notes that despite the physical and economic ruin of Germany after World War II, the payment of billions of dollars in compensation to Germany's war victims "was accompanied without any noticeable hardship to the average German citizen. The wise German leaders . . . considered the restitution to Nazi victims to be an essential moral prerequisite for Germany's readmission to the family of civilized nations." Benjamin Ferencz, "Compensating Victims of the Crimes of War," *Virginia Journal of International Law* 12 (1972): 3431.

19. A number of Japanese legislators have pressed for some form of compensation through legislation. Representative Sumiko Shimizu stated that she would "devote herself to adopting a resolution to the comfort women issue, including concrete measures for compensation." "Japan Asked to Compensate Asians," *Japan Times*, August 14, 1993. On August 30, 1993, a group of Japanese women members of the Diet announced efforts to compensate these victims, claiming urgency because of the advanced age of most of the survivors. "Japanese Women MPs Urge Compensation for 'Comfort Women,'" *Xinhua (New China) News Agency*, August 30, 1993 (available in LEXIS, Asiapc Library, Xinhua File).

An American Response

20 | Lipinski Resolution

CONCURRENT RESOLUTION

Expressing the sense of Congress concerning the war crimes committed by the Japanese military during World War II. Whereas during World War II the Government of Japan deliberately ignored and flagrantly violated the Geneva and Hague Conventions and committed atrocious crimes against humanity;

■　■　■

Whereas at the Japanese biochemical warfare detachment in Mukden, Manchuria, commanded by Dr. Shiro Ishii, experiments were conducted on living prisoners of war that included infecting prisoners with deadly toxins, including plague, anthrax, typhoid, and cholera;

■　■　■

Whereas the Japanese military invaded Nanjing, China, from December, 1937, until February, 1938, during the period known as the "Rape of Nanjing," and brutally and systematically slaughtered more than 300,000 Chinese men, women, and children and raped more than 20,000 women;

Whereas the Japanese military enslaved millions of Koreans during World War II and forced hundreds of thousands of women into sexual slavery for Japanese troops;

Whereas international jurists in Geneva, Switzerland ruled in 1993 that women who were forced to be sexual slaves of the Japanese military during World War II

House Concurrent Resolution, 105th Congress, 1st Session (July 9, 1997).

(known by the Japanese military as "comfort women") deserve at least $40,000 each as compensation for their "extreme pain and suffering";

Whereas the Government of Germany has formally apologized to the victims of the Holocaust and gone to great lengths to provide financial compensation to the victims and to provide for their needs and recovery; and

Whereas by contrast the Government of Japan has refused to fully acknowledge the crimes it committed during World War II and to provide reparations to its victims: Now, therefore, be it

Resolved by the House of Representatives (the Senate concurring), That it is the sense of Congress that the Government of Japan should—

(1) formally issue a clear and unambiguous apology for the atrocious war crimes committed by the Japanese military during World War II; and

(2) immediately pay reparations to the victims of those crimes, including United States military and civilian prisoners of war, people of Guam who were subjected to violence and imprisonment, survivors of the "Rape of Nanjing" from December, 1937, until February, 1938, and the women who were forced into sexual slavery and known by the Japanese military as "comfort women."

Suggested Readings

Chang, Iris. *The Rape of Nanking: The Forgotten Holocaust of World War II* (New York: Basic Books, 1997).

Hicks, George. *The Comfort Women* (New York: W. W. Norton, 1994).

Howard, Keith, ed. *True Stories of the Korean Comfort Women* (New York: Cassell, 1995).

Keller, Nora Okja. *Comfort Woman* (New York: Viking, 1997).

Weissbrodt, David, and Frank Newman. *Selected International Rights Instruments and Bibliography for Research on International Human Rights Law* (Cincinnati: Anderson Publishing Company, 1996).

4 | Japanese Americans

Introduction

21 | Japanese American Redress and the American Political Process

A Unique Achievement?

Roy L. Brooks

The success of any organized attempt to seek redress for human injustices is inextricably linked to politics, not justice or logic. Intuitions of public policy, the prejudices that legislators share with their constituencies, the willingness of political leaders to step forward and exercise political leadership, political inconvenience, and the simple exchange of favors have had the greatest impact on the fate of redress claims. Nowhere is this more evident than in the United States. Various groups have laid claim to reparations—primarily Native Americans, African Americans, and Japanese Americans—but only the latter have seen anything close to total vindication. By studying the experiences of Japanese Americans, we can glean important lessons about the redress of human injustices within the complex web of the American political system.

Noted historian Sandra Taylor opens Part 4 with an overview of the experience of Japanese people in America, focusing on the conditions that led to their evacuation and internment during World War II. Japanese immigrants first came to America in the 1880s. These immigrants are called the Issei, in contrast to the first generation of ethnic Japanese born in this country, who are referred to as the Nisei, and those who returned to Japan as children to be educated, who are known as the Kibei. Though many Issei lost cultural contact with their homeland, and even though their Nisei children were American citizens, assimilation in America proved difficult for them. In the eyes of many Americans, the Japanese represented "otherness" and were treated accordingly. The Issei were denied the right of naturalization and the right to purchase land. The 1924 National Origins Act banned further immigration from Japan. The stage was set for the increasingly hostile treatment of Japanese Americans that would follow the attack on Pearl Harbor.

On February 19, 1942, just two months after Pearl Harbor, President Franklin Delano Roosevelt issued Executive Order 9066. This important document, which follows Taylor's chapter, directed the secretary of war to prescribe military areas "from which any or all persons may be excluded" who might threaten national security by sabotage or espionage. Absent from the executive order were the requirements, fundamental to a democracy, that criminal charges be filed against the accused and that a trial soon follow. Japanese Americans on the West Coast and in western Arizona were forced to quickly sell or store their property and moved first to Assembly Centers, and later to the ten internment camps. More than 120,000 persons of Japanese ancestry, including over 77,000 American citizens, were confined to the internment camps under the authority of Executive Order 9066, even though the executive order did not specifically target them. What political forces allowed the order to be used as a means to deprive Japanese Americans of their fundamental constitutional right to due process?

The answer to this question lies in the report produced by the Commission on Wartime Relocation and Internment of Civilians (CWRIC), which Congress established in 1980 to review Executive Order 9066 and its impact on "American citizens and permanent resident aliens." A comprehensive series of hearings, including testimony by more than 750 witnesses, led the commission to conclude that Executive Order 9066 was not justified by military necessity but was fueled by racial prejudice, war hysteria, and a failure of political leadership. The CWRIC's analysis is supported by the dramatically different treatment of ethnic Japanese in Hawaii. Because those of Japanese ancestry represented more than 35 percent of the population in Hawaii, a strategically important area, the logical assumption would be that this area posed the greatest danger. And yet, only 1 percent of the ethnic Japanese in Hawaii were detained. This difference in policy is attributed to greater racial tolerance, the larger representation of ethnic Japanese in the population, and a restrained military commander who argued for a presumption of loyalty, absent evidence to the contrary. A very different political climate on the mainland allowed mass exclusion to occur.

Although the public's attention has focused primarily on Japanese Americans, the CWRIC report serves as a reminder that the United States has similarly mistreated other groups—for example, removing Aleuts from the Aleutian Islands to southeastern Alaska. Although the Aleuts were evacuated for a rational purpose—the military wanted to ensure their safety from Japanese invaders—they were subjected to deplorable living conditions, including inadequate housing, sanitation, and medical care. Evacuees were crowded into rotting buildings and epidemics raged throughout the camps. Equally disturbing, the Aleuts returned to their villages after the war only to find them looted by American military personnel.

Paralleling the complaints of the Aleuts, the narratives that follow the CWRIC report below vividly describe the conditions under which the internees had to live. Not only were the Japanese Americans uprooted from their homes and deprived of their property, but they were also denied their freedom. The sense of being a prisoner of war or a convicted criminal pervaded the camps, a mood reinforced by barbed-wire fences, watchtowers, armed guards, and a highly regimented lifestyle. Adding to the sense of incarceration and frequent terror was the attitude of the guards. As one lieutenant stated: "the guards were finding guard service very monotonous, and that nothing would suit them better than to have a little excitement, such as shooting a Jap."

Despite the inherent injustice of denying persons the right of due process, more than three decades passed before the movement for redress gained momentum. Roger Daniels, perhaps the leading scholar on Japanese Americans, chronicles the movement, noting that government support for reparations was unforeseeable even twenty-five years after the evacuation. A number of conditions made redress appear unlikely. Japanese Americans were considered the "model minority," and their socioeconomic progress was real. Increasing numbers of the Nisei and Sansei (grandchildren of Japanese immigrants) joined the American middle class. In addition, the Issei became eligible for citizenship in 1952 and the ban on Japanese immigration was lifted, although a quota was instituted in its place. Hawaii gained admittance to the union, and Asian American legislators arrived in Washington.

Notwithstanding these impressive gains, the lingering effects of internment continued to reverberate twenty-five years later. As Daniels points out, even though Japanese Americans on average had more education than whites, they earned less money. Japanese Americans were also denied the prosperity many white families enjoyed during the booming wartime economy that allowed debts to be paid and investments to accumulate. More significantly, the evacuation defined the experience of ethnic Japanese in America. Daniels informs us that in the eyes of Japanese Americans, "relocation was and is the central event in Japanese American history, the event from which all other events are dated and compared."

And yet, conflicting attitudes between generations made this an uneasy legacy. While the Nisei preferred to move beyond the traumatic experience, their Sansei children sought to confront the past. They wanted to restore ethnic pride to Japanese Americans. This change of attitude created an impetus to search for the truth, and brought survivors forward to testify before the CWRIC.

The second piece by Daniels details the CWRIC's recommendations, which followed its report. These included a joint congressional resolution acknowledging and apologizing for the wrongs committed; a presidential pardon for those who refused to comply with the evacuation order; restitution of status and entitlements lost due to discrimination; establishment of a foundation to sponsor educational activities; and compensation of twenty thousand dollars to each survivor. These recommendations served as the foundation for the Civil Liberties Act of 1988, which also included an apology and an award of twelve thousand dollars to each eligible Aleut.

Leslie T. Hatamiya follows with a powerful analysis of the Civil Liberties Act as a historic legislative achievement. Few Americans realize how difficult it is to pass legislation, how truly inaccessible Washington is to the average citizen. In *Arrogant Capital* (1994), political analyst Kevin Phillips argues that our lawmakers are mired in bureaucracy, captured by well-financed special interest groups who can influence the outcome of elections. Japanese Americans did not fit into this world in the 1980s. They were a numerical minority (less than 1 percent of the population), politically inactive as a group, and divided over whether to pursue a legislative or judicial route in the fight for redress. In addition, as the redress movement reached its peak in the 1980s, the federal budget deficit was nearing an all-time high, further dimming the prospects of an expensive reparations package. By all accounts, the Japanese American redress movement should have failed (like the African American redress movement for slavery and Jim Crow) or, at best, should have gained only marginal success (like the Native American redress movement). Why was it successful? How were Japanese Americans able to break through the political barriers that have stymied other groups? What conditions constitute a successful redress movement in the American political system? These are some of the tough questions Hatamiya tackles in her important essay.

Among the points Hatamiya makes is that the redress bill became a "free vote." Veterans' groups did not actively oppose the bill primarily because of the remarkable war record of Japanese American veterans (the Nikkei soldiers), who fought valiantly for a country that held their parents captive. The only group that opposed the redress movement, Americans for Historical Accuracy, lacked sufficient credibility to mount a threatening campaign. Their claim that internment was brought about not by racism but by military necessity was thoroughly rejected in the CWRIC report and various judicial proceedings regarding the internment matter. Thus, members of Congress were able to vote their conscience, without fear of paying a price at the polls—what is often called a "free vote."

The lobbying efforts of Japanese Americans also contributed to the bill's success. For example, the Japanese American Citizens League (which during the war had advised passivity rather than open resistance to evacuation and internment) was able to create a coalition of congressional supporters, including liberal Democrats and conservative Republicans, by framing the legislative issue as one of equal opportunity rather than as a claim for preferential treatment. Enhancing this support network, bonds were forged with other Asian American groups, as well as with civil rights organizations and various sympathizers, including "surrogate Nikkei," or white soldiers who fought alongside Japanese American soldiers during the war.

Notwithstanding the importance of the lobbying coalition and the lack of formidable opposition, Hatamiya suggests that the actions of key individuals within the government—legislative sherpa guides, if you will—decided the fate of the Civil Liberties Act. She notes that congressional committees serve a "gatekeeping" function in that they hold the power to advance or block legislation. While early chairs of the subcommittee hearing the bill failed to push for redress, Barney Frank made redress his top priority when he became subcommittee chair in 1987. After the bill was voted out of committee and presented to the House and Senate, four Japanese American members of Congress also vigorously fought for the cause, personalizing discussions with narratives of their own war experiences. These individuals provided the insider support that is integral to success in the American political process.

Reinforcing Hatamiya's analysis of the uniqueness of the Japanese American redress movement is Proclamation 4417, issued by President Gerald Ford on February 19, 1976. The proclamation acknowledges that we now know that the evacuation was wrong and hopes "that we have learned from the tragedy of that long-ago experience forever to treasure liberty and justice for each individual American, and resolve that this kind of action shall never again be repeated." Most importantly for Japanese Americans who feared evacuation and internment could happen to them again, the proclamation declares that Executive Order 9066 is obsolete and its effectiveness was terminated when the hostilities of World War II ceased. Even with this official recognition of the injustices perpetrated against Japanese Americans, it would take twelve years for the political climate to sufficiently ripen to allow passage of the reparations package.

Although Japanese Americans accomplished their legislative goals, the Civil Liberties Act and the redress movement behind it have come under criticism. Following President Ford's proclamation, Daniels, in his final piece, discusses the arguments raised by opponents of monetary redress. These critics fall at both ends of the political spectrum. Republican Rep. Daniel Lundgren, who adopted the CWRIC report as a commissioner but dissented from recommendations that included monetary reparations, believes that nothing more than an apology is required. While Lundgren argues that the passage of time makes monetary redress inappropriate—and fears its extension to the African American and Native American redress movements—Daniels counters that these arguments are irrelevant, because the bill provided money only for survivors or direct victims. Dissent against monetary reparations also arose in liberal newspapers such as the *New York Times*, which argued for a symbolic "gesture of atonement"—for example, a scholarship fund—as an alternative to monetary redress.

The testimony of former Rep. Norman Y. Mineta (D-Calif.), who was himself interned during World War II, also addresses criticisms of monetary redress. Mineta concedes that liberty is priceless, but argues that this does not make payments inappropriate. Japanese Americans did not sell their civil and constitutional rights. These rights were "ripped away," and that fact entitles survivors to compensation—that is, to atonement money. Most importantly, Mineta reminds us that "at issue here is the wholesale violation, based on race, of those very legal principles we were fighting to defend."

While some have argued that the Civil Liberties Act goes too far, others have argued that it does not go far enough. The latter argument was raised in the 1992 case of *Jacobs v. Barr*, wherein the constitutionality of the Act was challenged because of its failure to include internees of Italian or German descent. Arthur Jacobs, a German American who was interned with his father as a child, claimed that the Act denied him equal protection under the law, based solely on his racial classification. Race-conscious remedial measures are subject to the "strict scrutiny test," the most rigorous level of judicial review available. The court of appeals held that the Civil Liberties Act passed this test. Japanese Americans were interned en masse without due process as a consequence of racial prejudice, whereas Italian and German Americans received individual due process hearings. Wholesale evacuation of these groups was rejected because of widespread political opposition. Jacobs's father was interned following an individual hearing, not as the result of a mass evacuation. The court concluded that Congress's decision to limit compensation to Japanese Americans is substantially related (and narrowly tailored) "to the important (and compelling) governmental interest of compensating those who were interned during World War II because of racial prejudice."

Illustrating the narrow tailoring of the Civil Liberties Act, ethnic Japanese not classified as citizens or permanent resident aliens of the United States were also not eligible to receive atonement money under the Act. The CWRIC reported that approximately 2,300 Latin American residents of Japanese ancestry, primarily from Peru, were deported to the United States for internment during World War II. While the reasoning behind deportation was related to the fear of a Japanese attack near the Panama Canal, the commission concluded that political factors such as cultural prejudice and economic jealousy motivated the action taken by the Latin American countries. Deportees were shipped to the United States and classified as illegal aliens, meaning they were subject to repatriation to Japan. After the war, few wished to live in a devastated Japan, but Peru refused to allow these noncitizens to return. Japanese Peruvians lost their property and the country they called home, and many were separated from family members for years. And yet, redress would come from the United States only after the group brought a lawsuit to challenge the constitutionality of the Civil Liberties Act. On June 12, 1998, the lawsuit was settled, paying five thousand dollars to each plaintiff and issuing an apology.

Part 4 ends with further criticism of redress, in the form of letters from John J. McCloy and Karl R. Bendetsen. Assistant Secretary of War John J. McCloy participated in the decision to evacuate Japanese Americans, a position that he still vigorously defends in his letter as "entirely just and reasonable" based on the military situation of the time. McCloy, who was also a celebrated Wall Street lawyer, challenges the CWRIC report and suggests the Japanese American population benefited from relocation. Former U.S. Army Colonel Karl R. Bendetsen accuses the commission of inaccurately recording his testimony and maintains that Japanese Americans were evacuated, but not interned. Despite testimony and evidence to the contrary (such as the narratives presented here), he claims that everyone was free to leave the camps and those who chose to remain received such free benefits as medical care, food, and education. Perhaps these positions best illustrate the monumental—and unique—achievement of the Japanese Americans in advancing the redress bill through the American political system.

The Internment Experience

22 | The Internment of Americans of Japanese Ancestry

Sandra Taylor

Japanese immigrants first came to the United States beginning in the 1880s, seeking economic freedom and opportunity. When the National Origins Act was passed by Congress in 1924, a quota system was established for certain immigrant groups, but further immigration from Japan was banned. The congressional action reflected public opinion, especially on the West Coast, where the industrious newcomers had aroused racial animosity as well as economic envy. Most of the original settlers, the Issei, and their American-born children, the Nisei, lost contact with their homeland but were unable to assimilate into a country that was prejudiced against them because of their "otherness." The Japanese Americans, most of whom lived in the three urban centers of Los Angeles, San Francisco, and Seattle or in rural farming communities, turned inward, shunned by their neighbors. The Nisei were Americanized through public education, and English was their primary tongue. Many spoke only a little Japanese, despite efforts of their parents to provide for Japanese language instruction in after-school classes. Some of the first generation visited Japan, and some sent their children, called the Kibei, to be educated there so they would not lose their roots. But most gradually lost contact with their homeland.

Hostility against the Japanese community was deeply rooted in racism. The Issei were denied the right of naturalization, the last group of immigrants who were discriminated against in this manner. In 1913 they were also refused the right to purchase land, based on their resident alien status, although many circumvented the law by putting the land in the name of their citizen children. Most white Americans had little to do with them, believing they were "too different" and unassimilable.

Japanese Americans would have been accepted into the larger American culture had it not been for growing hostility against Japan. Fears of a "yellow peril" had been manifest ever since Japan defeated Russia in 1905, and hostilities increased with diplomatic clashes after World War I. In the 1920s, the U.S. Navy began preparing for war against Japan, assuming an eventual clash in the Pacific. Once the Pacific war did begin, with Japan's attack on Manchuria in 1931, the public's opinion became even more hostile toward a nation it saw as aggressive and barbaric. The stage was set for Pearl Harbor.

When Pearl Harbor was attacked on December 7, 1941, the Issei feared the worst, but assumed their children would be safe because of their citizenship. The Federal Bureau of Investigation (FBI) had already compiled a list of West Coast aliens considered dangerous, primarily community leaders—Buddhist priests, newspaper editors, Japanese language teachers, and the like. They were seized immediately and imprisoned in remote places in Montana and North Dakota. Neither they nor their families knew where they were taken. More than a month passed before the federal government, prodded by racist military leaders on the West Coast such as Colonel Karl Bendetsen and Lieutenant General John DeWitt, convinced President Franklin Roosevelt that all Japanese Americans should be removed. [See chapter 34 for Bendetsen's defense of this position.] The basic reasoning behind this conclusion was that there was no way to tell the innocent from the guilty. This led to the tortured logic that because no Japanese American had committed any act of espionage in the past, that only proved that they would do so in the future. Roosevelt had commissioned a private report by Curtis Munson that concluded this minority group posed no threat. The Justice Department also initially opposed the military's recommendations, since the FBI believed it could handle any problems that arose.

Executive Order 9066, which Roosevelt issued on February 19, 1942, specified exclusion of anyone who posed a threat to national security because of the commission of espionage or sabotage. Although the Order did not state that it targeted Japanese Americans alone, that was the clear intent.

The next steps followed in rapid succession. Japanese Americans in the areas designated Military Zones 1 and 2—basically the West Coast and western Arizona—were ordered to sell their property or provide for its storage. Families were registered and given a number. They were moved first to thirteen areas called Assembly Centers, while the ten internment camps (basically, concentration camps) were being constructed. The Assembly Centers were located in racetracks, fairgrounds, and other places that could immediately hold large numbers of people. For many, this was the cruelest action; being housed in former horse stalls was unsanitary, crude, and humiliating to people, many of whom had lived in middle-class comfort nearby. These centers were run by the Army's Wartime Civil Control Administration (WCCA) until the War Relocation Authority (WRA) camps were ready. The internees lacked the most basic medical, educational, and sanitary facilities. The situation improved only moderately in the concentration camps.

The Army located ten sites in seven states: two each in California, Arkansas, and Arizona; one each in Idaho, Wyoming, Utah, and Colorado. Sites were selected on the basis of remoteness, lack of physical resources, and, occasionally, political considerations. The inhabitants did not know in advance where they were going and were permitted to take only one bag apiece. They had anywhere from forty-eight hours to three weeks to dispose of all the remnants of their former lives. The trains they boarded to take them to their new homes had covered windows.

Life in camp was traumatic for the elderly, but occasionally a respite from stern parental authority for the young. Each camp, constructed of tarpaper, with a pot-bellied stove for heat, provided only basic facilities. Each family had one small room in a barracks with no privacy. Bathing facilities were in separate barracks, as were the mess and social halls. Each camp set up schools for the young and activities for the elderly, and also allowed the residents to work at camp jobs ranging from hospital staff to teachers to farmers to secretarial support for the administration. Some did leave the camps for seasonal agricultural work. The pay they earned could not be higher than that of an Army private (it ranged from nineteen to twenty-one dollars a month). The food was adequate but foreign and often made them sick. Churches provided comfort for believers, Buddhist and Christian alike. Students who had been in college were able to continue their higher education at schools in the Midwest and East willing to accept them.

Although the Japanese Americans had at first gone willingly, hoping to prove their loyalty, a few sought to test the legality of the Order; they were promptly jailed. The Supreme Court upheld internment on grounds of military necessity. Once in camp, conflicts did break out between the members of the Japanese American Citizen's League (JACL), who had supported cooperation, and those who believed passivity had been a mistake. Further friction developed when the U.S. Army called for volunteers and then instituted the draft. Many young men could not countenance going to war when their parents still remained behind barbed wire. There were also conflicts between the Kibei and the Nisei, and occasionally between Hawaiian Japanese, whose leaders had been transported to mainland prison camps, then moved to internment centers, over the whole matter of cooperation. Finally, the WRA administered questionnaires in order to facilitate the release of "loyal" internees to take jobs in the Midwest and East, and to move the "trouble-makers" to the camp at Tule Lake, California. Of those who moved to Tule Lake, 69 percent were citizens (mostly children). Some 39 percent had requested repatriation to Japan. (Many of these later recanted their decisions, but it took considerable legal aid from the ACLU to reverse their voluntary decision to leave.)

Fear of an invasion from Japan ended with the battle of Midway in the spring of 1942, but the internment continued. Although some left the camps after the loyalty screening, most did not, afraid to face a hostile public and eager only to return to their old homes on the West Coast. The Supreme Court reversed its previous decisions in December 1944 with *Ex Parte Endo*, ruling that citizens could not be held without due process of law. But before the Court decision was issued, President Roosevelt ordered the camps closed.

By 1946 some 60 percent of the internees had returned to their former homes, despite initial hostility and occasional acts of violence directed toward them. Gradually public opinion shifted, in large part due to the publicity given the conspicuous bravery of Japanese American units, the 100th Battalion and the 442nd Regimental

Combat Team, which saw action in North Africa and Europe. Others served valiantly in military intelligence in the Pacific.

The struggle for justice took considerably longer. Issei were allowed citizenship in 1952, but a quota system for Asians was established. In 1948, Congress passed legislation that allowed only minimal compensation for financial loss, given the fact that financial transactions had to be documented. By 1988, the convictions of Gordon Hirabayashi and Fred Korematsu had been set aside as the result of writs of *coram nobis*, meaning the decisions had been made in error, but one of the defendants, Minoru Yasui, was already deceased by then. [These cases are discussed in chapter 32 below.]

Financial redress was finally addressed in 1980, when Congress established the Commission on Wartime Relocation and Internment of Civilians. The commission took testimony and examined the matter, concluding that the internment was an injustice based on racism, not military necessity. The Civil Liberties Act of 1988 provided for an apology, acknowledged the injustice of internment, and sponsored public education activities regarding the harm done to the Japanese Americans. Signed by President Ronald Reagan on August 10, 1988, the bill also authorized payment of twenty thousand dollars to each survivor of the camps. Although many of the original internees were dead by then, at least Congress and the president had recognized the necessity of due process of law.

REFERENCES

Commission on Wartime Relocation and Internment of Civilians. *Personal Justice Denied.* Washington, D.C.: U.S. Government Printing Office, 1982.

Daniels, Roger. *Concentration Camps: North America.* Malabar, Fla.: Krieger Publishing, 1971; rev. ed., 1981.

———. *The Politics of Prejudice.* Berkeley: University of California Press, 1962; reprint, Magnolia, Mass.: Peter Smith, 1966.

Daniels, Roger, Harry H. L. Kitano, and Sandra C. Taylor. *Japanese Americans: From Relocation to Redress.* Salt Lake City: University of Utah Press, 1984; reprint, Seattle: University of Washington Press, 1986, 1988.

Irons, Peter. *Justice at War: The Story of the Japanese Internment Cases.* Oxford: Oxford University Press, 1983.

Taylor, Sandra C. *Jewel of the Desert: Japanese Internment at Topaz, Utah.* Berkeley: University of California Press, 1992.

Tatcishi, John. *And Justice for All: An Oral History of the Japanese American Detention Camps.* New York: Random House, 1984.

23 | Executive Order 9066

Authorizing the Secretary of War to Prescribe Military Areas

February 19, 1942

Whereas the successful prosecution of the war requires every possible protection against espionage and against sabotage to national-defense material, national-defense premises, and national-defense utilities:

Now therefore, by virtue of the authority vested in me as President of the United States, and Commander in Chief of the Army and Navy, I hereby authorize and direct the Secretary of War, and the Military Commanders whom he may from time to time designate, whenever he or any designated Commander deems such action necessary or desirable, to prescribe military areas in such places and of such extent as he or the appropriate Military Commander may determine, from which any or all persons may be excluded, and with respect to which, the right of any person to enter, remain in, or leave shall be subject to whatever restrictions the Secretary of War or the appropriate Military Commander may impose in his discretion. The Secretary of War is hereby authorized to provide for residents of any such area who are excluded therefrom, such transportation, food, shelter, and other accommodations as may be necessary, in the judgment of the Secretary of War or the said Military Commander, and until other arrangements are made, to accomplish the purpose of this order. The designation of military areas in any region or locality shall supersede designations of prohibited and restricted areas by the Attorney General under the Proclamations of December 7 and 8, 1941, and shall supersede the responsibility and authority of the Attorney General under the said Proclamations in respect of such prohibited and restricted areas.

I hereby further authorize and direct the Secretary of War and the said Military Commanders to take such other steps as he or the appropriate Military Commander may deem advisable to enforce compliance with the restrictions applicable to each Military area hereinabove authorized to be designated, including the use of

Federal troops and other Federal Agencies, with authority to accept assistance of state and local agencies.

I hereby further authorize and direct all Executive Departments, independent establishments and other Federal Agencies, to assist the Secretary of War or the said Military Commanders in carrying out this Executive Order, including the furnishing of medical aid, hospitalization, food, clothing, transportation, use of land, shelter, and other supplies, equipment, utilities, facilities, and services.

This order shall not be construed as modifying or limiting in any way the authority heretofore granted under Executive Order No. 8972, dated December 12, 1941, nor shall it be construed as limiting or modifying the duty and responsibility of the Federal Bureau of Investigation, with respect to the investigation of alleged acts of sabotage or the duty and responsibility of the Attorney General and the Department of Justice under the Proclamations of December 7 and 8, 1941, prescribing regulations for the conduct and control of alien enemies, except as such duty and responsibility is superseded by the designation of military areas hereunder.

Franklin D. Roosevelt
The White House
February 19, 1942

24 | Report of the Commission on Wartime Relocation and Internment of Civilians

SUMMARY

The Commission on Wartime Relocation and Internment of Civilians was established by act of Congress in 1980 and directed to

1. review the facts and circumstances surrounding Executive Order Numbered 9066, issued February 19, 1942, and the impact of such Executive Order on American citizens and permanent resident aliens;
2. review directives of United States military forces requiring the relocation and, in some cases, detention in internment camps of American citizens, including Aleut civilians, and permanent resident aliens of the Aleutian and Pribilof Islands; and
3. recommend appropriate remedies.

In fulfilling this mandate, the Commission held 20 days of hearings in cities across the country, particularly on the West Coast, hearing testimony from more than 750 witnesses: evacuees, former government officials, public figures, interested citizens, and historians and other professionals who have studied the subjects of Commission inquiry. An extensive effort was made to locate and to review the records of government action and to analyze other sources of information including contemporary writings, personal accounts and historical analyses.

By presenting this report to Congress, the Commission fulfills the instruction to submit a written report of its findings. Like the body of the report, this summary is divided into two parts. The first describes actions taken pursuant to Executive

Report of the Commission on Wartime Relocation and Internment of Civilians, *Personal Justice Denied* (Washington, D.C.: U.S. Government Printing Office, 1982), pp. 1–2, 16–23.

171

Order 9066, particularly the treatment of American citizens of Japanese descent and resident aliens of Japanese nationality. The second covers the treatment of Aleuts from the Aleutian and Pribilof Islands.

PART I: NISEI AND ISSEI

■   ■   ■

To either side of the Commission's account of the exclusion, removal and detention, there is a version argued by various witnesses that makes a radically different analysis of the events. Some contend that, forty years later, we cannot recreate the atmosphere and events of 1942 and that the extreme measures taken then were solely to protect the nation's safety when there was no reasonable alternative. Others see in these events only the animus of racial hatred directed toward people whose skin was not white. . . .

HAWAII

When Japan attacked Pearl Harbor, nearly 158,000 persons of Japanese ancestry lived in Hawaii—more than 35 percent of the population. Surely, if there were dangers from espionage, sabotage and fifth column activity by American citizens and resident aliens of Japanese ancestry, danger would be greatest in Hawaii, and one would anticipate that the most swift and severe measures would be taken there. But nothing of the sort happened. Less than 2,000 ethnic Japanese in Hawaii were taken into custody during the war—barely one percent of the population of Japanese descent. Many factors contributed to this reaction.

Hawaii was more ethnically mixed and racially tolerant than the West Coast. Race relations in Hawaii before the war were not infected with the same virulent antagonism of 75 years of agitation. While anti-Asian feeling existed in the territory, it did not represent the longtime views of well-organized groups as it did on the West Coast and, without statehood, xenophobia had no effective voice in the Congress.

The larger population of ethnic Japanese in Hawaii was also a factor. It is one thing to vent frustration and historical prejudice on a scant two percent of the population; it is very different to disrupt a local economy and tear a social fabric by locking up more than one-third of a territory's people. And in Hawaii the half-measure of exclusion from military areas would have been meaningless.

In large social terms, the Army had much greater control of day-to-day events in Hawaii. Martial law was declared in December 1941, suspending the writ of habeas corpus, so that through the critical first months of the war, the military's recognized power to deal with any emergency was far greater than on the West Coast.

Individuals were also significant in the Hawaiian equation. The War Department gave greater discretion to the commanding general of each defense area and this brought to bear very different attitudes towards persons of Japanese ancestry in Hawaii and on the West Coast. The commanding general in Hawaii, Delos Emmons, restrained plans to take radical measures, raising practical problems of labor shortages and transportation until the pressure to evacuate the Hawaiian Islands subsided. General Emmons does not appear to have been a man of dogmatic racial views; he appears to have argued quietly but consistently for treating the ethnic Japanese as loyal to the United States, absent evidence to the contrary.

This policy was clearly much more congruent with basic American law and values. It was also a much sounder policy in practice. The remarkably high rate of enlistment in the Army in Hawaii is in sharp contrast to the doubt and alienation that marred the recruitment of Army volunteers in the relocation camps. The wartime experience in Hawaii left behind neither the extensive economic losses and injury suffered on the mainland nor the psychological burden of the direct experience of unjust exclusion and detention.

■ ■ ■

[EXECUTIVE ORDER 9066]

The promulgation of Executive Order 9066 was not justified by military necessity, and the decisions which followed from it—detention, ending detention and ending exclusion—were not driven by analysis of military conditions. The broad historical causes which shaped these decisions were race prejudice, war hysteria and a failure of political leadership. Widespread ignorance of Japanese Americans contributed to a policy conceived in haste and executed in an atmosphere of fear and anger at Japan. A grave injustice was done to American citizens and resident aliens of Japanese ancestry who, without individual review or any probative evidence against them, were excluded, removed and detained by the United States during World War II.

In memoirs and other statements after the war, many of those involved in the exclusion, removal and detention passed judgment on those events. While believing in the context of the time that evacuation was a legitimate exercise of the war powers, Henry L. Stimson recognized that "to loyal citizens this forced evacuation was a personal injustice." In his autobiography, Francis Biddle reiterated his beliefs at the time: "the program was ill-advised, unnecessary and unnecessarily cruel." Justice William O. Douglas, who joined the majority opinion in *Korematsu* which held the evacuation constitutionally permissible, found that the evacuation case "was ever on my conscience." Milton Eisenhower described the evacuation to the relocation camps as "an inhuman mistake." Chief Justice Earl Warren, who had urged evacuation as Attorney General of California, stated, "I have since deeply regretted the removal order and my own testimony advocating it, because it was not in keeping with our American concept of freedom and the rights of citizens." Justice Tom C. Clark, who had been liaison between the Justice Department and the Western Defense Command, concluded, "Looking back on it today [the evacuation] was, of course, a mistake."

PART II: THE ALEUTS

During the struggle for naval supremacy in the Pacific in World War II, the Aleutian Islands were strategically valuable to both the United States and Japan. Beginning in March 1942, United States military intelligence repeatedly warned Alaska defense commanders that Japanese aggression into the Aleutian Islands was imminent. In June 1942, the Japanese attacked and held the two westernmost Aleutians, Kiska and Attu. These islands remained in Japanese hands until July and August 1943. During the Japanese offensive in June 1942, American military commanders in Alaska ordered the evacuation of the Aleuts from many islands to places of relative safety. The government placed the evacuees in camps in southeast Alaska where they remained in deplorable conditions until being allowed to return to their islands in 1944 and 1945.

■ ■ ■

The evacuation of the Aleuts had a rational basis as a precaution to ensure their safety. The Aleuts were evacuated from an active theatre of war; indeed, 42 were taken prisoner on Attu by the Japanese. It was clearly the military's belief that evacuation of non-military personnel was advisable. The families of military personnel were evacuated first, and when Aleut communities were evacuated the white teachers and government employees on the islands were evacuated with them. Exceptions to total evacuation appear to have been made only for people directly employed in war-related work.

■ ■ ■

Aleuts were subjected to deplorable conditions following the evacuation. Typical housing was an abandoned gold mine or fish cannery buildings which were inadequate in both accommodation and sanitation. Lack of medical care contributed to extensive disease and death.

Conditions at the Funter Bay cannery in southeastern Alaska, where 300 Aleuts were placed, provide a graphic impression of one of the worst camps. Many buildings had not been occupied for a dozen years and were used only for storage. They were inadequate, particularly for winter use. The majority of evacuees were forced to live in two dormitory-style buildings in groups of six to thirteen people in areas nine to ten feet square. Until fall, many Aleuts were forced to sleep in relays because of lack of space. The quarters were as rundown as they were cramped. As one contemporary account reported:

The only buildings that are capable of fixing is the two large places where the natives are sleeping. All other houses are absolutely gone from rot. It will be almost impossible to put toilet and bath into any of them except this one we are using as a mess hall and it leaks in thirty places. . . . No brooms, soap or mops or brushes to keep the place suitable for pigs to stay in.

People fell through rotten wooden floors. One toilet on the beach just above the low water mark served ninety percent of the evacuees. Clothes were laundered on the ground or sidewalk.

■   ■   ■

In the fall of 1942, the only fulltime medical care at Funter Bay was provided by two nurses who served both the cannery camp and a camp at a mine across Funter Bay. Doctors were only temporarily assigned to the camp, often remaining for only a few days or weeks. The infirmary at the mining camp was a three-room bungalow; at the cannery, it was a room twenty feet square. Medical supplies were scarce.

Epidemics raged throughout the Aleuts' stay in southeastern Alaska; they suffered from influenza, measles, and pneumonia along with tuberculosis. Twenty-five died at Funter Bay in 1943 alone, and it is estimated that probably ten percent of the evacuated Aleuts died during their two or three year stay in southeastern Alaska.

To these inadequate conditions was added the isolation of the camp sites, where climatic and geographic conditions were very unlike the Aleutians. No employment meant debilitating idleness. It was prompted in part by government efforts to keep the Pribilovians, at least, together so that they might be returned to harvest the fur seals, an enterprise economically valuable to the government. Indeed a group of Pribilovians were taken back to their islands in the middle of the evacuation period for the purpose of seal harvesting.

The standard of care which the government owes to those within its care was clearly violated by this treatment, which brought great suffering and loss of life to the Aleuts.

■   ■   ■

The Aleuts were only slowly returned to their islands. The Pribilovians were able to get back to the Pribilofs by the late spring of 1944, nine months after the Japanese had been driven out of the Aleutian chain. The return to the Aleutians themselves did not take place for another year. Some of this delay may be fairly attributed to transport shortage and problems of supplying the islands with housing and food so that normal life could resume. But the government's record, especially in the Aleutians, reflects an indifference and lack of urgency that lengthened the long delay in taking the Aleuts home. Some Aleuts were not permitted to return to their homes; to this day, Attuans continue to be excluded from their ancestral lands.

The Aleuts returned to communities which had been vandalized and looted by the military forces. Rehabilitation assessments were made for each village; the reports on Unalaska are typical:

> All buildings were damaged due to lack of normal care and upkeep. . . . The furnishings, clothing and personal effects, remaining in the homes showed, with few exceptions, evidence of weather damage and damage by rats. Inspection of contents revealed extensive evidence of widespread wanton destruction of property and vandalism. Contents of closed packing boxes, trunks and cupboards had been ransacked. Clothing had been scattered over floors, trampled and fouled. Dishes, furniture, stoves, radios, phonographs, books, and other items had been broken or damaged. Many items listed on inventories furnished by the occupants of the houses were entirely missing. . . . It appears that armed forces personnel and civilians alike have been responsible for this vandalism and that it occurred over a period of many months.
>
> Perhaps the greatest loss to personal property occurred at the time the Army conducted its clean up of the village in June of 1943. Large numbers of soldiers were in the area at that time removing rubbish and outbuildings and many houses were entered unofficially and souvenirs and other articles were taken.

■ ■ ■

The Aleuts suffered material losses from the government's occupation of the islands for which they were never fully recompensed, in cash or in kind. Devout followers of the Russian Orthodox faith, Aleuts treasured the religious icons from czarist Russia and other family heirlooms that were their most significant spiritual as well as material losses. They cannot be replaced. In addition, possessions such as houses, furniture, boats, and fishing gear were either never replaced or replaced by markedly inferior goods.

In sum, despite the fact that the Aleutians were a theatre of war from which evacuation was a sound policy, there was no justification for the manner in which the Aleuts were treated in the camps in southeastern Alaska, nor for failing to compensate them fully for their material losses.

25 | Japanese American Narratives

Roy L. Brooks

The evacuees received food, shelter, medical care, and education free of charge.[1] However, life in the Assembly Centers, which collected new evacuees, and in the Relocation Centers, which received evacuees from the Assembly Centers for more permanent placement, was depressing, to say the least: the loss of property and freedom was simply un-American.

A reporter from the *San Francisco Chronicle* described the living quarters, essentially military barracks, at one Relocation Center:

> Room size—about 15 by 25, considered too big for two reporters.
> Condition—dirty.
> Contents—two Army cots, each with two Army blankets, one pillow, some sheets and pillow cases (these came as a courtesy from the management), and a coal-burning stove (no coal). There were no dishes, rugs, curtains, or housekeeping equipment of any kind. (We had in addition one sawhorse and three pieces of wood, which the management did not explain.)[2]

Many internees complained about the lack of adequate accommodations and the lack of privacy:

> When we first arrived at Minidoka, everyone was forced to use outhouses since the sewer system had not been built. For about a year, the residents had to brave the cold and the stench of these accommodations.[3]

> There were 7,700 people crowded into space designed for 5,000. They were housed in messhalls, recreation halls, and even latrines. As many as 25 persons lived in a space intended for four.[4]

> Apartment is shared by married couple, age around 50 years, and our family of four, one girl just nine and one ten years old, my husband is out during the day on a

job. . . . The heat is terrific and the lady in our apartment is very sensitive to heat, so whenever her washing and ironing is done she is always taking naps—makes it hard for children to run in and out—for fear it may disturb her. She is an understanding person, but still there is time she wished she could have slept just another ten minutes.[5]

The daily routine in a Relocation Center was highly structured and dispiriting. Said one internee:

Life begins each day with a siren blast at 7:00 A.M., with breakfast served cafeteria style. Work begins at 8:00 for the adults, school at 8:30 or 9:00 for the children.[6]

Camp life was highly regimented and it was rushing to the wash basin to beat the other groups, rushing to the mess hall for breakfast, lunch and dinner. When a human being is placed in captivity, survival is the key. We develop a very negative attitude toward authority. We spent countless hours to defy or beat the system. Our minds started to function like any POW or convicted criminal.[7]

The sense of being a POW or a convicted criminal was reinforced by the physicality of the camps, most of which were surrounded by barbed-wire fences, watchtowers and armed guards.[8] A 1942 investigation of one camp reported that:

The guards have been instructed to shoot anyone who attempts to leave the Center without a permit, and who refuses to halt when ordered to do so. The guards are armed with guns that are effective at a range of up to 500 yards. I asked Lt. Buckner if a guard ordered a Japanese who was out of bounds to halt and the Jap did not do so, would the guard actually shoot him. Lt. Buckner's reply was that he only hoped the guard would bother to ask him to halt. He explained that the guards were finding guard service very monotonous, and that nothing would suit them better than to have a little excitement, such as shooting a Jap.

Some time ago, a Japanese [Nisei] was shot for being outside of a Center. . . . The guard said that he ordered the Japanese to halt—that the Japanese started to run away from him, so he shot him. The Japanese was seriously injured, but recovered. He said that he was collecting scrap lumber to make shelves in his house, and that he did not hear the guard say halt. The guard's story does not appear to be accurate, inasmuch as the Japanese was wounded in the front and not in the back.[9]

NOTES

1. U.S. Department of the Interior, *WRA: A Story of Human Conservation* (Washington, D.C.: U.S. Government Printing Office, 1947), p. 80.
2. *San Francisco Chronicle*, May 26, 1943, quoted in Lillian Baker, *The Concentration Camp Conspiracy* (Glendale, Calif.: AFHA Publications, 1981), p. 258.
3. Testimony of Shuzo C. Kato, taken before the Commission on Wartime Relocation and Internment of Civilians, Seattle, September 9, 1981, p. 201.

4. Report of the Commission on Wartime Relocation and Internment of Civilians, *Personal Justice Denied* (Washington, D.C.: U.S. Government Printing Office, 1982), p. 160.

5. Edward H. Spicer, Asael I. Hansen, Katherine Luomala, and Marvin K. Opler, *Impounded People: Japanese-Americans in the Relocation Centers* (Tucson: University of Arizona Press, 1969), p. 99.

6. *San Francisco Chronicle*, May 26, 1943, quoted in Baker, *Concentration Camp Conspiracy*, p. 258.

7. Testimony of Kinya Noguchi, taken before the Commission on Wartime Relocation and Internment of Civilians, San Francisco, August 11, 1981, p. 108.

8. Unsolicited testimony, George G. Muramoto.

9. Report by Philip Webster, WRA, August 31–September 2, 1942, quoted in Michi Weglyn, *Years of Infamy: The Untold Story of America's Concentration Camps* (New York: William Morrow, 1976), p. 91; see also testimony of Teru Watanake, taken before the Commission on Wartime Relocation and Internment of Civilians, Los Angeles, August 6, 1981, p. 246 (shooting at Manzanar).

The Redress Movement

26 | Relocation, Redress, and the Report
A Historical Appraisal

Roger Daniels

[In 1967,] twenty-five years after the evacuation, . . . Harry Kitano and I . . . organized what we believe was the first academic conference devoted to an analysis of the evacuation and some of its consequences. . . .

The atmosphere at and preceding that conference sixteen years ago was quite different from the atmosphere here in Salt Lake City in March 1983. There had been a good deal of genteel pressure from some of the leadership of the Japanese community in Los Angeles not to have the conference at all. Things were going well, some thought; why stir up old bad feelings. None of us thought that we were saying the last word about the relocation; but no one, I think, dreamed that less than two decades later there would be a mass movement for redress, a mass movement that may get significant support from an organ of the federal government. Our chief concern was the awful question "Can it happen again?" and our major suggestions for remedial legislation concerned the desirability of keeping the Japanese American Claims Act open and the possibility of having the preventive detention section of the Internal Security Act of 1950 repealed, since that legislation sanctioned procedures modeled directly on those used to incarcerate Japanese Americans in 1942.

It is not surprising, in retrospect, that our horizons were so limited. Great progress had been made by many if not most of the victims of Executive Order 9066. Sociologist William Petersen was already hailing Japanese Americans as "our model minority," as much, I suggest, a way of putting down groups he regarded as disruptive as a way of hailing the undoubted achievements of the Nikkei

From Keynote Address, International Conference on Relocation and Redress, Salt Lake City, Utah, March 10, 1983. Taken from Roger Daniels, Harry H. L. Kitano, and Sandra C. Taylor, *Japanese Americans: From Relocation to Redress*, revised ed. (Seattle: University of Washington Press, 1991), pp. 3–5, 8.

183

in recovering from the disasters of World War II. And the progress was real. There had been a Japanese American Claims Act in 1948, although with utterly inadequate funding, and in 1952 racial and ethnic bars were removed from the naturalization statutes—no longer were Issei "aliens ineligible to citizenship"—and a token immigration quota had been awarded to Japan. In 1959 Hawaii had been belatedly admitted to the Union, so from that point on, there were Asian American legislators in Washington. A people who had owned no political "clout" in 1942 were now, in a technical sense, overrepresented, an overrepresentation that would be increased when California began to send Asian Americans, one of them a naturalized citizen, to Washington.

By the 1960s the socioeconomic gains of the bulk of the Nisei and the Sansei were beginning to push many of them into the middle and upper-middle classes. Figures compiled by the state of California in 1965 showed that persons of Japanese ancestry had, on average, more education than whites, but, somewhat paradoxically, earned significantly less money: Japanese American males over fourteen had a median income of $4,388 as opposed to $5,109 for whites. If we look only at the well-to-do, the gap is even greater. Only 7.7 percent of Japanese American men twenty-five years of age and older earned as much as $10,000, while 12.1 percent of the similar white group did. There are many explanations for this discrepancy, including, of course, a reluctance by some employers to put Asian Americans in positions in which they supervised, hired, and fired whites. A major reason surely stemmed from the fact that the war years were, for most Americans, years of relative prosperity, years in which old debts were paid and savings and investments increased. But many Japanese Americans were simply financially wiped out, and they and their families would always suffer from being a step or two behind where they would have been if the government had only let them continue to live industrious, productive, law-abiding lives. A quarter of a century after the evacuation and twenty-one years after the last camp had closed, the effects of the wartime incarceration were still present. It was quite clear then, as it is today, that the relocation was and is the central event in Japanese American history, the event from which all other events are dated and compared. "Before the war" and "after camp" are the phrases that provide the essential periodization of Japanese American life.

Now, sixteen years later, some of us are again at a conference, but a conference with a different mood, in a different time, and with a different purpose. Perhaps the greatest single difference is the difference in community attitudes, a difference that was becoming apparent even before the traumatic Commission hearings began. No one has articulated that change better than the Nisei writer, Yoshiko Uchida, in her moving memoir, *Desert Exile*.

> Today some of the Nisei, having overcome the traumatizing effects of their incarceration and participated in a wide spectrum of American life with no little success, are approaching retirement. Their Sansei children, who experienced the Vietnam War, with its violent confrontations and protest marches, have asked questions about those early World War II years.

Why did you let it happen? they ask of the evacuation. Why didn't you fight for your civil rights? Why did you go without protest to the concentration camps? They were right to ask these questions, for they made us search for some obscured truths and come to a better understanding of ourselves and of those times. They are the generation who taught us to celebrate our ethnicity and discover our ethnic pride.

It is my generation, however, who lived through the evacuation of 1942. We are their link to the past and we must provide them all we can remember, so they can better understand the history of their own people. As they listen to our voices from the past, however, I ask that they remember they are listening in a totally different time; in a totally changed world.[1]

This generational difference is one of the hallmarks of American immigrant life. Almost half a century ago, the Norwegian American historian Marcus Lee Hansen, considered the father of immigration history, wrote that the second generation in its eagerness to become as fully Americanized as possible tends to reject the heritage of its fathers and mothers; while the third generation, to a degree, tends to reject the values and experience of their own parents, to embrace some of the cultural values of their grandparents' generation, and begin to try to recapture at least some of the ethnic past. Hansen, in the 1930s, did not have Issei, Nisei, and Sansei in mind; he was generalizing from his own Norwegian American experience. That his generalizations seem to have some relevance to the Japanese American experience testifies both to the relative universality of Hansen's insights and to the essential Americanness of the experience of the Nikkei here.

To anyone at all concerned or connected with the Japanese American community once the drive for redress had begun in the late 1970s, it was clear that the winds of change were blowing. Some of the change was not pretty: animosities and resentments, arising out of intracommunity conflicts in the months after Pearl Harbor, came to the surface after more than three decades of repression. The word *inu*, literally "dog," but in this context "informer" or, colloquially, "rat fink," began again to be applied to persons, living and dead, for what they allegedly had done or not done in late 1941 and early 1942. Even more common were displays of emotion: Time and time again, at meetings in various communities—Seattle, Cleveland, Philadelphia, Chicago—I saw grown men and women of my own age break down and cry in public as they spoke, or tried to speak, of those events during the war that affected them the most. The instance that sticks most in my mind is the man in Cleveland who couldn't quite finish his story about his military leave just prior to going overseas to fight with the 442nd Regimental Combat Team. His folks were still in camp at Minidoka, Idaho, so he went there. What he remembered most was his mother apologizing profusely because she simply was not able to prepare his favorite foods to give him the kind of meal appropriate for a soldier going off to battle. These, and other experiences, convinced me, even before the Commission was created, that the therapeutic effects of the struggle for redress were important events in the history of the community and would be so even if no Commission were established, even if its report papered over the truth.

That, happily, is not the case. On February 24th we got the Commission report, and it was a good one.

■   ■   ■

The Commission has, with its February report, *Personal Justice Denied*, fulfilled its first obligation. The report and its conclusions unambiguously establish that wrong was done to both the Japanese American people and the Aleuts. Some have been disappointed that no recommendations for redress were contained in the report and have been critical of this omission. The omission, of course, was deliberate, and I think that the Commission's strategy was both logical and effective. Had the report contained recommendations—especially recommendations involving monetary redress—public attention would have been diverted from the report's historical conclusions and focused on the proposed remedies. It was important that the Commission's conclusions—that the evacuation was not "justified by military necessity," that its root historical causes were "race prejudice, war hysteria, and a failure of political leadership"—be disseminated as widely as possible. With that accomplished, a predicate has been established for the Commission to perform its second task, to make its recommendations to the Congress by June 30, 1983, at which time it is slated to go out of existence.

■   ■   ■

NOTE

1. Yoshiko Uchida, *Desert Exile: The Uprooting of a Japanese American Family* (Seattle: University of Washington Press, 1982), p. 147.

Forms of Redress

27 Redress Achieved, 1983–1990

Roger Daniels

The Commission on Wartime Relocation and Internment of Civilians (CWRIC) . . . issued five recommendations for redress to Congress in June 1983. First, it called for a joint congressional resolution acknowledging and apologizing for the wrongs done in 1942. Second, it recommended a presidential pardon for persons who had been convicted of violating the several statutes establishing and enforcing the evacuation and incarceration. Third, it urged Congress to direct various parts of the government to deal liberally with applicants for restitution of status and entitlements lost because of wartime prejudice and discrimination. It gave as an example the less than honorable discharges that were given to many Japanese American soldiers in the weeks after Pearl Harbor which meant that they had no status as war veterans. Fourth, it recommended that Congress appropriate money to establish a special foundation to "sponsor research and public educational activities . . . so that the causes and circumstances of this and similar events may be illuminated." And fifth, in its most important recommendation, it called upon Congress to make a one-time, tax-free, per capita compensation of $20,000 to each survivor who had been incarcerated. An educated guess was that there were perhaps 60,000 such persons alive in 1983, so that the presumed cost was $1.2 billion.

■   ■   ■

What became the Civil [Liberties] Act of 1988 . . . wrote into law all five of the CWRIC's recommendations.

From Roger Daniels, Harry H. L. Kitano, and Sandra C. Taylor, *Japanese Americans: From Relocation to Redress*, rev. ed. (Seattle: University of Washington Press, 1991), pp. 219, 221.

28 | Institutions and Interest Groups

Understanding the Passage of the Japanese American Redress Bill

Leslie T. Hatamiya

On February 19, 1942, President Franklin D. Roosevelt issued Executive Order 9066, pursuant to which, over the next four years, the U.S. government incarcerated in internment camps more than 120,000 persons of Japanese ancestry, of whom 77,000 were American citizens, without criminal charges or a trial of any kind. Forty-six years and eight presidents later, in an effort to atone for the "grave injustice" suffered by Japanese Americans during the war, President Ronald Reagan signed the Civil Liberties Act of 1988, authorizing a national apology, an education fund, and individual payments of twenty thousand dollars to the surviving internees.[1] Never before had the government granted such redress to an entire group of citizens for a deprivation of their constitutional rights.

In terms of its impact on the direct beneficiaries and its reaffirmation of all citizens' constitutional rights, the historical significance of the Civil Liberties Act's passage is self-evident. What may not be so obvious is the Act's status as a historic legislative achievement. Although Congress typically passes less than 10 percent of the thousands of bills proposed each year, the redress bill's prospects for success were particularly dim when it was first brought to Congress's attention in the late 1970s. Japanese Americans were a small fraction of the American population (approximately three-tenths of one percent),[2] were concentrated in a few West Coast states, and had not been politically active as a community.[3] Those Japanese Americans who were determined to fight for redress could not agree on the route to take. While some thought the legislative route made the best sense, others preferred to seek a judicial remedy.[4] Such a small, inactive, and fragmented community was un-

The author would like to thank Randy Schieber, David Brady, and Jay Wexler for their editorial assistance in writing this essay.

likely to have much influence over reelection-minded members of Congress, who typically respond to well-organized interest groups that represent key components of their constituencies. As the fight for redress carried over into the 1980s, with the federal budget deficit nearing an all-time high[5] and Gramm-Rudman-Hollings spending restrictions coming into play in 1985,[6] the chances that Congress would pass a bill price-tagged at over $1.25 billion to compensate Japanese Americans, stereotypically thought to be a "model minority" (i.e., prosperous and high-achieving), for actions that occurred during wartime nearly forty years before seemed particularly low.

Given this backdrop, the Civil Liberties Act's passage provides an instructive window into the policy-making process on Capitol Hill. To a certain extent, it highlights the important role that interest-group pressures play in determining the fate of legislation. Motivated primarily by their interest in getting reelected,[7] legislators are most responsive to concentrated, well-organized interest groups that can be the greatest help—or the greatest threat—in terms of votes and campaign fundraising in the next election.[8] Interest groups, in turn, take action on a particular issue, depending on the preferences of their members, the intensity of those preferences, their incentives to act, the sufficiency of their resources, and the costs of mobilizing.[9]

Initially, the redress legislation faced formidable potential opposition. It seemed likely that veterans' groups would object to legislation giving $1.25 billion to Japanese Americans (often incorrectly associated with Japanese nationals) who suffered during the war but were still provided food and housing, while members of the U.S. armed forces risked their lives in combat. Yet no effective opposition materialized as a substantial impediment to the Civil Liberties Act's passage. Although some local chapters of veterans' groups came out against the legislation, the national organizations of the Veterans of Foreign Wars and the American Legion, both with the organizational structure and resources to mount a powerful opposition lobby, never officially opposed the bill. To the contrary, both passed general resolutions in support of redress at their national conventions, though neither actively lobbied Congress on the bill's behalf. The reason for these groups' quiescence was the distinguished record of the Japanese American veterans of World War II. Even with family and friends behind barbed wire, approximately thirty-three thousand Japanese Americans from Hawaii and the mainland valiantly and voluntarily served in the U.S. military.[10] The most heralded were the members of the 442d Regimental Combat Team, a segregated Japanese American unit made up of volunteers from the internment camps and Hawaii combined with the 100th Infantry Battalion of the Hawaiian National Guard. In seven major campaigns, more than eighteen thousand men served with the 442d, with over half suffering casualties and six hundred killed.[11] The 442d eventually became the most decorated American unit of its size in World War II. In addition, Japanese American contributions to the Military Intelligence Service have been credited with shortening the Pacific War by two years through skillful translations of battle plans, defense maps, tactical orders, intercepted messages, and diaries.[12] Supported by this remarkable wartime record in defense of a nation that incarcerated many of them as well as their families, Japanese American veterans convinced local and national veterans' groups not to oppose (if not to support) redress.[13]

With the veterans' lobby neutralized, the only group that actively opposed the legislation was Americans For Historical Accuracy (AFHA), a small but committed Gardena, California–based organization led by historian Lillian Baker that characterized itself as a "coalition against the falsification of U.S.A. history." Motivated by the belief that the internment was necessary for national security reasons and, in any event, not an unpleasant experience for Japanese Americans,[14] AFHA conducted letter-writing campaigns, held political rallies, and submitted testimony at congressional hearings. But the group, and particularly its leader Baker, whose writings had a racist flavor, had little credibility on the redress issue and was not taken too seriously on Capitol Hill.[15]

For many senators and representatives, with neither a noticeable Japanese American constituency nor a vocal and organized opposition, redress thus became a "free vote"—that is, they were free to vote for or against the legislation without fear of constituent backlash.[16] Representatives and senators thus had increased opportunities to engage in inside lobbying and the trading of favors to influence the votes of their colleagues. Legislators could also cast their votes on redress on the basis of ideological and personal reasons, rather than their constituents' economic or other interests.

The status of the redress issue as a free vote was particularly important because, while an organized opposition failed to emerge, key Japanese American organizations overcame the community's small size and historically apolitical disposition to develop into successful lobbying machines for redress. These organizations formulated an effective strategy, formed coalitions with other organizations, and secured crucial inside-the-Beltway support. In particular, during the early 1980s, the Japanese American Citizens League, the community's most established organization, created the Legislative Education Committee as an independent lobbying arm whose sole purpose was to get redress passed and which enjoyed strong community ties as well as Capitol Hill know-how.[17] By framing redress as an attempt to remedy a deprivation of the fundamental principle of equal opportunity, rather than as a racial issue or a form of affirmative action, redress supporters appealed to members across the political spectrum, forming a unique congressional coalition of supporters that included liberal Democrats and conservative Republicans.[18] Japanese American leaders also successfully expanded the movement's base of support. They reached out not only to other Asian American groups, but to civil rights groups generally (including the Leadership Conference on Civil Rights, the Anti-Defamation League of B'nai B'rith, the National Association for the Advancement of Colored People, and the American Civil Liberties Union) and to other sympathetic groups (including the National Education Association, the American Bar Association, some labor unions, and Protestant churches), taking advantage of those organizations' contacts, membership, resources, and political expertise to pressure Congress. Using every connection they could uncover, redress leaders also located "surrogate Nikkeis" in parts of the country with small or nonexistent Japanese American populations—for example, soldiers who had fought alongside Japanese American soldiers during the war and were sympathetic to the redress cause—who wrote letters to their own representatives and senators in favor of the legislation.[19] The support of both individual surrogate Nikkeis and other organized interest groups reinforced the notion that redress was not just a Japanese American issue, but an all-American, constitutional issue. With a broad arsenal of support, redress leaders coordinated letter-writing efforts with personal lobbying visits in order to magnify the intensity of the support for the legislation. For example, if a group of former internees planned to meet with a representative in his district office, a flurry of letters from constituents would coincide with the visit.[20] The combined effort was far more effective than either letter-writing or personal lobbying would have been alone.

Although the absence of organized opposition and the development of an effective and resourceful pro-redress lobbying machine go far in explaining the redress bill's passage, interest-group dynamics are never the sole determinants of legislative fate. The passage of the Civil Liberties Act demonstrates that successful legislative outcomes are the result of a combination of institutional and political variables. In fact, institutional factors may well have played the most critical role in determining the redress bill's fate. When the first redress bills were proposed, the committee system provided one of the biggest obstacles. Committees fulfill a powerful gatekeeping function in the policy-making process—namely, each committee, particularly its chair, sets the agenda for the policy issues under its jurisdiction. A single committee (or subcommittee) chair can decide a bill's fate simply by electing to hold—or, more importantly, not to hold—hearings on it.[21] In addition to their *ex ante* gatekeeping function, committees have *ex post* powers once similar bills pass both the House and the Senate. The chair selects the members who sit on the conference committee charged with reconciling the two bills, and in many cases, the compromises reached in conference determine whether or not the legislation will secure the votes needed in both chambers for final passage.[22]

The redress legislation presents a classic example of the powerful role of the committee system in the policy-making process. When the first redress bills emerged in the early 1980s, Sam Hall, a Texas Democrat, served as chair of the relevant Judiciary subcommittee. Representing a rural district in the northeastern corner of the state that most resembles the deep South, and with a voting record mirroring his conservative constituency, Hall had no interest in making redress a priority. He held hearings on the legislation in the 98th Congress, but skewed them to focus only on the issue of the MAGIC cables, intercepted Japanese diplomatic messages that supposedly gave reason to doubt the loyalty of Japanese Americans during World War II, not on the question of whether the internment of 120,000 people was justified even if a few Japanese Americans had been disloyal.[23] The redress bill never emerged from Hall's subcommittee for consideration by the full Judiciary Committee. During the 99th Congress, Hall resigned from the House to take a federal judgeship, and Dan Glickman, a moderate Democrat from Kansas, took over as chair of the Judiciary subcommittee. Although he was more sympathetic to redress than his predecessor, Glickman had aspirations of higher elected office in a state with little support for the bill, and was thus unwilling to push the legislation through the committee process.

With the start of the 100th Congress in 1987, however, the institutional tide turned dramatically for redress. When Glickman left the Judiciary Committee to take an open seat on the Agriculture Committee, Barney Frank became chair of the Judiciary subcommittee. That change in personnel was critical, giving the redress bill its first real chance for serious consideration, much less passage, by the House. Although Frank, representing a district in Massachusetts, had few Asian American constituents, he was a die-hard, uncompromising liberal, firmly committed to civil-rights causes.[24] Immediately after becoming chair, Frank made redress a top priority, using all of his institutional powers to the issue's best advantage.[25] Holding hearings on the legislation in April 1987, he stacked the panel of witnesses in favor of redress. Certain that the wartime internment had been wrong, Frank knew that selling the idea of twenty-thousand-dollar payments to all surviving internees was going to be the greatest hurdle in getting the legislation out of committee and passed by the full House. He therefore made sure that the testimony presented at the hearings focused on the appropriateness of that remedy to the injustices suffered during the war.[26] Frank also played a critical role when the differing redress bills passed by the House and Senate were sent to a conference committee for reconciliation. Wanting to prevent a stalemate, he skillfully navigated the negotiations to ensure that the differences in the bills were resolved and did not prevent the legislation from moving forward to final passage.

While Chairman Frank cleared the bill's procedural path, another key institutional factor—probably the most important factor behind the Civil Liberties Act's passage—gave the legislation the inside leadership and connections without which most bills have only the slimmest chance of passage. Four Japanese American members of Congress—Senators Daniel Inouye and Spark Matsunaga of Hawaii and Congressmen Norman Mineta and Bob Matsui of California—skillfully shepherded the redress bill through the legislative process. Each had a personal connection to the legislation, the Hawaiians as World War II veterans and the Californians as former internees. Although all four initially had their doubts about redress, given the unlikelihood of success, they used their status as high-ranking and well-respected members of the Senate and House[27] to win passage of the redress legislation, personally and vigorously lobbying their colleagues at some political risk to themselves.

On the Senate side, Inouye and Matsunaga assumed different roles in the redress effort. Senator Inouye took the lead early on, when leaders of the Japanese American Citizens League approached the four members of Congress for advice in January 1979. Inouye suggested the idea of lobbying for a congressional study commission that would issue a report on the factors behind the internment, rather than attempting to secure monetary compensation from the start. Once the other three members agreed, Inouye took the lead in getting the commission bill passed.[28] Because it merely authorized a study of wartime events without mandating that actual redress be made, the bill establishing the Commission on Wartime Relocation and Internment of Civilians was not particularly controversial. However, the commission's hearings, report, and recommendations were critical to laying the groundwork, both within the halls of Congress and in the Japanese American community, for redress's success.[29]

When it came to getting the Civil Liberties Act of 1988 passed, Inouye supported the legislation as one of its original cosponsors but let his fellow Hawaiian senator take the lead, and in the 100th Congress, Senator Matsunaga gave redress his all. Many people, including the other Japanese American members of Congress, credited Matsunaga with almost singlehandedly getting the legislation passed in the Senate. Known as one of the hardest working and most personable senators around, he personally lobbied all ninety-eight other senators at least once, talking to many about the legislation two or three times.[30] An individual legislator only expends such sustained personal effort for legislation at the top of his or her priority list, and Matsunaga in particular was not one to ask his colleagues for favors too frequently, making it especially difficult for his colleagues to refuse to support the redress bill when he approached them.[31] Matsunaga's extraordinary lobbying efforts and Inouye's support were particularly persuasive because both senators had fought in combat as members of the 442d Regimental Combat Team for a nation that had incarcerated fellow Japanese Americans, and Inouye had lost part of his right arm in the process. In the end, the redress bill had seventy-five Senate cosponsors, an unheard-of number for major civil rights legislation and well above the sixty votes needed to prevent a filibuster.

Because members of the House, who have smaller, more homogenous electorates than their Senate counterparts and are up for election every two years, are more apt to yield to constituency pressure in policy decisions, Congressmen Mineta and Matsui had a much tougher job of lobbying their colleagues and had to be more vigilant in securing the votes needed for the bill's passage. Moreover, they did so at greater political risk than Inouye and Matsunaga, since they had very small numbers of Asian Americans in their districts and thus potentially faced electoral backlash. The combined efforts of Mineta and Matsui were indispensable, especially in getting the bill out of committee. Even though Barney Frank, as subcommittee chair, was using his institutional powers to get the bill to the floor, there were many conservative members of the subcommittee and its parent Judiciary Committee who were not comfortable supporting redress. They questioned the premise that the internment was the result of racism, war hysteria, and failed political leadership, as the Commission on Wartime Internment had concluded,[32] and had a strong disinclination to "rewrite history" forty years after the fact. Influenced by the presence of Mineta and Matsui at the bill's final mark-up, however, Committee Republicans eventually voted for the bill in committee.[33] Mineta and Matsui continued to lobby their colleagues tenaciously once the redress bill was on the House floor. Throughout the fight, they personalized the issue by discussing their own experiences as children interned during the war, as well as emphasizing the merits of the bill.[34]

The efforts of Inouye, Matsunaga, Mineta, and Matsui should not be underestimated. Congress is a place where no single legislator can get a bill passed without the help of others; favors and bargaining are integral to the legislative process, especially with regard to bills like the Civil Liberties Act, where minimal opposition enables legislators to cast their vote free from threat of constituent backlash. Congressional peer pressure was also unusually significant in this case because all four members had personal ties to the legislation. Because the atmosphere in Congress, especially the Senate, is collegial, it is difficult for legislators to vote against legislation that directly affects their colleagues. Inouye, Matsunaga, Mineta, and Matsui were not just speaking for their constituents, as they might have been in asking for new Air Force bases or housing projects in their states or districts; when they lobbied other members, they were speaking for themselves and the injustices they had personally endured. In the end, the leadership and dedication of the four Japanese American members were indispensable; without their efforts, the Civil Liberties Act would have had only a minuscule chance of succeeding.

As an example of a successful legislative outcome, the Civil Liberties Act is particularly instructive. It qualifies the proposition that concern for reelection is the primary force behind congressional voting behavior, demonstrates how effective even a small and geographically concentrated interest group can be, highlights the importance of individual legislative champions, and underscores the critical role of institutional factors in making or breaking a bill. Like most legislation, the redress bill's success is attributable to a host of different factors that affect the policy-making process. Only by examining all of those factors can we appreciate the hard-fought and unlikely victory that the Civil Liberties Act and its supporters enjoyed.

NOTES

1. *U.S. Statutes at Large*, 102 (1988): 903. The House passed its version of the Civil Liberties Act, H.R. 442, without any major amendments, by a vote of 243–141 on September 17, 1987, the bicentennial of the U.S. Constitution. Seven months later, on April 20, 1988, the Senate passed companion bill S. 1009 by a margin of 69–27. By early August 1988, the two chambers approved the conference committee report reconciling the bill, sending the Civil Liberties Act to the White House for President Reagan's signature on August 10.

2. U.S. Bureau of the Census, *U.S. Census of Population, 1980* (Washington, D.C.: U.S. Government Printing Office, 1983).

3. Bruce Stokes, "Learning the Game," *National Journal* 43 (October 22, 1988): 2652–53.

4. Members of the Japanese American community who were actively involved with the redress issue generally favored the legislative route because they felt that no court decision could encompass a national apology, an educational fund, and individual monetary compensation and that the expired statute of limitations on the internees' claims against the government created an insurmountable obstacle to judicial relief. However, when the Japanese American Citizens League (JACL) decided that its first step into the congressional arena would be to seek the creation of a commission that would study the issue and make recom-

mendations for redress, other members of the community dissented, believing that the community should seek monetary compensation outright. One group, the National Council for Japanese American Redress (NCJAR), decided that the legislative route was a lost cause at that point and concluded that the best alternative was to seek redress through the judicial process. William Hohri, chair of the National Council for Japanese American Redress, telephone interview with author, 25 August 1989. In March 1983, NCJAR filed a class action suit with twenty-two causes of action against the federal government on behalf of twenty-five Japanese American plaintiffs. William Minoru Hohri, *Repairing America: An Account of the Movement for Japanese-American Redress* (Pullman, Wash.: Washington State University Press, 1988), pp. 191, 194.

5. In the early years of the Reagan Administration, the United States witnessed a historic and unprecedented rise in the federal budget deficit, from $59.6 billion in 1980 to $195.4 billion in 1983, when the redress bills were first introduced. It rose to $220.7 billion in 1986, decreasing to $155.1 billion in 1988, the year the Civil Liberties Act was passed. *Congressional Quarterly Weekly Report* 46, no. 8 (1988): 338.

6. The escalating deficits prompted the 1985 passage of the Gramm-Rudman-Hollings restrictions, which put stringent caps on federal spending and called for a balanced budget by fiscal year 1991, with intermediate targets that decreased continually from 1986 to 1990. If the estimated deficit for the upcoming year were to exceed its target (with a $10 billion tolerance range), then an automatic sequestration process would be triggered and across-the-board reductions for each federal account were to be made. See *U.S. Statutes at Large*, 99 (1985): 1038–1101.

7. See David Mayhew, *Congress: The Electoral Connection* (New Haven: Yale University Press, 1974), p. 16. "The electoral goal has an attractive universality about it. It has to be the *proximate* goal of everyone, the goal that must be achieved over and over if other ends are to be entertained" (ibid.).

8. See, e.g., Gary C. Jacobson, *The Politics of Congressional Elections*, 4th ed. (New York: Longman, 1997), p. 188. In particular, public choice theory emphasizes the central role of interest groups in the legislative process, by assuming that legislators typically act in their own self-interest and by viewing "legislation as an economic transaction in which interest groups form the demand side, and legislators form the supply side." William N. Eskridge, Jr., "Politics without Romance: Implications of Public Choice Theory for Statutory Interpretation," *Virginia Law Review* 74 (1988): 285; see also R. Douglas Arnold, *The Logic of Congressional Action* (New Haven: Yale University Press, 1990); Sam Peltzman, "Toward a More General Theory of Regulation," *Journal of Law and Economics* 19 (1976): 211.

9. See generally Mancur Olson, *The Logic of Collective Action* (Cambridge: Harvard University Press, 1971).

10. Commission on Wartime Relocation and Internment of Civilians (hereafter CWRIC), *Personal Justice Denied* (Washington, D.C.: U.S. Government Printing Office, 1982), p. 253. Once World War II began, the Selective Service System reclassified Japanese American servicemen as Class 4-C, enemy aliens ineligible for service. Knowing that a military record would prove their loyalty to the United States, however, Japanese American community leaders successfully lobbied the War Department to allow Japanese American men to fight in combat. Mike Masaoka, with Bill Hosokawa, *They Call Me Moses Masaoka: An American Saga* (New York: William Morrow, 1987), pp. 120–27.

11. CWRIC, *Personal Justice Denied*, p. 258.

12. Ibid., pp. 254–56. In addition to the 442d and the MIS, Japanese Americans also served in the Quartermaster Corps, the WACs, the Army Map Service, the Office of Strategic Services, and the Office of War Information. Ibid., p. 259.

13. Grant Ujifusa, former strategy chair of the Japanese American Citizens League Legislative Education Committee, interview with author, Chappaqua, New York, 15 July 1989.

14. See Lillian Baker, *The Concentration Camp Conspiracy: A Second Pearl Harbor* (Lawndale, Calif.: AFHA Publications, 1981).

15. See Norman Y. Mineta, former Congressman from California, interview with author, Washington, D.C., 19 July 1989.

16. See Dwight R. Lee, "Politics, Ideology, and the Power of Public Choice," *Virginia Law Review* 74 (1988): 194–95. According to Lee, "People put ideological considerations ahead of economic interests when voting for the simple reason that it costs them almost nothing to do so."

17. Leslie T. Hatamiya, *Righting a Wrong: Japanese Americans and the Passage of the Civil Liberties Act of 1988* (Stanford, Calif.: Stanford University Press, 1993), pp. 137–44. Another important pro-redress community group was the National Coalition for Redress/ Reparations (NCRR). In contrast to JACL, which had established Washington connections and focused on inside-the-Beltway lobbying, NCRR organized massive letter-writing and phone-calling campaigns and other grassroots efforts.

18. Ujifusa, interview with author.

19. Grayce Uyehara, former executive director of the Japanese American Citizens League Legislative Education Committee, Medford, New Jersey, 14 July 1989.

20. Ibid.

21. Nelson W. Polsby, *Congress and the Presidency*, 4th ed. (Englewood Cliffs, N.J.: Prentice-Hall, 1986), pp. 141–42.

22. Ibid., pp. 155–56.

23. Mineta, interview with author.

24. See Tom Morganthau et al., "Barney Frank's Story," *Newsweek*, 15 September 1989, pp. 14–16.

25. Belle Cummins, former majority assistant counsel to House Judiciary Committee, Subcommittee on Administrative Law and Governmental Relations, interview with author, Washington, D.C., 25 July 1989.

26. Mineta, interview with author; Uyehara, interview with author.

27. In the 100th Congress, Inouye was the Secretary of the Senate Democratic Conference and the third-ranking member of the Senate leadership; Matsunaga was the second-ranking Democrat on the Senate Finance Committee and Chief Deputy Majority Whip; Mineta was the third-ranking member on the House Public Works and Transportation Committee and a Deputy Majority Whip; and Matsui was an Assistant Majority Whip at Large and a member of the powerful House Ways and Means Committee.

28. John Tateishi, former chair of the Japanese American Citizens League, National Redress Committee, telephone interview with author, 1 November 1989.

29. In July 1980, Congress passed and President Jimmy Carter signed into law the legislation creating the CWRIC. Led by Chair Joan Z. Bernstein, a Washington attorney and former general counsel of the Department of Health and Human Services, the commission conducted extensive primary research and held twenty days of hearings in nine cities across the country. More than 750 witnesses testified, including former Japanese American internees, wartime government officials, academics, community leaders, and other interested people.

Releasing a 467-page report, entitled *Personal Justice Denied*, in December 1982, the CWRIC concluded:

> Executive Order 9066 was not justified by military necessity, and the decisions which followed from it—detention, ending detention and ending exclusion—were not driven by analysis of military conditions. The broad historical causes which shaped these decisions were race prejudice, war hysteria and a failure of political leadership. Widespread ignorance of Japanese Americans contributed to a policy conceived in haste and executed in an atmosphere of fear and anger at Japan. A grave injustice was done to American citizens and resident aliens of Japanese ancestry who, without individual review or any probative evidence against them, were excluded, removed and detained by the United States during World War II.

CWRIC, *Personal Justice Denied*, p. 18. Six months later, the Commission issued recommendations for remedies as an act of national apology, which became the basis for the Civil Liberties Act: enactment of a joint resolution of Congress acknowledging that a grave injustice had been done and offering a national apology; presidential pardons for those convicted of violating the wartime curfew or exclusion orders; liberal review of applications submitted to the federal government for restitution, status, or entitlements lost during the war; appropriation of funds for an educational foundation; and individual payments of twenty thousand dollars to surviving internees. CWRIC, *Personal Justice Denied, Part II, Recommendations* (Washington, D.C.: U.S. Government Printing Office, 1983), pp. 8–10. The commission's work was invaluable to the redress cause; the hearings, report, and recommendations both educated Congress and the public about the Japanese American experience and gave the redress legislation credibility. They also galvanized the Japanese American community, providing former internees with a forum through which to voice feelings of anger, frustration, despair, and bitterness about the internment that had been repressed for forty years.

30. Elma Henderson, former legislative assistant to Senator Spark Matsunaga, interview with author, Washington, D.C., 21 July 1989.

31. According to Mike Masaoka, a Japanese American lobbyist, JACL leader, and friend of Matsunaga's, "No doubt many who personally did not favor this corrective and remedial measure joined in the co-sponsorship and final endorsement of this extraordinary congressional language because of their personal friendship and affection for the Hawaiian lawmaker." Mike Masaoka, "In Tribute to Sen. Spark Matsunaga: Probably More Statutes of Benefit to Those of Japanese Ancestry," *Pacific Citizen*, 4 May 1990, p. 6.

32. CWRIC, *Personal Justice Denied*, p. 18.

33. Roger Fleming, former minority counsel to House Judiciary Committee, Subcommittee on Administrative Law and Governmental Relations, interview with author, Washington, D.C., 26 July 1989.

34. For example, after recalling "what it was like to be an American citizen in 1942 if you happened to be of Japanese ancestry," Congressman Matsui spoke poignantly on the House floor of the importance of the redress bill, just before the House first passed it:

> We have a responsibility to die for our country, but I tell you one thing, that in a democracy, this democracy, with [our] Constitution, a citizen does not have a responsibility . . . to be incarcerated by our own Government without charges, without trial, merely because of our race. That is what our constitutional fathers meant 200 years ago when they wrote the Bill of Rights. That is not a responsibility and an inconvenience of a democracy.

Congressional Record, 100th Cong., 1st Session, 1987, 133, pt. 17:24304. Soon after Matsui's remarks, Congressman Mineta put the task before the House in more personal terms:

> We lost our homes, we lost our businesses, we lost our farms, but worst of all, we lost our most basic human rights. Our own Government had branded us with the unwarranted stigma of disloyalty which clings to us still to this day.
>
> So the burden has fallen upon us to right the wrongs of 45 years ago. Great nations demonstrate their greatness by admitting and redressing the wrongs that they commit, and it has been left to this Congress to act accordingly. . . .
>
> I must confess this is a moment of great emotion for me. Today we will resolve, if we can finally lift the unjust burden of shame which 120,000 Americans have carried for 45 painful years. It is a day that I will remember for the rest of my life.

Ibid., pp. 24305–6.

29 | Proclamation 4417

Confirming the Termination of the Executive
Order Authorizing Japanese-American
Internment during World War II

February 19, 1976

**BY THE PRESIDENT OF THE UNITED STATES OF AMERICA
[GERALD R. FORD], A PROCLAMATION**

In this Bicentennial Year, we are commemorating the anniversary dates of many great events in American history. An honest reckoning, however, must include a recognition of our national mistakes as well as our national achievements. Learning from our mistakes is not pleasant, but as a great philosopher once admonished, we must do so if we want to avoid repeating them.

February 19th is the anniversary of a sad day in American history. It was on that date in 1942, in the midst of the response to the hostilities that began on December 7, 1941, that Executive Order 9066 was issued, subsequently enforced by the criminal penalties of a statute enacted March 21, 1942, resulting in the uprooting of loyal Americans. Over one hundred thousand persons of Japanese ancestry were removed from their homes, detained in special camps, and eventually relocated.

The tremendous effort by the War Relocation Authority and concerned Americans for the welfare of these Japanese-Americans may add perspective to that story, but it does not erase the setback to fundamental American principles. Fortunately, the Japanese-American community in Hawaii was spared the indignities suffered by those on our mainland.

We now know what we should have known then—not only was that evacuation wrong, but Japanese-Americans were and are loyal Americans. On the battlefield and at home, Japanese-Americans—names like Hamada, Mitsumori, Marimoto, Noguchi, Yamasaki, Kido, Munemori and Miyamura—have been and continue to be written in our history for the sacrifices and the contributions they have made to the well-being and security of this, our common Nation.

201

The Executive order that was issued on February 19, 1942, was for the sole purpose of prosecuting the war with the Axis Powers, and ceased to be effective with the end of those hostilities. Because there was no formal statement of its termination, however, there is concern among many Japanese-Americans that there may yet be some life in that obsolete document. I think it appropriate, in this our Bicentennial Year, to remove all doubts on that matter, and to make clear our commitment in the future.

Now, therefore, I, Gerald R. Ford, President of the United States of America, do hereby proclaim that all authority conferred by Executive Order 9066 terminated upon the issuance of Proclamation 2714, which formally proclaimed the cessation of hostilities of World War II on December 31, 1946.

I call upon the American people to affirm with me this American Promise—that we have learned from the tragedy of that long-ago experience forever to treasure liberty and justice for each individual American, and resolve that this kind of action shall never again be repeated.

In witness thereof, I have hereunto set my hand this nineteenth day of February in the year of our Lord nineteen hundred seventy-six, and of the Independence of the United States of America the two hundredth.

30 | Response to Criticisms of Monetary Redress

Roger Daniels

Although the CWRIC report, *Personal Justice Denied*, had been adopted unanimously, one commissioner, Rep. Daniel Lundgren (R-Calif.), dissented from all recommendations which involved the payment of money. He thought that an apology was enough. He argued that "it is inappropriate that present day taxpayers should be held accountable for actions that occurred 40 years ago. Should we pay monetary redress for survivors for the abhorrent practice of slavery or the inhumane treatment of Indians 100 years ago?"[1] As the bill provided redress for survivors only, Lundgren's arguments were a chain of nonsequiturs. Humorist Mark Russell put it nicely by noting that "one congressman is worried that the Chinese will want back pay for building the railroads in the last century. They'll be beefing up security in Washington for another Bonus March by angry Chinese railroad workers."[2]

There was, not surprisingly, significant public reaction against monetary redress, including frequent assertions, in editorials and letters to the editor, that since Japan had bombed Pearl Harbor the now rich Japanese government should make any payments that were due. More frequent were arguments that the United States couldn't afford it or that the Japanese didn't need the money. Often, the objections were accompanied by statements of regret that mass incarceration had occurred. An influential example of this was the *New York Times*. While noting that the incarceration was "a cruel and pointless surrender to panic"—something it had not said during World War II—and that the "lasting resentment" of Japanese Americans was "legitimate," the paper's editorial board found monetary redress inappropriate and suggested a symbolic "gesture of atonement" such as a "fund offering scholarships."[3]

From Roger Daniels, Harry H. L. Kitano, and Sandra C. Taylor, *Japanese Americans: From Relocation to Redress*, rev. ed. (Seattle: University of Washington Press, 1991), pp. 219–20.

NOTES

1. "Testimony of Congressman Daniel E. Lundgren, 42nd District, California, before the Senate Judiciary Committee Subcommittee on Administrative Practice and Procedure, July 27, 1983," 6 pp., mimeographed.

2. *Cincinnati Post*, August 8, 1983.

3. *New York Times*, August 4, 1981.

31 | Testimony of Representative Norman Y. Mineta

I realize that there are some who say that these payments are inappropriate. Liberty is priceless, they say, and you cannot put a price on freedom.

That's an easy statement when you have your freedom. But to say that because constitutional rights are priceless they really have no value at all is to turn the argument on its head.

Would I sell my civil and constitutional rights for $20,000? No. But having had those rights ripped away from me, do I think I am entitled to compensation? Absolutely.

We are not talking here about the wartime sacrifices that we all made to support and defend our nation. At issue here is the wholesale violation, based on race, of those very legal principles we were fighting to defend.

"Testimony in support of H.R. 442 by Norman Y. Mineta, M.C., Subcommittee on Administrative Law, House of Representatives, April 29, 1987," 4 pp., mimeographed, p. 3. Congressman Mineta was himself interned during World War II.

32 | German Americans, Italian Americans, and the Constitutionality of Reparations

Jacobs v. Barr Opinion for the Court
Filed by Chief Judge Mikva

Before Chief Judge Abner Mikva; Harry Edwards and Ruth Bader Ginsburg, Circuit Judges

Fifty years ago, President Roosevelt authorized his Secretary of War to send Japanese Americans to internment camps solely because of their race. Four years ago, Congress passed a Civil Liberties Act to compensate the victims of the policy, and to apologize for the "grave injustice" they had suffered. Today, Arthur Jacobs, an American citizen who says he was detained with his German father in 1945, argues unexpectedly that the Civil Liberties Act is unconstitutional. Because the Act compensates interns of Japanese and Aleutian, but not German, descent, he says it denies him the equal protection of the laws.

We disagree with the district court's conclusion that Mr. Jacobs has no standing to bring his suit. He alleges that he was denied compensation under the Act even though he, like the children of Japanese Americans, was interned by the United States government, and that is enough to establish injury under Article III. But we reject Mr. Jacobs's claim on the merits. After three years of testimony from hundreds of witnesses, Congress concluded that Japanese Americans were detained en masse because of racial prejudice and demagoguery, while German Americans were detained in small numbers, and only after individual hearings about their loyalty. Congress's conclusions, which are amply supported by the historical record, suggest that the decision to compensate Japanese but not German Americans can survive the most exacting equal protection review—let alone the intermediate scrutiny that the Supreme Court requires us to apply.

959 F.2d 313 (D.C. Cir. 1992), *cert. denied*, 506 U.S. 831.

I. BACKGROUND

Arthur Jacobs was born in Brooklyn in 1933 and was interned, along with his German father, at Ellis Island in February, 1945. His complaint alleges that he was interned "as a consequence of the internment of his father," but he provides no details about why, precisely, either he or his father was interned. (At oral argument, his counsel conceded that the father was interned after an individual hearing, rather than as part of a mass deportation program of the kind directed against the Japanese. She could not say, however, whether Mr. Jacobs was ordered by the government to accompany his father, or whether he went because his father chose to keep the family together. Transcript of Oral Argument at 12.) In April, 1945, the family was transferred to an internment camp at Crystal City, Texas, where they remained until the beginning of December. At Crystal City, Mr. Jacobs says that he was treated no differently than the children of Japanese interns, who taught him, he alleges, how to "eat sushi" and to make "sandals and kites."

On August 10, 1988, Congress passed the Civil Liberties Act of 1988, Title I of "An Act to Implement the Recommendations of the Commission on Wartime Relocation and Internment of Civilians." Recognizing that "a grave injustice was done both to citizens and permanent resident aliens of Japanese ancestry by their forced relocation and internment during World War II," Congress attempted to make amends by issuing a formal apology and $20,000 to each Japanese intern. In the same legislation, Congress passed the Aleutian and Pribilof Islands Restitution Act, which authorizes an apology and an award of $12,000 to each eligible Aleut. Congress found that the Aleuts were relocated to Alaska "long after any potential danger to their home villages had passed" and that the "United States failed to provide reasonable care" for them and for their property.

Congress passed the Civil Liberties Act after collecting volumes of evidence about the injustices suffered by Japanese Americans. It had previously authorized three years of investigation by a Commission on Wartime Relocation and Internment of Civilians. The Commission's conclusions, presented to Congress in a December 1982 report called *Personal Justice Denied* [Commission on Wartime Relocation and Internment of Civilians, *Personal Justice Denied* (Washington, D.C.: U.S. Government Printing Office, 1982)], relied on hundreds of thousands of documents and testimony from over 750 witnesses. Ibid. at vii, 1. The Commission found unambiguously that Executive Order No. 9066 and the military orders affecting Japanese Americans were the products of prejudice and demagoguery, rather than military necessity. *Personal Justice Denied* at 4–6, 27–46. But it also found that "no mass exclusion or detention, in any part of the country was ordered against American citizens of German or Italian descent," and that actions against German or Italian aliens were "much more individualized and selective than those imposed on the ethnic Japanese." Ibid. at 3.

In enacting the Civil Liberties Act, Congress noted that the premises relied on in Supreme Court decisions upholding the internment have been repudiated by scholars, by former government officials, and more recently, by courts. See, e.g., H.R.

Rep. No. 278, 100th Cong., 1st Sess. 9 (1987). In 1983, Fred Korematsu, Gordon Hirabayashi, and Minoru Yasui, who had challenged the constitutionality of the internment, reopened their landmark federal cases through writs of error coram nobis. Their wartime convictions for defying the internment policy were vacated, based on evidence that the government had misrepresented and suppressed evidence that racial prejudice, not military necessity, motivated the internment of Japanese Americans. *Korematsu v. United States*, 584 F.Supp. 1406 (N.D. Cal. 1984); *Hirabayashi v. United States*, 627 F.Supp. 1445 (W.D. Wash. 1986), aff'd in part and rev'd in part, 828 F.2d 591 (9th Cir. 1987); *Yasui v. United States*, 83-151 BE (D. Or. 1984), remanded, 772 F.2d 1496 (9th Cir. 1985). None of the decisions was reversed on appeal. For an admirable review of the history of the internment policy, see *Hohri v. United States*, 782 F.2d 227, 231-39 (D.C. Cir. 1986) (Wright, J.), vacated, 482 U.S. 64 (1987).

Mr. Jacobs filed this purported class action for injunctive and declaratory relief on March 9, 1989. Because only interns of Japanese and Aleutian ancestry are entitled to redress under the Civil Liberties Act, he alleges that it discriminates on the basis of national origin in violation of the Fifth Amendment. On January 22, 1991, the district court held that he had failed to allege facts establishing his standing to challenge the Civil Liberties Act and dismissed the action.

This appeal followed.

II. ANALYSIS

A. STANDING

The constitutional requirement for standing has three prongs. First, plaintiffs must allege that they have suffered some actual or threatened injury; second, the injury must be fairly traceable to the challenged official conduct and, third, there must be a substantial likelihood that the alleged injuries will be redressed by a judicial decision in the plaintiffs' favor. *Allen v. Wright*, 468 U.S. 737, 751 (1984).

The broad injury that Mr. Jacobs alleges is that the Civil Liberties Act of 1988 denies him the equal protection of the laws. When the injury alleged is the denial of equal protection, plaintiffs must also allege that they are being denied equal treatment solely as a result of the classification they are challenging. *Heckler v. Mathews*, 465 U.S. 728, 738 (1984).

The district court dismissed the complaint because it concluded that Mr. Jacobs had failed to allege any injury at all:

> The fact that he was interned is simply not enough to establish standing. As the government notes, the plaintiff does not allege that there is any similarity between his internment and that of those persons referred to in the above Acts. . . . [A]ll the plaintiff argues is that he was interned as the result of his father's internment. His father may well have been interned for valid reasons. . . . Mem. Op. at 13-14 ("This

Court cannot discern the basis upon which the plaintiff contends that he has been injured by the 1988 Act.").

We conclude that the district court has confused standing questions with defenses on the merits. Mr. Jacobs does allege that there is a similarity between his internment and that of the Japanese and Aleuts. In his complaint, he alleges: "Although Plaintiff experienced the precise harms and losses that the individuals of Aleutian or Japanese ancestry experienced, Plaintiff is not receiving compensation for his harm and losses." And in his response to defendant's motion to dismiss, he alleges: "Plaintiff suffered the same injury *as a result of the same governmental conduct* yet is denied the relief to which he is equitably entitled due to impermissible discrimination or exclusion and for no other reason."

Mr. Jacobs's complaint is imprecise, but it is sufficient to satisfy the *Heckler* test which merely requires him to allege that he suffered the same injuries as the Japanese and Aleuts, and that he has been denied compensation because of his national origin. The fact that Mr. Jacobs says he was interned, in other words, is enough to establish injury for standing purposes; he is not required to allege at the outset that he was interned for the same reasons as the Japanese and Aleuts, as the district court suggested. Evidence that the reasons were, in fact, radically different—that the Japanese children, for example, were interned because of virulent racial prejudice while Mr. Jacobs was interned after his father received an individualized hearing—is a defense on the merits, not a bar to standing.

■ ■ ■

The government urges us to impose an even higher standing barrier than the district court. To establish standing, it argues on appeal, Jacobs "must show that he satisfies all the statutory criteria for receiving compensation other than being a person of Japanese ancestry." In the government's view, the only people who have standing to challenge the Civil Liberties Act are those who, but for their race, would themselves have been victims of Executive Order No. 9066. Like the district court, the government confuses standing with merits questions. We reject its ingenious theory, which would have the effect of barring most equal protection challenges even before they have been presented.

Since we think Mr. Jacobs has adequately alleged injury, we turn to the remaining tests for standing, which he passes easily. The alleged injury (denial of the compensation that equal protection demands) is traceable to the asserted unconstitutional classification in the Civil Liberties Act. As for redressibility, the Supreme Court has noted that a court sustaining an equal protection challenge faces two remedial alternatives:

[it] may either declare [the statute] a nullity and order that its benefits not extend to the class that the legislature intended to benefit, or it may extend the coverage of the statute to include those who are aggrieved by the exclusion. For that reason, we have frequently entertained attacks on discriminatory statutes or practices even when the

government could deprive a successful plaintiff of any monetary relief by withdrawing the statute's benefits from both the favored and the excluded class.

Heckler v. Mathews, 465 U.S. at 738-39.

In this case, a court could order the benefits of the Civil Liberties Act to be extended to Mr. Jacobs, or it could declare the statute a nullity. Congress would then either rewrite the Act to include German Americans in Mr. Jacobs's class, or it would discard the legislation. In either case, the equal protection violation would be redressed.

B. FURTHER DISCOVERY

Although the district court did not reach the merits of the case, the government argues that they are ripe for decision, and a remand would not serve any useful purpose. Mr. Jacobs addressed the merits in his pleadings, and the government briefed them below and on appeal. At oral argument, Mr. Jacobs's counsel argued strenuously for further discovery, but was unable to show how it could strengthen her client's case. Her only suggestion was that examination of the War Department's files might uncover secret evidence that General DeWitt or Secretary of War Stimson said: "We don't like the Germans; let's gather them up and let's lock them up like we are doing the Japanese." She does not appear to have read the report of the Congressional Commission, which notes that General DeWitt did press for a program that would have allowed the removal of several thousand Germans and Italians from the West Coast. *Personal Justice Denied* at 286. But because of widespread political opposition to mass detention of Germans and Italians, Secretary Stimson persuaded President Roosevelt to reject the proposal. Ibid. at 287. Given the overwhelming evidence supporting Congress's conclusion that there was no mass detention of Germans, and given our deference to Congress's fact finding, we do not agree that further discovery on a scrupulously reported historical question would cast any useful light on the case.

In his pleadings below, Mr. Jacobs did make the remarkable (and entirely inconsistent) argument that further discovery would help him to prove that "there was a military justification for the large-scale exclusion of individuals of Japanese descent," because many Japanese were trying to organize "massive fifth-column activities." Access to government archives, Mr. Jacobs believed, would help him "demonstrate that there was a good faith basis for the government to promulgate the exclusion orders, that the wartime exclusion and relocation was undertaken in a reasonable manner, [and] that the Plaintiff is, in fact, similarly situated to the persons being compensated under the Acts."

It is not clear why Mr. Jacobs toyed with the idea of defending the internment policy, except to argue in the alternative that even if his father had been legitimately detained because his loyalty was suspect, many Japanese were disloyal as well. (The bizarre theory seemed to be that Congress deprived disloyal German interns of equal protection when it compensated disloyal Japanese interns.) Mr. Jacobs's appellate counsel, fortunately, suggested at oral argument that her client was no longer seeking discovery on the question of Japanese American treachery, and would concentrate instead on uncovering evidence of prejudice against German Americans. Since Congress has examined that evidence exhaustively, we conclude that the questions that remain in dispute are constitutional not factual, and we have all the information we need to decide them. We turn, therefore, to the merits.

C. THE MERITS

1. Standard of Review

There is an initial dispute about our standard of review. In *Metro Broadcasting Inc. v. FCC*, 497 U.S. 547 (1990), the Supreme Court held that "benign race-conscious measures mandated by Congress—even if those measures are not 'remedial in the sense of being designed to compensate victims of past governmental or societal discrimination'—are constitutionally permissible to the extent that they serve important governmental objectives within the power of Congress and are substantially related to the achievement of those objectives." Id. at 564–65 (quoting *Fullilove v. Klutznick*, 448 U.S. 448, 519 (1980)). [*Editor's Note: By the slimmest of margins (5–4) the Supreme Court overruled* Metro Broadcasting *in* Adarand Constructors, Inc. v. Peña, *515 U.S. 200 (1995), holding that the strict scrutiny test applies to congressionally mandated race-conscious measures. Judge Mikva's application of the strict scrutiny test to the Civil Liberties Act in this case (see below) makes this a moot point, but one worth mentioning.*]

It would seem hard to claim that the Civil Liberties Act of 1988—which was designed to compensate victims of past governmental discrimination—should be subject to even stricter scrutiny than the nonremedial measures upheld in *Metro Broadcasting*. Mr. Jacobs, however, insists that the Civil Liberties Act should be subject to strict scrutiny, and should be upheld only if it is narrowly tailored to meet a compelling governmental interest. *Metro Broadcasting* compels us to reject his argument.

There are not yet any cases applying strict scrutiny to remedial racial classifications approved by Congress; on the contrary, strict scrutiny has only been applied to race-conscious remedies designed by municipalities, or lower courts. See *Richmond v. J. A. Croson Co.*, 488 U.S. 469, 490 (1989) ("That Congress may identify and redress the effects of society-wide discrimination does not mean that, *a fortiori*, the States and their political subdivisions are free to decide that such remedies are appropriate."); see also *United States v. Paradise*, 480 U.S. 149 (1987) (district court's race conscious remedial order subjected to strict scrutiny). The *Paradise* Court, however, noted:

Although this Court has consistently held that some elevated level of scrutiny is required when a racial or ethnic distinction is made for remedial purposes, it has yet to reach consensus on the appropriate constitutional analysis. We need not do so in this case however, because we conclude that the relief ordered survives even strict scrutiny analysis.

Ibid. at 166–67.

Like the *Paradise* Court, we have no doubt that the Civil Liberties Act of 1988 could survive the strictest scrutiny, and like the *Paradise* Court, we will apply the more exacting test for demonstrative purposes only.

The *Metro* Court made another distinction that controls our decision in this case:

> Although we do not 'defer' to the judgment of the Congress and the Commission *on a constitutional question*. . . . [w]e must pay close attention to the expertise of the Commission and the factfinding of Congress *when analyzing the nexus* between minority ownership and programming diversity. With respect to this 'complex' *empirical question*, we are required to give '*great weight* to the decisions of Congress and the experience of the Commission.'

110 S.Ct. at 3011 (emphases added) (citations omitted).

The holding of *Metro*, in other words, is that although courts should not defer to Congress on constitutional questions, we should defer—or give "great weight"—to Congress on empirical questions. We see no difference between "great weight" and "deference," which the Supreme Court and this Court have consistently treated as synonyms. See, e.g., *Rostker v. Goldberg*, 453 U.S. 57, 64 (1981).

In light of *Metro* and its predecessors, we must give "great weight" to Congress's factual findings that the Japanese internment program was "motivated largely by racial prejudice, wartime hysteria, and a failure of political leadership," while the internment of Germans and Italians was not.

2. Congress's Conclusions

In enacting the Civil Liberties Act, Congress sought to remedy "a grave injustice" and "fundamental violations" of "basic civil liberties and constitutional rights." In particular, Congress found that the Japanese internment policies "were carried out without adequate security reasons" and "were motivated largely by racial prejudice, wartime hysteria, and a failure of political leadership." "The Government unquestionably has a compelling interest in remedying past . . . discrimination by a state actor," *United States v. Paradise*, 480 U.S. at 167, especially discrimination as ugly as the policies endorsed by the government in *Korematsu v. United States*, 323 U.S. 214 (1944). Unless Mr. Jacobs can show that he, like the children of Japanese descent, was interned because of racial prejudice, then it seems obvious that the remedy Congress chose in the Civil Liberties Act (compensating children of Japanese but not German descent) is substantially related to the ends of the Act (compensating those who were interned because of racial prejudice). The remedy, in fact, would represent a "perfect fit between means and ends." *Croson*, 488 U.S. at 526–27 (Scalia, J., concurring in the judgment).

But Mr. Jacobs cannot show—he does not even allege—that he was interned because of racial prejudice. The children of Japanese descent were not interned simply because their parents were interned, but because they themselves were subject to the Civil Exclusion Orders issued pursuant to Executive Order No. 9066. See, e.g., *Ex Parte Mitsuye Endo*, 323 U.S. 283, 288 (1944) (emphasis added) (Civilian Exclusion Order No. 52 excludes "all persons of Japanese ancestry, both alien and non-alien" from Sacramento, California). Mr. Jacobs, by contrast, alleges that he was interned not as a consequence of racial prejudice, but "as a consequence of the internment of his father." He provides no other details about why, precisely, his father was interned; but his counsel conceded at oral argument that the father was interned as a result of an individual hearing, rather than a mass deportation policy of the kind directed against the Japanese. She did not know whether Mr. Jacobs was ordered by the government to accompany his father, or whether he went because his father chose to keep the family together. But even if we assume that Mr. Jacobs was ordered to accompany his father, he cannot prevail unless he can prove the following, improbable proposition: that although his father was interned after a valid hearing, he, Jacobs, was ordered to accompany his father because of "racial prejudice, wartime hysteria, and a failure of political leadership."

After extensive testimony, however, Congress found that "*no* mass exclusion or detention, in any part of the country, was ordered against American citizens of German or Italian descent. Official actions against enemy aliens of other nationalities were much more individualized and selective than those imposed on the ethnic Japanese." *Personal Justice Denied* at 3 (emphasis added). Congress does not appear to have distinguished in its findings between the treatment of the children of German interns and the treatment of the interns themselves. We do not know, therefore, whether children like Mr. Jacobs were ordered to accompany their fathers as a matter of course; if so, whether they received hearings; or if not, whether it was simply assumed that families would stay together. But this much is clear: Congress's finding that "no mass exclusion or detention . . . was ordered against American citizens of German or Italian descent" is broad enough to cover children as well as adults, and it leaves no room for the unlikely suggestion that German American children were the victims of prejudice, while their fathers were not.

If evidence before Congress had suggested that German children experienced the same racial prejudice as Japanese children, Mr. Jacobs could certainly argue that Congress was wrong to extend benefits arbitrarily to the Japanese alone. Cf. *Katzenbach v. Morgan*, 384 U.S. 641, 657 (1966). Of course Congress cannot exclude an identifiable group from a remedial program because of racial or ethnic prejudice. *Regents of Univ. of Cal. v. Bakke*, 438 U.S. 265, 359–60 n. 35 (1978) (opinion of Brennan, White, Marshall, and Blackmun, JJ.). But Congress has concluded that Germans were not subject to the same prejudice as Japanese, and we must give its empirical conclusion "great weight." *Metro Broadcasting*, 110 S.Ct. at 3008.

Congress's findings, in any case, would survive any standard of review, since the historical evidence is hardly controversial. (The evidence is discussed in detail in chapter 12 of the Commission's report, "Germans and German Americans," *Personal Justice Denied*, at 283–93.) The report concludes that in the spring of 1942, the War Department debated whether the power of Executive Order No. 9066 should be used to exclude categories of German and Italian aliens. There were no serious proposals for the mass deportation of all Germans and Italians, but General DeWitt pressed for the removal of several thousand aliens from the West Coast. President Roosevelt rejected the proposal because of widespread political opposition to the detention of Germans and Italians. When the evacuation of the Japanese was about to begin, a congressional select committee called the mass movement of Germans and Italians "out of the question if we intend to win this war." Report of the Select Committee Investigating National Defense Migration, U.S. House of Representatives, 77th Cong., 2d Sess., H.R. Rep. No. 1911, p. 24. Accordingly, General DeWitt on the West Coast, and General Drum on the East Coast, issued individual exclusion orders to a small number of Germans and Italians. *Personal Justice Denied* at 288. The report concludes that visceral prejudice toward Asians, combined with the political influence of Germans accounted for the very different treatment of Japanese and German Americans. Ibid. at 289.

The report also points to cases reversing individual German American exclusion orders as further evidence of the lack of widespread prejudice toward Germans. Ibid. at 115–16 (discussing *Schueller v. Drum*, 51 F.Supp. 383 (E.D. Pa. 1943) and *Ebel v. Drum*, 52 F.Supp. 189 (D. Mass. 1943)). These cases are different from the Japanese cases in three respects. First, the exclusion of German Americans, unlike the mass exclusion of Japanese Americans, involved individual administrative and judicial proceedings which focused on the military threat posed in each case. *Personal Justice Denied* at 115–16. Second, courts in the German American cases took a skeptical, rather than deferential, view of the military's sweeping claims about the threat posed by the excluded person. Ibid. Comparing Mr. Ebel's case with Mr. Hirabayashi's, for example, the Ebel court concluded: "There is no such question of discrimination involved in this case. The plaintiff Ebel was not ordered excluded because he was a German or because he was a naturalized citizen, but only on the ground he was dangerous to the national defense." *Ebel v. Drum*, 52 F.Supp. at 194.

Finally, many of the German exclusions were reversed, even though the evidence against the individuals in question was much more compelling than the vague accusations directed at the Japanese. Mr. Ebel, for example, kept up intimate contacts with the German consul, and was an enthusiastic fundraiser for the Kyffhaeuser Bund. Ibid. at 192. The court described Mr. Scherzberg as someone "more imbued with Nazi principles than with American ideals," *Scherzberg v. Maderia*, 57 F.Supp. 42, 47 (E.D. Pa. 1944), especially since he called the British catastrophe at Dunkirk "a good thing," and had installed a short wave radio in his car to beam Nazi propaganda throughout greater Philadelphia. Ibid. at 43–44. Both men, nevertheless, were freed, while Japanese Americans, whose loyalty was never questioned, were imprisoned.

In debates over the Civil Liberties Act of 1988, individual members of Congress also emphasized the very different treatment of Japanese and German Americans. Representative Frank, for example, said: "I don't see how anybody can look at these historical events and deny that racial prejudice is there, when Japanese Americans were treated so differently than German Americans, Italian Americans, or Americans who had an ethnic ancestry affiliated with any other country." *Legislation to Implement the Recommendations to the Commission on Wartime Relocation and Internment of Civilians: Hearings Before the Subcomm. on Admin. Law and Governmental Relations of the House Comm. of the Judiciary*, 100th Cong., 1st Sess. 157 (April 29, 1987). Representative Lowry, similarly, explained that he had grown up in a part of Washington in which almost everyone was German, and none of them was interned during the War. *Civil Liberties Act of 1985 and Aleutian and Pribilof Islands Restitution Act Part 1: Hearings Before the Subcomm. on Admin. Law and Governmental Relations of the House Comm. on the Judiciary*, 99th Cong., 2d Sess. 61 (April 28 and July 23, 1986). Representative Panetta, a co-sponsor of the House bill, found it "bitterly ironic—and an unattractive reflection of fear and prejudice—that Americans of German or Italian ancestry were not considered a similar threat even though we were also at war with those countries." Ibid., 99th Cong., 2d Sess. 1520 (April 28 and July 23, 1986). And Representative Mineta, who had himself been interned, said: "We did not lock up German-Americans. We did not lock up Italian-Americans. . . . Why is it that we just happened to lock up an ethnic group subject to decades of blatant and cruel discrimination? Because this was the group that popular opinion . . . demanded to have locked up." *Japanese American and Aleutian Wartime Relocation: Hearings Before the Subcomm. on Admin. Law and Governmental Relations of the House Comm. on the Judiciary*, 98th Cong., 2d Sess. 75 (June 20, 21, 27, and Sept. 12, 1984).

All this is to say that Congress considered extensive evidence that Japanese Americans were the victims of widespread racial prejudice, while German Americans were not; and we would confidently uphold Congress's factual conclusions even if we were not compelled, as we are, to give them "great weight." We conclude, therefore, that Congress's decision to compensate Japanese but not German Americans is substantially related (as well as narrowly tailored) to the important (and compelling) governmental interest of compensating those who were interned during World War II because of racial prejudice.

The district court, finally, did not address Mr. Jacobs's claim that he is similarly situated to the Aleuts. And since Mr. Jacobs does not even allege that the United States failed to provide him with reasonable care, or that he was relocated from Brooklyn "long after any danger to his home village had passed," we will not address it either.

III. CONCLUSION

We vacate the district court's holding that Mr. Jacobs has no standing to bring his suit, but we reject Mr. Jacobs's claim on the merits. Congress's finding that Japanese Americans were the victims of prejudice, while German Americans were not, is broad enough to cover children as well as adults; and it is amply supported by historical evidence that the internment policy extended to Japanese American but not to German American children. Congress, therefore, had clear and sufficient reason to compensate interns of Japanese but not German descent; and the compensation is substantially related (as well as narrowly tailored) to Congress's compelling interest in redressing a shameful example of national discrimination.

We conclude, in short, that the Civil Liberties Act of 1988 does not deprive Mr. Jacobs of the equal protection of the laws, and we remand to the district court with instructions to enter judgment on the merits in favor of the defendants.

It is so ordered.

33 | The Case of the Japanese Peruvians

During World War II the United States expanded its internment program and national security investigations to Latin America on the basis of "military necessity." On the government's invitation, approximately 3,000 residents of Latin America were deported to the United States for internment to secure the Western Hemisphere from internal threats and to supply exchanges for American citizens held by the Axis. Most of these deportees were citizens, or their families, of Japan, Germany and Italy. Although this program was not conducted pursuant to Executive Order 9066, an examination of the extraordinary program of interning aliens from Latin America in the United States completes the account of federal actions to detain and intern civilians of enemy or foreign nationality, particularly those of Japanese ancestry.

What began as a controlled, closely monitored deportation program to detain potentially dangerous diplomatic and consular officials of Axis nations and Axis businessmen grew to include enemy aliens who were teachers, small businessmen, tailors and barbers—mostly people of Japanese ancestry. Over two-thirds, or 2,300, of the Latin American internees deported to the United States were Japanese nationals and their families; over eighty percent came from Peru.[1] About half the Japanese internees were family members, including Nisei, who asked to join their husbands and fathers in camps pending deportation to Japan; family members were classified as "voluntary internees."[2]

Underlying these deportations was the fear of Japanese attack in Latin America, particularly at the Panama Canal, which produced suspicion of Latin American Japanese. But a curious wartime triangle trade in Japanese aliens for internment

From Report of the Commission on Wartime Relocation and Internment of Civilians, *Personal Justice Denied* (Washington, D.C.: U.S. Government Printing Office, 1982), pp. 305–14.

developed, too. Some Latin American countries, particularly Peru, deported Japanese out of cultural prejudice and antagonism based on economic competition; the United States, in turn, sought Latin American Japanese internees to exchange with Japan for American citizens trapped in territories Japan controlled. The same dynamic often affected Germans and Italians.

■ ■ ■

The model of the Latin American deportation and internment program was developed in Panama. Before the war, the United States had agreed orally and informally with Panamanian officials to intern Japanese nationals during wartime. After the Pearl Harbor attack, Panama declared war on the Axis and froze Japanese assets. Japanese aliens were arrested by Panamanian and American agents for security reasons because they were near the Canal Zone. The War Department instructed the Commanding General of the Caribbean Defense Command to construct an internment camp in Panama for enemy aliens.[3] Panama later agreed to transfer internees to the United States to be traded for Western Hemisphere nationals held in Japan.[4]

In Peru, the State Department aimed to eliminate potential military threats and to integrate Peru's economy and government into the war effort. After war broke out, Peru notified the War Department that the United States could place military installations there; a small military force eventually encamped near the oil fields of northern Peru, and the United States promised $29 million in armaments through Lend-Lease agreements, the largest pledge to a Latin American state.[5] Peru moved quickly against its Japanese residents, whose newspapers, organizations and schools were closed after December 7. Japanese assets were frozen, and the Proclaimed Lists brought hardship to Japanese businesses; some Peruvian Japanese were asked to leave. Before any deportations occurred, almost 500 Japanese registered repatriation requests at the Spanish Embassy, which represented Japan's interests in Peru.[6] This group was among the first to be deported. The initial targets of the American-Peruvian deportation program were enemy alien diplomatic and consular officials and some business representatives of Japan. Peru wished to deport all Japanese and other Axis nationals as well, but the United States recognized its limited need of Latin American Japanese for exchange with Japan; the problems of limited shipping facilities; and the administrative burden of a full-scale enemy alien deportation program. The United States limited the program to deporting officials and "dangerous" enemy aliens.

■ ■ ■

During early 1942, approximately 1,000 Japanese, 300 Germans and 30 Italians were deported from Peru to the United States, along with about 850 German, Japanese and Italian aliens picked up in Ecuador, Colombia, and Bolivia[7] and an additional 184 men from Panama and Costa Rica.[8] Normal legal proceedings were ignored and none of the Peruvians were issued warrants, granted hearings, or indicted after arrest. On entering the United States, officials of Axis nations were placed in State Department custody and private citizens were sent to INS internment camps in Texas. In most cases passports had been confiscated before landing, and the State Department ordered American consuls in Peru and elsewhere to issue no visas prior to departure.[9] Despite their involuntary arrival, deportees were treated by INS as having illegally entered this country.[10] Thus the deportees became illegal aliens in U.S. custody who were subject to deportation proceedings, i.e., repatriation.

Most of the first group of deportees from Peru were men, primarily diplomatic and consular officials, representatives of Japanese business interests, and private citizens targeted as community leaders and thus "believed to be dangerous." . . .

■   ■   ■

The repatriation and exchange program proceeded slowly. In September 1943, over 1,300 Japanese left New York for Japan, over half from Peru, Panama, Costa Rica, Mexico, Nicaragua, Ecuador, Cuba, El Salvador and Guatemala; almost 40 percent of the entire contingent was from Peru.[11]

In the spring of 1944, the State Department realized that no more Axis nationals would be repatriated until the war was over. Nevertheless, from January to October 1944, over 700 Japanese men, women, children and 70 German aliens were deported from Peru to the United States, along with over 130 enemy aliens from Bolivia, Costa Rica and Ecuador.[12] Peru pushed for additional Japanese deportations, but the United States could not commit the shipping and did not want to augment the hundreds of Japanese internees awaiting repatriation. The State Department also decided not to repatriate Axis nationals against their will, realizing that many internees might not want to return to a devastated country. Thus deportation proceedings lagged and the INS internment camps became overcrowded.

Internees at INS camps in Crystal City, Kennedy and Seagoville, Texas, and Missoula, Montana, had two main concerns: having their families join them in the United States and repatriation to Japan. Living conditions at the camps were not unlike those in the war relocation centers. Confinement's bad effects were evident: lack of privacy, family breakdown, listlessness and uncertainty about the future. To safeguard the internees from unhealthy conditions, the camps were inspected routinely by Spain, the International Red Cross, the War Prisoners Aid of the YMCA and the YWCA, the American Friends Service Committee, and the National Catholic Welfare Conference. At the end of the war, approximately 1,400 Latin American Japanese, mostly from Peru, were interned in the United States, awaiting a decision on their destiny. Some wished to return to Latin America, others to Japan. To most it was a choice of the lesser of two evils: they had lost everything in Latin America, but Japan, which they had left to pursue greater economic opportunity, was devastated by the war. A number wanted to remain in the United States and begin anew.

■   ■   ■

In December 1945, approximately 800 Peruvian Japanese were voluntarily deported to Japan,[13] but in general the internment ended very slowly and tortuously. The United States sought to return internees, who were not classified as dangerous and who refused deportation to Axis countries, to their points of origin in Latin America. . . .[14]

. . . [T]he internees used litigation to block deportation to Axis states. Some German internees filed habeas corpus petitions challenging their detention by the United States, claiming that they were not alien enemies as defined by the Alien Enemy Act of 1798, because they were not natives or citizens of an enemy country. In January 1946, this effort failed when a federal district court ruled that the Latin America internees were "alien enemies" who could legally be detained.[15] After this decision, 513 Japanese (over ninety percent from Peru), 897 Germans and 37 Italians from Latin America in United States internment camps were granted hearings pending deportation to Axis countries.[16] The hearings were a formality leading inevitably to deportation to Axis countries, although most of the remaining Latin American Japanese wished to return to Peru. Voluntary repatriation continued into 1946, with at least 130 Peruvian Japanese returning to Japan by June.[17]

■   ■   ■

At the beginning of 1947, 300 Peruvian Japanese remained in the United States, the majority at Seabrook. Those with family ties in Peru entertained hopes of returning home. Talks between the United States and Peru were stalemated during 1947; negotiations were renewed with the Peruvian government which had come to power in a coup in the winter of 1948–49, but it refused to accept any non-citizens.

In the spring of 1949, exasperated State Department officials concluded that the only solution to the Peruvian Japanese internee problem was to give internees the status of "permanent legally admitted immigrants" who could remain in the United States.[18] Finally, in July 1952, the remaining Japanese Peruvian internees, having resided in the United States for seven years or more, petitioned the Board of Immigration Appeals to reopen hearings to suspend deportation orders, and Congress approved the deportation suspensions in 1953. The wartime deportation and internment program was finally at an end. But, for some, the emotional trauma of the program was endless. Peruvian deportee Ginzo Murono stated: "Some of the people from Peru who were interned with me were separated from their families for many years. In a few cases, the broken families were never reunited."[19]

■   ■   ■

[Editor's Note: In 1996, five Japanese–Latin American former internees filed suit in federal court claiming a violation of the constitutional right to equal protection stemming from a denial of reparations granted in the Civil Liberties Act of 1988. They were denied eligibility to receive the twenty thousand dollars paid to each of the Japanese American former internees because the Act limited eligibility to citizens and permanent resident aliens of the United States. On June 12, 1998, the U.S. Department of Justice settled the lawsuit, paying the plaintiff class five thousand *dollars each. The settlement was accompanied by an apology from President Clinton. Many of the estimated 2,200 Japanese–Latin American former internees currently live in Japan and Peru and may not be able to meet the two-month filing period for requesting payment.*]

NOTES

1. Edward N. Barnhart, "Japanese Internees from Peru," *Pacific Historical Review* 31 (1962): 169–78.

2. U.S. Department of Justice, *Annual Reports for Fiscal Years 1943–1946* (Washington, D.C.: U.S. Department of Justice, 1944–1947) (CWRIC 14641).

3. Telegram, U.S. Department of State to U.S. Ambassador to Panama, December 12, 1941. NARS. RG 59 (CWRIC 6944).

4. C. Harvey Gardiner, *Pawns in a Triangle of Hate: The Peruvian Japanese and the United States* (Seattle: University of Washington Press, 1981), p. 14; telegram, U.S. Embassy in Panama to Secretary of State, May 18, 1942. NARS. RG 59 (CWRIC 6944).

5. Gardiner, *Pawns*, pp. 20–21.

6. Ibid., p. 25.

7. Ibid., pp. 25–46.

8. Ibid., p. 58.

9. Ibid., p. 29.

10. Barnhart, "Japanese Internees," p. 175.

11. Gardiner, *Pawns*, p. 84.

12. Ibid., pp. 88–107.

13. Ibid., p. 124.

14. Barnhart, "Japanese Internees," p. 174.

15. Gardiner, *Pawns*, p. 133; one German internee, von Heymann, won a reversal in the Second Circuit Court of Appeals, *United States v. Watkins*, 159 F.2d 650 (2d Cir. 1947).

16. Gardiner, *Pawns*, p. 134.

17. Ibid., p. 130.

18. Ibid., p. 168.

19. Testimony, Ginzo Murono, New York, Nov. 23, 1981, p. 32.

34 | Letters from John J. McCloy and Karl R. Bendetsen

John J. McCloy [was] the ranking surviving individual who participated in the decision to relocate the Japanese Americans in the winter of 1941-42. Then assistant secretary of war, McCloy . . . had a distinguished career as a member of the New York bar and as an appointee of Democratic and Republican presidents from Franklin Roosevelt to Jimmy Carter. In this letter,[1] as in testimony before CWRIC [Commission on Wartime Relocation and Internment of Civilians], on the "op-ed" page of the New York Times, *and on television programs such as the* McNeil-Lehrer Report *and* Sunday Morning, *McCloy expresse[d] his dissatisfaction with both the substance of the commission's report and the form that the hearings took.*

LETTER FROM JOHN J. McCLOY TO JANE B. KAIHATSU

April 12, 1984

As you are perhaps aware, I have testified already at some length in response to the attempt to further recompense those who were temporarily relocated under the direct orders of President Roosevelt (who was the only official of the government who could order the step), as a defense to the surprise attack by the Japanese Navy and Air Force on Pearl Harbor, an event which plunged us into the Pacific War and shortly thereafter into the war with Germany. I hope to be given further opportunity to defend the country against what I feel would be a great injustice to the American taxpayer.

From Roger Daniels, Harry H. L. Kitano, and Sandra C. Taylor, *Japanese Americans: From Relocation to Redress*, rev. ed. (Seattle: University of Washington Press, 1991), pp. 213–16.

The President's action in ordering the relocation of Japanese/Americans from the sensitive military areas of the West Coast was entirely just and reasonable. He did not have the benefit of hindsight to see how we might recover from this devastating attack. It was a calculated attempt on his part to offset the great menace to our security caused by the sinking of our main Pacific Fleet. The President had ample and, indeed, striking evidence of the existence of subversive Japanese and Japanese/American agencies on the West Coast, poised to frustrate any defense against Japanese acts of aggression.

It is always difficult, if not impossible, to attempt to recreate the conditions as they existed long after the event and the Pearl Harbor attack and its consequences are no exception to this rule. The demand for the removal of the Japanese elements along our military installations on the West Coast after Pearl Harbor was very great. And there was good reason for alarm. A large part of our Pacific Fleet had been sunk and the installations on Pearl Harbor had been largely destroyed. The attacking forces had disappeared to the North practically unscathed. There was a constant danger of a recurring attack on what remained of our sensitive Western defenses. These mainly consisted of military installations on our West Coast particularly our bomber plants and it was in these areas that our Japanese/American population was largely congested and distributed. With our Pacific Fleet maimed, one of the chief elements of our national security was threatened at a critical time. If the "Miracle" at the Battle of Midway had not occurred, the loss of our second line of defense would certainly have put us in real jeopardy.

As a defense against this threat, the President saw fit to order the relocation of certain elements of our Japanese/American population. They were permitted to go anywhere else in the country they saw fit to go at the expense of the government. They were not "interned." The President insisted that the move be undertaken by the Army as he felt confident in the fact that the Army was best equipped to manage the operation efficiently and the Army's inspection system could be called on to insure that the operation was carried out humanely.

It is never possible to equate fully the inconveniences, sacrifices, dislocations or sufferings which all segments of a population endure in the time of war. I believe it would be most unjust to all Americans, indeed, to all nationalities who suffered as a result of the Japanese sneak attack on Pearl Harbor, to have those who were affected by the President's order be further compensated for their removal from the sensitive military areas of the West Coast in order to protect the interests of the entire country. Generally speaking, I would say that our Japanese/American population benefited from the relocation rather than suffered, as did so many others of our population as a result of the war.

The so-called investigation which sought to obtain unconscionably large unproven lump sums for added compensation for the relocation which had been given when evidence was fresh and witnesses were alive and in a position to testify was really outrageous. No serious attempt was made to recreate the conditions that the Japanese attack created on the West Coast, nor, the reasonableness of the steps that the President ordered to meet the devastating attack. Instead, a persistent Lobby sought only to support heavy additional unproven payments to the relocatees and this was done at government expense. The Lobby was able to obtain from U.S. taxpayers funds to actually bring a case against the U.S. for what was a perfectly reasonable precaution taken by the President, who did not have the benefit of hindsight, in time of war to protect the security of the whole country. The manner and the atmosphere in which the hearings were held was, as I say, outrageous and a disgrace to our Congressional Investigating Legislative System. It is the manner in which the "investigation" was conducted which should itself be investigated. It is much better for all concerned that Congress refuse these further attempts to compensate for the relocation which President Roosevelt ordered and which provided for our security after the Pearl Harbor attack.

As for myself, I could not and did not originate the order for the relocation of the Japanese/American population following this attack. I could not move a soldier, much less a civilian. I was simply asked to do what I could to assist the Army in carrying out the Commander in Chief's order. I urged that a civilian agency be put in charge of the relocation process as promptly as possible so that the Army could concentrate on the conduct of the war itself.

Our Japanese/American population was generally loyal. This was proven by a number of facts including the splendid record of the 442nd Combat Team, a unit I urged the Army to form. But, reasonable precautions had to be taken against those who might not be. What was needed on the West Coast after the Pearl Harbor attack was to protect against the consequences of the disaster and to deter any further acts such as the Japanese government was guilty of. I cannot prove it but I firmly believe that with the knowledge we now have and which, at the time, was available to the President of the U.S. of the existence of subversive agencies along the West Coast (I refer particularly to information revealed by MAGIC), that the relocation method against the Japanese was a good reason why serious acts of sabotage did not occur on the West Coast after the President's order was given. In short, I believe it was the effectiveness of the relocation order which added to the security of the West Coast and indirectly to the security of the country as a whole.

It is, of course, true that many of our citizens were never adequately compensated for the sacrifices they had to make as a result of the Pearl Harbor attack. Certainly not those whose bodies are still entombed in the sunken ships at Pearl Harbor or those American citizens who were killed in Italy with the 442nd Combat Team.

If there are any further hearings to be held on this subject, I hope in all fairness and in good conscious [sic] that a free and objective opportunity be given to those who would wish to support this entirely just order which President

Roosevelt issued for the relocation of certain segments of our Japanese/American population on the West Coast after the disasterous [*sic*] bombing of Pearl Harbor by the then Japanese Government.

Sincerely,
John J. McCloy
[signed]

While some of those involved in the decision to relocate Japanese Americans, such as Supreme Court Justice Tom C. Clark, later publicly stated that they regretted what they had done, others continue to believe that what they did was proper and something that, were the circumstances repeated, they would do again. Among these is former U.S. Army Colonel Karl R. Bendetsen, who, as he himself put it, "conceived method, formulated details and directed evacuation of 120,000 persons of Japanese ancestry from military areas."[2] Colonel Bendetsen's testimony before the CWRIC on November 2, 1981, took up some 150 pages of transcript. A recent succinct statement of his current views follows:[3]

LETTER FROM KARL R. BENDETSEN TO JANE B. KAIHATSU

April 9, 1984

I testified for several hours before the Commission with which you are certainly familiar. My official testimony as reproduced by the Commission was not filed in the archives as I had given it and did not accurately record what I had said. It had been deliberately changed after I had reviewed and corrected it.

Toward the close of my three-hour testimony, two hours of which was direct, and one hour in answering questions, one of the Commission members made this statement: Is it not your present opinion that the Executive Order of the President 9066 ordering relocation from the Western Sea Frontier was a mistake on the part of The President and those senior officials who recommended it? My answer was this:

> If The President who signed the Order and the senior officials who recommended it, including the Secretary of War Mr. Stimson, the Chief of Staff General Marshall, the Assistant Secretary of War Mr. McCloy and the Commanding General of the 4th Army and Western Defense Command General DeWitt, had known then what we know today, the Order would never have been issued at all. There would have been no evacuation. The unprovoked sneak attack of Japan had destroyed substantially all of the United States Pacific Fleet. The West Coast of the U.S. was literally defenseless. The Japanese forces invaded the Aleutian Islands and there was no way whatsoever that these officials could have known what we know today, that the Japanese forces would not ultimately attack.

If a major attack had come and if there had been no evacuation *most Japanese* residents along the Western Sea Frontier, whether U.S. or Japanese born, would have supported the invading forces, *even* though some would not have welcomed them. Under the circumstances of war, servicemen, families of servicemen, mothers and fathers, husbands, brothers and sisters, children, friends suffered a great deal. Those who were evacuated were not interned. It is a totally false claim. Everyone was completely free to leave the Western Sea Frontier. Many thousands did. Everyone was free to leave the assembly centers and the evacuation centers so long as they did not return to the Sea Frontier. Families were not separated.

The testimony before you has been false that evacuees' property was seized. It was not. Their household effects were stored with warehouse receipts issued to each. Their crops were harvested and sold. The proceeds of those sales were faithfully deposited to their bank accounts. Those who chose to stay in evacuation centers had many benefits. Their children were educated, they had free medical care and food. They administered their own centers. They had excellent food because the residents of the centers chose it. Those of that age were sent to college and university free, at Federal expense. No one was detained in a relocation center.

Everyone could have left at will, but many of them chose not to do so. They worked near by and had free room and board. They had protection. They did not suffer nearly as much as many citizens whose loved ones were killed, wounded and who never have been compensated.

No person of Japanese ancestry who lived east of the Western Sea Frontier was asked to move.

The hearings of this Commission on the West Coast were held without any protection of favorable, truthful Japanese witnesses who wished to speak the truth. They were violently treated by the many "anti-American" Japanese citizens who attended these hearings.

The Supreme Court of the U.S. ruled that the evacuation was constitutional. Notwithstanding, there were payments made to those who were relocated. They fared better than millions of non-Japanese, whether citizens or not. Under these circumstances, if you objectively consider what I have said, you would not make any additional redress but would objectively take into account the facts rather than the false allegations.

This then is my statement.

Sincerely,
Col. Karl R. Bendetsen,
U.S.A. (ret.)
[signed]

NOTES

1. Letter, McCloy to Jane B. Kaihatsu, April 12, 1984, enclosed in letter, McCloy to Sandra C. Taylor, May 22, 1984.

2. A. N. Marquis Company, *Who's Who in America, 1946–1947* (Chicago: A. N. Marquis Company, 1946), p. 173. See also Bendetsen's oral history at the Truman Library, Independence, Missouri.

3. Letter, Bendetsen to Jane B. Kaihatsu, April 9, 1984, enclosed in letter, Bendetsen to Sandra C. Taylor, May 22, 1984.

Suggested Readings

Baker, Lillian. *American and Japanese Relocation in World War II: Fact, Fiction and Fallacy*. Medford, Ore.: Webb Research Group, 1990.

Hohri, William Minoru. *Repairing America*. Pullman: Washington State University Press, 1988.

Krammer, Arnold. *Undue Process: The Untold Story of America's German Alien Internees*. New York: Rowman and Littlefield, 1997.

Tateishi, John. *And Justice for All*. New York: Random House, 1984.

5 | Native Americans

Introduction

35 | Wild Redress?

Roy L. Brooks

Some human injustices span the duration of a war, a political regime, or a historical era. Others persist much longer. The gross mistreatment of Indians in America is of the latter variety; it has lasted some five hundred years. Not only has this atrocity been remarkably prolonged, but it has covered a wide range of harms, including deprivation of life, sustenance, culture, language, land, liberty, religion, and self-sufficiency. Because of the duration and assortment of injustices committed against Native Americans, the question of redress raises intractable issues. Perhaps this helps to explain why the federal government's repeated attempts at redress seem as "wild" as the system of justice described in *Wild Justice*, a book by Michael Leader and Jack Page that details the federal government's shamefully result-oriented handling of Indian claims.

Laurence Armand French opens Part 5 with an outline of the Indian experience in America over five centuries. Initially, Native Americans were enslaved, along with Africans, and used by England to fight the French and Spanish. After its inception and many battles with the Indians, the United States government introduced a policy known as "Removal." The purpose of Removal was to create reservations. It was during this period, in 1838, that approximately one-fourth of the Cherokee nation died in the infamous "Trail of Tears," the thousand-mile trek from their eastern homeland to Indian Territory (Oklahoma). French takes us through the labyrinth of subsequent federal policies implemented during the nineteenth and twentieth centuries that, as he argues, were designed to eliminate Native American culture, language, and sovereignty.

Personal accounts taken from these different policy eras illustrate the variety of Indian suffering and claims for reparations. For example, during the Removal era, many treaties were broken. In 1865, a Yankton Sioux named Palaneapope spoke for many Indians when he complained: "When I signed the treaty I told them I never would sign for the pipestone quarry. I wanted to keep it for myself; but I understand white men are going there and getting and breaking up the stone." Removal also relocated many prospering tribes to barren land. The Winnebago Indians lived in Minnesota until they were moved to Nebraska. "We used to farm and raise a crop of our own. Each family had a span of horses or oxen to work, and had plenty of ponies; now, we have nothing."

Indiscriminate violence was among the common sufferings Native Americans experienced. As the narratives indicate, Indian men, women, and children were often killed as a result of white racism or aggression. "Big Snake said he had done nothing wrong," Hairy Bear tells us in his narrative. Yet he was needlessly shot dead in a confrontation with soldiers. The Wounded Knee Massacre testimony from 1890 shows that even those Native Americans who were loyal to the U.S. government were shocked by the violence. As American Horse, a Sioux Indian, expressed, "Of course it would have been all right if only the men were killed; we would feel almost grateful for it. But the fact of the killing of the women, and more especially the killing of the young boys and girls who are to go to make up the future strength of the Indian people, is the saddest part of the whole affair and we feel it very sorely."

The taking of land is the most enduring injustice committed against Native Americans. More than 2 billion acres of land were transferred from Native Americans to the United States in treaties. Understandably, then, most Native American claims for reparations seek the return and control of land. As Nell Jessup Newton, dean of the University of Denver College of Law, observes in her chapter, "Tribal people consistently asserted and demanded justice for wrongs committed against their property interests as well as their right to exist as independent peoples." Newton's fascinating study of litigation involving Indian land claims supports the contention in *Wild Justice* that redress through the courts was nothing if not wild. For example, in 1946, Congress created the Indian Claims Commission (ICC), a quasi-judicial tribunal empowered to hear the myriad of Indian tribe lawsuits pending against the federal government. The commission, which was dissolved in 1978, had authority to award monetary relief on any tribal claim, whether legal or "moral," that arose since 1776. Because it could only order monetary redress, the ICC was structurally precluded from offering redress for the most important Indian claim—the return of Indian lands. As Newton observes, "the decision to equate justice with money . . . was the most serious flaw in the commission's design and implementation." Congress failed to incorporate in the ICC's enabling legislation the Indian view of the relationship of people to land, Newton argues.

In addition to offering redress that was nonresponsive to Indian claims, the ICC's system of redress (both procedurally and substantively) was wild in other respects. Decisions regarding Indian claims were unabashedly result-oriented. When necessary or convenient, the commission ignored precedent or engaged in formalistic analysis. Worse, some decisions ordered forms of redress that were more harmful than helpful to Indian claimants. For example, many of the ICC's backers in Congress saw it as a means of terminating the tribal way of life and assimilating Indians into mainstream society. Most Native Americans deemed tribal termination and assimilation to be cultural genocide and, hence, more of an insult than a redress, let alone a reparation.

In fairness, land-claim litigation before the ICC and other federal tribunals raised very difficult legal questions. Given the absence of records and the government's Removal policy, how could a court determine what land a tribe occupied two centuries ago? How does a court place a monetary value on land that everyone concedes belongs to a tribal group? Should a court determine value by the subsistence the land in question afforded the tribe prior to its taking (the so-called "nuts and berries" method of valuation) or should it determine value in a Euro-American fashion by appraising its worth to white farmers or miners? As difficult as these questions are, they do not excuse or justify the courts' handling of Indian claims.

Wild redress may also be a proper characterization of the federal government's legislative approach to Indian claims. Much of the focus, once again, centers on land claims. Robert A. Williams, Jr., highlights one of the central problems in federal land claims legislation in his detailed analysis of the Supreme Court's most recent construction of a land claim statute, the 1971 Alaska Native Claims Settlement Act (ANCSA). The ANCSA provided for the largest Indian land claim settlement ever made by Congress. Alaska Natives received $962.5 million and approximately 44 million acres of Alaskan land to settle all aboriginal land claims. The federal government's desire to settle, Williams argues, "was driven by the need of the major oil companies to build a pipeline across Native-claimed lands, which could transport huge quantities of oil, discovered in 1968, from Prudhoe Bay." The statutory question before the Supreme Court was whether the grant of land to the Alaska Natives under the ANCSA carried with it the grant of sovereignty. A unanimous Court held that because the ANCSA was silent on the issue, it must be read to deny the grant of sovereignty. But what good is the return of land without the right to exercise tribal jurisdiction—"the institutional privilege of force"—Williams asks.

The repatriation of Native American religious and cultural artifacts is yet another example of wild redress. After years of denying repatriation demands, some museums are beginning to return religious and cultural artifacts. The Native American Graves Protection and Repatriation Act of 1990, a federal statute, requires museums that receive federal funding to inventory their Native American artifacts and, upon request, return "unassociated funerary objects" or "sacred objects." Not only does the statute have limited application, but Native American tribes must prove blood-lineage to be entitled to repatriation of the artifact. Proof of such lineage is greatly complicated by the governmental policy of forced Removal.

In the Larsen Bay case discussed in Rick Hill's chapter, the Smithsonian Institution doubted that there was a "reasonable relationship" between the modern Native American tribe and the disputed artifact. The irony in many cases is that the museum that wishes to maintain possession of the artifact for further research is the same entity that determines the validity of the blood-lineage claim. Because the determination to return an artifact is not made by a neutral party, repatriation may never occur. One Mohegan man, who had been dealing with Yale's Peabody

Museum, expressed frustration with the process by asking, "How would you feel if your grandmother was in a cardboard box?"

Not all Native American reparation claims stem from past injustices. One example is the recent claim of infringement on Native American sovereignty resulting from gaming regulations. Paralleling its response to other Indian claims, the government's treatment of sovereignty claims carries a hint of wildness.

The Indian Gaming Regulatory Act (IGRA), enacted in 1988, is at the center of the sovereignty controversy. A 1987 United States Supreme Court decision, *California v. Cabazon Band of Mission Indians*, gave impetus to the IGRA. In that case, the Supreme Court held that California had no authority to regulate bingo and card games run by the Cabazon Band absent express congressional consent. One year later Congress passed the IGRA to permit states to regulate gaming on Indian reservations.

Pursuant to the IGRA, the Pala Indian tribe of California signed a gaming compact on March 6, 1998, with the state's governor, Pete Wilson. The signing of the compact sparked great controversy, in large part because the terms of what is deemed to be a "model" compact purport to bind all other gaming tribes in California. If a gaming tribe does not sign the model compact, new terms will have to be negotiated in separate compacts with the state to avoid federal prosecution for illegal gaming. The legality of the model compact has not yet been resolved.

Governor Wilson, in his defense of the Pala Compact (chapter 44), maintains that the compact is beneficial for Native Americans because it encourages cooperation among tribal groups, as well as between tribal governments and state and county governments. Remote, nongaming tribes such as the Pala Indians can achieve self-sufficiency by licensing their allotment to gaming tribes, Governor Wilson argues. The Pala Indian tribe agrees that the model compact will likely lead to economic self-sufficiency and, hence, genuine tribal sovereignty.

Gaming tribes, on the other hand, fervently oppose the model compact. They see it as an infringement on their sovereignty, which could spread to other states where issues of tribal sovereignty have also arisen. The Viejas Band of Kumeyaay Indians of California, which has benefited greatly from its casino operations, has led the opposition against the Pala Compact. "How can you get to the goal post, when it keeps moving out of reach?" the Chairman of the Viejas tribe, the Honorable Anthony R. Pico, asks in his chapter, referring to the fact that the legality of gaming seems to change year to year. But more than that, Indian sovereignty is endangered, Pico argues, because the compact requires additional state and county regulation of Native American activity on reservations. As Pico states: "The last time Indians were left to the mercy of the state and county, they were almost entirely exterminated. We have survived, accomplished economic and government renewal, without the aid of government, and in spite of state government."

If the federal government, through the IGRA and the Pala Compact, grants Native Americans the (limited) right to game, can this be viewed as redress in the form of tribal rehabilitation, intended to help Native Americans achieve economic self-sufficiency and sovereignty? Or is this action more properly viewed as another form of wild redress—in this instance, a redress that engenders more harm than good for Indians?

Naomi Mezey analyzes these questions in her chapter. Mezey argues that the federal right to game created under the IGRA, whether conceived as individual compensation or as group rehabilitation, is a poorly constructed redress program for Native Americans. She maintains that redress must be redistributive to be meaningful; yet, the right to game transfers wealth not on the basis of individual or tribal need, but only on the basis of a tribe's willingness "to open gaming operations," and then only if the operations are profitable. Thus, "though some tribes profit handsomely, not all do, and most tribes do not profit at all." Mezey goes on to suggest that gaming rights can probably fit better under a different redistributive theory, namely that "the redistributive right arises from a group claim to sovereignty." The IGRA vindicates the basic desire for self-determination, which carries with it the *potential* for economic development and independence through the operation of racetracks, lotteries, and other tribal businesses, including gaming, on reservations free of state interference. As Toni Stanger of the National Congress of American Indians has said: "Sovereignty is the right to raise revenue on our land."

Thus, the sovereignty issue raised in Pico's statement goes to the heart of the gaming controversy, not only in California but in Oklahoma, Washington, and other states. But, ironically, as Mezey points out, the federal right to game cuts *against* tribal sovereignty in numerous ways. It "invites an influx of outsiders" on Native American lands; it "effects dramatic changes in the tribal economy" as well as "cultural sacrifices"; and it "brings about increased governmental scrutiny." On the other hand, the Pala Compact, which sets up a partial economic confederacy of gaming and nongaming tribes, also undercuts tribal sovereignty. Even though it would seem to meet Mezey's view of redress—namely, redress as wealth transfer—it ignores tribal autonomy and cultural distinctiveness. "It's as unrealistic to expect one tribe to use its gaming proceeds to support another as it would be to ask the state of New York to share its lottery earnings with Hawaii."

Mezey's observation goes to the heart of the matter: the sovereignty problem is structured into the enabling legislation. "The IGRA asks tribes to sacrifice some presumed sovereignty in exchange for a new federal right to exercise sovereignty." Is this not wild?

The Native American Experience

36 | Native American Reparations
Five Hundred Years and Counting

Laurence Armand French

PRE-COLUMBIAN AND COLONIAL PERIODS

For more than five hundred years attempts have been made to exterminate, assimilate, or otherwise eliminate Native Americans from the American hemisphere. Their privation knows no equal in American history. No other group within the United States has been subjected to such cruel, harsh, and deceptive exploits at the hands of the dominant society and for such a long period of time. Massacres at the hands of the military and civilians, slavery, wars, removal, treaty deceit, starvation, disease, genocide, forced sterilization, and cultural genocide are some of the methods used in the Euro-American effort to destroy the native peoples and their cultures in the American hemisphere. Claims of genocide continue in Latin America and Mexico, while Canada has made the most progress in reparations, offering the Inuit a massive homeland.

In the United States, Machiavellian policies directed toward the American Indian have been the norm since the colonial era. The noted Smithsonian anthropologist James Mooney estimated the U.S. pre-Columbian aboriginal population at 1,152,950.[1] Douglas H. Ubelaker contended that Mooney most likely did not factor in the death brought about by epidemics of European and African diseases such as smallpox, measles, and plague, and he added a million to Mooney's earlier calculations.[2] More recent research puts the American Indian population, in what is now the United States, at over 5 million. But by 1800, the American Indian population was estimated to be only six hundred thousand.[3] While the American Indian population was being reduced by disease, slaughter, slavery, wars, and cultural genocide (removal, concentration camps), some 15 million African slaves were brought to the Americas between the sixteenth and nineteenth centuries. Nearly half of the African slaves, 7 million, were brought to the Americas during the 1700s.[4]

Contrary to popular belief, Indian slavery was not unusual during the colonial era. It played a significant role in both colonial trade and in the extermination of most of the southeastern tribes. These dozens of tribes endured disease and slaughter, reducing them to the five durable groups that became known as the "Five Civilized Tribes"—the Cherokee, Choctaw, Chickasaw, Creek, and Seminole. Indian slavery emerged as a deliberate process of exploitation used mostly by the British as a lever for generating intertribal hostilities. Enslaved Indians were also forced to fight against other European colonial powers, notably the French and Spanish. Gary Nash noted that the Indian slave trade involved all the colonies and was especially crucial to the development of Charleston, South Carolina. In 1708, for example, the Carolina settlement consisted of 5,300 whites and 4,300 slaves, 1,400 of whom were Indian slaves.[5]

The Indian slave trade involved all the horrors long associated with the worst images of slavery, including beatings, killings, and tribal and family separation. It became routine policy to separate families, sending the Indian men off to the northern colonies while keeping the women and children in the south. This policy was justified on the ground that it minimized rebellion among Indian male slaves.

Much like the British in the eastern colonies, the Spanish exploited the Indian slaves in the western American colonies. In the east, Indian slaves became a viable component of trade, along with deer skins and furs; in the west, American Indians were enslaved by the Catholic Church in order to build and maintain its missions. Later, American Indians became landless peasants as a result of the large land grants awarded to colonists by the Spanish Crown.[6] American Indian slavery was, in short, an integral part of the colonial economy.

U.S. POLICIES OF DECEIT

REMOVAL

Through a trail of broken treaties and harsh policies, driven by the ethnocentric concept of "manifest destiny," the United States government continued to control the fate of the estimated six hundred thousand American Indians who survived the colonial period. Between 1778 and 1868, the United States negotiated 394 treaties with Indian groups. Federal, state, and local executive orders and statutes were also used in the continued control and exploitation of American Indians.[7]

Manifest destiny provided the justification for running roughshod over the American Indian. The term, coined in 1845 by John O'Sullivan, referred to a policy that began as reaffirmation of the United States' independence from Great Britain. Manifest destiny signified the moral and political imperative of the United States' domination of the continent from the Atlantic Ocean to the Pacific Ocean. It also provided intrinsic moral and ethnocentric justification for the exploitation of others.

American expansionism predates its formal expression in manifest destiny. With no expressed constitutional mandate for the federal government to acquire new territory by treaty, President Thomas Jefferson authorized his agents, James Monroe and Robert R. Livingston, to negotiate the purchase of the Louisiana territory. The purchase treaty was signed on April 30, 1802, and ratified by the Senate on October 20, 1803. It gave the United States needed space, what became known as the "Indian Territory," for the removal of American Indians from the eastern states.

President Andrew Jackson was a central figure in the removal of the eastern Indians. A strong proponent of states' rights, Jackson ignored two Supreme Court decisions upholding the rights of the Cherokee Nation against the state of Georgia. During Jackson's first term, Congress passed the Indian Removal Act on May 28, 1830. This act authorized the president to exchange lands west of the Mississippi River, not part of any state or organized territory, for the purpose of removing tribes residing east of the Mississippi River. The Indian Removal Act gave President Jackson the authority he desired to implement his infamous Removal Policy. Removal treaties could now be negotiated with the southern tribes and imposed on those who refused to negotiate.

The removal of the southeastern tribes, notably the Five Civilized Tribes, had the intended effect of opening the southern states to white domination. It also provided the desired buffer between the United States and the western Spanish territories. Thus, by virtue of President Jackson's Removal Policy, the southeast was not only rid of its Indian problem, but the removed tribes provided the first line of resistance to any Spanish aggression against the United States.[8]

In 1838, some sixteen thousand Cherokees who refused removal were led at gunpoint in the dead of winter on a thousand-mile trek from their eastern homeland to Indian Territory (Oklahoma). A quarter of the Cherokee population perished during what has come to be known as the "Trail of Tears." The Cherokee, along with the four other Civilized Tribes, recovered and rebuilt their communities in Indian Territory. The Civil War and Reconstruction halted this progress and brought considerable hardship to the Civilized Tribes. During Reconstruction, the tribes were forced to cede their western territory for the post–Civil War removal of the Plains tribes, including the Kaw, Osage, Pawnee, Tonkawa, Ponca, Oto-Missouri, Iowa, Sac and Fox, Kickapoo, Potawatomie, Shawnee, Cheyenne, Arapaho, Wichita, Caddo, Commanche, and Kiowa Apache.[9]

This new policy of removal also hurt the tribes of the southwest. In 1864, the Navajo were forced onto a reservation in New Mexico Territory, in what is now part of Arizona and New Mexico. General James H. Carleton became military commander in New Mexico in 1862. He was determined to remove the Navajo from the territory so that whites could settle there without fear of Indian reprisal. As a result, the Navajo were removed to a barren area in eastern New Mexico known as the Bosque Redondo. Under the command of Colonel Christopher "Kit" Carson, who was in charge of the Navajo removal, those who resisted were summarily executed, as were the sick who could not keep up on the forced march to

Fort Sumner. Hogans (family dwellings) and pastures were burned and livestock and game were destroyed in order to discourage those who attempted to resist removal. By December 1864, the 8,354 Navajos who survived the "Long Walk" were confined in a concentration camp near Fort Sumner at the Bosque Redondo.[10]

Following four years of Navajo starvation, disease, and death, the federal government in 1868 admitted the failure of the Carleton plan and signed a new treaty with the Navajo, returning a small portion of their original homeland. The 1868 treaty spelled out the accommodative conditions under which the Navajo now had to live. Among its legal stipulations was the authority of the U.S. Government to subject non-Indian lawbreakers on the reservation to federal rather than Indian laws. This legal philosophy was articulated by Indian Commissioner Hiram Price:

> Savage and civilized life cannot lie and prosper on the same ground. One of the two must die. If the Indians are to be civilized and become a happy and prosperous people, they must learn our language and adopt our modes of life. We are fifty million of people, and they are only one-fourth of one million. The few must yield to the many.[11]

The Plains Indian Removal Policy was promulgated in the 1868 Fort Laramie Treaty. It was nearly identical to that of the Navajo treaty forged the same year. The major exception was that the Sioux were to be allotted 80 acres per family on the reservation, instead of the Navajo's 160 acres. Hence, the Indian policy that emerged in 1868 was removal followed by reservation control (cultural genocide), regardless of the cultural uniqueness of the tribes involved.

On March 3, 1871, four months after President Ulysses S. Grant's Peace Policy purported to end the era of Indian wars, the various removal policies were terminated. Removal enforcement proved problematic. For example, the federal government either could not or would not enforce the Plains tribes' treaty once whites illegally found gold in the sacred Black Hills and Bad Lands of what is now western South Dakota. As with other removed tribes, starvation was the norm around the forts where the Plains tribes were concentrated under the control of a civilian agency and the U.S. Army. These conditions led to the Battle of the Little Big Horn in 1876, the assassination of Crazy Horse and Sitting Bull, and the massacre at Wounded Knee in 1890.[12]

DESTRUCTION OF INDIAN TERRITORY

As previously noted, specific allotments of deeded homesteads were made to the Navajo and Sioux in preference to collectively held reservations. In time, the federal government imposed the allotment policy on the tribes forcefully removed to Indian Territory (Oklahoma). Replacing earlier treaties, the allotment policy, like prior Indian policies, benefited whites and hurt Indians. In 1893, despite previous treaty obligations, Congress established a commission, headed by Senator Henry L. Dawes, to negotiate the allotment of lands belonging to the Five Civilized Tribes and the dissolution of their tribal governments. In 1889, President Benjamin Harrison supported Congress's effort to open up Indian Territory (Oklahoma) to white settlers.

The vehicle for breaking previous treaties was the Curtis Act of June 28, 1898. This act abolished tribal laws and tribal courts, mandating that all persons in Indian Territory, regardless of race, came under U.S. authority. The Curtis Act amended the earlier Dawes Act and, consequently, authorized the allotment of tribal lands, thus dissolving all tribes within Indian Territory. This process was completed in 1907 when Indian Territory became the state of Oklahoma. Finally, on June 2, 1924, nearly sixty years after all African Americans were granted citizenship, all Indians born within the United States were granted citizenship. New Mexico was the last state to enfranchise American Indians residing on Indian lands within the state, doing so in 1948.[13]

Despite citizenship status, many American Indians lost their allotments in Oklahoma due to a conspiracy of unsavory "boomers" and discriminatory white courts [discussed below in chapter 41]. Indeed, the current reservation system of federal trust tribal lands did not come about until 1934 with the enactment of the Wheeler-Howard Indian Reorganization Act. Yet, in the 1950s, under the Eisenhower Administration, another assault on Indian tribalism was initiated, this time under the guise of Termination and Relocation.

Termination began with House Concurrent Resolution 108. Pursuant to that resolution, on August 1, 1953, Congress began to terminate federal supervision over American Indians. All Indian tribes in California, Florida, New York, and Texas, along with the Flathead Tribe of Montana, the Klamath Tribe of Oregon, the Potawatomie Tribe of Kansas and Nebraska, the Chippewa Tribe of Turtle Mountain in North Dakota, and the Menominee Tribe of Wisconsin, were subjected to Termination. Public Law 280 augmented Termination by extending state jurisdiction over offenses committed by Indians in Indian counties (reservations). Initially, the Public Law 280 states were California, Minnesota, Nebraska, Oregon, and Wisconsin.

Relocation was yet another attempt at cultural genocide of the American Indians. This plan was to entice young adult Indians off the reservation and into magnet urban areas. The goal was to separate subsequent generations of American Indians from their traditional language, culture, and customs.

Between Termination and Relocation, the federal government attempted to strike the fatal blow against American Indians and their distinctive cultures. Relocation created large urban populations of "marginal Indians," who were cut off from their former culture and language. These people belong neither to the larger dominant society nor to their traditional Indian culture. Cultural genocide was the goal of the federal government's policy. A dire failure, Termination ended with the Menominee Restoration Act of 1973, which restored the Menominee tribe to federal status.[14]

THE CURRENT STATUS OF U.S. INDIAN POLICIES

Indian radicalism emerged in the 1960s and 1970s as part of the general unrest in America over the Vietnam War. The American Indian Movement (AIM) wanted an end to what it termed "white colonialism." The November 1972 "Trail of Broken Treaties" march on Washington, D.C., was followed a year later by the bloody confrontations between AIM and the federal government on the Pine Ridge Reservation at Wounded Knee, the site of the massacre in 1890. Leonard Peltier, a Turtle Mountain Chippewa, is currently serving a life sentence within the federal prison system for his conviction in the death of two FBI agents. Many contend that he was framed and that he is in fact a political prisoner of the federal government.[15]

Ironically, while the United States often criticizes other countries for their civil and human rights violations, it has a long history of such abuses when dealing with the indigenous people of this hemisphere. These policies and practices of slaughter, slavery, wars, physical and cultural genocide (ethnic cleansing), death marches, and concentration camps have not sufficiently shamed the federal government into providing meaningful reparations. The United States is even reluctant to offer an apology for these practices. This certainly does not bode well for future governmental relations with Indians, nor for the United States' credibility in passing judgment on other societies for similar practices.

NOTES

1. James Mooney, "The Aboriginal Population of America North of Mexico," *Smithsonian Miscellaneous Collections*, vol. 80, ed. John R. Swanton (Washington, D.C.: Smithsonian Institution, 1928), pp. 1–40.

2. Douglas H. Ubelaker, "Prehistoric New World Population Size: Historical Review and Current Appraisal of North American Estimates," *American Journal of Physical Anthropology* 45 (1976): 661–66.

3. Russell Thornton, *American Indian Holocaust and Survival* (Norman: University of Oklahoma Press, 1987).

4. W. D. Borrie, *The Growth and Control of World Populations* (London: Weidenfeld and Nicolson, 1970).

5. Gary Nash, *Red, White and Black: The Peoples of Early America* (Englewood Cliffs, N.J.: Prentice-Hall, 1974).

6. Rupert Costo and Jeannete Henry Costo, *The Missions of California* (San Francisco: Indian Historical Press, 1987).

7. Rupert Costo and Jeannette Henry Costo, *Indian Treaties: Two Centuries of Dishonor* (San Francisco: Indian Historical Press, 1977).

8. Anders Stephanson, *Manifest Destiny* (New York: Hill and Wang, 1995).

9. Wilson Lumpkin, *The Removal of the Cherokee Indians from Georgia 1827–1841* (New York: A. M. Kelly, 1971).

10. Garrick Bailey and Roberta Glen Bailey, *A History of the Navajos* (Sante Fe, N.M.: School of American Research Press, 1986).

11. Hiram Price, *Annual Report of the Commissioner of Indian Affairs* (Washington: House Executive Document no. 1, 47th Congress, 2nd Session, 1882, Serial 2110), pp. 3–4.

12. Laurence A. French, "Foundations of Indian Justice," in *The Winds of Injustice*, ed. Laurence A. French (New York: Garland Publishing, 1994),
pp. 3–74.

13. U.S. Congress, *Indian Citizenship Act*, vol. 43 U.S. Statutes at Large (1924), p. 253.

14. U.S. Congress, *Menominee Restoration Act*, vol. 87 U.S. Statutes at Large (1973), p. 700 ff.

15. Yvonne Bushyhead, "In the Spirit of Crazy Horse: Leonard Peltier and the AIM Uprising," in *The Winds of Injustice*, ed. Laurence A. French (New York: Garland Publishing, 1994), pp. 77–112.

Native American Narratives

37 | The Killing of Big Snake, a Ponca Chief, October 31, 1879

Hairy Bear

Big Snake said he had done nothing wrong; that he carried no knife; and threw off his blanket and turned around to show he had no weapon. The officer again told him to come along. Big Snake said he had done nothing wrong, and that he would die before he would go. I then went up to Big Snake and told him this man (the officer) was not going to arrest him for nothing, and that he had better go along, and that perhaps he would come back all right; I coaxed all I could to get him to go; told him that he had a wife and children, and to remember them and not get killed. Big Snake then got up and told me that he did not want to go, and that if they wanted to kill him they could do it, right there. Big Snake was very cool. Then the officer told him to get up, and told him that if he did not go, there might something happen. He said there is no use in talking; I came to arrest you, and want you to go. The officer went for the handcuffs, which a soldier had, and brought them in. The officer and a soldier then tried to put them on him, but Big Snake pushed them both away. Then the officer spoke to the soldiers, and four of them tried to put them on, but Big Snake pushed them all off. One soldier, who had stripes on his arms, also tried to put them on, but Big Snake pushed them all off. They tried several times, all of them, to get hold of Big Snake and hold him. But Big Snake was sitting down, when six soldiers got hold of him. He raised up and threw them off. Just then one of the soldiers, who was in front of him, struck Big Snake in the face with his gun, another soldier struck him along side the head with the barrel of his gun. It knocked him back to the wall. He straightened up again. The blood was running down his face. I saw the gun pointed at him, and was scared, and did not want to see him killed. So I turned away. Then the gun was fired and Big Snake fell down dead on the floor.

From Senate Executive Document No. 14, 46th Congress, 3d Session (January 5, 1881), p. 13.

251

38 | The Massacre at Wounded Knee, South Dakota, December 29, 1890

Turning Hawk and American Horse (Sioux)

The furor that the appearance of the ghost dance religion created among the Sioux brought about a concomitant hysteria in the white community, even far from Indian country. There were numerous public demands that the whole thing be stopped by the army. On December 14, 1890, Sioux police were sent to arrest Sitting Bull, and in the ensuing fracas the old chief was killed. Some of Sitting Bull's followers fled and joined a band of Sioux under Big Foot. A few days later, in this emotionally charged situation, the appearance of soldiers caused the band to flee toward the Pine Ridge reservation. At Wounded Knee Creek, they were surrounded by army troops, and surrendered. This was on the evening of December 28, ironically enough, the day on which the Christian church has long celebrated the festival of the Massacre of the Holy Innocents. The following morning, in a search for weapons, shooting started, whereupon ensued the indiscriminate slaughter of Indians by members of the 7th Cavalry, Custer's old regiment. The following account is taken from reports given to the Commissioner of Indian Affairs on February 11, 1891.

TURNING HAWK, Pine Ridge (Mr. Cook, interpreter): Mr. Commissioner, my purpose to-day is to tell you what I know of the condition of affairs at the agency where I live. . . .

■　■　■

When we heard that these people were coming toward our agency we also heard this. These people were coming toward Pine Ridge agency, and when they were al-

From *Fourteenth Annual Report of the Bureau of American Ethnology* (1896), Part 2, pp. 884–86.

most on the agency they were met by the soldiers and surrounded and finally taken to the Wounded Knee creek, and there at a given time their guns were demanded. When they had delivered them up, the men were separated from their families, from their tipis, and taken to a certain spot. When the guns were thus taken and the men thus separated, there was a crazy man, a young man of very bad influence and in fact a nobody, among that bunch of Indians fired his gun, and of course the firing of a gun must have been the breaking of a military rule of some sort, because immediately the soldiers returned fire and indiscriminate killing followed. . . .

■　■　■

AMERICAN HORSE: There was a woman with an infant in her arms who was killed as she almost touched the flag of truce, and the women and children of course were strewn all along the circular village until they were dispatched. Right near the flag of truce a mother was shot down with her infant; the child not knowing that its mother was dead was still nursing, and that especially was a very sad sight. The women as they were fleeing with their babes were killed together, shot right through, and the women who were very heavy with child were also killed. All the Indians fled in these three directions, and after most all of them had been killed a cry was made that all those who were not killed or wounded should come forth and they would be safe. Little boys who were not wounded came out of their places of refuge, and as soon as they came in sight a number of soldiers surrounded them and butchered them there.

Of course we all feel very sad about this affair. I stood very loyal to the government all through those troublesome days, and believing so much in the government and being so loyal to it, my disappointment was very strong, and I have come to Washington with a very great blame on my heart. Of course it would have been all right if only the men were killed; we would feel almost grateful for it. But the fact of the killing of the women, and more especially the killing of the young boys and girls who are to go to make up the future strength of the Indian people, is the saddest part of the whole affair and we feel it very sorely.

■　■　■

TURNING HAWK: I had just reached the point where I said that the women were killed. We heard, besides the killing of the men, of the onslaught also made upon the women and children, and they were treated as roughly and indiscriminately as the men and boys were.

Of course this affair brought a great deal of distress upon all the people, but especially upon the minds of those who stood loyal to the government and who did all that they were able to do in the matter of bringing about peace. They especially have suffered much distress and are very much hurt at heart.

■　■　■

39 | How the Indians Are Victimized by Government Agents and Soldiers

Palaneapope

The following testimony by a Yankton Sioux was given in August 1865, to a commissioner of Indian affairs, A. W. Hubbard, at the Yankton agency in South Dakota. "Grandfather" is an Indian way of referring to the United States government.

When I went to make my treaty, my grandfather agreed, if I would put three young men to work, he would put one white laborer with them to learn them; that I should put three young men to learn ploughing, and he would put one white man to learn them; also, three to sow, three to learn the carpenter's trade, three to learn the blacksmith's trade, and such other trades as we should want; and my great grandfather was to furnish one white man for each trade to learn the young men. My grandfather also said that a school should be established for the nation to learn them to read and write; that the young boys and girls should go to school, and that the young men who worked should have the same pay as the whites. My grandfather told me if my young men would go to work that the money going to those who would not work should be given to those who would work. None of these things have been fulfilled. . . .

My friend, I think if my young men knew how to sow, farm, carpenter, and do everything else, I could send the white men away; we ourselves should have the money paid the white men, and we should have plenty of money. If we had been learned all these things we could support ourselves, have plenty of money, have schools, and I could have written my great grandfather, and have got a letter from him; I could have written him myself what I wanted.

■　　■　　■

From Senate Report No. 156, 39th Congress, 2d Session (March 3, 1865), pp. 366–72.

I think I gave my land to my grandfather. When I signed the treaty I told them I never would sign for the pipestone quarry. I wanted to keep it myself; but I understand white men are going there and getting and breaking up the stone.

I would have to tell my grandfather that I made a treaty with him, and I would have to ask him how many goods he is going to give me; and I would tell him that I want him to give me the invoices of my goods, that I may know what I am entitled to. I do not want corn thrown to me the same as to hogs. If I could get my invoices I should always know what belongs to me. Every time our goods come I have asked the agent for the invoices, but they never show me the invoices; they can write what they please, and they go and show it to my grandfather, and he thinks it all right. I think, my friend, my grandfather tells me lies. My friend, what I give a man I don't try to take back. I think, my friend, there is a great pile of money belonging to us which we never yet have received.

. . . My grandfather . . . told me I should take one hundred and sixty acres of land for my own use, and that I should have plenty of land to raise hay for the stock. All the hay on my bottom land is cut by the white man to sell. I asked for hay, but I can get none—white man cut it; I can't tell who gets the money for the hay, but I think Redfield got some money for hay; my ponies can have no hay. . . .

■　■　■

. . . If I had understood from what my grandfather told me, that I was to be treated as I have been, I would never have done as I have done; I never would have signed the treaty. . . .

■　■　■

A steamboat arrived with our goods, and the goods were put out; Burleigh said they were our goods, and they were marked for us; there were five boxes. There were some officers and soldiers there. The boxes remained there on the bank until the next day. At night somebody scratched the marks off and put on other marks. (This statement was witnessed by Medicine Cow and Walking Elk.) They saw it done. . . .

■　■　■

. . . I think the way the white men treated us is worse than the wolves do. We have a way in winter of putting our dead up on scaffolds up from the ground, but the soldiers cut down the scaffolds and cut off the hair of the dead, and if they had good teeth they pulled them out, and some of them cut off the heads of the dead and carried them away. . . . Another time when General Sully came up he passed through the middle of our field, turned all his cattle and stock into our corn and destroyed the whole of it. The ears of some were then a foot long; the corn was opposite Fort Randall, and they not only destroyed the corn but burnt up the fence. I think no other white man would do so; I do not think my grandfather told them to do so. The soldiers set fire to the prairie and burnt up four of our lodges and all there was in them, and three horses. When my corn is good to eat they cross the river from Fort Randall and eat it, and when it is not good they throw it in the river. . . . Before the soldiers came along we had good health; but once the soldiers came along they go to my squaws and want to sleep with them, and the squaws being hungry will sleep with them in order to get something to eat, and will get a bad disease, and then the squaws turn to their husbands and give them the bad disease.

■　　■　　■

. . . My friend, what I am going to tell you is the truth. We only get five dollars apiece; we have only had one trader; he often makes us feel bad; he sells us goods so high it makes us cry; I think there ought to be two traders; I want two traders. . . .

■　　■　　■

40 | Forced Removal of the Winnebago Indians, Nebraska, October 3, 1865

Chief Little Hill

Formerly I did not live as I do now. We used to live in Minnesota. While we lived in Minnesota we used to live in good houses, and always take our Great Father's advice, and do whatever he told us to do. We used to farm and raise a crop of all we wanted every year. While we lived there we had teams of our own. Each family had a span of horses or oxen to work, and had plenty of ponies; now, we have nothing. While we lived in Minnesota another tribe of Indians committed depredations against the whites, and then we were compelled to leave Minnesota. We did not think we would be removed from Minnesota; never expected to leave; and we were compelled to leave so suddenly that we were not prepared; not many could sell their ponies and things they had. The superintendent of the farm for the Winnebagoes was to take care of the ponies we left there and bring them on to us wherever we went; but he only brought to Crow Creek about fifty, and the rest we do not know what became of them. . . . After we got on the boat we were as though in a prison. We were fed on dry stuff all the time. We started down the Mississippi river, and then up the Missouri to Dakota Territory, and there we found our superintendent, and stopped there (at Crow Creek). . . . After we got there they sometimes give us rations, but not enough to go round most of the time. Some would have to go without eating two or three days. It was not a good country; it was all dust. Whenever we cooked anything it would be full of dust. We found out after a while we could not live there. Sometimes the women and children were sick, and some of them died; and we think many of them died because they could not get enough to eat while they were sick. . . .

Now, I will speak about our annuity goods. I think some of our goods—I know pretty near where they have gone to. . . . I know one thing certain, that the pork

From Senate Report No. 156, 39th Congress 2d Session (March 3, 1865), pp. 416–17.

and flour we left in Minnesota, that belonged to us, was brought over to Crow Creek and sold to us by Hawley & Hubbell, our storekeepers at Crow Creek. I will pass and not say more about the provision, and say of things since we left Crow Creek. For myself, in the first place, I thought I could stay there for a while and see the country. But I found out it wasn't a good country. I lost six of my children, and so I came down the Missouri River.

The Redress Movement:
Land Claim Litigation

41 | Indian Claims for Reparations, Compensation, and Restitution in the United States Legal System

Nell Jessup Newton

Treaties with American Indian Tribes transferred more than 2 billion acres of land to the United States.[1] These treaties also recognized tribes as sovereigns with respect to their internal affairs. Although some treaties were negotiated from a position of strength, many others were the product of fraud or coercion rather than consent. Cultural differences marred this treaty process. In addition to the obvious problem of negotiating in an unfamiliar language, tribal people had different concepts of the relationship of people to land than those encapsulated in the concept of property in Euro-American cultures. A treaty that seemed fair on its face, for example, might well have been based on a tribe's understanding that the treaty granted only rights to use the land, or that the grant of permanent occupation to others (what Euro-Americans would conceptualize as fee simple title) did not change the tribe's sovereignty—its authority to control activities on the land.[2]

Disputes over the interpretation or breach of treaties began almost as soon as the first treaties were made and continue to this day. In addition to treaty disputes, tribes complained of interference with tribal sovereignty or of confiscation of their original land by settlers and miners, often with federal approval. In short, tribal people consistently asserted and demanded justice for wrongs committed against their property interests as well as their right to exist as independent peoples. Claims phrased in the language of property and sovereignty are in turn integral components of Indian tribes' attempts to retain their cultural identity.[3]

Yet the wrongs inflicted by colonialism do not fit neatly into the constructs of the American legal culture. As a result, the legal claims systems created to provide Indian tribes with redress have failed them in multiple ways. The failure was caused

Adapted from "Compensation, Reparations, and Restitution: Indian Property Claims in the United States," *Georgia Law Review* 28 (1994): 454.

both by the cultural assumptions embedded in the deep structure of Euro-American law and by the imposition of formal substantive rules of American Indian law that seem to have been constructed to benefit the government at the expense of Indian tribes.

An example of the interplay of these factors is the history of the Court of Claims and the Indian Claims Commission. In 1855, Congress created the Court of Claims to provide a forum for those with claims for money damages against the government, including compensation for property seized by the government.[4] Shortly thereafter, an amendment excepted any claims based on treaties with Indian tribes and foreign nations from the new court's jurisdiction.[5] The legal community assumed that the exception for Indian treaties barred Indian tribes from bringing any kinds of claims to the Court of Claims. As a result, tribes with land claims were relegated to Congress for relief until after World War II. Tribes with the resources to hire lobbyists obtained what were called "special jurisdictional acts" permitting claims to be brought in the Court of Claims seeking compensation for a variety of wrongs, including seizures of land.[6] Nevertheless, the Court of Claims interpreted these special acts so narrowly that few tribes prevailed.[7] In addition, the special statutes often permitted the court to offset against the damages awarded any gratuities the federal government had given the tribe and to recoup the cost of administering any Indian programs that had benefited the tribe. Since gratuities included everything the government could prove it had given the tribe, such as blankets and food, the final net judgment was considerably reduced.[8]

World War II and its aftermath dramatically affected the United States' treatment of Indian tribes. Indian people fought in great numbers during the war, acquitting themselves with honor. The Holocaust in particular impelled policymakers to consider the human rights dimensions of its treatment of Native Americans. For example, those arguing for fairer treatment of Indian land claims noted that Hitler himself had invoked the example of the treatment of Western Indians during the period of "manifest destiny" in the United States as justification for the Nazi invasion of Czechoslovakia and Poland to gain more *lebensraum* for the German people.[9] The differential treatment of Indian tribes' land claims conflicted with the spirit of postwar egalitarianism and visions of restorative justice.

In 1946, Congress enacted a comprehensive method to settle ancient Indian claims for all time. The Indian Claims Commission Act (ICCA) granted tribes access to the Court of Claims for any future claims, including property claims, redressible by private parties in that Court. The act also created a commission to investigate and settle any and all claims arising before 1946 that tribes wished to bring forward. The ICCA held out much promise. The law provided for the creation of an Investigation Division, with access to all government documents, which could then report to the Indian Claims Commission. This provision and other aspects of the law permitted adoption of a cooperative rather than a strict adversarial model. The law also assigned the commission jurisdiction over so-called "moral" as well as legal claims, by granting it jurisdiction over "claims based upon fair and honorable dealings that are not recognized by any existing rule of law or equity."[10]

A coalition of different visions and interests created the majority needed for passage of the ICCA. These visions might be labeled assimilationist, distributive, and restorative. For example, in addition to the high-minded reasons mentioned above, many supported the ICCA as a mechanism to convince tribal people to abandon their outmoded notions of tribalism. They reasoned that only when Indian tribes settled their ancient grievances would they be able to cast off the last of their bitterness toward the United States and assimilate fully into the dominant culture. This vision is essentially assimilative and thus perpetuates the legacy of colonialism. Others saw the ICCA as a form of distributive justice that would benefit all tribes, who were then the poorest minority group in the United States, with per capita incomes below the levels of those in so-called Third World nations. Instead of a direct transfer from the treasury to all tribes, which might be politically unpalatable, these advocates believed that provisions permitting the Indian Claims Commission to award damages for so-called moral claims would permit all tribes to recover money damages. Still others believed the ICCA provided an opportunity for true restorative justice. The Investigative Division could listen to the tribes' stories of mistreatment without having to fit these histories into formal legal structures, investigate the relations between the particular tribe and the United States, and make recommendations to the commission for each tribe that could include both monetary compensation and restoration of land. The idea was not merely to transfer money to all tribes, but to tailor justice in light of each tribe's history.[11]

The ICCA failed to meet the expectations of nearly everyone involved in its creation. To begin with, the newly constituted Indian Claims Commission adopted an adversary system with all the procedural rules such a system requires. The commission interpreted its mandate very narrowly and held that it was only empowered to award monetary compensation. It also failed to create the Investigative Division permitted by the law. These initial decisions barred tribes from seeking the kind of declaratory and injunctive relief that might have permitted the commission to dispense restorative justice. With the commission thus organized as a court, the Justice Department acted like attorneys: they fought each claim as tenaciously as would be expected of attorneys defending their clients. The commission also adopted technical rules that made the Court of Claims, long criticized as overly technical and biased toward the government, seem enlightened. Fine distinctions and legal niceties multiplied, with the tribes often on the wrong side of the legal rule or the "exception to the exception." Expert witnesses, such as anthropologists, were pitted against one another. Most disappointing were the commission's rulings that effectively nullified the provision permitting broad moral claims, the fair and honorable dealings clause. This clause was so narrowed as to become redundant and useless for the most serious claims, those based on destruction of tribal identity.[12]

The Indian Claims Commission did not even fulfill the expectations of those who merely sought redistribution of wealth to Indian Tribes. While some tribes succeeded in obtaining large money judgments, many who had been harmed the most seriously were awarded nothing because their claims were merely "moral" and not "legal." Even when tribes were awarded compensation, the distribution plans created by the Department of the Interior provided that the money was to be distributed per capita to all members of the tribe, whether they lived on or off the reservation and whether or not they maintained any ties to the modern-day tribe. This distribution mechanism considerably lessened the amount available to the tribe for such purposes as economic development.[13]

The Indian Claims Commission's procedures and substantive rules thus divided tribes into winners and losers based not on the amount of land taken from them by the government or the degree of physical or cultural harm suffered, but on the niceties of legal doctrines developed to protect the Treasury, as well as the degree of skillfulness and honesty of the attorneys who represented them. Tribes with treaties received better compensation than those who had relied on the government's word, for example, because some of the treaties could be read as creating a property right in land retained. But the decision to equate justice with money, taken in early commission decisions, was the most serious flaw in the commission's design and implementation.

There were also statutory flaws in the prosecution of Indian claims. The ICCA's attorneys' fee provision created conflicts of interest. Ten percent of the judgment is paid to the attorney as a contingency fee. This has led attorneys to advise tribes to drop any claims for present possession of property, even though the tribe could prove that the government had not in fact formally confiscated its land. A claim for present possession could not be brought before the Indian Claims Commission, and while it might be brought in federal court, the attorney would not be guaranteed a fee. As a result, tribes were sometimes urged to concede that they no longer owned the land and to sue instead for a taking of property.[14]

More seriously, the ICCA permitted any "tribe, band, or identifiable group of Indians" to press a redressible claim. This gave rise to great injustices in cases where an attorney in effect "created" a tribe for the purpose of pressing a land claim. Members of such a constructed tribe might find that the land they presently occupy had been forfeited in a claim brought on their behalf by an entity to which they had never belonged.

Tribes complained that the claims system created conflicts of interest for attorneys, and charged attorney misconduct. Charges included allegations that attorneys had stipulated, without tribal permission, to boundaries of taken land that encompassed land still being used by tribal members.[15] Some tribal people also charged that those chosen to represent a tribe before the Indian Claims Commission had no such authority. Most notable is the story of the Dann family and other Western Shoshone tribes who unsuccessfully challenged a stipulation entered into by an attorney representing an entity called the Western Shoshone Identifiable Group, which had no authority to represent the many individual bands of Shoshone Indians.[16] Because of this stipulation, the Supreme Court held that land occupied by the Dann family had been taken, despite the fact the family had continuously lived on and used the land for grazing.[17]

An example of the Indian Claims Commission's overly formalistic method of dealing with claims is illustrated by *Fort Sill Apache Tribe*.[18] The entire Chiricahua

Apache tribe had been incarcerated, after the defeat of Geronimo, as prisoners of war in Florida, Alabama, and finally Fort Sill, Oklahoma, for twenty-seven years. Most Chiricahua members had not supported Geronimo, and even the government acknowledged that the tribe's incarceration had been illegal. The Indian Claims Commission dismissed the remaining tribe members' suit, however, on several grounds. First, the commission held that an unlawful imprisonment claim could not be brought by the collective, but only as an ordinary tort claim affecting individual members of the tribe. Since the ICCA had created a forum only for group harms, the tribe could not bring this suit on behalf of its individual members. The tribe had also based a claim on the fair and honorable dealings clause, arguing that the imprisonment had destroyed the tribe's integrity. The commission dismissed this group harm by holding that there must be a statutory basis for such a claim. Since the United States had never made a treaty or statutory promise not to imprison the tribe, the tribe had no claim. After this case, the fair and honorable dealings clause became a dead letter; the only successful case regarding the clause involved a group of Alaskan natives who had been held in virtual slavery for over seventy years. In short, as Nancy Lurie has eloquently argued in her work on the Indian Claims Commission, the adversary system moved the commission in the direction of very simple, easily quantifiable claims.[19]

In addition to these structural barriers to restorative justice, the Indian Claims Commission and its reviewing courts, the Court of Claims and the Supreme Court, created legal doctrines that seriously impeded tribes' attempts to gain even monetary damages. In particular, the Supreme Court created rules of formal *in*equality, with the most notable ruling coming in 1955, a year after the Court had resoundingly denounced such rules in *Brown v. Board of Education*.

In *Tee-Hit-Ton Indians v. United States*,[20] the Court drew a distinction between aboriginal Indian land, which was land owned by the tribe since time immemorial, and land conveyed to a tribe by an official act of Congress or by a treaty.[21] The opinion is a model of formalistic analysis, holding that the word "property" in the Fifth Amendment Takings Clause does not include aboriginal Indian land. An ironic consequence is that this decision favored hostile tribes over those who allied themselves with the United States. Tribes like those of the Northern Plains that fought settlement usually entered into a treaty afterward, recognizing the boundaries of their reservation land; tribes that dealt amicably with the government's representatives received no such protection. For example, the California Indian tribes believed they had entered into treaties. Because the Senate never ratified the treaties, the tribe had no "property" rights.[22] The Inuits, Tlingits, and other people of Alaska had never fought a war with the United States; the *Tee-Hit-Ton* decision thus legitimated the taking of Alaska when its vast mineral resources were discovered.[23]

In 1980, the Supreme Court also adopted a rule distinguishing treaty-recognized title from other non-Indian owned land by labeling nonconsensual transfers of Indian tribal land to third parties not to be takings when the government acts as guardian of the tribe rather than as a sovereign. When the government can show it "fairly (or in good faith) attempt[ed] to provide [its] ward with property of equivalent value," its actions are insulated from the Takings Clause.[24] Under this standard, a tribe whose land, recognized by title, was or is being taken by Congress without tribal consent must overcome the good faith effort test in order to recover any compensation at all. This standard acts most harshly against ancient claims. A tribe may still sue for breach of trust if the government's actions as trustee do not measure up to the fairly high standards imposed on fiduciaries, but interest is only paid on constitutional claims against the government.[25] Because the Sioux Nation was successful in demonstrating that the government had acted not as a guardian but as a sovereign in acquiring the Black Hills, the tribe's $17 million judgment based on the fair market value at the time of taking was augmented by over $100 million in interest damages accruing up to the date of the decision. Nevertheless, the rule serves as a reminder that the American legal system still accepts rules of formal inequality when dealing with Indian land. The Sioux people do not regard this legal case as a victory. Money is not the remedy that will restore them for the loss of their most sacred place.

CONCLUSION

Indian tribal people, depicted as on the brink of extinction since contact with Euro-American society, are very resilient. Despite the procedural, structural, and substantive hurdles presented by the American legal system, or perhaps because of them, Indian tribes have increasingly sought the restoration of land by petitioning Congress or by purchasing land and asking the Secretary of the Interior to take it into trust or add it to the tribe's existing reservation. Since 1970, the United States has restored 540,000 acres of public domain lands to various Indian tribes.[26] Perhaps the most famous such restoration was the return of the Blue Lake to the Taos Pueblo in New Mexico. Despite great concern that this restoration would create dangerous precedents for those tribes who had lost in the Indian Claims Commission, Congress restored this land in part because of its great religious significance to the people of the Taos Pueblo.[27] Since that restoration, tribes have continued to lobby for further restoration of public domain land to tribal control. Some tribes have successfully negotiated for land in addition to money in out-of-court settlements of legal claims,[28] or successfully used public relations to garner public support for attempts to keep their land.[29]

Restoration of land enables tribal people to retain their distinctiveness. As important, the process of seeking restoration can include an opportunity to narrate a story of the past wrongs without the need to fit these wrongs into narrow legal constructs or to quantify unquantifiable injuries. Such restoration efforts, when successful, can bring about reconciliation and understanding; while even a multi-million-dollar monetary judgment obtained after more than fifty years of litigation, as occurred with the Sioux Nation in the Black Hills case, can foster enmity and distrust. Although the money judgment in the Black Hills case has grown to over $500 million, the Sioux people have refused to accept the money. Since the Supreme Court awarded them compensation in 1980, they have continued to state that only a solution that returns some land in the Black Hills will ever be acceptable.

NOTES

1. Russell Lawrence Barsh, "Indian Land Claims Policy in the United States," *Notre Dame Law Review* 58 (1982): 7.

2. See references cited in Nell Jessup Newton, "Compensation, Reparations, and Restitution: Indian Property Claims in the United States," *Georgia Law Review* 28 (1994): 453, 459–60n. 20.

3. By cultural identity I do not mean a frozen, timeless stereotype of the traditional Indian, but the fluctuating identity exhibited by all modern societies. Cultural identity claims are often made by indigenous people as a way of arguing their right to be independent peoples, free from the control of the dominant society in which they are located.

4. See Act of February 24, 1855, Chapter 122, 10 Statute 612, 612 (creating Court of Claims).

5. Act of March 3, 1863, Chapter 92, § 9, 12 Statute 765, 767 (excluding claims dependent on treaty stipulations entered into with Indians).

6. See Petra T. Shattuck and Jill Norgren, *Partial Justice: Federal Indian Law in a Liberal Constitutional System* (New York: St. Martin's Press, 1991), p. 143 (noting problems created by this system).

7. Francis Paul Prucha, *The Great Father: The United States Government and the American Indians*, vol. 2 (Lincoln: University of Nebraska Press, 1984), p. 1018 (reporting that only twenty-nine out of nearly two hundred claims survived dismissal on technicalities).

8. For example, the Indians of California were awarded $17,053,941 before offsets reduced the award to $5,024,842. *Indians of California v. United States*, 102 Ct. Cl. 837 (1944).

9. Creation of Indian Claims Commission, Hearings Before the Committee on Indian Affairs, House of Representatives, 79th Congress, 1st Session 79, p. 108 (1945) (statement of Ernest L. Wilkinson, Esq.).

10. Indian Claims Commission Act of 1946, Public Law Number 726, Chapter 959, § 2(5), 60 Statute 1049.

11. Robert N. Clinton, Nell Jessup Newton, and Monroe Price, *American Indian Law: Cases and Materials*, 3d ed. (Charlottesville, Va.: Michie Company, 1991), pp. 721–24 (reviewing explicit and implicit justifications for Indian Claims Commission).

12. See generally Nell Jessup Newton, "Indian Claims in the Courts of the Conqueror," *American University Law Review* 41 (1992): 753, 776–84 (discussing, inter alia, refusal to compensate Apache Tribe for twenty-seven years of wrongful imprisonment).

13. See, e.g., Nancy O. Lurie, Epilogue to *Irredeemable America: The Indians' Estate and Land Claims*, ed. Imre Sutton (Albuquerque: University of New Mexico Press, 1985), p. 363 (criticizing per capita payments and arguing that tribal people were often not aware that payments were compensation for tribal land).

14. Shattuck and Norgren, *Partial Justice*, pp. 151–55 (criticizing the Indian Claims Commission's methods of determining that land had been taken in order to proceed to money damages phase of litigation). See also Charles F. Wilkinson, "Home Dance, the Hopi, and Black Mesa Coal: Conquest and Endurance in the American Southwest," *Brigham Young University Law Review* (1996): 449, 460–61 (relating charges that attorney for Hopi misrepresented the scope of the commission's powers in order to press a land claim and obtain appointment as tribal general counsel).

15. See, e.g., *Pueblo of Santo Domingo v. United States*, 647 F.2d 1087 (Ct. Cl. 1981), *cert. denied*, 456 U.S. 1006 (1982) (order denying tribe's request to withdraw from 1969 stipulation made by its attorney without its permission as untimely).

16. See *United States v. Dann*, 470 U.S. 39, 48–49 (1985) (holding that appropriation of funds to pay judgment in Indian Claims Commission Act case precluded any further litigation regarding land).

17. Ibid., p. 49. See generally Carolyn Orlando, "Aboriginal Title Claims in the Indian Claims Commission: *United States v. Dann* and Its Due Process Implications," *Boston College Environmental Affairs Law Review* 13 (1986): 241, 261 (giving full background of *Dann* case and arguing that Supreme Court overlooked due process implications).

18. 477 F.2d 1360 (Ct. Cl. 1973).

19. See Lurie, Epilogue to *Irredeemable America*, p. 363.

20. 348 U.S. 272 (1955).

21. Ibid., p. 279.

22. See *Indians of California v. United States*, 102 Ct. Cl. 837 (1944) (awarding California Indians $5,024,842); Ralph L. Beals, "The Anthropologist as Expert Witness," in *Irredeemable America: The Indians' Estate and Land Claims*, ed. Imre Sutton (Albuquerque: University of New Mexico Press, 1985), p. 139 (describing California land claim case).

23. For a discussion of the case and its implications, see Nell Jessup Newton, "At the Whim of the Sovereign: Aboriginal Title Reconsidered," *Hastings Law Journal* 31 (1980): 1215.

24. *United States v. Sioux Nation*, 448 U.S. 371, 416 (1980).

25. See ibid., p. 415 (stating Congress is "subject to limitations inhering in . . . a guardianship").

26. See Russell Barsh, "Indian Land Claims Policy in the United States," *Notre Dame Law Review* 58 (1982): 7, 73n. 358 (collecting statutes reflecting instances where the United States has reconveyed over 500,000 acres to public domain in western states to tribes between 1970 and 1982). For citations to statutes restoring land, see references cited in Newton, "Compensation, Reparations, and Restitution," 477n. 98.

27. See Imre Sutton, "Incident or Event? Land Restoration in the Claims Process," in *Irredeemable America: The Indians' Estate and Land Claims*, ed. Imre Sutton (Albuquerque: University of New Mexico Press, 1985), p. 211 (discussing Blue Lake restoration as very flawed precedent because process took forty years and the Pueblo received only 46,000 acres).

28. For example, the Maine Tribes received a fund of $54 million earmarked for the purchase of valuable timber land within their aboriginal territory when they settled an ancient claim against the United States. Maine Indian Claims Settlement Act, 25 U.S.C. §§ 1721, 1724 (1988) (providing $27 million in appropriations, $54.5 million for land acquisition, and giving tribes option to purchase 300,000 acres).

29. See Wendy Espeland, "Legally Mediated Identity: The National Environmental Policy

Act and the Bureaucratic Construction of Interests," *Law and Society Review* 28 (1994): 1149 (relating the successful methods by which the Yavapai of Fort McDowell used legal methods provided by the National Environmental Policy Act, publicity generating events such as marches, and the invocation of their unique history to resist relocation from their reservation and halt the construction of a dam).

The Redress Movement:
Land Claim Legislation

42 | The True Nature of Congress's Power over Indian Claims

An Essay on *Venetie* and the Uses of Silence in Federal Indian Law

Robert A. Williams, Jr.

CONGRESS'S POWER OVER INDIAN CLAIMS

According to well-established principles of federal Indian law, Congress has plenary power to manage Indian affairs.[1] This broad power has given Congress extraordinary flexibility in approaching the difficult questions of law and justice that arise in addressing the claims of Indian tribes conquered and colonized by the United States.

Prior to World War II, Congress used its broad power over Indian claims to pass special jurisdictional acts permitting some Indian tribes to seek compensation for treaty violations and other claims for reparations before the Court of Claims. The great degree of power and flexibility that Congress possesses in this arena of Indian affairs is signified by its decision following World War II to settle *all* outstanding Indian claims against the United States by passage of the 1946 Indian Claims Commission Act.[2]

In more recent decades, Congress has used its broad power over Indian affairs as a basis for passing special claims legislation. There are laws on the books, in other words, that make reparations to Indian tribes for what has been lost through the processes of colonization and conquest by the United States.[3]

It is tempting to look at this flexible and broad power that Congress possesses over Indian claims and conclude that it represents a practical and even very wise approach to a very complex subject. Many difficult questions of law and justice can arise when Congress considers Indian claims. The power Congress exercises over this area enables it to respond sensitively and intelligently to Indian claims in different contexts. But to fully understand the true nature of this power Congress possesses under principles of federal Indian law, it is necessary to look beyond the visible signs of Congress's efforts over time to settle Indian claims.

If all we consider are the legislative acts approved by Congress, then all we can know about are the Indian claims Congress has chosen to recognize and redress. What of those claims that Congress will not hear, or refuses to address? As has been noted, Congress has many means at its disposal to deal with Indian tribes and their claims for reparations. Under principles of federal Indian law, silence is one of these means. Congress can say nothing about the rights that should be restored to an Indian tribe and, in effect, deny the tribe's claims to law and justice.

THE SUPREME COURT'S VENETIE DECISION

Consider, for example, the Supreme Court's 1998 decision in *Alaska v. Native Village of Venetie Tribal Government*.[4] The Court's unanimous decision in *Venetie*, written by Justice Clarence Thomas, denied the claims of Alaska's Native peoples to sovereignty and self-government over the 44 million acres of lands they had acquired under the 1971 Alaska Native Claims Settlement Act (ANCSA).[5]

ANCSA was the largest Indian land claims settlement ever enacted by Congress. It was a comprehensive statute, designed to settle all aboriginal land claims by Alaska Natives. It was driven by the need of the nation's major oil companies to build a pipeline across Native-claimed lands, which could transport huge quantities of oil, discovered in 1968, from Prudhoe Bay.

ANCSA extinguished all aboriginal claims to Alaskan land, including rights to hunt and fish. Alaska Natives received from Congress the transfer of $962.5 million in federal funds and approximately 44 million acres of Alaskan land as reparations for the extinguishment of their claims. The settlement did not go directly to Alaska Natives, but to state-chartered private business corporations that were to be formed pursuant to the statute. All the shareholders of these corporations were required to be Alaska Natives; however, because ANCSA corporations received title to the transferred land in fee simple (i.e., by absolute title), and no federal restrictions applied to subsequent land transfers by them, the ANCSA lands would be subject to creditors and liquidation.

The Native village of Venetie, Alaska, is home to the Neets'aii Gwich'in Indians of the Arctic Circle. In 1943, the secretary of the interior created a reservation for the Neets'aii Gwich'in about the size of Delaware (approximately 1.8 million acres) out of the land surrounding Venetie and another nearby tribal village, Arctic Village. By enacting ANCSA in 1971, Congress expressly terminated the Venetie Reservation and established two Native corporations for the Neets'aii Gwich'in, one in Venetie and one in Arctic Village. In 1973, those corporations, under a provision in ANCSA allowing Native corporations to take title to former reservation lands in lieu of ANCSA's monetary payments and transfers of nonreservation land, received absolute title to the former Venetie Reservation from the United States. The corporations then transferred their title to the land to the Native Village of Venetie Tribal Government.[6]

In 1986, the Venetie Tribal Government, claiming that its ANCSA lands constituted "Indian country" within the meaning of federal statute 18 U.S.C. § 1151, asserted taxing jurisdiction over a private contractor hired by the State of Alaska to
construct a state-financed public school in Venetie. Under 18 U.S.C. § 1151, enacted by Congress in 1948 for purposes of establishing federal criminal jurisdiction
over Indian-held lands, the term "Indian country" includes reservations established
by treaty or statute (18 U.S.C. § 1151(a)), "all dependent Indian communities
within the borders of the United States" (18 U.S.C. § 1151(b)), or Indian allotments (18 U.S.C. § 1151(c)). Under well-established principles of federal Indian
law, primary jurisdiction over lands recognized as Indian country rests with the federal government and the Indian tribe inhabiting it, and not with the surrounding
state government.[7]

Recognition of an Indian tribe's claim to Indian country status for its land is very
important from the tribe's perspective. Under principles of federal Indian law, Indian country status for its lands gives the tribe jurisdiction, "the institutional privilege of force" as Robert Cover has defined the term.[8] With Indian country jurisdiction, a tribe can exercise sovereignty and self-government. In Indian country, control of tribal membership, family law matters, the way that children are to be
raised, securing life and sustenance from the land, and other basic human rights of
cultural survival and cultural self-determination belong to the tribe. These are
rights subject to diminishment only by Congress acting under its plenary power in
Indian affairs. Most importantly, Indian country status for Indian lands protects
the tribe from the jurisdictional encroachments of often hostile surrounding state
governments.[9]

When the Venetie Tribal Government attempted to collect its tax in tribal court,
claiming that its ANCSA lands met the "dependent Indian communities" prong of
§ 1151(b) for Indian country status, the State of Alaska filed suit in federal court
seeking to enjoin its collection. Alaska contended that the tribe had no jurisdiction
to impose its tax because its ANCSA lands were not Indian country. The lands were
held in fee simple under Alaska state law as proscribed by ANCSA, free of federal
supervision, ownership, or control, and therefore the tribe was not a dependent Indian community under Section 1151(b).

In ANCSA itself, Congress never mentioned the issue of jurisdiction over Native-
claimed lands or Indian country status for those lands. In its major amendments to
ANCSA in 1991, in fact, Congress went out of its way to say *nothing* on the issue
of Native village powers of self-government and Indian country status of ANCSA
lands: "No provision of this Act . . . shall be construed to validate or invalidate or
in any way affect—(1) any assertion that a Native organization . . . has or does not
have governmental authority over lands . . . or persons within the boundaries of the
State of Alaska, or (2) any assertion that Indian country . . . exists or does not exist
within the boundaries of the State of Alaska."[10]

Potentially all of the 44 million acres selected by Alaska Natives under ANCSA
could have been affected by a finding that Venetie's ANCSA lands constituted

Indian country.[11] At stake for Alaska Natives in *Venetie,* therefore, was whether their rights of cultural self-determination and survival were going to be recognized and protected by the federal government.

The Supreme Court began its Indian country analysis in *Venetie* by first interpreting the term "dependent Indian communities" in § 1151(b):

> Since 18 U.S.C. § 1151 was enacted in 1948, we have not had an occasion to interpret the term "dependent Indian communities." We now hold that it refers to a limited category of Indian lands that are neither reservations nor allotments, and that satisfy two requirements—first, they must have been set aside by the Federal Government for the use of the Indians as Indian land; second, they must be under federal superintendence.[12]

In applying these two requirements, Justice Thomas held for a unanimous Court as follows: "The Tribe's ANCSA lands do not satisfy either of these requirements. After the enactment of ANCSA, the Tribe's lands are neither 'validly set apart for the use of the Indians as such,' nor are they under the superintendence of the Federal Government." The Court said that with respect to the federal set-aside requirement, "it is significant that ANCSA, far from designating Alaskan lands for Indian use, revoked the existing Venetie Reservation." Further, because ANCSA revoked the Venetie Reservation, and Congress stated explicitly that ANCSA's settlement provisions were intended to avoid a "lengthy wardship or trusteeship," it was equally clear, to the Court, at least, that "ANCSA ended federal superintendence over the Tribe's lands."[13] Because the tribe's ANCSA lands did not meet the "dependent Indian communities" test for Indian country, it did not have jurisdiction to impose its tax.

The *Venetie* Court derived its two requirements of federal set-aside and superintendence for Indian country status under § 1151(b) by citing three of its own prior cases, which had discussed the concept of "dependent Indian communities" and were decided long before Congress's enactment of § 1151 in 1948. According to Justice Thomas, Congress "codified" the federal set-aside and superintendence requirements that the Court's prior precedents "had held necessary for a finding of 'Indian country' generally."[14] Therefore, Congress, by failing to take explicit action in ANCSA to create or recognize Indian country status for ANCSA lands, extinguished any rights to sovereignty and self-government Alaska Natives might claim over those lands. The true nature of Congress's power over Indian affairs is such, according to the Supreme Court in *Venetie*, that the principles of federal Indian law do not recognize an Indian tribe's basic rights to cultural survival and self-determination until Congress has chosen to act on the tribe's claims to those rights.[15]

CONCLUSION

What Congress did not want to create was a relationship with Alaska Natives by which the federal government recognized and protected their rights of sovereignty and self-government over their ANCSA-claimed lands. The "principal architect of ANCSA" was Senator Henry "Scoop" Jackson of Washington,[16] a long-time critic of the reservation system based on the experiences of his state with its Indian reservations. Speaking in Alaska, Jackson decried: "It is high time to stop treating the Indians as second-class citizens. Indians ought to be treated just as other citizens and assimilated into our population."[17] Jackson's staff assistant at the time of ANCSA's passage, William Van Ness, admitted that "[t]he act was . . . a very radical effort at social engineering and it was done on a very, very calculated basis."[18] Alaska's governor, Ernest Gruening, argued that creating reservations for Alaska natives was "wholly destructive."[19]

Congress, however, never expressly revoked the right of Alaska Natives to exercise jurisdiction over their lands in ANCSA. Congress was silent on that issue in ANCSA and in its subsequent amendments to the legislation. Yet the Supreme Court held in *Venetie* that by this silence, Congress denied Alaska Natives their claims to sovereignty and self-government over their ANCSA lands. Congress never articulated an expressed intent to bring ANCSA lands under federal superintendence and control.

A racist attitude toward Indian tribes is reflected in Congress's longstanding policy of silence on the issue of Alaska Native sovereignty. Congress chose to say nothing because of the racist belief that Indian country status for Alaska Native–held lands would retard the assimilation of Alaska Natives to the norms and values of a superior race of European-derived, "civilized" peoples. In essence, the Court's opinion in *Venetie* holds that a racist attitude toward Indian tribes justifies denying those tribes jurisdiction over their lands without Congress ever saying a word. Under the principles of federal Indian law, the State of Alaska has been given the right by Congress to exercise the institutional privilege of force over Alaska Natives and their ANCSA lands.

NOTES

1. "Plenary authority over the tribal relations of the Indians has been exercised by congress from the beginning, and the power has always been deemed a political one, not subject to be controlled by the judicial department of the government." *Lone Wolf v. Hitchcock,* 187 U.S. 553, 565 (1903). On the plenary power of Congress in Indian affairs, see Felix Cohen, *Handbook of Federal Indian Law* (Charlottesville, Va.: Michie Company, 1982), pp. 207–16.

2. 25 U.S.C.A. §§ 70–70(v). See, generally, David H. Getches, Charles F. Wilkinson, and Robert A. Williams, Jr., *Federal Indian Law: Cases and Materials,* 3d ed. (St. Paul, Minn.: West Publishing Company, 1993), pp. 311–18 (describing the history of the special jurisdictional acts and the establishment of the Indian Claims Commission). The Indian Claims Commission was given broad jurisdiction by Congress. It was empowered by Congress to "hear and determine" claims cases arising in law or equity based on the Constitution, laws, treaties, or executive orders or sounding in tort. In addition, in a section of the act vesting an unprecedented form of jurisdiction for any court in the United States, Congress empowered

the Indian Claims Commission to hear "claims based upon fair and honorable dealings that are not recognized by any existing rule of law or equity." 25 U.S.C.A. § 70a.

3. For example, in the eastern land claims cases of the 1970s and 1980s, Congress was able to use its broad power over Indian affairs to intervene in ongoing court cases in which the Indian tribe clearly appeared to be winning its claim. States such as Maine, Connecticut, and Rhode Island had purchased Indian lands nearly two centuries ago in violation of federal laws and jurisdiction over Indian land sales. Congress used its power over the Indian claims process to legislate and fund major settlements agreed to by both sides in these highly contested cases. See Getches, Wilkinson, and Williams, *Federal Indian Law*, pp. 116–17, 382–87.

4. 118 S.Ct. 948 (1998).

5. See 43 U.S.C.A. §§ 1601–1628. The history leading up to the passage of ANCSA by Congress and an analysis of its provisions are provided in David H. Getches, "Alternative Approaches to Land Claims: Alaska and Hawaii," in *Irredeemable America: The Indians' Estate and Land Claims*, ed. Imre Sutton (Albuquerque: University of New Mexico Press, 1985), pp. 311–18.

6. See 118 S.Ct. 948, 951 (1998).

7. As Justice Thomas explained in *Venetie*: "Generally speaking, primary jurisdiction over land that is Indian country rests with the Federal Government and the Indian tribe inhabiting it, and not with the States." Ibid., note 1.

8. Robert M. Cover, "Foreword: *Nomos* and Narrative," *Harvard Law Review* 97 (1983): 4, 54.

9. In the seminal case of *Worcester v. Georgia*, 31 U.S. (6 Pet.) 515 (1832), the United States Supreme Court, in an opinion authored by Chief Justice John Marshall, described the practical effects of this foundational principle of state jurisdictional exclusion from Indian country. *Worcester* involved a challenge to the efforts of the State of Georgia to exercise jurisdiction over the Cherokee Indians' reservation:

> The Cherokee nation, then, is a distinct community, occupying its own territory, with boundaries accurately described, in which the laws of Georgia can have no force, and which the citizens of Georgia have no right to enter, but with the assent of the Cherokees themselves, or in conformity with treaties, and with the acts of congress. The whole intercourse between the United States and this nation, is, by our Constitution and laws, vested in the government of the United States.

Ibid., p. 561.

The policy reasons supporting Indian country designation by the federal government are deeply ingrained in the principles of federal Indian law. History has demonstrated time and time again that the individual states surrounding Indian country cannot be trusted to deal fairly with Indian tribes. As the Supreme Court itself stated in *United States v. Kagama*, 118 U.S. 375 (1886), in one of the most famous and frequently cited passages in all of federal Indian law: "Because of the local ill feeling, the people of the States where they [Indian tribes] are found are often their deadliest enemies." Ibid., p. 384.

10. Public Law Number 101-214, § 17, 43 U.S.C. § 1601 note. See also Senate Report Number 201, 100th Congress, 1st Session, p. 41 (1987).

11. See 101 F. 3d 1286, 1303–1304 (9th Cir. 1996) (where Judge Fernandez, writing separately, noted that the majority's holding called into question the status of all 44 million acres of land conveyed by ANCSA).

12. 118 S.Ct., p. 953.

13. Ibid., pp. 955–56.

14. Ibid., p. 953.

15. Ibid., p. 955n. 6.

16. Thomas R. Berger, *Village Journey: The Report of the Alaska Native Review Commission* (New York: Hill and Wang, 1985), p. 20.

17. Ibid., p. 134.

18. Ibid., p. 21. Douglas Jones, staff assistant to Alaska's Senator Mike Gravel, also admitted that ANCSA was a form of social engineering. Ibid.

19. Ibid., p. 134.

Repatriation of Religious and Cultural Artifacts

43 | Repatriation Must Heal Old Wounds

Rick Hill

This essay discusses the Larsen Bay repatriation case arising from the excavation in the 1930s of Native American property from Kodiak Island, Alaska. After four years of controversy, the property was returned.

In the past, Indian peoples have been looked upon by museums as suppliers of material culture or as performers to celebrate the opening of exhibitions. Few museums have actually developed their policies and programs with native peoples in mind. Although American Indian topics are a major part of the educational mission in over four hundred United States museums, the communities discussed have not been perceived as part of the public trust of those museums. Despite their centrality to the museum world, American Indians are often viewed as being outside the fiduciary and moral mandate of those institutions. This must change, and repatriation has begun to open the doors to a new relationship with the native people of this land.

The majority of museums have failed to identify native communities as their primary or target audience. Few have attempted to develop educational programs for people living on reservations or sought to circulate their collections among native communities. Fewer still have American Indians in decision-making positions. The lack of emphasis on establishing relationships or providing educational opportunities for Native Americans has led to a communications gap between museums and Indian people.

Rick Hill, "Repatriation Must Heal Old Wounds," pp. 184–86. From *Reckoning with the Dead*, edited by Tamara L. Bray and Thomas W. Killion; © 1994; published by the Smithsonian Institution. Used by permission of the publisher.

Discussions surrounding the issue of repatriation within the museum profession have generally been very anti-Indian. This is true to the extent that American Indians seeking the repatriation of remains and objects have not infrequently been labeled as acculturated militants, and their requests categorized as political rather than religious in nature. The story of the Larsen Bay request is a case in point. This type of defensive reaction on the part of museums is a way of discrediting the moral basis of the repatriation request. It raises questions about the moral obligations of museums to respect the religious concerns of those they study. It also foregrounds the question of the museum's educational obligations to assist in the cultural rejuvenation of the communities that produced the objects of interest in the first place.

Many of the museums' arguments against repatriation suggest that these institutions consider Native Americans to be outside of their institutional mandates. Should Native Americans be excluded from a museum's fiduciary or legal responsibilities? Are American Indians part of the public trust envisioned by museums? Is there not a moral obligation for museums to assist in the cultural development of American Indians as well as the general public? The failure on the part of many museums to address such questions, and their general response to the repatriation issue, has had the effect of casting Native Americans as anti-social, anti-science, and anti-progress.

Museums must stop thinking of Native Americans as adversaries and begin to view them more responsibly as constituents. American Indians must become part of the program mandate for museums with Native American collections. Museums must develop new partnerships with American Indians for the sake of cultural management within American Indian communities. This partnership needs to be based on the recognition of the fact that museums possess objects that are critical to the spiritual, cultural, and social well-being of American Indians. Native American identity is often manifested in these objects. The loss of these objects from native communities, ritual sites, the classrooms, and homes has caused great deprivations within American Indian society. The museums' possession of our dead and our religious objects has become the main wound that exists between our peoples. The time for healing has come—as mandated by Congress.

In the Larsen Bay case, the Smithsonian questioned whether there was a "reasonable relationship" between the contemporary native community that has made the repatriation request and the human remains in question. Prior to legislation, the Smithsonian would only consider the return of human remains in cases where direct descent could be proven or the name of the individual was known. Embedded in this policy was the assumption that modern native people lacked sufficient ties to their ancient ancestors. The irony is that scholars have defined American Indian cultures on the basis of archaeological evidence and created such entities as "paleo-Indians" as if they were genetic and cultural mutants that had no relationship to modern Native Americans. The denial that there is any spiritual affinity with native ancestors who died before the arrival of the Europeans is in itself unreasonable.

With regard to cultural patrimony, the validity of Indian beliefs is often questioned, bringing the resistance to repatriation to a new level of paternalism. Indian concepts of sacredness, spirit, and religion differ from those of other cultures. Some scholars have questioned those beliefs and want to act as judge, jury, and executioner in order to dismiss American Indian notions of sacredness. Yet their own scholarship identifies native concepts of community property as different from those of Western cultures. Museums know that there is a spiritual relationship between Native Americans and the objects they created or they would not be interested in collecting the objects in the first place. Their own research describes the emotional, spiritual, and cultural importance of ritual objects to Native American identity.

The possession of native dead is seen as a violation of a sacred trust of an entirely different kind. Coming to grips with that reality can lead to new perspectives on the value of information and an increase in knowledge among native people, as demonstrated in the Larsen Bay case. The repatriation of the human remains from the Uyak site stimulated research on the native people of the region and forced anthropologists to think about the significance of the remains. The difference in this case was that new voices were heard and questions about morality were seriously addressed. In the end, both science and religion were advanced.

The museums claim that the repatriation process will take several years and more than $60 million to identify and investigate Native American remains, funerary offerings, sacred objects, and the cultural patrimony of American Indian nations in their possession. They claim that they do not know what they have, yet they argue that these sacred materials are essential to maintaining the integrity of their collections and that the remains of our dead are part of the national heritage. How do you create respect and understanding for American Indian burial customs by desecrating their beliefs? How do you present American Indian grave materials intelligently given the professed lack of information?

The integrity of American Indian religious practices must be taken into account. Museums must examine their legal and moral responsibilities to ensure the preservation of American Indian culture where it still exists. It is hard to imagine that museums are willing to stand by and watch American Indian languages disappear, witness the dismantling of Native American religious freedom, or think of living elders as potential specimens for the future generations of archaeologists and museum collections. There must be museum professionals who want to assist American Indians in these matters. It is time for those people to step forward.

This is not to say that some museums have not taken a proactive approach to assisting American Indians in their cultural development or that human remains and sacred objects have not been repatriated successfully. Where such events have occurred without the force of law, one is apt to find more secure relationships between the native community and the museums in question. The Smithsonian Institution and the New York State Museum are two examples of institutions that have successfully negotiated the return of sacred objects. Native Americans have actively participated in and benefited from such initiatives. The public is also better served insofar as their awareness of modern American Indian traditions and concerns is increased, and a more realistic education about contemporary American Indian culture achieved. In responding to the real needs of Native Americans, museums come to be seen as a social force for cultural development rather than simply as temples of the past.

In most cases, however, it has only been the force of law that has brought museums to the negotiating table. The history of the relationship between American Indians and museums proves this to be true. Only when Native Americans arm themselves with lawyers can they obtain audiences with museum boards of trustees to discuss their concerns. The majority of museums will return items requested by American Indians only if legally required to do so. The Larsen Bay case and the other acts of repatriation by the Smithsonian send a positive signal to both the Native American and the museum community. The Smithsonian, in reversing its previous stance on the repatriation issue, is setting a national model. This precedent must be seen in the broader context of other issues of religious freedom with which native peoples are still struggling. The use and protection of sacred sites, the right to participate in religious ceremonies without fear of persecution, and the right to define one's own culture and beliefs all play a part in the relationship of Native Americans to other Americans. Museums must do more to reflect current social, political, and religious trends in order to better educate museum visitors about the dynamics of contemporary native cultures.

Despite some unethical practices in the past, museums will have served the long-term educational needs of American Indians if they now proceed to assist American Indian communities in the creative use of archival material, objects of cultural identity, and other educational resources to help foster a new era of cultural development for American Indians. By creating new opportunities for American Indians to learn about their artistic, religious, literary, and musical traditions and beliefs, museums will share the responsibility of preserving American Indian culture for many generations to come.

Museums have preserved many objects of American Indian pride and belief. The time has come to recognize that this act of holding objects has really been for the sake of the American Indians themselves. This generation of Native Americans needs to be associated with those objects. It is critical. Time is taking its toll on tribal elders who still remember when many of the contested objects were in native hands. If we wait much longer, much of the remaining oral traditions surrounding these objects could be lost.

Museums can have a positive impact on the future cultural diversity of this nation. They hold the balance of power. They retain the objects that American Indians believe are essential for their survival. If museums fail to respond, they will have to bear responsibility for the demise of the American Indian cultures that they profess they want to preserve. American Indians have made their interests in these matters very clear over the last one hundred years. The time has come for museums to act.

American Indians also have a responsibility in resolving these matters. As we have seen in repatriation cases around the country, native peoples have taken different approaches to the problem based on the initial responses they have received from museums. The museums that want to lock dead Indians in and keep live ones out will find themselves faced with Native American lawyers and mired in court battles. Those that show genuine concern and negotiate in good faith will find that Native Americans will share in the responsibility of the resolution. We have made great strides with human remains and the dead are now returning home to their original resting places. Ironically, the recognition of American Indian religious rights has led to greater self-awareness within the native community. The act of reburial is a highly charged emotional and spiritual event. The fulfillment of this simple moral act opens the doors to museums to participate in the cultural management of Indian communities while at the same time acknowledging the rights of native peoples to manifest their own spiritual destiny.

Wealth, Redistribution, and Sovereignty

44 | Office of the Governor, Pete Wilson, State of California, Press Release

Sacramento, March 6, 1998

Governor Pete Wilson today signed an historic compact with the Pala Band of Mission Indians to allow legal gaming on tribal lands. The Pala-State compact is a comprehensive model agreement that authorizes the tribe to conduct legal gaming as required under federal law, but also includes fundamental protections for both employees and patrons, provides for local community involvement and tribal sharing of revenues with non-gaming tribes, and restrains the expansion of gaming in California.

"Today, I'm announcing that we have finalized a compact with the Pala Tribe so that it may proceed with legal gaming on its reservation," Wilson said. "This compact is more than a legal document. It is a ground-breaking agreement. As such, it is more comprehensive and visionary than any other previous compact in the United States. It is a model to be replicated by other tribes."

"I wish to express my respect for the Pala Band," Wilson said. "They have conducted themselves honorably and in good faith and have negotiated a compact that will benefit not only the members of their own tribe but those of all other tribes who choose wisely to follow their example. Indeed, this compact is a model to be replicated in subsequent agreements between the state and other tribes and will afford to tribes who choose to do so the right to license their allocation of gaming devices to other tribes."

The Pala-State compact allows the tribe to conduct any kind of gaming that the California State Lottery may conduct. The compact is for a ten-year term, with two five-year renewal periods. This ground-breaking agreement provides:

- No slot machines; only legal lottery devices will be permitted.
- A statewide limit on the number of devices of 19,900 is included, given that there are 100 federally recognized tribes in California, each of which could

291

open up a gaming facility. Accordingly, the State has allocated 199 devices to the Pala Band; however, the Pala Band can increase the number of its devices—up to 975—by licensing them from other tribes, who would then forego operating the devices themselves.

- Non-gaming tribes, many of whom are located in remote areas, can thereby share in the gaming revenues by licensing their allocation of 199 lottery devices to tribes in better locations for operating a gaming facility. This will allow non-gaming tribes to benefit (annual revenues for a license of the full 199-device allocation is expected to be as high as $1 million) and will discourage a proliferation of small gaming centers throughout this State.
- The Legislature will be encouraged to enact economic development zones, which generate revenues that can substitute for the gaming revenues. The compact calls for a reduction in lottery devices that represent 50 percent of the net income from the new investments generated by these zones for the tribe, thereby giving the tribe an incentive to have diverse economic investments.
- Employees at tribal facilities will be under the protection of the State's workers' compensation, unemployment insurance and disability insurance laws. And, for the first time anywhere in the United States, service employees (any housekeeping, cleaning, food and beverage, or hotel employees) will be granted the same collective bargaining rights that employees at non-tribal facilities have.
- The local community will be given a significant voice in the provisions of the compact over all local issues, including the environment and compensation for local police and other services. Before the tribe commences the authorized gaming, it must agree with the county to mitigate all significant environmental effects. In addition, the local electorate will have the right to an advisory vote over the compact. A majority vote against the compact will be taken into account in negotiating the county's agreement with the tribe and can trigger a renegotiation of the compact.
- Patrons will be protected against injury and property damage through requirement that the tribe maintain public liability insurance in the amount of $5 million per occurrence. Moreover, if the tribe refuses to pay any patron who wins a lottery game, the patron has the right to require binding arbitration of the dispute.
- Compliance with California's casino prohibition: The tribe may not offer its gaming devices in a hotel; it may not have card games in the same room as the gaming devices; and complimentary alcoholic beverages are prohibited. These restrictions are designed to comply with the California constitutional prohibition against casinos of the type operating in Nevada and New Jersey [Article IV, section 19(e)].

The State is now prepared to enter into compacts with other tribes. Any tribe with jurisdiction over Indian lands in California will now have sixty days (1) to agree to enter into an identical compact, or (2) if it ceases all illegal gaming, to negotiate a different compact. The U.S. Attorneys have agreed to take enforcement action against any tribe that is unlawfully gaming and does not elect one of these options.

Today, we expect [at least 6] California tribes to indicate their endorsement of the Pala compact. . . .

The United States Department of Justice has committed to taking enforcement action against any tribe that is engaged in illegal gaming in California unless it agrees within 60 days to enter into the Pala compact or cease its unlawful gaming and negotiate a new compact. To demonstrate its good faith, the State will agree not to invoke its Eleventh Amendment sovereign immunity in any lawsuit which claims that it has not negotiated in good faith with a tribe that ceases its unlawful gaming within 60 days.

45 | Statement of the Honorable Anthony R. Pico, Chairman, Viejas Band of Kumeyaay Indians, Press Conference

San Diego, March 13, 1998

For the past seven years we've been negotiating off and on, more off than on, with Governor Pete Wilson for a compact that would legalize our video electronic machines.

And here it is. I guess it's like Christmas, you wait and wait for it. When it finally comes you're either overjoyed or disappointed.

To say we, the Viejas Band, are disappointed with the Pala Compact would be a gross understatement. The reaction of the Viejas Tribal council and tribal members ranges from shock, disbelief, and disappointment, to anger and outrage. Unlike the governor, who has had seven years to make and prepare his case for what he wants, and the Pala Band, which had 17 months to consider and debate the implications of the 132-page legal document, we've only had a week to study it.

Despite my strong feelings, I want to try to be as objective about his document as I can be, given the circumstances.

First, however, we want people to know that we believe this is not the end of the battle over a class three gaming compact, but another obstacle, another hurdle. We are not ready to say this compact, or its conditions, is the last or final judgment on our future.

No one wants to see an end to this contentious, divisive, costly and prolonged political and legal battle more than the Viejas People.

But, we are committed to pursuing legislative, political, and legal options, including further negotiations to win a more acceptable compact. And, we will fight until there are no options left. We will not agree to something that is not fair and mutually acceptable to the tribes, as well as the state.

■　■　■

. . . [T]here is the very real threat of 60-day enforcement actions by U.S. attorneys and the Department of Justice against tribes who do not sign.

The gun to our backs gives the Pala Compact a legitimacy it does not deserve. There's more.

■　■　■

What I want to bring to your attention is the sacrifice this compact requires in terms of our sovereignty. We are being asked to give up the rewards of the long, hard-fought struggle of our ancestors and elders for legal, constitutional and treaty guarantees of self-government and political jurisdiction.

The ultimate price, the price each tribe may have to finally measure and weigh, will be what is the cost of state reporting, control and intrusion into what are considered the governmental affairs of tribes and the federal government.

This compact goes well beyond questions of gaming regulation, or scope and types of games, as set forth by federal law. It sets a nationwide precedent over all other tribal-state compacts. The Pala compact puts California once again in the history books for its extreme punitive treatment of Indians.

It extracts more rights from tribal governments than have ever been taken or negotiated in a gaming compact. The state interjects itself into the political and governmental jurisdiction of tribal governments in ways it would not dare dictate to, or interfere in the constitutional authority of a city, or another state.

The price we are being asked to pay to engage in economic revitalization is a heavy one. Perhaps too heavy. What is at stake is our most sacred commodity—our sovereignty, our right to control our destiny as governments.

Few people understand we are governments. This is because we have not had the resources to exercise our governmental rights or responsibilities. You can't get blood from a turnip, and you can't get taxes to run a government from poor people. Reservations are populated by poor people.

First, we needed a business to help individuals become self-sufficient through jobs, then we needed a source of revenue to fund the typical programs and services constituents of other governments take for granted. Gaming was our solution.

The only thing we have ever asked of the state is that we have a level playing field. That wasn't enough. We were naive. What we needed was a guarantee that everybody had to play by the same rules, and that the rules could not constantly change.

The governor said in 1995, 1996 and 1997, he could not negotiate or sign a compact without state authorization. We worked with the legislature to provide him just such a bill—twice. He vetoed both bills. Today, the governor has signed a compact without legislative approval or authorization in place, saying he really doesn't need it. How can you get to the goal post, when it keeps moving out of reach?

Would the city of El Cajon give up its right and responsibility to comply with the wishes and policy expressed by its voters to the demands of La Mesa? Would La Mesa City Hall give up its right to hire its own people, set their salaries, establish its own building codes and compliance, or make agreements with neighboring governments? I think not. Yet, the Viejas Government is being asked to do just that.

■ ■ ■

Article 5.1.4 of the Pala Compact expands the state's civil, criminal and regulatory jurisdiction to cover all persons and entities who are associated with the tribe's gaming operations. Obviously the state doesn't trust the FBI, because every Viejas employee associated with our gaming operations has an FBI background check and licensing by the National Indian Gaming Commission, charged along with tribes for regulating gaming.

Article 5.1.5 requires employees to pay a licensing fee to the state, the amount to be determined by the state. This would also amount to a business tax on our vendors and suppliers.

Article 5.1.7 states that employees denied a gaming license by the state, including tribal members, have no appeal or remedy.

Every business and every government would object to hav[ing] these terms dictated to them. We want to do everything it takes to prevent fraud or criminal activities in our gaming operations, we welcome help from the state. But, we do not need hindrance or unnecessary, costly duplication of our own strict controls through the office of our gaming commissioner, the National Indian Gaming Commission, the Federal Bureau of Investigation, the Justice Department, the Treasury Department and the Internal Revenue Service.

■ ■ ■

There is also the unknown factor. The factor of cost.

Assuming state regulation is $200,000 per tribe, that's $10 million for the state to regulate us. What the ultimate cost might be this year, or four years from now, cannot even be anticipated, let alone budgeted.

Currently, we pay the Federal Government to regulate and process tribal gaming employment applications, licenses, review of financial audits, allocation of earnings, etc. State regulation costs alone may drive us out of business.

■ ■ ■

One of the most onerous articles in the Pala Compact is number 15, the "County Participation Agreement." This article gives government control belonging to the Viejas Government to the county supervisors. The county has never had jurisdiction on tribal land, nor even wanted the responsibilities for providing for our people or services.

Now, even though we have no say about county zoning on our borders, or traffic, air or water pollution impact on our reservation, the [county] board of supervisors will have the right to force tribes to pay for environmental mitigation for every land use decision the tribe makes. The county will be given authority to approve building and design standards, the right to approve the location of any new gaming facility and "to protect the public health and safety from the activities of the tribe."

This makes me angry.

Historically, this reservation was created to protect us from genocide and a state and county policy of legalized slavery and extermination, and to keep us from causing any problems for those rushing to steal our land and homes. The county has never given tribes one dollar to build roads, garbage collection, fire services, or housing. And, we have never asked, because we choose to do without, rather than pay the price of intervention in our lives. In the 1950s, the Indians had to sue in this county for indigent health care, educational and other monies for Indian programs given to this state by the federal government that never resulted in Indian services.

In every case from water to health care, to criminal justice, and education, to our people's public safety, the tribes paid for it themselves, through the limited resources of the federal government, or went without. Mostly, we went without.

Now we are being told the county is needed to protect our customers and neighbors from our activities! We establish our own zoning and land use policies, the county has no place, right or reason to usurp this authority.

We comply with strict federal environmental law, BIA oversight, building codes, and our own policies, which are as strict, if not stricter, than those of the state or the county. But they are tailored to our circumstances, which are very unique, and are within our governmental jurisdiction according to federal law, policy, and court decisions.

This compact constitutes a radical and dangerous departure from the federal tribal relationship grounded in the Constitution, and reduces our governments to adjuncts of counties and states. The last time Indians were left to the mercy of the state and county, they were almost entirely exterminated. We have survived, accomplished economic and government renewal, without the aid of government, and in spite of state government. And we not only do not need, nor want other governments in our lives, but we fear it.

46 | The Distribution of Wealth, Sovereignty, and Culture through Indian Gaming

Naomi Mezey

POSTMODERN CONSUMERISM AND GAMING

■　■　■

From racetracks and lotteries to riverboat and reservation gambling to full-scale Las Vegas casinos, gambling has ballooned into a $30 billion industry,[1] and some form of legalized gambling now exists in every state except Utah and Hawaii.[2]

■　■　■

Growing gambling revenues have enormous redistributive potential, and state governments stand to be the predominant beneficiaries. But the potential for profit from a once-nefarious industry has engendered widespread debate about the growth of legalized gambling. Oddly enough, the eye of this political and rhetorical storm has centered on the relatively small take by Indian gaming. Of the $30 billion in gambling profits made in 1992, Indian gaming claimed less than 5 percent.[3] Nevertheless, the Indian right to game,[4] clarified by the passage of the Indian Gaming Regulatory Act (IGRA) in 1988,[5] has generated both enormous revenues and enormous controversy.

The federal right of Indians to run gambling operations on tribal land within limits set by state law brings the issues of tribal sovereignty and cultural identity into stark relief and reorients the debate about what kind of rights Native Americans might have or desire in the goods the IGRA redistributes.

From Naomi Mezey, "The Distribution of Wealth, Sovereignty, and Culture through Indian Gaming," *Stanford Law Review* 48 (1996): 711–16, 736–37. © 1996 by the Board of Trustees of the Leland Stanford Junior University.

■ ■ ■

First, to the extent the IGRA seeks to give a gaming right to all tribes without considering the external impediments to gaming profits many tribes face, it does not distribute the benefits of the gaming right equally. Second, to the extent the IGRA does not recognize either the heterogeneity of tribal cultures or the cultural choices gaming entails, it cannot distribute the benefits of gaming effectively. Gaming, with its concomitant postmodern consumerism, forces tribes that seek to engage in it to assess the commensurability of wealth, cultural identity, and sovereignty. In doing so, gaming complicates the distinction between the material and nonmaterial.

Finally, for tribes that choose to game under the IGRA, the choice may entail significant political constraints. By allocating some control of gaming rights to the states, the IGRA necessarily redistributes sovereignty. And by subjecting tribal gaming to federal regulation and oversight, the IGRA asks tribes to sacrifice some presumed sovereignty in exchange for a new federal right to exercise sovereignty. The federal entitlement of Native Americans to game on tribal lands does not implicate economic development policy and wealth distribution alone. By redistributing culture and sovereignty, the IGRA fuels the tribes' long battle for cultural survival and political autonomy.

GAMING AND REDISTRIBUTION

INDIAN POVERTY: THE NEED FOR ECONOMIC DEVELOPMENT

■ ■ ■

For some tribes, . . . [gaming] has fundamentally transformed their economies. For others, desperate economic conditions still prevail. And the IGRA plays out the same ironic and unintended consequences.

According to Stephen Cornell and Joseph Kalt, researchers with the Harvard Project on American Indian Economic Development, "American Indian reservations are notable for their extreme and persistent poverty—reservation Indians are the poorest minority in the United States."[6] More than 27 percent of all Native American households fall below the poverty line,[7] and in some tribes, such as the Navajo, more than 45 percent of families live in poverty.[8]

Indian reservations also experience overwhelming unemployment, with a national average of 46 percent in 1989.[9] The average masks a range from a low of 17 percent on the Jicarilla Apache Reservation in New Mexico to a high of 90 percent unemployment on the Rosebud Reservation in South Dakota.[10] The average rate of unemployment in 1989 for all races in the United States was 5 percent.[11] Of the sixty-seven reservations surveyed by the Bureau of Indian Affairs in 1989, twenty-nine had unemployment rates of 50 percent or higher.[12] Not surprisingly, there is a correspondingly high dependence among reservation Indians on transfer economies of public assistance and other governmental programs.[13]

GAMING AS DISTRIBUTION ON THE BASIS OF WHAT?

In presenting these rather bald statistics, I am not unaware of the larger constellation of social institutions and practices (both within tribes and between tribes and the federal government) into which such figures fit.[14] I have left these statistics free of causation claims partly because standing alone they convey the dramatic inequalities in wealth between most Native Americans and the rest of the nation. But this [essay] does consider whether these inequalities by themselves are sufficient to understand gaming as a new source of tribal wealth; in other words, is a federal entitlement to gaming on reservations an income distribution policy aimed ultimately at helping poor individuals, or does it distribute something else for other reasons?

There are a number of grounds on which Native Americans might base a claim for a federal right to game. The first is a standard individual rights claim to income based on wealth inequities and the redistributive potential of gaming. Yet running a gaming operation is neither an individual enterprise, nor does it guarantee that the profits will be distributed to individuals according to need.

The well-known historical injustices that amplify the meaning of the statistics on Indian poverty offer another explanation for the gaming entitlement: that it is a kind of reparations program directed at tribes as social groups that have suffered past injury at the hands of the government. In fact, American Indians may make the strongest case for Mari Matsuda's call for reparations as a group-based claim.[15] The historical abuses are well-documented, the victimized group is identifiable because it has remained largely unassimilated both culturally and geographically,[16] and the current members of the group continue to suffer harm in that the vitality of each tribe's cultural identity and autonomy is threatened by the social and economic desperation of reservation life.[17] Moreover, the present harms are causally connected to past wrongs. But a group claim based on past cultural wrongs raises the question of whether the form of the reparation—entitlement to reservation gaming—is not in fact an opportunity for further infliction of cultural harm.

The right of Native Americans to operate gambling facilities under either an individual rights claim to income or a group rights claim to reparations is a poor fit. The right does not function as an across-the-board wealth transfer because only those tribes that choose to open gaming operations, and then only those whose operations are profitable, actually benefit. In addition, to the extent a successful gaming operation invites an influx of outsiders, effects dramatic changes in the tribal economy, and brings about increased governmental scrutiny, it may entail cultural sacrifices that do not support a reparations claim based on harm to cultural vitality.

A third explanation of gaming rights sees them as redistributive under a different kind of group rights claim. According to this theory, gaming rights redistribute an opportunity to increase wealth, though not explicitly on the basis of a lack of wealth. Rather, the redistributive right arises from a group claim to sovereignty. Because of the historical sovereignty of Native Americans as a group, they have a right to operate gaming on tribal lands with limited state interference.[18]

■   ■   ■

SOME THOUGHTS ON INDIAN GAMING

■   ■   ■

Since the IGRA's enactment, gaming has become "the single largest source of economic activity for Indian tribes."[19] Tribal gaming grossed $1.5 billion in revenues in 1992,[20] and an estimated $4 billion in 1993.[21] While these figures represent a small percentage of the total profits from gambling nationwide,[22] they are particularly significant when compared to the poverty statistics for reservations. But the numbers hide two substantial problems with gaming as a mechanism for wealth redistribution.

The first problem is the scope of the distribution. If the IGRA means to benefit all Indians as a group, then the legislation is woefully inadequate to the task. Though some tribes profit handsomely, not all do, and most tribes do not profit at all. Of the 550 federally recognized tribes, only 91 of them operate high-stakes gaming facilities.[23] If Congress envisioned the individual tribes, rather than all Indians, as the IGRA's beneficiaries, then the Act is better suited to its goal. Yet it still fails to create a right to which all tribes have equal access. As a way to bridge the gap between tribes with respect to both access and actualization of profits, some people advocate an economic confederacy of gaming and nongaming tribes that pool their resources.[24] Because the trust status of tribal lands makes obtaining loans difficult, gaming tribes could at least make loans to nongaming tribes to support other economic development projects.[25] Others argue that tribes are distinct nations with distinct cultures and "[i]t's as unrealistic to expect one tribe to use its gaming proceeds to support another as it would be to ask the state of New York to share its lottery earnings with Hawaii."[26]

The second problem is one of instability. Even if the IGRA works well for the moment, which is questionable, it is tremendously short-sighted. Assuming states do not take over gaming by competing with tribes themselves, or prohibit gaming altogether, there remains the problem of saturation. Successes have already brought intense competition, and those casinos that are not in heavily populated areas are deeply dependent on the fluctuations of tourism. Economic dislocation is inevitable as the market for gaming levels out.[27]

The lesson is that most—though not all—cities, states and Indian tribes should resist the lure of the green felt and find other answers to their economic woes. The belief that every town or reservation can capture a lion's share of the tourist pot is as unrealistic as it is for players around a poker table.[28]

To exhaust the metaphor, the IGRA is gambling against some fundamental economic principles.

■   ■   ■

NOTES

1. Francis X. Clines, "Gambling, Pariah No More, Is Booming Across America," *New York Times*, December 5, 1993, p. A1. In addition to enormous revenues, widespread legalized gambling has created an estimated 500,000 jobs. Ibid.

2. Ibid.

3. *Implementation of Indian Gaming Regulatory Act: Oversight Hearing before the Subcommitte on Native American Affairs of the House Committee on Natural Resources*, 103d Congress, 1st Session (1993) pt. III, p. 73 [hereinafter Hearings] (statement of Will E. Cummings, Managing Director of Christiansen/Cummings Associates, Inc., on the "Gross Annual Wager" of the U.S.).

4. Indian tribes began gaming during the 1980s in an effort to generate revenues and to alleviate desperate economic conditions. See notes 6–13 below and accompanying text. This attempt to achieve economic self-sufficiency, however, brought the tribal nations into conflict with the states as each body claimed a sovereign right to control gaming. Litigation over this conflict signaled to Congress a need for federal intervention in the regulation of gaming on Indian lands. See, e.g., *California v. Cabazon Band of Mission Indians*, 480 U.S. 202 (1987) (limiting state regulatory power over Indian gaming).

5. 25 U.S.C. §§ 2701–2721 (1988). Under the IGRA, "Indian tribes have the exclusive right to regulate gaming activity on Indian lands if the gaming activity is not specifically prohibited by Federal law and is conducted within a State which does not, as a matter of criminal law and public policy, prohibit such gaming activity." Ibid. § 2701(5).

6. Stephen Cornell and Joseph P. Kalt, Malcolm Wiener Center for Social Policy, *Where's the Glue? Institutional Bases of American Indian Economic Development* 6 (Harvard Project on American Indian Economic Development, Report No. 52, 1991).

7. Gary Fields and Linda Karnamine, "Indian Data Shows 27% Live in Poverty," *USA Today*, November 17, 1994, p. A3 (citing 1990 Census).

8. Bureau of the Census, U.S. Department of Commerce, *1990 Census of Population: Characteristics of American Indians by Tribe and Language* (Washington, D.C.: U.S. Government Printing Office, 1994), tbl. 6, p. 197.

9. Cornell and Kalt, *Where's the Glue?* at tbl. 1 (citing Bureau of Indian Affairs, U.S. Department of the Interior, "Indian Service Population and Labor Force Estimates" [January 1989]). The statistics from the Bureau of Indian Affairs use the Bureau of Labor Statistics' definition of unemployment. Under this definition, unemployment figures count those who are unemployed but actively seeking work. If the figures included those who had given up on finding work, they would be much higher. Stephen Cornell and Joseph P. Kalt, Malcolm Wiener Center for Social Policy, *Pathways from Poverty: Development and Institution-Building on American Indian Reservations* 6 (Harvard Project on American Indian Economic Development, Report No. 32, 1989).

10. Cornell and Kalt, *Where's the Glue?* at tbl. 1.

11. See Cornell and Kalt, *Pathways from Poverty*, at tbl. 1.

12. Cornell and Kalt, *Where's the Glue?* at tbl. 1.

13. See Bureau of the Census, *1990 Census of Population: Characteristics of American Indians*, tbl. 6, p. 182.

14. See Michael J. Piore, "Historical Perspectives and the Interpretation of Unemployment," *Journal of Economic Literature* 25 (1987): 1834.

15. See Mari J. Matsuda, "Looking to the Bottom: Critical Legal Studies and Reparations," *Harvard Civil Rights–Civil Liberties Law Review* 22 (1987): 323, 362.

16. One of the standard doctrinal objections to group-based reparations claims stems from a perceived inability to identify the perpetrators and the victims. Ibid., pp. 374–80.

17. Reparations claims should be based on continuing stigma and economic harm. Ibid., pp. 380–85.

18. Given the federal government's role as paternal trustee, it is not clear that the claim based on group sovereignty operates independently of blatant wealth inequities.

19. 141 *Congressional Record* § 3401 (daily ed., March 2, 1995) (statement of Sen. Mc-Cain).

20. Hearings, pt. III, p. 77 (testimony of Will E. Cummings, Managing Director, Christiansen/Cummings Assoc., Inc.).

21. 141 *Congressional Record* § 3401 (daily ed., March 2, 1995) (statement of Sen. Mc-Cain).

22. Ben Campbell notes that Indian gaming revenues relative to the national total are far smaller than the media portrays them to be. Ben Campbell, "Indian Gaming Is No Economic Panacea," *Denver Post*, December 26, 1994, p. 7B.

23. Ibid.

24. Conversation with Justice Raymond Austin, Navajo Supreme Court, in Stanford, Calif. (March 16, 1995).

25. Ibid.

26. Campbell, "Indian Gaming Is No Panacea," p. 7B.

27. See, e.g., William R. Eadington, "Casinos Are No Economic Cure-All," *New York Times*, June 13, 1993, p. F13.

28. Ibid.

Suggested Readings

Anaya, S. James. *Indigenous Peoples in International Law*. New York: Oxford University Press, 1996.

Carrillo, Jo, ed. *Readings in American Indian Law: Recalling the Rhythm of Survival*. Philadelphia: Temple University Press, 1998.

Deloria, Vine, Jr. *Custer Died for Your Sins*. New York: Macmillan, 1969.

Fortunate Eagle, Adam. *Alcatraz! Alcatraz! The Indian Occupation of 1969–1971*. Berkeley, Calif.: Heyday Books, 1992.

Hoxie, Frederick E., ed. *Encyclopedia of North American Indians*. New York: Houghton Mifflin, 1996.

Lieder, Michael, and Jake Page. *Wild Justice*. New York: Random House, 1997.

Mankiller, Wilma Pearl. *Mankiller: A Chief of Her People*. New York: St. Martin's Press, 1993.

Marks, Paula Mitchell. *In a Barren Land*. New York: William Morrow, 1998.

Matsuda, Mari J. "Looking to the Bottom: Critical Legal Studies and Reparations." *Harvard Civil Rights–Civil Liberties Law Review* 22 (1987): 323.

Rhea, Joseph Tilden. *Race Pride and the American Identity*. Cambridge: Harvard University Press, 1998.

Shattuck, Petra T., and Jill Norgren. *Partial Justice: Federal Indian Law in a Liberal Constitutional System*. New York: Berg Publishers, 1991.

Smith, Paul Chaat, and Robert Allen Warrior. *Like a Hurricane: The Indian Movement from Alcatraz to Wounded Knee*. New York: New Press, 1996.

Williams, Robert A., Jr. *The American Indian in Western Legal Thought: The Discourses of Conquest*. New York: Oxford University Press, 1990.

6 | Slavery

Introduction

47 | Not Even an Apology?

Roy L. Brooks

Few today would condone human bondage or fail to see the stain slavery has left on the American moral character. Nor would many Americans spurn the ideal of justice and atonement for wrongdoing. Nevertheless, the slavery redress movement has met resistance at every turn. Unlike the atrocities addressed elsewhere in this book, the question of whether an official apology for slavery should be issued has not been settled, not to mention the critical question of whether the U.S. government should pay reparations for its involvement in slavery. Although these issues have been debated extensively, the federal government has been reluctant to issue an apology, let alone provide reparations for an era generally regarded as one of the most shameful in all of history.

Distinguished judge and legal scholar A. Leon Higginbotham, Jr., opens Part 6 with a description of the precarious legal status of blacks during the colonial period. Beginning with their arrival in 1619, blacks experienced steadily decreasing social, political, and economic freedom, eventually leading to legal enslavement. Even in more progressive colonies, such as Massachusetts, the ownership of slaves was a right protected by law.

This downward spiral in the sociolegal status of blacks was enshrined in the infamous case of *Dred Scott v. Sandford,* which follows Higginbotham's chapter. In *Dred Scott,* the Supreme Court affirmed the view that blacks were not intended by our Founding Fathers to be protected by the Constitution. Blacks, Chief Justice Roger Taney ruled, were "beings of an inferior order . . . unfit to associate with the white race" and, as such, "they had no rights which the white man was bound to respect." Accordingly, "the negro might justly and lawfully be reduced to slavery for his benefit." The Supreme Court's articulation of the status of blacks in decisions such as *Dred Scott* not only justified chattel slavery on legal and constitutional grounds, but also effectively placed the federal government's imprimatur on human bondage.

Contrary to the testimonials of some "benevolent" slaveholders, such as Confederate president Jefferson Davis, the typical slave experience was a nightmarish and demeaning one that took a tremendous personal toll on victims and their descendants. The narratives presented here provide a glimpse into the slave's world, where appalling living conditions and psychological, emotional, and physical persecution were the norm.

Analogous to Ruth Levor's account of the lingering effects the Holocaust has had on survivors and subsequent generations, Jennifer Fleischner finds a similar connection in slave and free black narratives. Fleischner's insightful essay provides an analysis of the complex family relationships that have caused the psychological legacy of slavery to be passed from one generation to the next. Based on a reading of Harriet Jacobs's 1861 narrative, Fleischner argues that although slaveholders attempted to break the chain of memory by urging slaves to "never think of it," it was only by facing these memories that slaves—and subsequent generations—could (and can) regain their "selves."

Fleischner focuses on portions of an 1879 narrative of a freeborn daughter of emancipated slaves, Julia A. J. Foote, to illustrate the maternal inheritance of slavery's memories, including beatings, running away, and lynchings. Although Foote was born free, many of her experiences parallel those of her mother. But while Foote's mother is unable to free herself from these memories—and in turn almost "enslaves" her daughter—Fleischner argues that Foote is able to rewrite her mother's slavery experience by refusing to submit to those who would chain her down. She will not ignore the past—the chain of memories that is the legacy of slavery—but neither will she submit to what Orlando Patterson calls the cult of victimology.

James Grahame, an English barrister who lived in America during the slavery era, offers poignant observations about the experiences of free blacks during the antebellum years. Grahame's critique chastises the South's efforts to restrict the freedoms of blacks, including the prohibition of black education and the denigrating treatment both slaves and free blacks received. In the North, where slavery had ceased to be a viable economic option, free blacks were similarly denied social and legal equality with whites. The North's treatment of blacks, in fact, tended to parallel that of the South. Free blacks were denied citizenship and the right to vote and were the subjects of "degradation *inevitable and incurable.*"

Joe R. Feagin and Eileen O'Brien discuss the growing redress movement and its two core goals: an apology and reparations. Although claims for redress have been pressed for more than a century, the movement did not gain significant momentum until the escalation of the civil rights movement in the 1950s and 1960s. Since the rise of black activism in the 1960s, calls for reparations (such as James Forman's 1969 "Black Manifesto," which demanded the economic rehabilitation of the African American infrastructure) have occupied a more prominent place in the American dialogue on race, especially among mainstream African American leaders (such as Rep. John Conyers [D-Mich.] and the NAACP) and a few white neoconservatives (such as Charles Krauthammer). Organizations such as the National Coalition of Blacks for Reparations in America (commonly known as N'COBRA) have brought the redress issue to the forefront of contemporary discussion by filing lawsuits. For example, N'COBRA has demanded the present-day equivalent of the "forty acres and a mule" promised by the federal government during Reconstruction. Despite increasing public consciousness and support from mainstream groups, the redress movement is still viewed by many as a radical or fringe concern. This image of the movement has hampered its efforts to gain an apology or reparations for slavery.

The merits of the redress movement's fundamental components—an apology and reparations—are taken up in the remainder of Part 6. James Grahame, in his 1842 book, *Who Is to Blame? Or Cursory Review of "American Apology for American Accession to Negro Slavery,"* offers what may be one of the first recorded demands for an apology for slavery. Grahame criticizes the United States for its hypocrisy in celebrating principles of individual liberty, while the North smugly condoned, and the South brazenly defended, human bondage. In his scathing indictment of American society, Grahame declares, "In no age or country have tyrannical invaders and usurpers of other men's rights been without apologies and apologists." Grahame suggests that southerners knew in their hearts that slavery was an unquestionably immoral institution, but found its abolition too inconvenient and too contrary to their material interests.

But why should the federal government issue an official apology now, some 130 years after slavery has ended? Rep. Tony Hall (D-Ohio) attempts to answer this question in chapter 55. In 1997, Hall sponsored House Concurrent Resolution 96, calling on the federal government to apologize for slavery. The apology itself is a simple, symbolic gesture that does not provide for monetary compensation. Yet, as Hall argues, it has deep meaning to both the apologizers and those who have been wronged. But, as Camille Paglia contends in her essay, symbolic gestures are devoid of any meaningful importance to African Americans. As Paglia argues, rather than benefiting African Americans, an official apology for slavery, taken alone, would serve to tether African Americans to the "bankruptcy" of identity politics; they would continue to identify with, and be identified as, former slaves. Paglia suggests that African Americans should instead concentrate their efforts on substantive reforms, rather than dwell on the past.

Hall and Paglia also disagree on a related question: Why should the government offer an apology to those who were not slaves themselves? Hall asserts that an apology is fundamental to racial reconciliation and rebuilding, all the while acknowledging the absence of privity between victim and perpetrator—no slaves or slaveholders are alive today. Hall, who is white, argues that the lingering effects of slavery and the necessity of atoning for a past wrong justify an apology. Taking a different approach, Paglia argues that because most people in the United States today have no direct connection to slavery, they bear no responsibility for it. An apology can only come from those who committed the acts in question. Our current government did not itself engage in slavery; thus, a formal apology from that government does not logically follow. Hall counters with the observation that Congress *as an institution* bears much responsibility for perpetuating slavery, and must make amends to form the groundwork for social healing. Finally, Hall sees privity as a nonissue given, for example, the government's recent apology to native Hawaiians for its participation in the overthrow of the Kingdom of Hawaii more than a hundred years ago.

The issue of an apology for slavery has resulted in an interesting alliance between Paglia and President Bill Clinton. As chapter 56 shows, President Clinton has strongly opposed issuing an apology for fear that its legal and social implications would not be in the country's best interest. A formal apology, he believes, could increase pressure to pay reparations and could inflame racial tensions.

African participation in the slave trade further complicates the movement toward redress. Paglia argues that if any apology from the federal government is to be given, it must be accompanied by apologies from all African nations that took part in the slave trade as well. Howard W. French, a celebrated *New York Times* correspondent, seems to agree that an apology is due from both sides of the Atlantic. However, French notes the particularly devastating effects of the transatlantic slave trade. He argues that although slavery existed in Africa before the intervention of Europeans, the European slave trade, unhampered by ethical conventions that constrained African slavery, devalued human life to a much greater degree. Furthermore, European demand for African slaves sparked rampant predatory behavior among African societies, motivating them to capture and sell Africans on a scale never seen before. In a strange twist of logic, this wholesale trade in human flesh by Africans negatively shaped European perceptions of Africans. Africans were viewed as savages, and the slave trade was thereby deemed to be morally acceptable.

Although the apology question is not new, fundamental disagreements and misperceptions persist. Robert S. McElvaine's chapter first appeared as an op-ed piece in the *Los Angeles Times* in 1997 and generated thousands of angry responses—a testimony to the controversy surrounding the apology question. McElvaine debunks the popular notion that the North's motive for fighting the Civil War was to free the slaves, and thus, that it was tantamount to an apology for slavery. Equally inaccurate is the related belief, held mostly by what McElvaine calls "neo-confederates," that the South fought to protect liberty and "states' rights." In fact, McElvaine maintains, the North fought to preserve the Union, while the South fought to deny the slaves' liberty and to preserve its way of life. Consequently, the North's participation in the Civil War cannot be seen as an apology for slavery, and the South's participation can only be seen as a defense of slavery. Even so, some, such as attorney Thomas Geoghegan, insist that an official apology for slavery is unnecessary because it has already been issued in Abraham Lincoln's Second Inaugural Address. Clearly, the apology question is far from resolved.

The final component of the slavery redress movement concerns reparations, usually in the form of atonement money, although other forms of reparations, such as affirmative action, are sometimes mentioned. This portion of the reparations movement is in many ways derived from Special Field Order No. 15. Issued near the end of the Civil War as Union troops led by General William Tecumseh Sherman burned a path through the South, the order was intended to destabilize the southern economy by authorizing newly freed slaves to settle liberated Confederate territory. The order was understood to be the federal government's pledge of "forty acres and a mule" for each black settler, but this deal was never carried out.

Present-day attempts to revive the promise of "forty acres and a mule" have met with little success. Each year since 1988, the Honorable John Conyers of Michigan has proposed House Resolution 40, its numerical designation a respectful reference to the "forty acres and a mule" slogan. The resolution, however, has never even made it out of committee. Regardless of its success, it is significant because it urges the formation of a congressional commission to study the reparations proposals for African Americans and addresses the apology question.

Opposition to reparations has not been limited to Congress. Law student Mary E. Smith analyzes both conservative and liberal opposition to the reparations movement, finding significant resistance across political lines. Although President Clinton has publicly conceded the residual effects of slavery, he has also advanced the major argument against reparations—lack of privity. Rather than reparations, President Clinton prefers a policy of reconciliation to erase the present effects of past racial discrimination. But can reconciliation be achieved without reparations? This is the question Smith asks.

The final two chapters in Part 6 provide some insight into the practical and legal problems that could derail the black reparations movement. Darrell L. Pugh begins with an examination of the potential problems surrounding the administration of reparations payments. Two areas are central to the analysis: the amount to be paid per capita and the form of distribution. Pugh theorizes that monetary reparations could be calculated in a manner sensitive to the income gap between blacks and whites, similar to a formula first proposed in Boris I. Bittker's book, *The Case for Black Reparations*. After calculating the amount of funds to be paid, Pugh considers whether payments should be distributed individually or collectively. He argues that to the extent that individual payments would likely be expended as personal consumption, and in a sense "wasted," collective reparations in the form of community investment and institutional rebuilding may be the more desirable method of distribution. To the extent that Paglia's argument that rehabilitative reparations make more sense than offering a mere apology can be read as an argument for a particular form of reparations (which I doubt it can), there is agreement between Paglia and Pugh.

While Pugh is mostly concerned with the logistics of reparations, Bittker and I probe the critical issue concerning the constitutionality of monetary reparations. We argue that the issue is problematic because recent Supreme Court cases, culminating in *Adarand Constructors, Inc. v. Peña*, approach the issue from the "color-blind" racial perspective that results in the application of the almost-fatal "strict scrutiny" standard of review to race-based compensatory legislation. But there is also legal support for black reparations. Such support comes less from the recent case of *Jacobs v. Barr,* which upheld the constitutionality of monetary reparations for Japanese Americans to the exclusion of German and Italian Americans (see Part 4 for the case and a discussion), than from the Supreme Court's affirmative action cases. These cases uphold the constitutionality of race-specific measures designed to redress a public institution's past discrimination. This rule could result in the beneficiary of the remedy and the victim of the discrimination being different persons, decades apart. Accordingly, extant caselaw may resolve the most serious legal challenge to black reparations (an issue not presented in *Jacobs v. Barr*): namely, the lack of privity between victim and perpetrator.

The privity issue might also be resolved through the enactment of redress legislation patterned after a famous civil rights statute, Title VII, which provides relief to victims of employment discrimination. Interpreting Title VII, the Supreme Court has held that courts may award preferential, race-conscious remedies that benefit nonvictims. Hence, it is not unprecedented in American law for there to be a separation between the victims of institutional discrimination and the beneficiaries of remedial legislation.

The Slave and the Free
Black Experience

48 | The Legal Status of African Americans during the Colonial Period

A. Leon Higginbotham, Jr.

VIRGINIA: AN EVALUATION

After the first blacks landed in 1619, they had an uncertain legal status for at least four decades. But as the years passed the freedom of blacks decreased and the deprivations they were forced to endure were transformed into legal dogma. By 1705 Virginia had rationalized, codified, and judicially affirmed its exclusion of blacks from any basic concept of human rights under the law. After the 1705 slave code, Virginia made several revisions, in acts passed in 1710, 1723, 1726, 1727, 1732, 1744, 1748, 1753, 1765, 1769, 1778, 1782, 1785, 1787, 1789, and 1792.[1] The 1792 act was the last and most comprehensive codification of the slave codes in eighteenth-century Virginia. Yet, from 1705 to 1792 there was no change of substantial significance to improve the status of slaves or free blacks.

In 1723, for instance, a free Negro or mulatto who was a housekeeper could keep one gun "[a]nd . . . all negroes, mullattoes or Indians bond or free, living at any frontier plantation [were] permitted to keep and use guns."[2] In this respect Virginia was not as restrictive as some other colonies and states. A 1769 provision banned the dismemberment of blacks because it was often "disproportioned to the offense and contrary to the principles of humanity";[3] nevertheless, the statute authorized the castration of any slave who attempted to ravish a white woman, but it had no similar provision when white men either attempted to or in fact ravished black women.[4]

From A. Leon Higginbotham, Jr., *In the Matter of Color: Race and the American Legal Process: The Colonial Period* (Oxford: Oxford University Press, 1978), pp. 58, 98–99, 252–55, 262–63. © 1978 by Oxford University Press, Inc. Used by permission of Oxford University Press, Inc.

In proceedings involving solely blacks, blacks were allowed to testify in court. But their testimony was admissible only against blacks.[5] No white man could ever be found guilty of a crime on the word of a black person.[6]

Thus, even upon reading all the late eighteenth-century legislative modifications in the light most favorable to Virginia, the pattern of debasement and degradation remains. The black slaves' plight was one of daily imposition of brutality by the laws which sanctioned his enslavement; no part of the legal process was his ally, the courts not his sanctuary. . . .

■ ■ ■

MASSACHUSETTS: AN EVALUATION

Perhaps, as some historians have suggested, Massachusetts colonists spoke out in moral outrage against the institution of slavery in 1636. Yet, ownership of human property was endorsed by the power structure, for throughout the colonial period statutes sanctioned the ownership of human beings and the colonial courts protected the masters' ownership interests. Merchants from Massachusetts, the most vigorous slave traders in the New World, made enormous profits from the slave trade. Judicial records are scarce, but those available reveal the prevalence of slavery in the colony.

The institution of slavery remained ambivalently defined in colonial Massachusetts, however. The earliest cases and statutes suggest that at first slavery was viewed as punishment for criminal conduct. Slaves, who were sometimes white, were generally not thought to be perpetually bound to serve. But with succeeding decades, enslavement became perpetual for nonwhites. By 1700 slavery had evolved into a racially identifiable institution. Blacks were imported into the colony as perpetual chattel slaves; Indians were captured and made perpetual slaves. Color itself began to indicate a separate, and lower, social class; free nonwhites were statutorily limited in their movements and in the occupations they could pursue. Despite these deprivations, one factor was crucial and must not be omitted; the nonwhite population in Massachusetts never lost the right and ability to seek judicial determination of the legitimacy of their individual enslavement.

Domestic slavery never assumed the economic importance in Massachusetts that it had in the more southern colonies. In fact, a combination of this lack of economic dependence on the institution, an expanding white labor population, a nonwhite population able and eager to sue for its freedom in the courts, and a burgeoning moral and intellectual commitment to political and economic liberty contributed to the increase in the number of nonwhites who were granted their freedom.

The political milieu that produced much of the revolutionary ferment during the War of Independence aided the blacks and Indians enslaved in Massachusetts to obtain their freedom either through manumission or through the courts. Moreover, this milieu resulted in a 1780 constitution with a Declaration of Rights which, if read literally, prohibited slavery in the new state. This interpretation was adopted and sustained by the Chief Justice of the Massachusetts Supreme Court in his 1783 charge to the jury in the *Quock Walker* case. Admittedly, slavery continued after the *Quock Walker* decision; judicial decrees tend to affect immediately only the rights of the litigants involved in the case. However, by judicial activism, the state of Massachusetts signaled that it would no longer protect the legality of slavery, regardless of social custom.

■ ■ ■

THE SLAVE CODES OF GEORGIA

THE 1755 SLAVE CODE

In 1755 royal Georgia passed its first law comprehensively regulating the status of slaves, entitled "An Act for the Better Ordering and Governing Negroes and Other Slaves in This Province."[7] This law, along with several others passed at the same time, immediately adopted many of the restrictions on slaves that had taken decades to develop in South Carolina and Virginia.

The contrast between the 1755 law and the 1750 law is dramatic. The new law increased the number of slaves that could be legally held on each plantation. It ended the protection of a slave's life by adding a host of special justifications and reduced penalties for the murder of a slave. It created numerous new crimes for which slaves could be executed and placed strict limitation on slaves' everyday activities and movements. It introduced procedural requirements in a slave's suit for freedom, which made it difficult for a slave ever to gain his freedom. Georgia was quickly and tragically catching up with the slave colonies immediately to her north.

The very first provision of the new law exemplified the greater hostility that would characterize the remainder of the code toward blacks. While the 1750 law had *permitted* the enslavement of blacks, the 1755 act established at the outset a firm presumption in favor of the enslavement of *all* blacks and certain Indians.

> [A]ll Negroes Indians (free Indians in Amity with this Government and Negroes Mulatos or Mestizos who are now free Excepted) Mulatos or Mestizos who now are or shall hereafter be in this Province and all their Issue and offspring Born or to be Born shall be and they are hereby declared to be and remain for ever hereafter absolute Slaves and shall follow the Condition of the Mother and shall be deemed in Law to be Chattels personal in the Hands of their Owners and possessors and their Executors Administrators and Assigns to all intents and purposes whatsoever.[8]

A later provision indicated that Georgia slaves could theoretically gain their freedom, since it gave white "guardians" of slaves the right to prosecute a slave's suit for freedom. Unfortunately, the provision implied that slaves could not institute such suits without a guardian.[9] Moreover, the burden of the proof lay upon the plaintiff. It was "always presumed that every Negro Indian Mulato and Mestizo is a Slave unless the Contrary can be made appear (the Indians in Amity with this Government Excepted) in which Case the burthen of the proof shall lie on the Defendant."[10] If the slave lost the suit, the court could "Inflict such Corporal punishment not Extending to Life or Limb of the [slave] as they in their Discretion shall think fit."[11] Thus, the law proclaimed that all blacks were to be considered slaves; required slaves to secure a guardian to prosecute a suit for their freedom; placed the legal burden of proof on slaves to demonstrate that they were not slaves; and subjected slaves to corporal punishment if they unsuccessfully prosecuted a suit under this extra burden.

■   ■   ■

Protection of the Slave's Life under the Code

The life of the slave was no longer protected by the laws of England, as it had been under the 1750 trustee law. In the case where a person "willfully" murdered his own or another person's slave he was merely "adjudged guilty of Felony for the first Offense and [had] the Benefit of the Clergy making Satisfaction to the Owner of such Slave.[12] Only on the second offense of *willful* murder did the "offender Suffer for the said Crime according to the Laws of England except that he shall forfeit no more of his Lands and Tenements Goods and Chattels than what may be Sufficient to Satisfy the owner of such Slave so killed as aforesaid."[13] Conviction for willful murder of a slave also required after 1755 the "oath of two witnesses," an extremely difficult burden of evidence for most criminal prosecutions.[14]

In other circumstances, the new law reduced or even eliminated the penalty for killing a slave because the murderer was supposedly justified or excused. A defendant merely forfeited fifty pounds sterling if he killed his own or another person's slave "on a Sudden heat or Passion or by undue Correction."[15] He received no penalty if he killed a slave who refused to "undergo examination" outside his master's property and assaulted and struck the white person.[16]

■   ■   ■

Assaults on Slaves

The assembly expressed their "humanitarian" concerns for blacks by providing that if any person

> wilfully cut the Tongue put out the Eye Castrate or Cruelly Scald burn or deprive
> any Slave of any Limb or Member or shall inflict any other Cruel punishment other
> than by whipping or beating with a Horse Whip Cow Skin Switch or Small Stick or

by putting Irons on or Confining or Imprisoning such Slave every such person shall for every such Offence forfeit the Sum of Ten pounds Sterling.[17]

However, in those rare instances when such cruelty could be proven, the maximum penalty was merely a fine. Furthermore, the acts of whipping or beating, even if done cruelly, were not crimes under this provision.[18] The statute added another fine of six shillings if a slave was "beaten Bruised Maimed or Disabled" at the hands of "any person or persons not having sufficient Cause or Lawfull Authority for so doing." In such cases the master was entitled to reimbursement for his economic loss. However, these cruel acts of bruising, maiming, or disabling became a crime only when perpetrated without the master's authorization. Thus, the determining factor was not the slave's well-being, but solely whether an outsider was damaging the master's economic interest in the slave.[19]

■　■　■

THE 1765 AND 1770 SLAVE CODES

While most of the provisions in the main 1755 slave law were continued in the 1765 and 1770 slave laws, both of those later laws introduced several harsher provisions that progressively tightened the restraints on blacks.[20] The greatest number of changes appeared in the new list of capital crimes that could be committed by "slaves, free negroes, Indians, mulattoes, or mestizoes." Both the 1765 and 1770 laws held that it was a capital offense for a slave, free black, mulatto, or mestizo to fail to reveal "the furnishing, procuring, or conveying of any poison to be administered to any person"; to "teach or instruct another Slave in the Knowledge of any Poisonous Root, Plant, Herb, or other sort of a poison whatever"; or to be convicted for the *second* time of striking a white person.[21] A slave who was "convicted of having given false information, whereby any other slave may have suffered wrongfully" would "suffer the same punishment as was inflicted upon the party accused," including death.[22]

Under the 1770 statute any slave, free black, mulatto, mestizo, or Indian (not in amity with the government) could be executed if he should attempt to rape or rape any white person; "break open, burn or destroy any dwelling house or other building whatsoever"; or be "accomplices, aiders, and abettors" of anyone who did.[23] The 1770 law also made several capital crimes, which had formerly pertained only to slaves, applicable to free blacks, mulattoes, mestizos, and some Indians.[24]

Many of the modest protections of slaves written into the 1755 code were dropped from the 1765 and 1770 laws. After 1765, there was no requirement that a slave's work day be limited to sixteen hours or that he be provided with "sufficient" food and clothing. After 1770 the provision shifting the burden of proof in certain cases to the person accused of assaulting a slave disappeared. The 1755 limitation on the permissible number of slaves for each white servant on a plantation was modified by both laws to permit more slaves.[25]

A few new provisions in the 1765 and 1770 laws were a marginal improvement for blacks. One provided that a person convicted for the first time of willfully killing a slave should, in addition to paying the fine imposed in the 1755 law, be "forever uncapable of holding any place of Trust, or exercising, enjoying or receiving the profits of any Office, place or employment, civil or Military within this Province."[26] Another unique provision contained in the 1765 law but dropped in 1770 provided that mulattoes and mestizos born outside Georgia should under certain circumstances be admitted into Georgia with many of the rights of British citizens.[27] This relatively benign statutory policy toward mulattoes was a sign of the new colony's uncertain military position. The threat of slave or Indian uprisings as well as external attack made the immigration of free mulattoes seem militarily advantageous to the Georgia legislators. Unfortunately, the provision never aided mulattoes since no one was ever naturalized during the life of the act. When the legislators wrote the 1770 slave law they dropped the protection from the code.[28]

■ ■ ■

NOTES

1. William W. Hening, *Statutes at Large; being a Collection of all the Laws of Virginia* (Richmond, Va.: Franklin Press, 1823), Chapters 16, 17 (1710), vol. 3, pp. 537–540; Chapter 4 (1723), vol. 4, pp. 126–134; Chapter 4 (1726), vol. 4, pp. 169–175; Chapter 15 (1727), vol. 4, pp. 222–228; Chapter 3 (1732), vol. 4, pp. 317–321; Chapter 6 (1732), vol. 4, pp. 324–325; Chapter 7 (1732), vol. 4, pp. 325–326; Chapter 12 (1744), vol. 5, p. 244; Chapter 13 (1744), vol. 5, pp. 244–245; Chapter 32 (1748), vol. 6, p. 31; Chapter 2 (1748), vol. 5, pp. 432–439; Chapter 14 (1748), vol. 5, pp. 547–558; Chapter 21 (1748), vol. 5, p. 38; Chapter 41 (1748), vol. 6, pp. 121–123; Chapter 38 (1748), vol. 6, pp. 104–112; Chapter 7 (1753), vol. 6, pp. 356–357; Chapter 24 (1765), vol. 8, pp. 133–137; Chapter 26 (1765), vol. 8, pp. 137–139; Chapter 27 (1769), vol. 8, pp. 374–377; Chapter 37 (1769), vol. 8, p. 393; Chapter 19 (1769), vol. 8, pp. 358–361; Chapter 1 (1778), vol. 9, pp. 471–472; Chapter 21 (1782), vol. 11, pp. 39–40; Chapter 32 (1782), vol. 11, p. 59; Chapter 78 (1785), vol. 12, p. 184; Chapter 78 (1786), vol. 12, p. 345; Chapter 22 (1787), vol. 12, p. 505; Chapter 37 (1787), vol. 12, p. 531; Chapter 45 (1789), vol. 13, p. 62. Samuel Shepherd, ed., *The Statutes at Large of Virginia*, Chapter 41 (1792), vol. 1, pp. 122–130; Chapter 42 (1792), vol. 1, pp. 130–136.

2. Hening, *Statutes*, vol. 4, p. 131.

3. Ibid., vol. 9, p. 358.

4. Ibid.

5. Shepherd, *Statutes at Large*, Chapter 41, vol. 1, p. 123.

6. The statute limits the admissibility of testimony by blacks to those situations where either a criminal charge is brought against another black or in the case of civil suits to those in which blacks *alone* are parties.

7. Albert Saye, *New Viewpoints in Georgia History* (Athens: University of Georgia Press, 1943), pp. 102–143.

8. Allen D. Candler, ed., *Colonial Records of Georgia* (Atlanta: Franklin Printing and Publishing Co., 1904), vol. 18, pp. 102–103 (hereafter cited as CROG).

9. Ibid., p. 103.

10. Ibid., p. 104.

11. Ibid. However, "if Judgment shall be given for the plaintiff a Special Entry shall be made declaring that the Ward of the Plaintiff is free and the Jury shall assess Damages which the Plaintiffs Ward hath sustained and the court shall give Judgment and award Execution Against the Defendant for such Damages with full Costs of Suit." Ibid., pp. 103–104.

12. Benefit of clergy originally meant the exemption of clergymen from the secular courts. Afterward it came to mean an exemption from the punishment of death and was extended to "clerks" or those who could read. The privilege greatly mitigated the criminal law, but led to such abuse that Parliament began to enact that certain felonies should be without benefit of clergy. See June Purcell Guild, *Black Laws of Virginia*, reprint edition (New York: Negro University Press, 1969), p. 154n. 2.

13. CROG, vol. 18, p. 132.

And in case any shall not be able to make the Satisfaction hereby required every such person shall be sent to any Frontier Garrison of this province or committed to the Goal at Savannah and there to remain at the public Expence for the Space of Seven years and to serve or to be kept to hard Labour and the pay usually allow'd by the public to the Soldiers of such Garrison or the profits of the Labour of the Offender shall be paid to the owner of the Slave murdered. (Ibid.)

14. Ibid., p. 132. However, if there were no reliable white witnesses, this requirement might be waived and the burden of proof shifted to the defendant charged with murdering the slave. CROG, p. 134.

15. Ibid., p. 132.

16. Ibid., pp. 105–106. A white person could "moderately correct" any slave who refused to be searched while outside his master's property. Ibid.

17. Ibid., vol. 18, pp. 132–133.

18. Ibid. Another provision implicitly gave a master the right to brand his slaves. Ibid., p. 120.

19. Ibid., pp. 106–107.

20. Technically, the 1765 law was never officially approved by the governor, though it served as the Georgia Slave Code until the passage of the 1770 law.

21. Ibid., vol. 18, pp. 661, 662–663, 669–670; CROG, vol. 19, part 1, pp. 221–223, 228–229.

22. CROG, vol. 18, p. 662; CROG, vol. 19, part 1, p. 222.

23. CROG, vol. 19, part 1, p. 220.

24. Any slave, free black, mulatto, or Indian (not in amity with the government) "shall . . . thereof suffer death" if "he shall be guilty of homicide of any sort upon any white person," except if the act was committed by "misadventure, or in defense of his or her owner or other person under whose care and government such slave shall be." The sentence of death would also be imposed if he shall "delude or entice any slave or slaves to run away" so that the owner was or would have been "deprived" of the slaves; or "shall raise or attempt to raise any insurrection." CROG, vol. 19, part 1, p. 220.

25. Compare CROG, vol. 18, p. 137 (1755) with Ibid., vol. 18, pp. 685–686 (1765) and CROG, vol. 19, part 1, pp. 245–246 (1770).

26. CROG, vol. 18, p. 682; CROG, vol. 19, part 1, p. 244.

All Persons male and Female of what Nation or Colour soever being born of free parents and now are or hereafter may come into this Province and give good Testimony of their humble duty and loyalty to his Majesty and their Obedience to the Laws and their Affection to the Inhabitants of this Province may be intituled to an Act of Assembly for Naturalizing them, and each of them, whereby they, their Wives, and Children may have, Use and enjoy, all the Rights, Privileges, Powers and Immunities whatsoever which any person born of British parents within this Province, may, can, might, could or of Right ought to have, Use or enjoy except to vote for or be Elected a Member to serve in the general Assembly of this Province and from thenceforth be adjudged, reputed and taken to be in every Condition, Respect and Degree as free to all Intents, Purposes and Constructions as if they had been and were born of British Parents within this Province, anything herein contained to the contrary Notwithstanding.

27. CROG, vol. 18, p. 659.

28. See Winthrop Jordan, *White over Black* (New York: W. W. Norton, 1968), pp. 169–171.

49 | African Americans under the Antebellum Constitution

Supreme Court of the United States

■ ■ ■

In the opinion of the court, the legislation and histories of the times, and the language used in the Declaration of Independence, show, that neither the class of persons who had been imported as slaves, nor their descendants, whether they had become free or not, were then acknowledged as a part of the people, nor intended to be included in the general words used in that memorable instrument.

It is difficult at this day to realize the state of public opinion in relation to that unfortunate race, which prevailed in the civilized and enlightened portions of the world at the time of the Declaration of Independence, and when the Constitution of the United States was framed and adopted. But the public history of every European nation displays it in a manner too plain to be mistaken.

They had for more than a century before been regarded as *beings of an inferior order* [emphasis added], and altogether unfit to associate with the white race, either in social or political relations; and so far inferior, that *they had no rights which the white man was bound to respect* [emphasis added]; and that the negro might justly and lawfully be reduced to slavery for his benefit. He was bought and sold, and treated as an ordinary article of merchandise and traffic, whenever a profit could be made by it. This opinion was at that time fixed and universal in the civilized portion of the white race. It was regarded as an axiom in morals as well as in politics, which no one thought of disputing, or supposed to be open to dispute; and men in every grade and position in society daily and habitually acted upon it in their private pursuits, as well as in matters of public concern, without doubting for a moment the correctness of this opinion.

From *Dred Scott v. Sandford*, 60 U.S. 393 (1856).

And in no nation was this opinion more firmly fixed or more uniformly acted upon than by the English Government and English people. They not only seized them on the coast of Africa, and sold them or held them in slavery for their own use; but they took them as ordinary articles of merchandise to every country where they could make a profit on them.

■　■　■

50 | Slave Narratives

Roy L. Brooks

If we were to listen only to slaveholders, we would be compelled to conclude that American slavery, that "peculiar institution," was benevolent. Jefferson Davis, the president of the Confederacy, certainly saw slavery in this fashion. Unlike most of his fellow slaveholders, Davis spoke from experience. Apparently, neither he nor his older brother, the patriarch of the family, mistreated slaves under their control. As one scholar has observed, "The slaves judged and punished themselves. Families were kept together." And, as one of Davis's slaves stated, "We had good grub and good clothes and nobody worked hard." Similarly, Davis treated his black body-servant "with exquisite courtesy and put him in charge of his plantation when he was away."[1]

The slave narratives, taken as a whole, paint a very different picture of slavery. These testimonies of ex-slaves give us a vivid view of the horrors of human bondage. They tell us without hesitation that slavery had no redeeming value. One narrative in particular, that of escaped slave turned abolitionist Frederick Douglass, most assuredly spoke for the vast majority of slaves:

> What, to the American slave, is your Fourth of July? I answer: a day that reveals to him, more than all other days in the year, the gross injustice and cruelty to which he is the constant victim. To him, your celebration is a sham; your boasted liberty, an unholy license; your national greatness, swelling vanity; your sounds of rejoicing are empty and heartless; your denunciation of tyrants, brass-fronted impudence; your shouts of liberty and equality, hollow mockery; your prayers and hymns, your sermons and thanksgivings, with all your religious parade and solemnity, are, to Him, mere bombast, fraud, deception, impiety, and hypocrisy—a thin veil to cover up crimes which would disgrace a nation of savages. There is not a nation of savages, there is not a nation on the earth guilty of practices more shocking and bloody than are the people of the United States at this very hour.[2]

Douglass's narrative is atypical in one important respect: he wrote it down himself. Most slave narratives were recorded by others. In addition, most slave narratives were collected during the first half of the nineteenth century and during the 1930s. These two collections, separated by generations, differ from one another in that the former narratives were recorded by white abolitionists who rewrote the interviews to conform to the literary standards of the day, whereas the latter were transcribed word-for-word by the Federal Writers' Project (FWP). The FWP was a federally funded program whose main objectives were to preserve the ex-slaves' language and speech patterns and to gather information about slavery. Slave narratives give us an inside view of slavery, from capture in Africa through emancipation in America.

Africans were taken into slavery through several methods. Kidnaping and tribal wars were the most common practices. Some tribal wars were staged for the sole purpose of capturing slaves. The victorious African chief would trade his prisoners to white slave traders for guns, ammunition, tobacco, liquor, and the like.[3]

We were alarmed one morning, just at the break of day, by the horrible uproar caused by mingled shouts of men, and blows given with heavy sticks, upon large wooden drums. The village was surrounded by enemies, who attacked us with clubs, long wooden spears, and bows and arrows. After fighting for more than an hour, those who were not fortunate enough to run away were made prisoners. It was not the object of our enemies to kill; they wished to take us alive and sell us as slaves. I was knocked down by a heavy blow of a club, and when I recovered from the stupor that followed, I found myself tied fast with the long rope I had brought from the desert. . . .

We were immediately led away from this village, through the forest, and were compelled to travel all day as fast as we could walk. . . . We traveled three weeks in the woods—sometimes without any path at all—and arrived one day at a large river with a rapid current. Here we were forced to help our conquerors to roll a great number of dead trees into the water from a vast pile that had been thrown together by high floods.

These trees, being dry and light, floated high out of the water; and when several of them were fastened together with the tough branches of young trees, [they] formed a raft, upon which we all placed ourselves, and descended the river for three days, when we came in sight of what appeared to me the most wonderful object in the world; this was a large ship at anchor in the river. When our raft came near the ship, the white people—for such they were on board—assisted to take us on the deck, and the logs were suffered to float down the river.

I had never seen white people before and they appeared to me the ugliest creatures in the world. The persons who brought us down the river received payment for us of the people in the ship, in various articles, of which I remember that a keg of liquor, and some yards of blue and red cotton cloth were the principal.

CHARLES BALL[4]

Although impossible to confirm, it is estimated that from 14 to 21 million Africans were pressed into slavery between the sixteenth and nineteenth centuries, that as many as one-third of them died resisting capture or struggling to survive the "middle passage," as the voyage to the Americas is commonly called. The middle passage was a "veritable nightmare." Slaves were packed in ships like sardines, disease was epidemic, and food was scarce and little more than garbage. Many committed suicide rather than endure the middle passage or live as slaves.[5]

[The ship's doctor] made the most of the room, and *wedged them in*. They had not so much room *as a man in his coffin*, either in length or breadth. It was impossible for them to turn or shift with any degree of ease. He had often occasion to go from one side of their room to the other, in which case he always *took off his shoes*, but could not avoid pinching them; he has the marks on his feet where they bit and scratched him. In every voyage when the ship was full they complained of heat and want of air. Confinement in this situation was so injurious that he has known them *go down apparently in good health at night and found dead in the morning*. On his last voyage he opened a stout man who so died. He found the contents of the thorax and abdomen healthy, and therefore concludes *he died of suffocation in the night*.

NAME UNKNOWN[6]

At the time we came into this ship, she was full of black people, who were all confined in a dark and low place, in irons. The women were in irons as well as the men.

About twenty persons were seized in our village at the time I was; and amongst these were three children so young that they were not able to walk or to eat any hard substance. The mothers of these children had brought them all the way with them and had them in their arms when we were taken on board this ship.

When they put us in irons to be sent to our place of confinement in the ship, the men who fastened the irons on these mothers took the children out of their hands and threw them over the side of the ship into the water. When this was done, two of the women leaped overboard after the children—the third was already confined by a chain to another woman and could not get into the water, but in struggling to disengage herself, she broke her arm and died a few days after of a fever. One of the two women who were in the river was carried down by the weight of her irons before she could be rescued; but the other was taken up by some men in a boat and brought on board. This woman threw herself overboard one night when we were at sea.

■   ■   ■

We had nothing to eat but yams, which were thrown amongst us at random—and of these we had scarcely enough to support life. More than one third of us died on the passage and when we arrived at Charleston, I was not able to stand. It was more than a week after I left the ship before I could straighten my limbs. I was bought by a trader with several others, brought up the country and sold to my present master. I have been here five years.

CHARLES BALL[7]

Having survived the middle passage, the slave now faced the auction block, here to be sold to the highest bidder. During his life, a slave could expect to be sold at least two times, and many more times if his owners were in the slave-breeding business. Slaves were inspected by prospective buyers and even curious nonbuyers, as though they were chattel. Perhaps the most atrocious and crushing aspect of the slave market, whether at the auction block or in a less formal venue, was the breakup of families.

Every first Tuesday slaves were brought in from Virginia and sold on the block. The auctioneer was Cap'n Dorsey. E. M. Cobb was the slave-bringer. They would stand the slaves up on the block and talk about what a fine-looking specimen of black manhood or womanhood they was, tell how healthy they was, look in their mouth and examine their teeth just like they was a horse, and talk about the kind of work they would be fit for and could do.   MORRIS HILLYER[8]

Never knew who massa done sold. I remember one morning ol' white man rode up in a buggy and stop by a gal name Lucy that was working in the yard. He say, "Come on. Get in this buggy. I bought you this morning." Then she beg him to let her go tell her baby and husband goodbye, but he say, "Naw! Get in this buggy! Ain't got no time for crying and carrying on." I started crying myself, 'cause I was so scared he was gonna take me, too. But ol' Aunt Cissy, whose child it was, went to massa and told him he was a mean dirty nigger-trader. Ol' massa was sore, but he ain't never said nothin' to Aunt Cissy. Then Hendley what was next to the youngest of her seven children got sick and died. Aunt Cissy ain't sorrowed much. She went straight up to ol' massa and shouted in his face, "Praise God! Praise God! My little child is gone to Jesus. That's one child of mine you never gonna sell."
                        NANCY WILLIAMS[9]

I said to him, "For God's sake! Have you bought my wife?" He said he had. When I asked him what she had done, he said she had done nothing, but that her master wanted money. He drew out a pistol and said that if I went near the wagon on which she was, he would shoot me. I asked for leave to shake hands with her which he re-fused, but said I might stand at a distance and talk with her. My heart was so full that I could say very little. . . . I have never seen or heard from her from that day to this. I loved her as I love my life.   MOSES GRANDY[10]

For the great majority of slaves, life on the plantation was far removed from Jef-ferson Davis's idyllic portrait. Even among Davis's "kindly treated" slaves, to be a slave was to be "owned by another person, as a car, house, or table is owned, . . . to live as a piece of property that could be sold—a child sold from its mother, a wife from her husband, . . . [and to be a] 'thing' whose sole function was determined by the one who own you."[11]

We didn't know nothing like young folks do now. We hardly knowed our names. We was cussed for so many bitches and sons of bitches and bloody bitches and blood of bitches. We never heard our names scarcely at all. First young man I went with wanted to know my initials! What did I know 'bout initials? You ask 'em ten years old now and they'll tell you. That was after the war. Initials!!!   SALLIE CRANE[12]

Slaves were not only dehumanized but were typically treated with vicious brutality—worked from dawn to dusk, whipped at the whim of the overseer.

One day while my mammy was washing her back my sister noticed ugly disfiguring scars on it. Inquiring about them, we found, much to our amazement, that they were Mammy's relics of the now gone, if not forgotten, slave days. This was her first reference to her "misery days" that she had made in my presence. Of course we all thought she was telling us a big story and we made fun of her. With eyes flashing, she stopped bathing, dried her back and reached for the smelly ol' black whip that hung behind the kitchen door. Bidding us to strip down to our waists, my little mammy with the boney bent-over back, struck each of us as hard as ever she could with that black-snake whip. Each stroke of the whip drew blood from our backs. "Now," she said to us, "you have a taste of slavery days."   FRANK COOPER[13]

My master used to throw me in a buck and whip me. He would put my hands together and tie them. Then he would strip me naked. Then he would make me squat down. Then he would run a stick through behind my knees and in front of my elbows. My knee was up against my chest. My hands was tied together just in front of my shins. The stick between my arms and my knees held me in a squat. That's what they call a buck. You couldn't stand up and you couldn't get your feet out. You couldn't do nothing but just squat there and take what he put on. You couldn't move no way at all. Just try to. You just fall over on one side and have to stay there till you were turned over by him. He could whip me on one side till that was sore and full of blood and then he would whip me on the other side till that was all tore up. I got a scar big as the place my ol' mistress hit me. She took a bull whip once. The bull whip had a piece of iron in the handle of it—and she got mad. She was so mad she took the whip and hit me over the head with the butt end of it and the blood flew. It ran all down my back and dripped off my heels.   ELLA WILSON[14]

Blackshear had them take their babies with them to the field and it was two or three miles from the house to the field. He didn't want them to lose time walking backward and forward nursing. They built a long trough like a great long old cradle and put all these babies in it every morning when the mother come out to the field. It was set at the end of the rows under a big cottonwood tree. When they were at the other end of the row, all at once a cloud no bigger than a small spot came up and it grew fast, and it thundered and lightened as if the world were coming to an end, and the rain just came down in great sheets. And when it got so they could go to the other end of the field, the trough was filled with water and every baby in it was floating round in the water, drowned. They never got nary a lick of labor and nary a red penny for any of them babies.   IDA HUTCHINSON[15]

NOTES

1. Paul Johnson, *A History of the American People* (New York: HarperCollins, 1997), p. 471.

2. William J. Bennett, ed., *The Book of Virtues* (New York: Simon and Schuster, 1993), p. 256. See, generally, Fredrick Douglass, *Life and Times of Frederick Douglass* (New York: Collier, 1962), originally published as *Narrative* in 1845.

3. Julius Lester, *To Be a Slave* (New York: Dell, 1968), pp. 20–21.

4. Charles Ball, *A Narrative of the Life and Adventures of Charles Ball, A Black Man*, 3d ed. (Pittsburgh: John T. Shryock, 1854), pp. 158–59.

5. Howard W. French, "The Atlantic Slave Trade: On Both Sides, Reason for Remorse," *New York Times*, April 15, 1998, sec. 4, p. 1. See also John Hope Franklin and Alfred A. Moss, Jr., *From Slavery to Freedom: A History of Negro Americans*, 6th ed. (New York: Alfred A. Knopf, 1988), pp. 36–39 (estimating a high of 9.5 million); Lester, *To Be a Slave*, pp. 26–27 (estimating a high of 50 million).

6. *Evidence on the Slave Trade* (Cincinnati: American Reform Tract and Book Society, 1855), p. 47.

7. Ball, *A Narrative of the Life and Adventures of Charles Ball*, pp. 159–60.

8. *Slave Narratives: A Folk History of Slavery in the United States from Interviews with Former Slaves Prepared by The Federal Writers Project, 1936–1938* (assembled by the Library of Congress, 1941).

9. Ibid.

10. Charles H. Nichols, *Many Thousand Gone: The Ex-Slaves' Account of Their Bondage and Freedom* (Leiden: E. J. Brill, 1963), p. 20.

11. Lester, *To Be a Slave*, p. 28.

12. *Slave Narratives: A Folk History of Slavery.*

13. Ibid.

14. Ibid.

15. Ibid.

51 Remembering Slavery

Jennifer Fleischner

It took two hundred years to create the antebellum slave culture of the United States—a culture born of generations of social, psychological, and biological crossings between black and white, slave and free. It was a mixed, complex world whose very existence contradicted the assumptions of racial purity and difference used to justify slavery. Masters and slaves shared in this contradictory world of "family" relations in the context of radical social and political separation. Slave narratives, in revealing just how conflicted, desperate, and internalized a world this was, suggest that the psychological legacy of slavery may take two centuries to unmake.

Slave narratives have been overlooked as a source for exploring this legacy, both for the individual and the culture. In the experiences of the individual slave narrator and his or her "family" (black and white) we see a history of suffering transmitted across generations. The two narratives discussed in this chapter—one from a mother's perspective, the other from a daughter's—illustrate this legacy.

When Dr. Flint, the master of Harriet Jacobs, whose 1861 narrative *Incidents in the Life of a Slave Girl* is considered the classic antebellum woman's slave narrative, tells his young slave girl that he "wish[es] the past [his sexual persecution of her] to be forgotten, and that we might never think of it,"[1] he is enjoining her to concede to her own further abuse. More profoundly, he is inviting her to be complicit in her own self-annihilation. Identity is made up of memories, and to suppress memories consciously or repress them unconsciously is to do away with the self. Against the weight of her master's wish, against her own self-doubts and her need to escape unbearable memories, Jacobs struggles to remember, knowing that this struggle is not hers alone. Writing about how she had to hide from her own children to escape Dr. Flint's menacing threats, she despairs that her daughter will grow up "without a mother's love . . . almost without memory of a mother!"[2]

The slaveholder's power to break the chain of memory—and love—that holds a family or a people together was one of the most destructive forces in the lives of slaves. But memories are persistent, and they are transmitted in subtle ways. And though what is remembered may be painful, forgetting is more devastating to the self and destructive of the human spirit.

The next slave narrative is not properly a slave narrative, since the narrator, Julia A. J. Foote, was the freeborn daughter of emancipated slaves. But her inner world, as she discloses it in *A Brand Plucked from the Fire: An Autobiographical Sketch* (1879, 1886), seems shaped by her conflicted identification with her once-enslaved mother. In her narrative, Foote strives to free herself from this maternal inheritance and to place herself beyond the reach of the trauma of this history: to be a brand plucked from the fire. To do this, however, she cannot break from her mother's memories; she must transform them.

The keys to Foote's narrative struggle are in the opening chapter. Here Foote gives her narrative's founding memory—a gruesome and extended account of how her mother was whipped for disobedience to her former master:

> This man, whom she was obliged to call master, tied her up and whipped her. . . .
> After the whipping, he himself washed her quivering back with strong salt water. At the expiration of a week she was sent to change her clothing, which stuck fast to her back. Her mistress, seeing that she could not remove it, took hold of the rough tow-linen under-garment and pulled it off over her head with a jerk, which took the skin with it, leaving her back all raw and sore.[3]

The memory is very much alive for Foote, as she emphasizes the sadism of the master and mistress and the protracted nature of her mother's suffering.

A later chapter, "The Undeserved Whipping," shows how Foote transforms her mother's transmitted memory as a way to order her own remembered experiences. "The Undeserved Whipping" most directly echoes her mother's memories, in that Foote tells of being whipped by Mrs. Prime, the mistress to whom she was indentured when she was ten. Reinforcing the link to her mother, this chapter evokes the structure, style, and themes of more obvious slave narratives. Foote's dependence upon Mrs. Prime as a maternal surrogate recalls numerous women's slave narratives, in which the slave girl, separated from her mother, turns to her mistress for love, comfort, and support. Foote tells us that "[a]ll this time the Primes had treated me as though I were their own child."[4] But she discovers the limits of this bond when Mrs. Prime wrongfully accuses her of theft: "She who had always been so kind and motherly, frightened me so by her looks and action that I trembled so violently I could not speak. This was taken as evidence of my guilt. The dear Lord alone knows how my little heart ached, for I was entirely innocent of the crime laid to my charge."[5]

When Foote runs away after the beating, her description recalls the plight of fugitive slaves. She describes the "long, lonely road, through the woods . . . [where] every sound frightened me, and made me run for fear some one was after me."[6] Finally, when she explains how her mother returns her to the Primes, "very much against my will,"[7] she underlines how the mother turns the "free" daughter's servitude into a veritable enslavement, not unlike her own.

However, the psychological goal of Foote's remembering is to rewrite her mother's—and her own—slavery experience. Where she depicts her mother as passive victim, whose confession of her "disobedience" fuels her mistress's jealous rage, Foote disobeys by *refusing* to confess. Although Mrs. Prime offers to cease the whipping if Foote confesses, Foote responds, "This, of course, I could not do."[8] More startlingly, Foote counters Mrs. Prime's torment of her victim with her own rage-filled fantasies and violent outbursts. She resists being a victim by becoming an aggressor. Foote "carried the rawhide out to the wood pile, took the axe, and cut it up into small pieces, which [she] threw away, determined not to be whipped with that thing again."[9] But the raging child who mutilates the whip is still subject to the adults (the Primes, her mother) who control her fate.

In telling her story, Harriet Jacobs sought (among other things) to restore the chain of memory between herself and her daughter—to recreate the maternal circle of protection, memory, love, and hope. As the daughter, Foote was faced with a related, though different task: to deal with the legacy of abuse suffered by her enslaved mother. Where aggression was forbidden but submission repugnant, narrative (fantasy and memory) provided some relief.

NOTES

1. Harriet Jacobs, *Incidents in the Life of a Slave Girl: Written by Herself* (1861), ed. Jean Fagan Yellin (Cambridge: Harvard University Press, 1987), p. 145.

2. Ibid., p. 2.

3. Julia A. J. Foote, *A Brand Plucked from the Fire: An Autobiographical Sketch* (Cleveland: Lauer and Yost, 1886), reprinted in *Spiritual Narratives*, ed. Henry Louis Gates, Jr. (New York: Oxford University Press, 1988), pp. 9–10.

4. Ibid., p. 24.

5. Ibid.

6. Ibid., p. 26.

7. Ibid.

8. Ibid., p. 25.

9. Ibid., p. 26.

52 | Life as a Free Black

James Grahame, Esq.

■　■　■

In the Northern States, where the inhabitants were never exposed to the temptations by which slavery was invited and extended in the South,—where the slaves were few, the white population numerous and rapidly increasing, and white labour at once easily procurable and fittest for the soil—there, where slavery reflected the greatest disgrace on the national name, afforded the least profit to the slave-owners, and injured the community by discrediting the occupation of free labourers,—a *gradual* abolition of slavery was brought to pass by laws which indulged the slave-owners with the choice of selling their negroes to the Southern planters, or of retaining their service for a limited period deemed sufficient for their own protection from pecuniary loss. In the Southern States, widely differenced from their northern sisters in all the circumstances which I have particularized, the number of slaves was progressively augmented by copious importations, and their bondage aggravated by laws restricting manumission, prohibiting negro education, and subjecting even freed men of colour to such privations and indignities as must repress the desire as well as the hope of freedom in the bosoms of the negro slaves. This last feature of Southern policy has been responsively copied in the manners and even in the laws of those Northern States within which slavery has ceased to exist,—where free persons of colour are sternly excluded from all social equality with the whites, from all political franchises and most civil rights,—and where in the year 1828, it was decided by the legal tribunals of Connecticut that "free people of colour are *not* citizens of the United States." Harsh as this may appear, it is milder than the sentiments which are openly avowed in the South, where the *right* of free people of colour even to breathe nature's air in America is disputed. . . . A late address published by the *Colonization Society* of Connecticut (a State, be it remarked, which

From James Grahame, Esq., *Who Is to Blame? Or Cursory Review of "American Apology for American Accession to Negro Slavery"* (London: Smith, Elder and Co., 1842), pp. 51–57.

has long plumed itself on the abolition of negro slavery within its limits) contains the following presentation:—"The habits, the feelings, all the prejudices of society—prejudices which neither refinement, nor argument, nor education, *nor even religion itself* can subdue—mark the people of colour, whether bond or free, as the subjects of a degradation *inevitable and incurable*." And in another recent American publication, the author frankly avows that "I am clear that whether we consider it with reference to the welfare of the State or the happiness of the blacks, *it were better to have left them in chains than to have liberated them to receive such freedom as they enjoy*: and greater freedom we *cannot, must not* allow them."[1] Even in Pennsylvania, so renowned for the equity of her laws and the liberality of her citizens, the French writer De Tocqueville informs us that no free man of colour dare present himself to vote at an election. Nominally enfranchised by the laws of the State, they are actually disfranchised by the more powerful manners of the people. . . . Such has been the result of that measure of the American Convention, and of those measures of the Northern States where slavery has been nominally abolished, that La Fayette, after his last visit to America, protested with grief and surprise that the achievement of American Independence had brought only increased misery and oppression on the African race. . . . Africa indeed has had reason to curse the Independence of North America.

No man is so blind as he that will not see. With such damning facts staring him in the face, the American writer who addresses himself to Lord Brougham persists in asserting that the generality of his countrymen treat free persons of colour with liberality, and slaves with kindness; that they deplore the subsistence of negro slavery among them; and that, entertaining a fixed purpose of purging their pure soil from such poisonous product, they are steadily and successfully pursuing the wisest means of accomplishing this desirable consummation. Such assertions from such a writer can have no weight with any impartial mind. . . .

That free people of colour are *not* treated with liberality but are subjected to the vilest indignities in the United States, is manifest not only from the American avowals which I have already cited, but from the concurring reports of *every traveller of every nation* that has recently visited America, and communicated his observations in discourse or by the press. With close (though perhaps unconscious) copy of the policy of ancient Egypt towards the children of Israel, America denies to free men of colour every liberal motive and every generous style, solace, and recompense of industry; and then insults them with the calumnious reproach "Ye are idle, ye are idle." The Americans themselves admit that (from the evil tempers of individual white masters) many of their slaves are treated with a cruelty far exceeding the necessary rigour of bondage: and I, on the other hand, admit that very many of their slaves, *as long* as they show themselves so brutalized by slavery as to be content with their degradation, and willing to display the mirth and sing the songs that were required of the enslaved Jews by their Babylonian captors, are treated with a kind, patient forebearance unexampled in the intercourse of masters with hired servants.

■   ■   ■

The Redress Movement

53 The Growing Movement for Reparations

Joe R. Feagin and Eileen O'Brien

In its modern phase, the African American redress movement encompasses a number of different goals. The most overt goals are (1) to secure compensation for the labor and lives stolen from the ancestors of African Americans by the oppressive systems of slavery and segregation and (2) to secure a national and public apology for that racial oppression. Robert Browne has underscored the related goal of providing African Americans today with a fair share of the national wealth, one that they would have had if given the same inheritances, opportunities, and privileges that white Americans had over the last four centuries.[1] In his book *The Case for Black Reparations* (1973), Boris I. Bittker argued that the oppression faced by African Americans was more extensive and longer in duration than that faced by other American racial groups. In his view, large-scale reparations are required to compensate African Americans.[2]

These demands and arguments for reparations may give the false impression that the African American redress movement is a recent phenomenon. Claims for reparations were, in fact, made many decades earlier. Black and white leaders, such as the abolitionists of the nineteenth century and the civil rights leaders from the 1940s to the 1960s, called for governmental action beyond the eradication of slavery or segregation to the provision of economic resources. The demand that the federal government follow through on its promises of "forty acres and a mule" after the Civil War and major job training programs during the 1960s are examples of economic claims made in the past.

Marcus Garvey, Dr. Martin Luther King, Jr., and Robert Penn Warren are among the diverse voices that have called for black reparations. Black activists, however, have been in the forefront of the redress movement, especially since the 1960s. One of the most active of these is James Forman. His appeal for reparations for African Americans is documented in his famous "Black Manifesto."

Originally delivered as an unwelcome interruption at a Riverside Church service in New York City in 1969, and addressed to the "white Christian Churches and Jewish Synagogues in the United States of America and All Other Racist Institutions," this manifesto was adopted by the National Black Economic Development Conference. "Black Manifesto" outlined in detail many economic demands, including the creation of banks, presses, universities, and training centers for African Americans, all to be established as repayment for centuries of racist degradation and exploitation.[3] While these earlier arguments for compensation were not always framed in terms of a theory of reparations, the essential elements of the theory were usually present.

Over the past few decades, numerous African American leaders have called for various forms of reparations for the years of slavery and segregation, as well as for contemporary racial oppression. Dr. Martin Luther King, Jr., Whitney Young, Jesse Jackson, and Louis Farrakhan have all spoken of the need for major compensation programs for African Americans. In 1994, the Nation of Islam petitioned a United Nations human rights commission to investigate the issue of reparations for African Americans and to "intervene based on international laws protecting the rights of minorities." The United Nations has yet to respond.[4] And since the late 1980s, Rep. John Conyers (D-Mich.) has regularly filed a bill (H.R. 40) calling for a commission to study the matter of reparations for African Americans. As of 1998, this bill is still being considered by a House subcommittee.[5]

Some African Americans have generated new organizations and efforts to work for reparations. The National Coalition of Blacks for Reparations in America (N'-COBRA) was created in the early 1990s to press for monetary compensation and other forms of reparations. Several important lawsuits have been filed. In Oakland, California, African American plaintiffs including some members of N'COBRA filed a lawsuit seeking $380 million in reparations for themselves and for local black communities. According to one plaintiff, "We're seeking reparations for our ancestors who aren't here to bear witness. . . . Nobody was paid 40 acres and a mule because Lincoln was assassinated before it could go through."[6] Although these lawsuits have not yet gone to trial, they have given the issue of reparations greater attention within black and white communities.

Another tactic has been especially attention-getting. A number of African Americans have filed "Black Tax" claims with the Internal Revenue Service, following a suggestion made by L. G. Sherrod in a 1993 article in *Essence* magazine. The claim was for $43,209 each, the estimated value of "40 acres and a mule" today. Several demands have been honored by mistake.[7]

In spite of the fact that it can trace its intellectual genealogy back to the likes of Martin Luther King, Jr., the African American redress movement is often seen today, especially by white Americans, as a "fringe" group movement, involving only groups such as N'COBRA. Recently, however, as the issue has gained more support and visibility nationally, other supporters have come forward. Several mainstream civil rights organizations, including the National Association for the

Advancement of Colored People (NAACP) and the Southern Christian Leadership Conference (SCLC), now officially support the reparations movement. There is even a small white group, Caucasians United for Reparation and Emancipation (CURE), formed in 1992 in Chicago, that actively supports reparations measures for African Americans.[8] Unexpected support has come from a few white neoconservatives such as Charles Krauthammer, who says he would support monetary reparations for African Americans if affirmative action programs were ended.[9]

In 1997 an important white supporter, Rep. Tony Hall (D-Ohio), proposed a congressional resolution (cosponsored by sixteen other House members) that provided a national public apology for slavery. Although modest, this resolution, Hall has said, does not rule out the possibility of investigating monetary reparations as well. Hall's resolution has received the backing of the Promise Keepers, a conservative religious group. In addition, several state and city governments have passed supportive resolutions calling for a national commission to investigate the issue of reparations for African Americans.[10]

Recent moves by a few white leaders in the direction of redress does not mean there is substantial support among white Americans for an apology, let alone reparations. In fact, a recent poll taken by ABC News indicates that while two-thirds of the black respondents thought the federal government should both apologize and pay money to them to "compensate for slavery," two-thirds of the white respondents resisted the idea of even an apology, and 88 percent rejected the notion of paying reparations.[11] Clearly, an apology and reparations are considered much too radical by a large majority of white Americans.

NOTES

1. Robert S. Browne, "The Economic Basis for Reparations to Black America," *Review of Black Political Economy* 21 (January 1993): 99.

2. Boris I. Bittker, *The Case for Black Reparations* (New York: Random House, 1973).

3. Ibid., pp. 161–75.

4. Linda Jones, "Closing the Books on Slavery? African American Groups Seek Reparations on Ancestors' Behalf," *Dallas Morning News*, June 15, 1996, p. 1C.

5. Salim Muwakkil, "Time to Redress Slavery's Damage," *Chicago Sun Times*, February 27, 1994, p. 45. See also N'COBRA's Home Page at http://www.ncobra.com.

6. Stephen Magagnini, "Descendants Suing U.S. over Slavery," *Sacramento Bee*, April 14, 1994, p. A1. This paragraph draws in part on Joe R. Feagin and Hernan Vera, *White Racism: The Basics* (New York: Routledge, 1995), p. 186.

7. Jones, "Closing the Books on Slavery?" p. 1C; Wes Smith, "40 Acres, a Mule plus 132 Years' Interest; Man's Crusade for Slavery Reparations Picks up Momentum," *Chicago Tribune*, July 10, 1997, p. 1N.

8. Lori S. Robinson, "Growing Movement Seeks Reparations for U.S. Blacks," *Arizona Republic*, June 22, 1997, p. H1.

9. S. A. Reid, "Account Past Due," *Atlanta Journal and Constitution*, October 24, 1993, p. G1.

10. Jonathon Tilove, "Congressman's Call for Slavery Apology Jolts U.S.; Reparations Issue Gains Attention," *New Orleans Times-Picayune*, July 6, 1997, p. A24.

11. ABC News Poll, June 18, 1997 (Accession number 0288792-0288793, University of Connecticut: Roper).

Forms of Redress: Apology

54 | Why the North and South Should Have Apologized

James Grahame, Esq.

"If there be," said that generous friend of America and of human nature, Thomas Day, (chiefly known as the author of *Sandford and Merton*,)—"if there be an object truly ridiculous in the universe, it is an American patriot signing resolutions in favour of liberty with the one hand, and with the other, brandishing a whip over his affrighted slaves." These words express the sentiment of all civilized men—except the Americans themselves—who, in reference to the system of negro slavery which they continue to uphold, so far from admitting the reproach of peculiar iniquity, boldly challenge a right to peculiar indulgence.

■   ■   ■

In no age or country have tyrannical invaders and usurpers of other men's rights been without apologies and apologists. Tears have been shed to palliate the rapacity of Xerxes, and disguise the ambition of Cromwell. But time-born Truth has always unmasked the hypocrite and his hypocrisy, and disclosed the falsehood of the allegations on which the oppressor sought to rear his unsound and iniquitous plea. Perhaps the well known fable of *the wolf and lamb* would be rendered truer to nature,—at least to the new disclosures of nature that the new world has produced,—if the wolf were made to say to his victim, "I am sorry to destroy you; but can neither restrain nor condemn the appetite which I indulge. That appetite was awakened in me by the power and artifice of a stronger brute that once domineered over myself: and though I have exerted sufficient vigour to reject *his* tyranny over *me*, yet I feel quite unable to forego the evil appetite against yourself which he taught

From James Grahame, Esq., *Who Is to Blame? Or Cursory Review of "American Apology for American Accession to Negro Slavery"* (London: Smith, Elder and Co.: 1842), pp. 1, 6–10.

me, or to overcome the prejudice against you which his lessons impressed on my innocent, reluctant, but tenacious mind."

The Americans, with continual application of flattering unction to their own souls, and ostentatious challenge of the world's admiration, plume themselves on being, of all the nations who have flourished in ancient or in modern times, the people by whom civil and political liberty has been most justly and nobly appreciated, most gallantly achieved, and most faithfully and successfully cultivated, preserved, and extended. To the plain uncorrupted understandings of honest men in every other country, this American claim appears seriously impeached in truth and value by the actual subsistence of negro slavery in America; and the Americans are everywhere taxed with the disgrace of peculiar treachery to those generous principles of which they profess themselves the most ardent and praiseworthy votaries.

Manifold and various are the defensive pleas by which Americans attempt to repel, elude, or extenuate the heavy charge. The citizens of those States, members of the Federal Union, within whose territory negro slavery has been actually abolished, protest that *their* conduct is not only irreproachable, but deserves the praise of generous sacrifice of their private interests on the altar of universal justice and liberty:—a protestation of which I shall presently do my endeavour to ascertain the value. They further protest against any responsibility for the actual retention of negro slavery within the Southern confederated states,—on the plea that by the constitutional compact of their National Union, the federal government is debarred from all interference with the social economy and domestic concerns of the particular provinces,—to whose local governments respectively is reserved the paramount and exclusive power of regulating such matters within the limits of their own separate and independent jurisdiction. They claim at once the praise of piety for disallowing within their private limits a practice repugnant to the will of God and the rights of man; and the praise of justice for their faithful adherence to a voluntary compact that blends their national name, character, and power with the support and perpetuation of that practice. On the other hand, the citizens of those States in which negro slavery still subsists, repel the charge against themselves in a tone as confident as that of their slaveless colleagues, but with greater variety of pleading. At once seeking their own vindication, and retorting the implied censure conveyed in the language of their national though not provincial colleagues, they contend that negro labour is essential to the peculiar culture of the soil which they possess; and that negro slave-labour, after having been employed in *every one* of the older American States (even in those whose soils demanded preferably the labour of free and white men) has never been abandoned in *any one* where the whites could retain it without manifest disadvantage to themselves. Some of them protest that, deploring the existence of slavery as a hated outrage on human nature, they acquiesce in it as a rooted and irremovable evil, of which the blame (if there be any) mainly lies with the Almighty, in creating its necessity by creating such climes and other circumstances of such potent invitation as to render the temptation to the practice irresistible by any exertion of the virtuous force which he has imparted to man. I have heard many of these persons profess, with every appearance of vehement sincerity, their desire to discover some *practicable* plan of abolishing negro slavery; but have almost invariably found that they required the *impracticability* of redressing long and enormous injustice without any atoning sacrifice or reparatory expence,—of restoring and elevating, as if by magic, and without any surrender of interest or convenience, the rights and the dignity of a numerous race of men whom they and their fathers have ruined and degraded. Others of them, and these by no means the least respected, enlightened, and zealous of their party, acquitting both their Creator and themselves from blame, courageously defend the system of negro slavery, and challenge not the indulgence but the applause of the world for their retention of it. They represent it as enhancing the sense and the value of liberty in the white masters, and fostering the dull and undeveloped intelligence of the black slaves; as establishing between different classes of men patriarchal relationships, liable indeed to abuse, but of which the proper and reasonable use opens new fields of virtue and happiness to mankind; and as enlarging the physical as well as the moral welfare of the human race, by cheaply supplying those tropical luxuries and commodities which only negro labour is competent to produce. Negro slavery, they contend, is, of all existing human institutions, the one which, rightly used, has the strongest tendency to promote the glory of God and the dignity and felicity of men. They have certainly found a new field for the exercise and expatiation of the human faculties, by a brave bound over the ordinary limits of impudence, absurdity, and impiety.

■　■　■

55 | Defense of Congressional Resolution Apologizing for Slavery

Congressman Tony P. Hall of Ohio

Mr. Speaker, last week, I introduced House Concurrent Resolution 96. This is a resolution that apologizes for slavery in the United States. It is rather simple. It is only one sentence long. Let me read it:

> Resolved by the House of Representatives that the Congress apologizes to African-Americans whose ancestors suffered as slaves under the Constitution and the laws of the United States until 1865.

That is simply what it says. It is a very simple idea. The Congress apologizes. It is a powerful message.

When a brother wrongs a brother, he apologizes. That is the foundation for beginning again. That is the price for restoring lost trust. This is the only way to start over. It is a simple gesture. It carries deep meaning. And it is the right thing to do.

When an institution wrongs a people, so it is again the right to do. . . .

■   ■   ■

It has been 134 years since slavery ended. Since that time, Congress has taken proud strides forward, done some wonderful things, including civil rights laws. But it is not enough.

Look around. The effects still linger today. Through my work as chairman of the former House Select Committee on Hunger and through my efforts to improve the lives of America's poor, I have seen the effects firsthand. We as a nation must do more. This is not a political gesture, it is not a partisan gesture, it is a very simple gesture and it certainly is the right thing.

143 Congressional Record H3890-H3891, 105th Congress, 1st Session (June 18, 1997).

The slaves and slave holders are long gone. No one alive today is responsible for slavery. No one alive today was shackled by the chains of slavery in America. Indeed, most Americans arc the descendants of people who came to the United States after slavery ended.

All of us today, white and black, live in the shadow of our past. African-Americans today still suffer from the lingering effects. We all pay the price of slavery.

The hatred and racial divisions springing from slavery are very much alive. Let us take this step to bury that hatred with the bones of the slaves and the slave holders.

No Member of Congress today voted on measures to perpetuate slavery. But the Congress as an institution does bear responsibility. The laws we passed ignored, even encouraged slavery. Our Constitution, the foundation for the Congress, and our Government even declared at one time that a black man was only three-fifths of a person.

Congress is a great institution. It is the most respected deliberative body in the world. At least three times in recent years, Congress formally apologized.

In 1988, it apologized to the Japanese-Americans who were interned in the United States during World War II.

In 1993, Congress offered a formal apology to native Hawaiians for the role the United States and U.S. citizens played in the overthrow of the government of the Kingdom of Hawaii 100 years earlier.

In 1990, Congress apologized to uranium miners, people affected by nuclear tests in Nevada, and their families.

An apology by Congress is rare, it is special, but it is not without precedence. Apologizing is symbolic, but it has a great meaning for those who are apologizing and it has power for those who are wronged.

Why apologize to just African-Americans for slavery? What about all the other people who have been wronged by laws passed by the Congress? The wrongs against African-Americans are clear to everyone. The consequences are severe. Maybe we have wronged others. Maybe an apology to them is due. I do not know. That is another issue. I do know that we need to apologize to African-Americans.

Many people have told me that apologizing is an empty, meaningless gesture. If it was so meaningless, why has the resolution erupted a fire storm of controversy throughout this Nation? If apologizing were so easy, then why is this resolution so difficult?

No, it is not easy to apologize. It is the right thing to do. Today 134 years later, it is not too late, but let us wait no longer. We are a nation of immigrants. Those who came as free men went in one direction. Those who came from slave ships, another. If we are to travel towards a common future, we owe it to our children to clearly mark that the early fork in the road was the wrong way.

■　■　■

56 | Clinton Opposes Slavery Apology

In stopovers in Africa last week, President Clinton was careful not to issue a formal apology for America's slave past, but rather to express regret and contrition. One reason, aides say, was to avoid being unnecessarily divisive at home. But another important factor—rarely discussed by the White House—is concern over the legal implications of a formal apology. If Clinton, as head of the U.S. government, issues such a statement, it could increase legal, as well as moral, pressure for reparations to the descendants of slaves, much as many Japanese-Americans won reparations for their illegal incarceration at the outbreak of World War II. That could not only prove very expensive, it could itself further inflame racial tension. That's why the White House is particularly grateful for the Rev. Jesse Jackson's defense of Clinton's handling of the issue. White House officials say privately that Jackson, who accompanied Clinton to Africa, has been especially effective in giving Clinton credibility on the apology question within the press corps and, they believe, with many African-Americans. "Jackson has given us a lot of help on this, and we'll all remember him for it," said one senior official.

■   ■   ■

From *U.S. News & World Report*, April 6, 1998, p. 7.

57

Ask Camille
Camille Paglia's Online Advice for the Culturally Disgruntled

Camille Paglia

WHO IS REALLY TO BLAME FOR THE HISTORICAL SCAR OF BLACK SLAVERY?

O Wise One.

I would be most interested to know if you think the U.S. government should apologize to African-Americans for the existence of the institution of slavery.

P.S. Keep *thinking*, Camille. It certainly sets you apart from most public voices in America Today.

Over it in D.C.

Dear Over it:

An apology can be extended only by persons who committed the original offense. Slavery was a commercial operation tolerated but not invented by government. Therefore the government cannot logically apologize for it.

Second, the United States consists today of a diverse population, much of which had no connection whatever to the slave-holding era. Italian immigration, for example, did not begin en masse until after the Civil War. All four of my grandparents were born in Italy; my mother did not arrive here until the 1930s. My people had nothing to do with the African slave trade, nor did most Asian immigrant groups.

Third, slavery was a worldwide phenomenon that still exists undercover in some Third World countries. It has been estimated that as many as nine out of ten people living in classical Athens were slaves. Euripides' play, *The Trojan*

Originally published by *Salon Magazine* at http://www.salonmagazine.com, "Ask Camille" column, July 8, 1997. Reprinted by permission.

Women (made into an all-star movie by Michael Cacoyannis), is all about the wretched enslavement faced by the queen and princesses of fallen Troy. The movie *Spartacus*, starring Kirk Douglas, is based on a real-life rebellion of slaves in ancient Rome, where slavery was the norm. The Aztecs of pre-Columbian Mexico not only enslaved but ritually slaughtered conquered peoples in staggering numbers.

Fourth, any official apology out of Washington, D.C., must be coordinated with apologies from all of the nations of West and Central Africa. Without the active collaboration of Africans, who did the actual reconnoitering, kidnapping, and transporting of tribal young along caravan routes to commercial ports on the West African coast, the slave trade would not have flourished as it did. Slavery was an established feature of African culture long before white men arrived. From the Nuremberg trials to *Schindler's List,* we are used to critiquing individuals' implications in or moral response to the arrest, abuse and extermination of innocent fellow citizens. Why should African history remain immune?

Fifth, this whole issue illustrates the bankruptcy of liberal identity politics, which has sharpened racial consciousness in this country to a dangerous degree. Apologies are empty gestures; substantive reform must be our aim. The state and federal government should be more concerned about decaying public education and the disgusting physical conditions of inner-city neighborhoods. We need public clinics to provide walk-in medical services to the poor. We need job-training programs and better public transit so that the poor can find work where it exists in the suburbs.

Finally, we need a more sophisticated multiculturalism that stops reductively identifying African-Americans as former slaves and instead introduces the young of all races to the enormity and complexity of world civilizations. Let Swahili, Hindi and Chinese be taught in our primary schools; let geography, with its crazily ever-shifting national borders, be memorized; let the full range of human history be revealed, with all its atrocities. Western imperialism is not the serpent that brought evil into paradise. The obsession with slavery—abolished here nearly a century and a half ago—is itself a form of enslavement.

58 | The Atlantic Slave Trade

On Both Sides, Reason for Remorse

Howard W. French

From the moment the White House announced that President Clinton would stop at Senegal's Gorée Island, one of this continent's most famous monuments to the Atlantic slave trade, a polemic was re-launched in the United States and in much of Africa over how and indeed whether Mr. Clinton should apologize for the centuries-long capture and sale into bondage of millions of Africans.

For some, the very idea of an apology was offensive. Weren't Africans engaging in slavery themselves well before the first Europeans came and carried off their first human cargoes? Didn't African chiefs themselves conduct razzias, or slaving raids, on neighboring tribes and march their harvest to the shores for sale?

For others, though, the Atlantic trade in Africans was one of the greatest crimes humanity has known, and remains one that has never been properly acknowledged. "The Holocaust was certainly a great tragedy, but it only lasted a few short years," said Joseph Ndiaye, the curator of the Maison des Esclaves, the featured stop on Mr. Clinton's trip to Gorée. "We never stop hearing about the Holocaust, but how often do we dwell on the tragedy that took place here over 350 years; a tragedy that consumed tens of millions of lives?"

In the end, an appropriately solemn Mr. Clinton stopped short of an outright apology for America's part in the slave trade, finding other ways to express his regret as he focused on the future. That Mr. Clinton so artfully chose to sidestep African slavery's long history should have come as no surprise to anyone familiar with its cruel and complicated details. Even today, few subjects are so prone to passionate disagreement. As ever, people from each leg of the triangular Atlantic trade—Europe, Africa and the Americas—still use the slave experience as a vacant screen upon which they project their own misperceptions and justifications.

From the *New York Times*, April 5, 1998, sec. 4 (Week in Review), p. 1.

THE COLONIAL VIEW

In the United States, the conservative columnist Patrick Buchanan recently echoed a sentiment heard often from whites who resent attempts to make them feel guilty for slavery: "When Europeans arrived in sub-Saharan Africa, the inhabitants had no machinery and no written language. When the Europeans departed, most of them by 1960, they left behind power stations, telephones, telegraphs, railroads, mines, plantations, schools, a civil service, a police force and a treasury."

Even disregarding the wildly benign view of Europe's colonial legacy, many historians say Mr. Buchanan's assumptions—of a savage continent being blessed with the gift of European civilization—are as erroneous as they are widespread. Early European travelers to West Africa, in fact, found societies that by many measures, from commonly available technology to general living standards, were not so different from home.

"The smelting of iron and steel in West Africa was similar to that in Europe in the 13th century, before the advent of power driven by the water wheel," wrote Hugh Thomas, the author of *The Slave Trade* (Simon and Schuster, 1997). "Senegambia had iron and copper industries, and the quality of African steel approached that of Toledo before the 15th century."

It would be dishonest to lay all of Africa's subsequent problems on the slave trade. But most experts do not doubt that the forces unleashed by Europe's demand for slaves, gold and other African goods radically destabilized societies that were embarking on their own path toward development, and laid waste to whole regions of this continent. "The discussion of how Africa became what it did subsequent to 1500 very quickly becomes an argument over what the slave trade did to the continent," said John Reader, a fellow of the British Royal Anthropological Institute and author of *Africa, a Biography of the Continent*. "Africa clearly would not have had an easy time even if there had not been an Atlantic slave trade," he wrote. "But one can easily imagine entirely different trajectories for the continent."

A cold look at the nature of the Atlantic slave trade makes it very difficult to overstate its impact.

Until recently, Africa's economic development has always been hindered by low population densities. Africa's population in 1500 has been estimated by some at 47 million. Over the next 350 years, between 10 and 15 million Africans were landed in chains in the New World, and 4 to 6 million more are thought to have died during their capture or the Atlantic crossing—a total of between 14 and 21 million people. History has seen few social disruptions on that scale.

In the end, however, many specialists in African history consider the process by which slavery worked to be as destructive as the sheer numbers involved.

Few African slaves were enchained by Europeans themselves. Instead, massive slave raids, huge marches of captives from inland areas and continuous rivalries between coastal kingdoms and local ethnic groups were driven by demand for Europe's coveted goods—cloth and candles, grain, horses, spiced wine, pots and pans.

For centuries in Africa, ethical conventions had governed the taking and use of slaves, who in most cases resembled the serfs of Europe more than the chattel of the Americas. These suddenly dissolved.

"The trans-Atlantic slave trade vastly devalued human life compared to what existed virtually anywhere on the continent before," said the historian Basil Davidson. "Things were not a peaceful Garden of Eden in Africa beforehand. But all of the evidence combines to show that the level of civilization in pre-colonial Africa was degraded and depressed by the onset of widespread violence related to the slave trade."

And here one begins to touch upon one of the cruelest ironies of the slave trade and enter into an area that many Africans and African-Americans are often unaware of or uncomfortable confronting directly.

African slavery, albeit of a very different kind, began long before the arrival of Europeans, and continued well after slavery's abolition in the West. And the slavery of the Americas could never have approached the scale it attained without the active and widespread collaboration of Africans. Most troubling, perhaps, are how European perceptions of Africans and their behavior lent seeming moral acceptability to the commerce.

The free-for-all among African societies to capture slaves from their neighbors and rivals for sale to whites was deliberately stimulated by the Europeans who anchored offshore with their cloth and trinkets. And this same state of chaos comforted whites in their view of Africans as ignoble savages.

Today Africans and African-Americans may often share a common view of slavery as the evil work of whites. But the very notion of shared Africanness so commonplace today existed only in the minds of foreigners during the time of this trade. To Africans, their own divisions on ethnic and linguistic lines mattered far more. The lack of solidarity served, in the European mind, as another easy rationale for enslaving them.

Contrast this to the attitude Europeans took toward the New World's Indians. Recorded instances of Indians selling each other into plantation slavery are rare. Less than 100 years into the colonization of the New World, calls were spreading for the abolition of Indian slavery.

"The Indians were seen by and large as a people unknown to the ancients who had somehow remained innocent and noble," said David Brion Davis, the Sterling Professor of History at Yale University. "At the very same time, mariners going up and down the African coast spread tales of Africans as savage barbarians who sold slaves themselves."

59 | They Didn't March to Free the Slaves

Robert S. McElvaine

It is generally accepted that the Civil War was the most important event in American history. Yet, as two current controversies remind us, we disagree on what that war was about.

The question of whether the nation should make a formal apology for slavery has brought forth from such authorities as former history professor Newt Gingrich and columnist George F. Will the declaration that we fought the war to end slavery. Meanwhile, across the South, where battles continue over the display of Confederate flags and related symbols, white defenders of their "heritage" argue that the Civil War was not about slavery but about states' rights and "Southern independence." *Orlando Sentinel* columnist Charley Reese has gone so far as to assert that the Confederacy was fighting for "liberty."

All of these beliefs are based on misreadings of history and taken together, they have the reality exactly backward. The Civil War was not fought to end slavery; it was fought to defend slavery.

The confusion stems from the failure to realize that the two sides in a war need not be fighting over the same issue. The objective of the North was not to end slavery but to preserve the Union. What the South sought was not to end the Union but to preserve slavery.

Few major historical events can properly be attributed to a single cause. But it is accurate to say that slavery was the cause of the Civil War. There would have been no secession, no Confederacy and no war had the South not been intent on maintaining its "peculiar institution." Slavery was the *raison d'etre* of the Confederacy.

Robert S. McElvaine, "They Didn't March to Free the Slaves," *Los Angeles Times*, July 25, 1997, p. B9.

The "liberty" the Confederacy sought to preserve was the liberty to own human beings.

The question that must be asked of those who believe that the Confederacy's purpose was to defend states' rights is this: Just which rights of the states were so important that they were worth splitting the nation in two and fighting a terrible war over, at the cost of 600,000 lives? Can anyone seriously contend that the tariff or any other matter of disagreement between the states and the federal government besides slavery would have produced majority sentiment for secession anywhere, save possibly South Carolina?

The only "right" that the Southern states were sufficiently intent on perpetuating that they would destroy the Union and fight a war over was the "right" to hold people as property—and that is in no sense a right. The Confederate flag never has been a symbol of states' rights. The state powers it has represented during and since the Civil War—slavery, segregation, lynching, racism—are all states' wrongs.

Many whites, particularly young whites in the South, say that they should not be blamed for what their ancestors did. Fair enough. But if they want to be emancipated from that legacy, they must reject it. The first symbolic step for the younger generation in separating itself from the wrongs of its forebears is not to apologize for slavery, but to stop venerating a heritage that was centered on slavery and a flag that came into existence to represent the defense of slavery.

It is time for white Southerners finally and unequivocally to accept the obvious truth: The Lost Cause was a bad cause.

It also is time for other white Americans to recognize that although the cause for which so many Northern soldiers died was a good one (preservation of the Union), it wasn't about ending slavery.

Leaving aside the question of whether a national apology for slavery at this late date would be wise or meaningless, this much can safely be said: The Southern cause in the Civil War is part of what the nation would be apologizing for, but the Northern cause in that war did not constitute such an apology.

60 | Lincoln Apologizes

Thomas Geoghegan

It's strange that there's a debate over whether our President should apologize for slavery. I thought our greatest President, Abraham Lincoln, already did, in his Second Inaugural Address.

It's an apology so poetic, so biblical, so Shakespearean, that I doubt any words read on a teleprompter could improve it.

The Second Inaugural is worth a book as good as the one Garry Wills wrote on the Gettysburg Address. Because the apology builds and rebuilds as it goes along, I only mar it by quoting in the middle. But in any case, here's just a part:

> It may seem strange that any men should dare to ask a just God's assistance in wringing their bread from the sweat of other men's faces but let us judge not that we be not judged.

(O.K., that's not an apology yet.)

> [But], the Almighty has His own Purposes. "Woe unto the world because of offences! for it must needs be that offences come; but woe to that man by whom the offence cometh!" If we shall suppose that American Slavery is one of those offenses

(He is supposing, but wait.)

> which, in the providence of God, must needs come, but which, having continued through His appointed time, He now wills to remove, and that He gives to both North and South, this terrible war, as the woe due to those by whom the offence came

(Yes, both North and South deserve to suffer this awful war.)

> shall we discern therein any departure from those divine attributes which the believers in a Living God always ascribe to Him?

360

(No, God wills this.)

Fondly do we hope—fervently do we pray—that this mighty scourge of war may speedily pass away. Yet, if God wills that it continue, until all the wealth piled by the bondsman's two hundred and fifty years of unrequited toil shall be sunk

(This national debt won't vanish quickly.)

and until every drop of blood drawn with the lash, shall be paid by another drawn with the sword

(Saying "sorry" isn't enough, and even money isn't enough.)

as was said three thousand years ago, so still it must be said "the judgments of the Lord are true and righteous altogether."

What's so strange is not that Lincoln apologized. What's so strange or scary is that such an apology would drop out of our heads. What is the reason, I wonder?

Too Shakespearean? Yes, but we have elites who claim to follow every word of *King Lear* and *Macbeth* and *The Comedy of Errors*, but their eyes glaze over when they read Lincoln.

Too biblical? That may be the problem. Any reference to the "Almighty," and people get nervous. Even the Religious Right seems tone-deaf to a President who speaks of the wrath of God.

Too violent? Yes, that's what I think. This apology for us is too strong in its emotion. Lincoln isn't saying, "Sorry! Have a nice day!" He rends his garments, he talks of blood, the blood sacrifice. He seems to hint at the sacrifice of his own life a few weeks later.

When Lincoln gave this speech, did he sense he would die, too? He must have recalled, as he spoke, that he too, had defended slavery, that he had promised to accept slavery if he could save the Union. Wasn't he apologizing not just for the country, but for himself?

You'd think the whole drama of apology—followed by assassination—would be burned in our brains, but it's apparent people have forgotten. All that we remember from the Second Inaugural is the conclusion, the words, "with malice toward none, with charity for all."

We have forgotten the words that precede this phrase, the terrible words, words about sacrifice. The whole careful edifice of the speech has somehow collapsed over the decades into a single sound bite:

All you need is love.

That attitude is what's sweeping the country. It's even swept away that terrifying apology, for that terrifying sin, completely from modern memory.

Forms of Redress: Reparations

61

Special Field Order No. 15

"Forty Acres and a Mule"

Headquarters, Military Division of the Mississippi, in the Field, Savannah, Georgia, January 16, 1865

1. The islands from Charleston south, the abandoned rice-fields along the rivers for thirty miles back from the sea, and the country bordering the St. John's River, Florida, are reserved and set apart for the settlement of the negroes now made free by the acts of war and the proclamation of the President of the United States.

2. At Beaufort, Hilton Head, Savannah, Fernandina, St. Augustine, and Jacksonville, the blacks may remain in their chosen or accustomed vocations; but on the islands, and in the settlements hereafter to be established, no white person whatever, unless military officers and soldiers detailed for duty, will be permitted to reside; and the sole and exclusive management of affairs will be left to the freed people themselves, subject only to the United States military authority, and the Acts of Congress. By the laws of war, and orders of the President of the United States, the negro is free, and must be dealt with as such. He cannot be subjected to conscription, or forced military service, save by the written orders of the highest military authority of the department, under such regulations as the President or Congress may prescribe. Domestic servants, blacksmiths, carpenters, and other mechanics, will be free to select their own work and residence, but the young and able-bodied negroes must be encouraged to enlist as soldiers in the service of the United States, to contribute their share toward maintaining their own freedom, and securing their rights as citizens of the United States.

Negroes so enlisted will be organized into companies, battalions, and regiments, under the orders of the United States military authorities, and will be paid, fed, and clothed, according to law. The bounties paid on enlistment may, with the consent of the recruit, go to assist his family and settlement in procuring agricultural implements, seed, tools, boots, clothing, and other articles necessary for their livelihood.

3. Whenever three respectable negroes, heads of families, shall desire to settle on land, and shall have selected for that purpose an island or a locality clearly defined

within the limits above designated, the Inspector of Settlements and Plantations will himself, or by such subordinate officer as he may appoint, give them a license to settle such island or district, and afford them such assistance as he can to enable them to establish a peaceable agricultural settlement. The three parties named will subdivide the land, under the supervision of the inspector, among themselves, and such others as may choose to settle near them, so that each family shall have a plot of not more than forty acres of tillable ground, and, when it borders on some water-channel, with not more than eight hundred feet water-front, in the possession of which land the military authorities will afford them protection until such time as they can protect themselves, or until Congress shall regulate their title. The quarter-master may, on the requisition of the Inspector of Settlements and Plantations, place at the disposal of the inspector one or more of the commercial points heretofore named, in order to afford the settlers the opportunity to supply their necessary wants, and to sell the products of their land and labor.

4. Whenever a negro has enlisted in the military service of the United States, he may locate his family in any one of the settlements at pleasure, and acquire a homestead, and all other rights and privileges of a settler, as though present in person. In like manner, negroes may settle their families and engage on board the gunboats, or in fishing, or in the navigation of the inland waters, without losing any claim to land or other advantages derived from this system. But no one, unless an actual settler as above defined, or unless absent on Government service, will be entitled to claim any right to land or property in any settlement by virtue of these orders.

5. In order to carry out this system of settlement, a general officer will be detailed as Inspector of Settlements and Plantations, whose duty it shall be to visit the settlements, to regulate their police and general arrangement, and who will furnish personally to each head of a family, subject to the approval of the President of the United States, a possessory title in writing, giving as near as possible the description of boundaries; and who shall adjust all claims or conflicts that may arise under the same, subject to the like approval, treating such titles altogether as possessory. The same general officer will also be charged with the enlistment and organization of the negro recruits, and protecting their interests while absent from their settlements; and will be governed by the rules and regulations prescribed by the War Department for such purposes.

6. Brigadier-General R. Saxton is hereby appointed Inspector of Settlements and Plantations, and will at once enter on the performance of his duties. No change is intended or desired in the settlement now on Beaufort Island, nor will any rights to property heretofore acquired be affected thereby.

By order of Major-General W.T. Sherman.

I. M. Dayton, Assistant Adjutant-General

62 | The Commission to Study Reparations Proposals

Congressman John Conyers of Michigan

In 1989 I first proposed that a commission be created to study the institution of slavery in this country from 1619 to 1865, and subsequent de jure and de facto racial and economic discrimination against African-Americans, as well as the impact of these forces on living African-Americans, and to make recommendations to the Congress on appropriate remedies.

One of the remedies in this Congress is H.R. 40, with the number of the resolution selected for the "Forty Acres and a Mule" rallying cry of 1865 when Civil War General Tecumseh Sherman issued Special Field Order 15, declaring the Georgia Sea Islands and a strip of South Carolina rice country as black settlements. Each family of freed slaves was to be given 40 acres and the loan of an Army mule to work the land.

■   ■   ■

HOUSE RESOLUTION 40

Be it enacted by the Senate and House of Representatives of the United States of America in Congress assembled,

SECTION 1. SHORT TITLE

This Act may be cited as the "Commission to Study Reparation Proposals for African-Americans Act."

From 143 Congressional Record E1548-E1549, 105th Congress, 1st Session (July 29, 1997).

SECTION 2. FINDINGS AND PURPOSE

(a) Findings: The Congress finds that—

  (1) approximately 4,000,000 Africans and their descendants were enslaved in the United States and the colonies that became the United States from 1619 to 1865;

  (2) the institution of slavery was constitutionally and statutorily sanctioned by the Government of the United States from 1769 through 1865;

  (3) the slavery that flourished in the United States constituted an immoral and inhumane deprivation of Africans' life, liberty, African citizenship rights, and cultural heritage, and denied them the fruits of their own labor; and

  (4) sufficient inquiry has not been made into the effects of the institution of slavery on living African-Americans and society in the United States.

(b) Purpose: The purpose of this Act is to establish a commission to—

  (1) examine the institution of slavery which existed from 1619 through 1865 within the United States and the colonies that became the United States, including the extent to which the Federal and State Governments constitutionally and statutorily supported the institution of slavery;

  (2) examine de jure and de facto discrimination against freed slaves and their descendants from the end of the Civil War to the present, including economic, political, and social discrimination;

  (3) examine the lingering negative effects of the institution of slavery and the discrimination described in paragraph (2) on living African-Americans and on society in the United States;

  (4) recommend appropriate ways to educate the American public of the Commission's findings;

  (5) recommend appropriate remedies in consideration of the Commission's findings on the matters described in paragraphs (1) and (2); and

  (6) submit to the Congress the results of such examination, together with such recommendations.

SECTION 3. ESTABLISHMENT AND DUTIES

(a) Establishment: There is established the Commission to Study Reparation Proposals for African Americans (hereinafter in this Act referred to as the "Commission").

(b) Duties: The Commission shall perform the following duties:

■ ■ ■

  (7) Recommended appropriate remedies. . . . In making such recommendations, the Commission shall address, among other issues, the following questions:

(A) Whether the Government of the United States should offer a formal apology on behalf of the people of the United States for the perpetration of gross human rights violations on African slaves and their descendants.

(B) Whether African-Americans still suffer from the lingering effects of . . . [slavery and Jim Crow].

(C) Whether, in consideration of the Commission's findings, any form of compensation to the descendants of African slaves is warranted.

(D) If the Commission finds that such compensation is warranted, what should be the amount of compensation, what form of compensation should be awarded, and who should be eligible for such compensation.

■　■　■

63 | Clinton and Conservatives Oppose Slavery Reparations

Mary E. Smith

The question of whether the United States should make reparations for slavery has led to outspoken opposition from a number of individuals. This opposition to compensation for slavery comes not only from conservatives, but from liberals as well, the most prominent of which is President Bill Clinton.

Clinton supports the major argument that has been made against the payment of reparations of slavery. He does not favor compensating the victims of slavery "because the nation is so many generations removed from that era that reparations for black Americans may not be possible."[1]

Although Clinton opposes compensating the descendants of slaves, he has suggested an alternative to reparations. He believes "the nation needs to continue to work to erase the effects of past discrimination."[2] In order to do so, Clinton has called for a new national dialogue on race, with the hope that the nation can become a "truly multiracial democracy."[3]

Prominent conservatives such as Speaker of the House and former history professor Newt Gingrich and columnist George F. Will also oppose compensation for slavery, but for another reason. They argue that we fought the Civil War to end slavery.[4] Although other conservatives agree with the more widely held view that the Civil War was fought to preserve the Union, rather than to end slavery,[5] they maintain that the North's participation in the Civil War makes the issue of an apology and reparations moot. Conservatives such as Terence P. Jeffrey have furthered this position by arguing that

> [t]he United States of America formally outlawed the importation of slaves in 1808. Slavery itself, the worst blight on the history of our nation, was obliterated from our law by the 13th Amendment to the Constitution that was ratified through an open democratic process by the American people in 1865.[6]

Thus, he argues that expiation by the United States has already taken place in the "form of a bloody Civil War that took the lives of almost 500,000 Americans" and resulted in the abolition of slavery.[7]

NOTES

1. "Clinton Opposes Slavery Reparations," http://allpolitics.com/1997/06/17/clinton.race.

2. Ibid.

3. Ibid.

4. Robert S. McElvaine, "They Didn't March to Free the Slaves," *Los Angeles Times*, July 25, 1997, p. B9.

5. See Paul Johnson, *A History of the American People* (London: Weidenfield and Nicolson, 1997), p. 470; Derrick Bell, *Race, Racism and American Law*, 3d ed. (Boston: Little, Brown, 1992), p. 9.

6. Terence P. Jeffrey, "Clinton Apologizes to Africa for Sins U.S. Never Committed," *Human Events: The National Conservative Weekly*, April 3, 1998, p. 1.

7. Ibid.

64 Collective Rehabilitation

Darrell L. Pugh

Should Congress muster the courage to proceed with a plan of reparations for African Americans, important issues of how to structure such payment need to be worked out. Specificially, two critical decisions need to be made: (1) How much money is to be paid out? and (2) How is the money to be paid out (i.e., whether to individuals in the form of compensation or to the class as a whole in the form of collective rehabilitation)?

Perhaps the most difficult decision facing Congress in enacting a public policy of reparations will be in determining the appropriate amounts to be awarded. Critical issues include whether the program would be largely symbolic or whether it would be seriously intended to close the large economic gap between African Americans and Caucasians. Assuming that the purpose will be the latter, it might be prudent to look to a proposal offered by Boris I. Bittker some thirty-five years ago.[1] In considering this very issue, Bittker suggested taking the gap between the average earnings for whites and blacks and multiplying this figure by the number of African Americans, to arrive at a sum that might suggest an annual level of funding.[2] Since it could be assumed that capacity building among African Americans would take time, some number of years of funding might be required to sustain such building efforts.[3]

Another approach might be to take the racial income gap figure and capitalize this value to determine the amount of investment required to realize the income necessary to close the gap. For example, assume an average income gap of $5,000 a year and an average market rate of return of 10 percent. Under the capitalization approach, it would take $50,000 of investment capital per eligible worker to close the gap (5,000/.10 = 50,000). This figure could then be multipled by the number of African Americans available in the adult workforce. Again, funding could be phased in over time, not only to encourage capacity building but to make the funding more politically feasible.

The second issue that must be addressed is how the payments would be made, whether to individuals or to and on behalf of the class as a whole. The fact that the reparations being suggested are prospective and primarily benefit nonvictims argues against the individual payment approach. Bittker persuasively argued that collective reparations would be used for institution building within the African American community, as an investment in its future, whereas money given to individuals would be used to finance consumption—"groceries, automobiles, occupational training, lottery tickets, and mutual-fund shares."[4] Whether or not Bittker is right in predicting how the money would be spent, one thing is certain, some portion of individual reparations would go toward consumption, thus reducing the amount available for investment. Legislation could require that all collective reparations paid to a legally authorized organizational entity be invested. Individuals could then apply according to established criteria for funds that would be used to foster the goals that "self-help" sought to achieve—namely, economic independence and self-sufficiency.

Creation of a national trust fund, administered by "legitimate" representatives of the African American community with oversight by Congress, might be one answer. Another approach might be the creation of a governmental entity structured along the lines of the Small Business Administration, headed by a board of governors appointed by the president with the advice and consent of the Senate. No doubt there are other possible administrative configurations worthy of consideration. The point is that collective investments would more than likely pay substantial dividends to the African American community that payments to individuals alone could not provide.

The prospect of reparations to African Americans is an exciting one. Many important political and legal constraints, as well as significant structural issues, need to be addressed. Nevertheless, there seems to be promising answers to some of these obstacles, bringing the potential for such a bold public policy step within the realm of possibility. What lies ahead is building the necessary national consensus required to support such a critical undertaking.

NOTES

1. Boris I. Bittker, *The Case for Black Reparations* (New York: Random House, 1973), p. 131.
2. Ibid.
3. Ibid.
4. Ibid., p. 72.

65 The Constitutionality of Black Reparations

Boris I. Bittker and Roy L. Brooks

In 1973, Boris Bittker discussed the constitutionality of black reparations in a chapter of his book, The Case for Black Reparations.[1] *In the following essay, Roy L. Brooks updates that discussion with Bittker's permission.*

Does the Constitution permit the federal government to establish and finance a program of reparations whose benefits would go to black citizens exclusively? It is, of course, common practice for governmental benefits to be distributed to a limited class of persons. Thus, we take it for granted that poor people but not rich ones get welfare payments, that veterans but not nonveterans qualify for benefits under the G.I. Bill of Rights, that homeowners but not tenants qualify for home-mortgage guarantees, and that farmers but not city people qualify for farm price supports and agricultural extension services. Moreover, in an earlier age the lines of demarcation drawn by Congress or the state legislature in the distribution of benefits were virtually immune to judicial review; echoing the popular maxim that beggars can't be choosers, it was said that no one has a constitutional right to public "largesse." This curt response is no longer in vogue, and the courts are now more willing to review the qualifications laid down in legislation on the complaint of an aggrieved person to see if his or her exclusion is so unreasonable as to violate the Fifth Amendment's guarantee of "due process of law" or the Fourteenth Amendment's guarantee of "equal protection of the laws."[2] In these judicial forays, however, the courts acknowledge that legislative bodies have an exceedingly wide range for the exercise of discretion, and the legislative judgment is rarely overturned.

Against this background, black reparations might be regarded as simply a routine legislative action to meet the claims of one defined group of citizens by establishing a program from which others (viz., whites) are excluded. Asked to enlarge the program to include whites (for example, on the ground that many whites have

374

also suffered from governmental neglect or misconduct), or to enjoin its operation entirely, the Supreme Court might repeat what it said when an Oklahoma optician argued that he was denied the equal protection of the laws by a state law that regulated his business but exempted the sellers of ready-to-wear eyeglasses with which his products competed:

> The problem of legislative classification is a perennial one, admitting of no doctrinaire definition. Evils in the same field may be of different dimensions and proportions, requiring different remedies. Or so the legislature may think. Or the reform may take one step at a time, addressing itself to the phase of the problem which seems most acute to the legislative mind. The legislature may select one phase of one field and apply a remedy there, neglecting the others. The prohibition of the Equal Protection Clause goes no further than the invidious discrimination.[3]

In a similar vein, the Supreme Court upheld the conviction of a Maryland storekeeper for selling a loose-leaf binder and a can of floor wax in violation of the state's Sunday closing laws, despite the fact that the laws exempted the sale of cigarettes, gasoline, candy, and a bewildering array of other products. Rejecting the defendant's argument that these statutory distinctions were so arbitrary and capricious as to deny him the equal protection of the laws, the Court said:

> Although no precise formula has been developed, the Court has held that [the equal-protection clause of] the Fourteenth Amendment permits the States a wide scope of discretion in enacting laws which affect some groups of citizens differently than others. The constitutional safeguard is offended only if the classification rests on grounds wholly irrelevant to the achievement of the State's objective. State legislatures are presumed to have acted within their constitutional power despite the fact that, in practice, their laws result in some inequality. A statutory discrimination will not be set aside if any state of facts reasonably may be conceived to justify it.[4]

Although expressed in cases involving the constitutionality of state action under the equal protection clause of the Fourteenth Amendment, judicial deference to the legislature's judgment is an equally common response when federal action is attacked under the due process clause of the Fifth Amendment.[5]

This reluctance to interfere with legislative solutions, however, does not extend to laws embodying distinctions based on race, color, or religion. They encounter a more skeptical reception, epitomized in the Supreme Court's statement that: "[d]istinctions between citizens solely because of their ancestry are by their very nature odious to a free people whose institutions are founded upon the doctrine of equality."[6] More succinctly, Justice John Marshall Harlan said in 1896 that the "Constitution is color-blind." He made this remark in his dissenting opinion in *Plessy v. Ferguson*,[7] where the majority upheld a state segregation statute; but it is often said that his view was vindicated and endorsed by *Brown v. Board of Education*[8] in 1954, when the Supreme Court rejected the *Plessy* precedent.[9]

Years later, Justice Antonin Scalia, quoting one of Boris I. Bittker's colleagues, would articulate a similar view of the Constitution:

The difficulty of overcoming the effects of past discrimination is as nothing compared with the difficulty of eradicating from our society the source of those effects, which is the tendency—fatal to a Nation such as ours—to classify and judge men and women on the basis of their country of origin or the color of their skin. A solution to the first problem that aggravates the second is no solution at all. I share the view expressed by Alexander Bickel that "[t]he lesson of the great decisions of the Supreme Court and the lesson of contemporary history have been the same for at least a generation: discrimination on the basis of race is illegal, immoral, unconstitutional, inherently wrong, and destructive of democratic society."[10]

Can these generalizations, founded on the equal protection clause of the Fourteenth Amendment and also on a more basic theory of democracy, be squared with racial distinctions having a compensatory purpose? Or do they confine governmental actions to the elimination of racial disparities for the future, requiring us to let bygones be bygones?

It is interesting to discover that Section 5 of the Fourteenth Amendment, authorizing Congress to enact appropriate legislation to enforce the amendment's prohibitions, was once described by the Supreme Court as having an exclusively racial purpose. "We doubt very much," said the Court in 1872, "whether any action of a State not directed by way of discrimination against the negroes as a class, or on account of their race, will ever be held to come within the purview of this provision."[11] This prophecy was not borne out, however, and, as we shall see, the Supreme Court in recent years has often asserted that legislation for the exclusive benefit of one racial group would ordinarily violate the Fourteenth Amendment and, by extension, the Fifth Amendment, even if animated by a benign purpose.[12]

Three decades ago, Bittker struggled with these issues in an article entitled "The Case of the Checker-Board Ordinance: An Experiment in Race Relations."[13] His arena was an imaginary lawsuit brought by a black who had been denied the right to buy a house designated for "white occupancy only" in New Harmony, Illinois, a utopian community in which every dwelling was assigned to either black or white occupancy in a checkerboard pattern. In this fable the ordinance was enacted to achieve integration by legal compulsion, following testimony by students of American race relations that private discrimination and prejudice are heightened by segregated housing patterns but lowered by integrated patterns; that a community with a stable pattern of integrated housing would enrich the lives of all its citizens by enlarging their relations with persons of the other race; and that whites either would not move to New Harmony or would tend to leave if they thought they would be greatly outnumbered by Negroes. The central issue in this hypothetical lawsuit was whether the equal protection clause of the Fourteenth Amendment permits citizens to be classified by race in the administration of a "benign" governmental program.

Because Bittker found the question troublesome and resistant to a clear solution, he cast the discussion in the form of separate opinions by three appellate judges. The first judge wrote the briefest opinion, concluding that the Constitution prohibits the use of race or color as a criterion of state action, at least in regulating the ownership and occupancy of land. He relied primarily on two Supreme Court decisions. One, decided in 1917, held that a municipal ordinance forbidding blacks to move into or occupy houses in residential blocks that were predominantly occupied by whites (and imposing reciprocal restrictions on whites) violated the due process clause of the Fourteenth Amendment.[14] The other, announced in 1948, cited the equal protection clause in holding that state courts could not enforce restrictive covenants voluntarily adopted by private landowners to preserve the racial character of their neighborhoods, even though the state courts stood ready to enforce such covenants against potential white occupants as well as against blacks:

> The rights established [by the Fourteenth Amendment] are personal rights. . . . Equal protection of the laws is not achieved through indiscriminate imposition of inequalities.[15]

The hypothetical judge's conclusion that New Harmony's checker-board ordinance was inconsistent with these cases was reinforced, in his opinion, by the Supreme Court's 1954 condemnation of public school segregation in *Brown v. Board of Education*. Not unlike proponents of California's Proposition 209,[16] the judge read *Brown* as a vindication of Justice Harlan's color-blind principle.

For Bittker's second hypothetical judge, this conclusion was an unacceptable interpretation of the Constitution. He accused his colleague of mechanically applying constitutional provisions designed to prevent discrimination against the newly emancipated slaves to a very different area, namely, remedial or compensatory legislation:

> The Fourteenth Amendment is almost one hundred years old, and its life has been replete with irony: railroads, utility companies, banks, employers of child labor, chain stores, money lenders, aliens, and a host of other groups and institutions have all found nurture in the due process and equal protection clauses, leaving so little room for the Negro that he seemed to be the fourteenth amendment's forgotten man. This despite the Supreme Court's early recognition that "the one pervading purpose" of the thirteenth, fourteenth, and fifteenth amendments was to insure "the freedom of the slave race, the security and firm establishment of that freedom, and the protection of the newly-made freeman and citizen from the oppressions of those who had formerly exercised unlimited dominion over him." . . . The kaleidoscope of life often refuses to reflect our confident predictions, but seldom has a forecast been so completely lost to sight. Even so, the crowning irony comes today, when the racial zoning, restrictive covenant and school segregation cases, which had begun to restore the fourteenth amendment to the Negro, are used as weapons to destroy the first local legislation to ameliorate the condition of the Negro that has passed in review before this court.[17]

In harmony with this approach, the second judge distinguished the cases on which the first judge had relied, arguing that racial classifications are not unconstitutional per se, but only if they impute inferiority to one of the groups:[18]

Any legislation that treats individuals (minors, women, men of draft age, veterans, lawyers, Indians, etc.) as members of a class necessarily distinguishes them from others; but the legislation does not "discriminate" (in an invidious sense) if the classification is validated by some appropriate purpose or effect.[19]

To illustrate this principle (now commonly called the "non-subordination principle"),[20] the second judge pointed out that race has often been used by the courts as a factor in passing on the constitutionality of criminal convictions:

In reviewing criminal cases in which violations of the due process clause have been alleged (e.g., denial of counsel, involuntary confessions, unreasonable delays in arraignment, etc.) the federal courts have often referred to the defendant's race or color. Without suggesting that race or color were crucial in all of these cases, or indeed in any, I cannot believe that they were merely neutral circumstances, like the defendant's social security number. Race, to the contrary, has been treated as a relevant circumstance, like the defendant's youth, poverty, illiteracy, or friendlessness, in judging whether he received due process of law. Rigorous proof of racial prejudice has not been demanded, however, and it would not be unreasonable to describe these cases as exercises of benevolent vigilance thought necessary to protect Negroes as a class from improper practices by the police and trial courts.[21]

Other racial classifications that are permitted because of their "remedial" character, according to the second judge, are the restricted rights of certain American Indians to dispose of their property until the Secretary of the Interior certified them as competent to handle their own affairs,[22] and cases permitting a black defendant in a criminal case to get a new trial if blacks were systematically excluded from his jury.[23] He went on to conclude that the checker-board ordinance, though it restricted the freedom of the black plaintiff to live where he wished, was a similarly reasonable effort to correct a social evil, and that it was consistent with the constitutional guarantees of due process and equal protection.

Recent scholarship finds additional support for the non-subordination principle in several other Supreme Court opinions. Three of the most unlikely sources are *Plessy, Brown,* and *Bolling v. Sharpe*:[24]

Plessy upheld a statute that separated African American passengers from white passengers in railway cars. The Supreme Court accepted the argument that the statute's racial distinction "has no tendency to destroy the legal equality of the races, or reestablish a state of involuntary servitude." This view of the statute gave birth to the Court's "separate but equal" doctrine. What is so revealing about this opinion is that the Court addressed the contention of the plaintiff that the statute stamped African Americans with a "badge of inferiority." The Court responded that such a suggestion of inferiority did not arise from the statute itself but from its interpretation by African Americans. It is of some moment that the Court felt it necessary to rebut the charges of racial subordination. If the 14th Amendment vindicated only the colorblind principle, there would be no need to discuss the issue of racial subordination. Because the Court did not find racial subordination in *Plessy*, it concluded that the statute was constitutional. . . .

■   ■   ■

Proponents of the colorblind principle invariably cite *Brown* as support for the principle. But the opinion does not even so much as mention the word "colorblind" or cite to Justice Harlan's dissent in *Plessy* wherein the term is actually used. The Supreme Court in *Brown* ruled that "separate educational facilities are inherently unequal." At the time of *Brown*, that was certainly true, not only in Topeka, Kansas, but in most other Jim Crow school districts across the country. "[T]he policy of separating the races is usually interpreted as denoting the inferiority of the Negro group," the Court noted. Thus, a close reading of *Brown* seems to indicate that the Court only intended to invalidate those racial classifications that subordinate or stigmatize a racial group. The same must be said of *Bolling v. Sharpe*, in which the Court, on the same day that it decided *Brown*, overturned a school segregation law in Washington, D.C. School segregation in the nation's capital was unconstitutional, the Court said, because it was not "reasonably related to any proper governmental objective, and thus it imposes on Negroes a burden." Arguably, neither *Brown* nor *Bolling* stand for the colorblind principle; both vindicate the nonsubordination principle.[25]

The non-subordination principle and the color-blind principle cannot easily coexist, if at all. Color-blindness is less concerned with social equality (what is sometimes called "measurable equality"); non-subordination is less concerned with legal equality (what is sometimes called "formal equal opportunity"). This tension is highlighted, yet often overlooked, in Justice Harlan's dissent in *Plessy*, in which he believed that color-blindness would *not* lead to a restructuring of the social order. Instead, he believed that whites would retain their social dominance under a color-blind Constitution. The very paragraph that sets forth the color-blind principle begins as follows:

> The white race deems itself to be the dominant race in this country. And so it is, in prestige, in achievements, in education, in wealth and in power. So, I doubt not, it will continue to be for all time, if it remains true to its great heritage and holds fast to the principles of constitutional liberty.[26]

Proponents of the non-subordination principle might ask: What good is legal equality without social equality?

This is not to say that the non-subordination principle rejects a fundamental tenet of our liberal democratic society—namely, the belief that the state should remain neutral as to race. The non-subordination principle accepts this command, but asserts that the lingering effects of slavery and Jim Crow implicate the state in a continuing regime of racial subordination that, at times, can only be brought to an end through a benign use of race.[27]

The third judge in the checkerboard fable argued that the distinction between benign and malevolent uses of racial classifications threatened to undermine the constitutional objective of equality. If a checkerboard pattern of individual houses is permissible, why not a checkerboard of city blocks or wards, or a local white-black ratio corresponding to the state or national ratio or to a sociologist's recipe for a "good mix" of racial groups? If housing is a permissible area for experimentation, why not proportional racial representations in schools, employment, or voting? If these quotas, limitations, and privileges are permissible ways to compensate for past injustices toward blacks, why not similar devices for other minorities, distinguished by religion, national origin, or economic status?

At a more fundamental level, the third judge, similar to today's proponents of California's Proposition 209,[28] rejected his colleague's theory that benign racial legislation can be distinguished from legislation that imputes inferiority to one of the groups:

> [E]ven the most well-intended legislation may be felt as humiliating by its objects, and especially so in a country that professes that "all men are created equal." . . . Viewed in this light, [New Harmony's] ordinance carries with it the offensive implication that is the unfortunate but seemingly inevitable concomitant of official charity or paternalism. Beyond that, it rests on, or is tantamount to, an official finding that whites will not live side-by-side with Negroes except under legal compulsion. Perhaps this will be regarded by some as an official condemnation of the attitude of whites, in no sense reflecting adversely on Negroes; but just as many Negroes could not write off racial segregation in the public schools as merely a monument to white inhumanity, so I doubt if the implications of New Harmony's ordinance will leave them unscathed. Rather, many Negroes may ask themselves, as victims of private prejudice often do, what they have done to instill such distaste in others; and this inward search—made more acute by the fact that similar legal measures are not deemed necessary for other minority groups—may be equally destructive of self-esteem whether the finding that integrated housing cannot be achieved without legal compulsion is correct or not.[29]

As to the Indian cases cited by his colleague to establish that the Constitution permits racial classifications of a remedial character, the third judge argued that they should serve instead "to warn us that the role of the Great White Father may be bitterly resented by those in his tutelage and that a guardian ordinarily prefers to postpone rather than to advance the day when his wards must face the rigors of freedom."[30] He went on to say that even if the criminal cases involving black defendants, on which his colleague relied, display a rule of "benevolent vigilance" for the rights of blacks, this does not "lead to the conclusion that legislatures may exercise in other areas of life whatever benevolent supervision they may believe is required by the social problems they perceive."[31]

The hypothetical third judge anticipated the views held by conservative black Americans in the 1990s. For example, Justice Clarence Thomas argued in *Adarand Constructors, Inc. v. Peña*[32] that there is [no] "paternalism exception to the principle of equal protection, . . ." and that "there can be no doubt that racial paternalism and its unintended consequences can be as poisonous and pernicious as any other form of discrimination." So-called "benign" discrimination teaches many that because of chronic and apparently immutable handicaps, minorities cannot compete with them without their patronizing indulgence. . . . [S]uch programs . . . stamp minorities with a badge of inferiority and may cause them to develop dependencies or to adopt an attitude that they are "entitled" to preferences. [33]

Likewise, another prominent black American, the author and academician Shelby Steele, has argued that the use of benign race-conscious programs in higher education has caused blacks to suffer "inferiority anxiety"—that is, self-doubt and a fear of competing with white Americans.[34]

In 1962, when Bittker argued all three sides in this inconclusive debate, the constitutionality of a "remedial" racial classification was only a cloud on the horizon. It was perceived as a problem by a few public housing agencies that were covertly applying a "benign" quota on black occupancy to prevent it from reaching the "tipping point" at which whites were expected to move out. Since then, however, the cloud has moved directly overhead, blown by the winds of change let loose by *Brown v. Board of Education*.

When *Brown* was decided, it was widely thought that compliance with its mandate "to admit [school children] to public schools on a racially nondiscriminatory basis"[35] could be achieved by the repeal of all school segregation laws and the assignment of pupils to schools on the basis of school districts with "neutral" boundaries (e.g., highways, rivers, railroad tracks, and political subdivisions). Thus, the plaintiffs in *Brown* framed the basic question in the case as whether the State of Kansas had the power to enforce the state statute by which racially segregated public elementary schools were maintained.[36] This suggested that the existence of predominantly or wholly black or white schools would not violate the Constitution, provided the new school-attendance zones followed "neutral" boundaries and were not gerrymandered to perpetuate a division along racial lines. The goal of *Brown*, proponents of this limited mode of compliance argued, was not integration but the elimination of compulsory segregation. Indeed, some argued that the deliberate selection of boundaries to achieve a "desirable" racial mix would be improper, based on the theory of a color-blind Constitution.

In the ensuing years, the Supreme Court has revisited this issue on numerous occasions. The tension between integration and color-blindness, two morally defensible perspectives on civil rights, came before the Court in a variety of contexts (primarily education, employment, and voting)[37] under the rubric of affirmative action. Beginning in 1978 with *Regents of the University of California v. Bakke*[38] and ending in 1995 with *Adarand Constructors, Inc. v. Peña*,[39] these cases, all of which deal with constitutional challenges to the use of racial preferences or quotas in the public sphere, provide the legal framework for assessing the constitutionality of black reparations. This framework begins with an understanding of the "strict scrutiny test," as explained by Brooks on another occasion:[40]

> The strict scrutiny test is nowhere to be found in the Constitution or in its legislative history. It is a legal doctrine made up entirely by judges. Developed as a means to facilitate close judicial review of Jim Crow and other "suspicious" legislative enactments, the strict scrutiny test applies to lawsuits brought under the equal protection clause of the Fourteenth Amendment or the equal protection component of the Fifth Amendment's due process clause. The former constitutional provision protects against state actions[41] and the latter against federal actions.[42]

> Now a fixture in constitutional law, the strict scrutiny test is the legal system's primary means of implementing . . . [the color-blind principle]. It commands the omission of race in the government's formulation of laws and public policies. More importantly, it operates to strike down, as a denial of equal protection of the laws, any governmental activity or legislation that is either predicated upon an explicit racial or other "suspect classification"[43] or violative of a "fundamental personal interest."[44] The act under scrutiny is saved from judicial strangulation only if the government can meet a two-fold burden. First, the classification must be justified by a "compelling governmental interest." Second, the means chosen to achieve that purpose must be the least restrictive, narrowly tailored means available.[45]

> As applied by the Supreme Court, the strict scrutiny test sets up a standard of judicial review so rigorous as to be fatal to most applicable legislative acts. The first burden is particularly difficult to meet. Protecting national security[46] and remedying past institutional or individual discrimination[47] are among the few (if not the only) times the government has been able to demonstrate a compelling governmental interest to the Supreme Court's satisfaction.

> The Court, however, has attempted to balance the interventionist proclivity of the strict scrutiny test with a more deferential form of judicial review. Legislative acts not predicated on a suspect classification or violative of a fundamental personal interest—which is where the great majority of legislative acts fall—do not offend constitutional equal protection if they can be rationally related to a legitimate governmental purpose. The "rational basis test" provides the widest degree of judicial comity to even speculative legislative judgments.[48]

Explicit gender-based classifications are not suspect classifications and, hence, are not subject to strict scrutiny. Neither are they reviewed under the rational basis test. Rather, the Supreme Court employs a "middle-tier" or an "intermediate level" of scrutiny. Under this standard, the classification in question must serve important governmental objectives and must be substantially related to the achievement of those objectives.[49]

> [T]he strict scrutiny test and the rational basis test are so predictably applied that the judicial outcome is virtually determined by the type of legislation under review. Legislation involving a suspect classification or a fundamental personal interest most likely will not survive constitutional scrutiny; whereas legislation involving economic

classifications probably will be sustained. The Supreme Court's analysis for equal protection claims is in this sense outcome-determinative.

Prior to *Adarand Constructors, Inc. v. Peña*,[50] the Supreme Court seemed to suggest that the strict scrutiny test did not apply to race-based affirmative action plans created by Congress. Indeed in *City of Richmond v. Croson Co.*,[51] the first case in which a majority of justices held that the strict scrutiny test governed the benign use of race by state or local government, Chief Justice William Rehnquist and Justices Sandra Day O'Connor and Byron White ruled that Congress, as a coequal branch of government, is entitled to greater deference than cities and states.[52] Agreeing with *Croson*'s dicta, a majority of the justices in a subsequent case, *Metro Broadcasting, Inc. v. FCC*,[53] applied the intermediate standard of review in upholding the constitutionality of a congressional affirmative action plan favoring racial minorities. Speaking for the Court, Justice William Brennan wrote:

> We hold that benign race-conscious measures mandated by Congress—even if those measures are not "remedial" in the sense of being designed to compensate victims of past governmental or societal discrimination—are constitutionally permissible to the extent that they serve important governmental objectives within the power of Congress and are substantially related to the achievement of those objectives.[54]

The decision in this case was split by the narrowest of margins, five to four.

Demonstrating a fair amount of indecision, the Supreme Court just five years later, and by another five-four margin, reversed *Metro Broadcasting*. The *Adarand* majority accused the *Metro Broadcasting* majority of taking a "surprising turn" in treating benign racial classifications by the federal government "less skeptically than others." Not unlike the first and third hypothetical judges in Bittker's checkerboard fable presented some thirty-six years ago, the *Adarand* majority believed that the color-blind principle should be vindicated. As a matter of basic democratic theory, the Court wrote:

> [T]he Fifth and Fourteenth Amendments to the Constitution protect persons, not groups. It follows from that principle that all governmental action based on race—a group classification long recognized as "in most circumstances irrelevant and therefore prohibited"—should be subjected to detailed judicial inquiry to ensure that the personal right to equal protection of the laws has not been infringed. These ideas have long been central to this Court's understanding of equal protection, and holding "benign" state and federal racial classifications to different standards does not square with them.[55]

Adarand would seem to sound the death knell for black reparations, unless they can be tendered as compensation for the government's racial discrimination against blacks. A recent circuit court opinion, *Jacobs v. Barr*,[56] makes this clear.

Jacobs dealt with the constitutionality of the Civil Liberties Act of 1988.[57] In this unprecedented legislation, Congress, on behalf of the federal government, apologized and provided atonement money of twenty thousand dollars each to citizens and permanent resident aliens of Japanese ancestry who were forcibly relocated and placed in internment camps during World War II. The Act also apologized and provided reparations awards of twelve thousand dollars each to the Aleuts who were forcibly relocated from their homelands to Alaska during that time. (See Part 4.) No other groups are entitled to compensation under the Act. In *Jacobs*, the plaintiff, a German American who was detained with his German father during the war, challenged this feature of the Act on grounds that it denied him equal protection of the laws. The court found ample evidence in the legislative history of the Act that Japanese American and Aleutian internees were the victims of racial prejudice at the hands of the federal government, whereas German American internees were not. For example, no mass exclusion or detention of German or Italian Americans was ordered, and those detained, including the plaintiff and his father, were first given due process hearings to establish their threat to national security. The circuit court therefore ruled that the Act passed constitutional muster under both the intermediate scrutiny test, which was the controlling standard of review at the time the case was brought, and the strict scrutiny test. "Congress . . . had clear and sufficient reason to compensate interns of Japanese but not German descent; and the compensation is substantially related (as well as narrowly tailored) to Congress's compelling interest in redressing a shameful example of national discrimination."[58]

Slavery and Jim Crow are undeniably shameful episodes of "national discrimination" (discrimination as official federal policy, not mere societal discrimination) against black Americans. Congress can certainly find ample evidence of this in the historical record should it decide to enact legislation for blacks similar to the Civil Liberties Act of 1988.[59] Legislation may be the only realistic way to proceed given the reluctance of courts to fashion their own monetary remedies. Indeed, it was in large part the failure of Japanese Americans to obtain monetary reparations through the courts that led to the pursuit of legislation resulting in the Civil Liberties Act. (See Part 4.)

But will the beneficiaries of black reparations, like those of the Civil Liberties Act, have to be actual victims of federal discrimination? As we move farther away from the Jim Crow era (circa 1865–1968), establishing privity between the wrongdoer and victim will become as problematic as it is for slavery-based claims. For this reason, proponents of reparations have argued for "new connections between victims and perpetrators," including the recognition that today's blacks belong to the same victim class as prior generations of blacks, that many black families can trace their genealogy to identifiable victims of slavery or Jim Crow, and that the U.S. government, even though it no longer officially discriminates, assumes the liabilities of past administrations and congresses.[60] These arguments are based on public policy considerations and not on legal doctrine. Indeed, they assume the absence of legal support for paying reparations to nonvictims, which may not be the case entirely.

Arguably, legal support for atonement money going to nonvictims can be based on two grounds—one constitutionally based, the other statutorily created. As to the first, we have already seen that the Supreme Court's affirmative action case law upholds race-conscious remedies designed to redress the perpetrator's past discrimination. Because such discrimination can occur years, even decades, prior to the crafting of the remedy, the beneficiary and victim need not be, and often are not, the same person. Victim-beneficiary alienation seems to be built into the controlling constitutional law.[61]

Second, Congress has enacted legislation that provides relief to certain nonvictims of employment discrimination. Section 706(g) of Title VII of the 1964 Civil Rights Act, the nation's primary employment discrimination law, empowers a court to order, upon a finding of unlawful discrimination, specific forms of relief "or any other equitable relief as the court deems appropriate."[62] This provision was intended, Congress said, "to give the courts wide discretion in exercising their equitable powers to fashion the most complete relief possible."[63] The Supreme Court has held that the last sentence of section 706(g), which prohibits a court from ordering a Title VII defendant to hire, reinstate, promote, or provide payback to an individual for any reason "other than" discrimination in violation of Title VII, does not prohibit a court from awarding (or an employer from granting through a consent decree) preferential, race-conscious remedies that benefit nonvictims.[64] On its face, the Court said, the last sentence does not "state that all prospective remedial orders must be limited so that they only benefit the specific victims of the employer's or union's past discriminatory acts."[65] While it is true that the nonvictims in these cases were incidental beneficiaries of nonmonetary relief, and that nonvictim black Americans would be targeted beneficiaries of monetary relief under most reparations plans, the Supreme Court's reasoning could easily extend beyond the specific facts of the cases. The purpose of such relief, the Court has reasoned, is "not to make identified victims whole," but to dismantle the lingering effects of prior discrimination and to prevent discrimination in the future.[66]

Using section 706(g) and the Civil Liberties Act as models, Congress might be able to enact a statute that made a legislative finding of past governmental discrimination against blacks as a group and then proceeded to award atonement money or other forms of reparations (e.g., affirmative action) to contemporary blacks. The purpose of the award would be atonement for past sins and not compensation to actual victims. This reasoning provides a logical basis for benefiting nonvictims. To borrow from the Supreme Court, "Such relief is provided to the class as a whole rather than to individual members; no individual is entitled to relief, and beneficiaries need not show that they were themselves victims of discrimination."[67]

The remarkable regularity and balance between the constitutional and statutory standards should not go unnoticed. Both are group- rather than individual-focused, and, more importantly, both seek to deal with the residual effects of prior acts of discrimination. The latter purpose would seem to provide the necessary legal grounds for deciding the privity issue. But in the end, a judicial resolution of that and other legal questions surrounding black reparations might well turn on public policy considerations, as is usually the case.

NOTES

1. Boris I. Bittker, *The Case for Black Reparations* (New York: Vintage Books, 1973), chap. 11. For reviews of Bittker's book, see Ira B. Shepard, "Book Review," *Georgia Law Review* 7 (1973): 587; Derrick A. Bell, Jr., "Dissection of a Dream," *Harvard Civil Rights–Civil Liberties Law Review* 9 (1974): 156; Mark Tushnet, "The Utopian Technician," *Yale Law Journal* 93 (1983): 208. For other discussion of the constitutionality of black reparations, see, e.g., Mari J. Matsuda, "Looking to the Bottom: Critical Legal Studies and Reparations," *Harvard Civil Rights–Civil Liberties Law Review* 22 (1987): 323; Rhonda V. Magee, "The Master's Tools, from the Bottom Up: Responses to American Reparations Theory in Mainstream and Outsider Remedies Discourse," *Virginia Law Review* 79 (1993): 863, 897–904.

2. See, e.g., *Adarand Constructors, Inc. v. Peña*, 518 U.S. 200 (1995) (race); *United States v. Virginia*, 518 U.S. 515 (1996) (gender); *City of Cleburne v. Cleburne Living Center, Inc.*, 473 U.S. 432 (1985) (discussing various standards of judicial review). See, generally, Erwin Chemerinsky, *Constitutional Law: Principles and Policies* (New York: Aspen Law and Business, 1997), pp. 638–746; Van Alstyne, "The Demise of the Right-Privilege Distinction in Constitutional Law," *Harvard Law Review* 81 (1968): 1439.

3. *Williamson v. Lee Optical Co.*, 348 U.S. 483, 489 (1955).

4. *McGowan v. Maryland*, 366 U.S. 420, 425–426 (1961).

5. See, e.g., *Adarand Constructors, Inc. v. Peña*, 515 U.S. 200 (1995); *Bolling v. Sharpe*, 347 U.S. 497 (1954).

6. *Hirabayashi v. United States*, 320 U.S. 81, 100 (1943).

7. *Plessy v. Ferguson*, 163 U.S. 537, 559 (1896).

8. *Brown v. Board of Education*, 347 U.S. 483 (1954).

9. There is disagreement over how to read *Brown*. *Brown* is commonly understood as overturning *Plessy* and the "separate but equal" doctrine. Some scholars, however, argue that the *Brown* court attempted to distinguish *Plessy* instead of overruling it. See, e.g., Lino Graglia, *Disaster by Decree: The Supreme Court Decisions on Race and the Schools* (Ithaca: Cornell University Press, 1976), pp. 26–30. Note that the *Brown* court found it necessary to mention that *Plessy* "involv[ed] not education but transportation." 347 U.S. at 491. For a detailed discussion and scholarly analysis of *Brown*, see, generally, Leon Friedman, ed., *Argument: The Oral Argument before the Supreme Court in Brown v. Board of Education of Topeka, 1952–55* (New York: Chelsea House Publishers, 1969); "Symposium: *Brown v. Board of Education*," *Southern Illinois University Law Journal* 20 (1995): 1.

10. *City of Richmond v. J. A. Croson Co.*, 488 U.S. 469, 520–521 (1989) (Scalia, J., concurring in the judgment) (quoting Alexander Bickel, *The Morality of Consent* [New Haven: Yale University Press, 1975], p. 133).

11. *Slaughter-House Cases*, 83 U.S. 36, 81 (1872).

12. See, e.g., *Adarand Constructors, Inc. v. Peña*, 515 U.S. 200 (1995); *City of Richmond v. Croson*, 488 U.S. 469 (1989).

13. Boris I. Bittker, "The Case of the Checker-Board Ordinance: An Experiment in Race Relations," *Yale Law Journal* 71 (1962): 1387.

14. *Buchanan v. Warley*, 245 U.S. 60 (1917).

15. *Shelley v. Kraemer*, 334 U.S. 1, 22 (1948).

16. Proposition 209 (or the "California Civil Rights Initiative") amended the California Constitution in 1996. Section 31(a) of the California Constitution now reads: "The State

shall not discriminate against or grant preferential treatment to any individiual or group on the basis of race, sex, color, ethnicity, or national origin in the operation of public employment, public education, or public contracting." California Constitution, Article 1, Section 31(a). Put simply, Proposition 209 ends most governmental affirmative action in California. The subsequent constitutional challenge to Proposition 209 was unsuccessful. See *Coalition for Economic Equity v. Wilson*, 110 F.3d 1431 (1997) (vacating the preliminary injunction and finding no unequal "political structure" that obstructs minorities from receiving protection against unequal treatment). For a more detailed analysis of Proposition 209, see Eugene Volokh, "The California Civil Rights Initiative: An Interpretive Guide," *University of California Los Angeles Law Review* 44 (1997): 1335. For a criticism of Proposition 209, see Derrick A. Bell, "California's Proposition 209: A Temporary Diversion on the Road to Racial Disaster," *Loyola Law Review* 30 (1997): 1447.

17. Bittker, "The Case of the Checker-Board Ordinance," p. 1393.

18. For a more detailed discussion, see, e.g., Roy L. Brooks, *Integration or Separation?* (Cambridge: Harvard University Press, 1996), pp. 199–213.

19. Bittker, "The Case of the Checker-Board Ordinance," p. 1394.

20. Brooks, *Integration or Separation?* p. 208.

21. Bittker, "The Case of the Checker-Board Ordinance," p. 1407.

22. *Squire v. Capoeman*, 351 U.S. 1 (1956).

23. See *Batson v. Kentucky*, 476 U.S. 79 (1986). See also *Powers v. Ohio*, 499 U.S. 400 (1991) (civil cases).

24. *Bolling v. Sharpe*, 347 U.S. 497 (1954).

25. Brooks, *Integration or Separation?* pp. 208, 210–211 (citations omitted).

26. *Plessy v. Ferguson*, 163 U.S. at 558 (Harlan, J., dissenting).

27. For a more detailed discussion, see Roy L. Brooks, *Critical Procedure* (Durham, N.C.: Carolina Academic Press, 1998), pp. 5–7.

28. See the discussion of Proposition 209 above.

29. Bittker, "The Case of the Checker-Board Ordinance," pp. 1419–1420.

30. Ibid., p. 1422.

31. Ibid., p. 1423.

32. *Adarand Constructors, Inc. v. Peña*, 515 U.S. 200 (1995).

33. Ibid., pp. 240–241.

34. See Shelby Steele, *The Content of Our Character: A New Vision of Race in America* (New York: St. Martin's Press, 1990), pp. 47, 55, 62–63, 68–70, 108–109, 113–125, 156–157.

35. *Brown v. Board of Education*, 349 U.S. 294, 301 (1955) (*Brown II*).

36. See Friedman, ed., *Argument*, p. 15.

37. For a discussion of these cases, see, e.g., Roy L. Brooks, Gilbert P. Carrasco, and Gordon A. Martin, *Civil Rights Litigation: Cases and Perspectives* (Durham, N.C.: Carolina Academic Press, 1995), chap. 10; Jed Rubenfeld, "Affirmative Action," *Yale Law Journal* 107 (1997): 427.

38. *Regents of the University of California v. Bakke*, 438 U.S. 265 (1978). In *Bakke*, a divided Supreme Court ruled five to four that state educational institutions could not set aside a specific number of slots for which only racial minorities could compete. Although important as a starting point for any discussion of benign racial classification, *Bakke*'s precedential value is rather questionable. *Bakke* is a poor case from which to draw conclusions about the application of the equal protection clause in general and the controlling standard of judicial

review for black reparations as well as other forms of race-based affirmative action. Only Justice Lewis Powell invalidated the racial quota on equal protection grounds. He was also the only justice to use the strict scrutiny test as the constitutional standard of review for race-based affirmative action. Significantly, the four justices who would not scrutinize benign quotas strictly—William Brennan, Thurgood Marshall, Harry Blackmun, and (possibly) Byron White—have not won the day in subsequent benign quota or preference cases. Since *Bakke*, a majority of Supreme Court justices have taken the position that all explicit racial classifications—whether racially exclusive or inclusive—are subject to strict scrutiny, and that only national security or the defendant's past or current intentional discrimination—not societal discrimination—will justify the use of such a classification. See, e.g., *City of Richmond v. Croson,* 488 U.S. 469 (1989); *Adarand Constructors, Inc. v. Peña,* 515 U.S. 200 (1995).

39. *Adarand Constructors, Inc. v. Peña,* 515 U.S. 200 (1995)

40. Roy L. Brooks, *Rethinking the American Race Problem* (Berkeley: University of California Press, 1990), pp. 51–52 (internal citations renumbered).

41. See, e.g., *United States v. Paradise,* 480 U.S. 149, 166 (1987) (cases cited therein). See also *Brown v. Board of Education,* 347 U.S. 483 (1954); *City of Richmond v. Croson,* 488 U.S. 46 (1989).

42. See, e.g., *Local 28 of Sheet Metal Workers v. EEOC,* 478 U.S. 421, 479–480 (1986) (cases cited therein). See also *Bolling v. Sharpe,* 347 U.S. 497 (1954).

43. See, e.g., *McDonald v. Board of Election Commissioners of Chicago,* 394 U.S. 802, 807 (1969). See, generally, Polyvios G. Polyviou, *The Equal Protection of the Laws* (London: Duckworth, 1980); Note, "Developments in the Law—Equal Protection," *Harvard Law Review* 82 (1969): 1065.

44. See, e.g., *Reynolds v. Sims,* 377 U.S. 533, 561–562 (1964). Fundamental personal interest includes the right to procreate, *Skinner v. Oklahoma,* 316 U.S. 535 (1942); the right to vote, *Reynolds,* 377 U.S. 533; and the right to interstate travel, *Shapiro v. Thompson,* 394 U.S. 618 (1969).

45. See, e.g., *Wygant v. Jackson Board of Education,* 476 U.S. 267, 273–274 (1986) (Powell, J., concurring); *Palmore v. Sidoti,* 466 U.S. 429, 432 (1984); *Loving v. Virginia,* 388 U.S. 1, 11 (1967). See also *McLaughlin v. Florida,* 397 U.S. 184 (1964); *Shelley v. Kraemer,* 334 U.S. 1 (1948).

46. See *Korematsu v. United States,* 323 U.S. 214 (1944).

47. See *Paradise,* 480 U.S. at 166 (cases cited therein).

48. See, e.g., *McDonald v. Board of Election Commissioners of Chicago,* 394 U.S. 802, 809 (1969). "Legislatures are presumed to have acted constitutionally." Ibid.

49. See, e.g., *United States v. Virginia,* 518 U.S. 515 (1996); *Craig v. Boren,* 429 U.S. 191 (1976). See also, Gerald Gunther, *Constitutional Law,* 11th ed. (Mineola, N.Y.: Foundation Press, 1985), pp. 642-664; Craig C. Ducat and Harold W. Chase, *Constitutional Interpretations,* 3d ed. (St. Paul, Minn.: West, 1983), pp. 692, 861–871.

50. *Adarand Constructors, Inc. v. Peña,* 515 U.S. 200 (1995).

51. *City of Richmond v. Croson,* 488 U.S. 469 (1989).

52. Ibid., pp. 486–494 (Part II of Justice O'Connor's opinion in which Chief Justice Rehnquist and Justice White joined).

53. *Metro Broadcasting, Inc. v. FCC,* 497 U.S. 547 (1990).

54. Ibid., pp. 564–565.

55. *Adarand Constructors, Inc. v. Peña,* 515 U.S. at 227.

56. *Jacobs v. Barr*, 959 F.2d 313 (D.C. Cir. 1992), *cert. denied* 506 U.S. 831 (1992).

57. 50 App. U.S.C., Sections 1989(a)-1989(d).

58. *Jacobs v. Barr*, 959 F.2d at 322.

59. See, e.g., Brooks, Carrasco, and Martin, *Civil Rights Litigation*, pp. 5–8; Bittker, *The Case for Black Reparations*, pp. 8–26.

60. See, e.g., Matsuda, "Looking to the Bottom," pp. 374–385.

61. See, e.g., *Fullilove v. Klutznick*, 448 U.S. 448, 478 (1980) (Congress had "evidence of a long history of marked disparity in the percentage of public contracts awarded to minority business enterprises").

62. 42 U.S.C., Sections 2000(e)–2005(g).

63. *Congressional Record* 118 (1972): 7168.

64. *Local 28, Sheet Metal Workers' International Association v. Equal Employment Opportunity Commission*, 478 U.S. 421, 424, 446–447 (1986); *Local Number 93, International Association of Firefighters v. City of Cleveland*, 478 U.S. 501, 516 (1986).

65. *Sheet Metal Workers'*, 478 U.S. at 474 n.46.

66. See ibid., p. 474.

67. Ibid.

Suggested Readings

Bontemps, Arna, and Langston Hughes, eds. *The Book of Negro Folklore*. New York: Dodd, Mead, 1959.

Davidson, Basil. *The African Slave Trade*. Boston: Atlantic–Little, Brown, 1961.

Dennett, John Richard. *The South as It Is: 1865–1866*. New York: Viking Press, 1967.

Federal Writers' Project. *The Negro in Virginia*. New York: Hastings House, 1940.

Genovese, Eugene D. *The Political Economy of Slavery*. New York: Vintage Books, 1967.

Morgan, Philip D. *Slave Counterpoint: Black Culture in the Eighteenth Century Chesapeake and Lowcountry*. Chapel Hill: University of North Carolina Press, 1998.

Munford, Clarence J. *Race and Reparations: A Black Perspective for the Twenty-First Century*. Trenton, N.J.: Africa World Press, 1996.

Osofsky, Gilbert. *Puttin' On Ole Massa*. New York: Harper and Row, 1969.

Stampp, Kenneth. *The Peculiar Institution*. New York: Random House, Vintage Books, 1956.

Verdun, Vicene. "If the Shoe Fits, Wear It: An Analysis of Reparations to African Americans." *Tulane Law Review* 67 (1993): 597–668.

Wade, Richard C. *Slavery in the Cities*. New York: Oxford University Press, 1964.

Wish, Harvey, ed. *Slavery in the South*. New York: Noonday Press, 1964.

7 | Jim Crow

Introduction

66 Redress for Racism?

Roy L. Brooks

"[T]he negro would appear to stand on a lower evolutionary plane than the white man, and to be more closely related to the highest anthropoids." This conclusion, memorialized in the 1910 edition of the prestigious *Encyclopaedia Britannica*, provided the "scientific" justification for the systematic, government-sanctioned exclusion of African Americans from mainstream society between the end of Reconstruction (circa 1875) and the late 1960s/early 1970s. Known as the "Jim Crow" era, this nearly one-hundred-year period was America's Age of Apartheid. It was a time in which nonwhites were accorded second-class citizenship under the law, and in which African Americans were singled out for particularly harsh treatment. African Americans lived in a world of fear—beatings, maimings, murder, and constant racial indignities—as well as limited opportunities. Despite the special nature of their suffering, despite the freshness of their claims—the absence of which, it was said, was fatal to their slavery claims—African Americans still have not received so much as an apology from the federal government. Why this is so is the focus of Part 7.

The distinguished scholar John Hope Franklin (with Alfred A. Moss, Jr.) begins our study with a brief overview of nearly a hundred years of legalized discrimination and segregation. Circumventing the recently adopted Fifteenth Amendment, which gave African Americans the right to vote, the South created numerous schemes to prevent them from exercising this key civil right. The intent was not just to deny the franchise to former slaves, but to all African Americans. As one white southerner expressed it: "I am just as opposed to Booker Washington as a voter, with all his Anglo-Saxon re-enforcements, as I am to the coconut-headed, chocolate-colored, typical little coon, Andy Dotson, who blacks my shoes every morning. Neither is fit to perform the supreme function of citizenship."

Anchored by political control, the South proceeded to construct a comprehensive regime of racial subordination. Schools, businesses, transportation, libraries, stores, parks, restrooms, and even drinking fountains were segregated. A dual system of justice also developed, frequently punctuated by lynchings—2,500 between 1883 and 1899, and 1,100 between 1900 and World War I, Franklin reports. Lynchings took place only because state and local governments were willing to look the other way or sometimes actively participate in the lawlessness. The federal government refused to pass antilynching legislation despite repeated requests by civil rights groups. So rampant and targeted were lynchings, often taking place in a carnival-like atmosphere, that a white poet and songwriter named Abel Meeropol (a.k.a. Lewis Allan) wrote a musical protest titled "Strange Fruit." Made famous in 1939 by Billie Holiday, the celebrated African American blues singer, the ballad gives a lyrical description of black bodies left hanging from trees for all to see. It goes in part:

> Southern trees bear a strange fruit;
> Blood on the leaves and blood on the root;
> Black body swinging in the Southern breeze;
> Strange fruit hanging from the poplar trees.

No other group in America not at war with the United States has experienced such injustice, hatred, and racism at the hands of its own government.

Jim Crow was not limited to the South. The North, including our nation's capital, also discriminated against African Americans and segregated them, both physically and psychologically. As the white southern author, Harry Ashmore, observed during his first visit to the North in the 1930s: "Proudly cosmopolitan New York was in most respects more thoroughly segregated than any Southern city: with the exception of a small coterie of intellectuals, musicians, and entertainers there was little traffic between the white world and the black enclave in Upper Manhattan called Harlem."

The narratives included in Part 7 provide personalized accounts of life under Jim Crow. One involves the infamous Tuskegee Syphilis Experiment conducted by the U.S. Public Health Service over a forty-year period. The testimony of one of the survivors is reminiscent of stories told of Jewish "guinea pigs" in Part 2. John Lewis's tale of police abuse and violence is played out in countless American cities even today. A few statistics are presented along with the narratives to convey a sense of the damage Jim Crow has wrought (and continues to work) upon African Americans.

Having touched upon the Jim Crow redress movement in the discussion of slavery (Part 6), we now move into the arguments for and against redress. Bernard H. Siegan contends that the issue of an apology for Jim Crow is moot, because the United States, through the enactment of numerous civil rights laws, beginning with the Civil Rights Act of 1957, and the issuance of many judicial decisions, the last significant one being the Supreme Court's decision in *Adarand Constructors, Inc. v. Peña* (1995), upholding the color-blind principle, has already apologized for Jim Crow. All branches of the federal government have "expressly or constructively condemned and repudiated racial discrimination as wrongful and unjust," Siegan argues.

Joe R. Feagin and Eileen O'Brien maintain that although *de jure* discrimination has ended, Jim Crow enjoys a thriving afterlife. They argue that the federal government should offer an official apology for Jim Crow because many whites still discriminate individually or institutionally against African Americans. Also, whites are the beneficiaries of a hundred years (and more) of "unjust enrichment." Legalized discrimination and segregation prevented African Americans from accumulating wealth that could be bequeathed to their children and grandchildren. At the same time, Jim Crow gave whites disproportionate access to the nation's wealth, which has been passed down to future generations of whites. Because the preferences whites have enjoyed during Jim Crow fuel present-day racial inequality between whites and blacks, whites should, at the very least, apologize to blacks, Feagin and O'Brien argue. Perhaps the difference between these scholars and Siegan turns on the question of whether the government, when it extends an apology, apologizes for its formal acts or for the consequences of those acts (or for both).

Turning to the reparations form of redress, two essays bring the reader face-to-face with an internal dialogue among African Americans that has been in progress some time. Both essays are written by highly regarded scholar/activists, and both recognize (and proceed from the assumption) that reparations are not a top priority among most African Americans today. The first essay, by C. J. Munford, professor of Black Studies at the University of Guelph in Canada, sees reparation claims as essential to nation-building and self-determination (Black Nationalism) and, hence, as key "to regenerat[ing] the mass Black liberation movement which has languished in suspended animation since the 1970s." In pursuit of that goal (and reminiscent of the Japanese American redress movement discussed in Part 4), Munford argues that "[s]upporters of reparations must strive to create an alternative discourse with the Black community. . . . Reparations' slogans and buzzwords must become household words across Black America." Along the way, Munford considers several questions important to African Americans and others, such as whether reparations constitute an attack on capitalism.

Robert Johnson, Jr., continues this internal dialogue. Johnson not only makes what at first glance might seem to be an anomalous juxtaposition—repatriation and reparations—but reveals through historical analysis that at several times in the past African Americans have viewed repatriation as a core reparations claim. Rather than having the victim of racial injustice shoulder the financial burden of repatriation—an unusual method of implementing a reparations scheme, to say the least—Johnson proposes that Congress fund a comprehensive repatriation plan developed by African Americans. He cites as precedent the Marshall Plan, federal support for Israel, and, most on point, Congress's substantial funding of the American Colonization Society's return-to-Africa program in the nineteenth century. Johnson addresses many of the "internal and external" obstacles to the success of his theory of repatriation as reparations, as well as the forces and factors that may help to advance it. It remains to be seen whether the largest experiment with repatriation—Liberia, where the African American resettlers oppressed the native

Africans for 160 years, culminating in a bloody civil war that remains unresolved to this day—will scare away African Americans.

The last essay in Part 7 concerns a settlement of Jim Crow claims, not by the national government, but by a state government. In 1994, the Florida Legislature enacted the Rosewood Compensation Act, designed to pay victims or their families for the white violence that destroyed the predominantly black town of Rosewood in 1923. Kenneth B. Nunn argues in his marvelous essay that missing from the Act are two important redress elements: an official apology and reparations. Although the Act declares that the State of Florida officially acknowledges that white violence demolished Rosewood, no apology was offered. Florida clearly desired to effectuate a settlement rather than pay reparations. (See Part 1 for the distinction between settlement and reparations.) Some of the settlement payments are designed to be compensatory, while others are intended to be rehabilitative. An example of the latter is the establishment of a Rosewood Family Scholarship Fund granting twenty-five scholarships a year, each worth four thousand dollars, for postsecondary education. The scholarships are available to minorities, not just direct descendants of Rosewood families. Nunn concludes that although only modest payments have been made pursuant to the Rosewood Compensation Act, it is nevertheless a "remarkable first step."

Perhaps a strategy for the assertion of Jim Crow claims can be patterned after Rosewood. Rather than pushing for a nationwide response from the federal government, African Americans could seek redress at the state and local levels. This would significantly reduce the size of the claimant class—a formidable obstacle to nationwide redress—and place the claims in a venue over which African Americans may have more control. An emphasis on community rehabilitation rather than individual compensation—even more so than under the Rosewood Compensation Act—might add to the feasibility of redress. On the other hand, some African Americans might reject a settlement approach and strongly favor reparations, which state and local governments may be just as adamantly unwilling to make as Florida. Currently, however, the biggest obstacle to reparations, not only for Jim Crow but also for slavery, is the lack of broad support among African Americans themselves.

The Jim Crow Experience

67 The Triumph of White Supremacy

John Hope Franklin and Alfred A. Moss, Jr.

When it became evident that white factions would compete with one another for the Negro vote, and thus frequently give the Negro the balance of power, it was time for the complete disfranchisement of the Negro, the Fifteenth Amendment to the contrary notwithstanding. On this, most Southern whites were agreed. They differed only over the method of disfranchising blacks. The view prevailed that none but people of property and intelligence were entitled to suffrage. As one writer put it, white Southerners believed that "no person should enjoy the suffrage unless he gives sufficient evidence of his permanent interest in and attachment to the community." And yet there were many who opposed such stringent disfranchisement because it would disqualify numerous whites. Not surprisingly, the poor whites were especially apprehensive. Some of them had been disfranchised by earlier measures; and when competition grew keen between rival white groups, the Conservatives actually barred Radical whites from the polls and, at the same time, permitted their own black supporters to vote. More poor whites were bound to be disfranchised by any new measures. The sponsors of a stricter suffrage had to be certain that they did not contravene the Fifteenth Amendment. Despite the fact that the Supreme Court had refused to apply the [the Fifteenth Amendment in early] cases, there was no guarantee that the Court would view so favorably any state action obviously designed to disfranchise a group because of its race.

These were the problems that had to be solved by state constitutional conventions when they undertook to write into their fundamental law a guarantee of white supremacy. It was in Mississippi, where a majority of the population was black, that the problem was first faced and solved. As early as 1886 sentiment was

From John Hope Franklin and Alfred A. Moss, Jr., *From Slavery to Freedom: A History of Negro Americans*, 6th ed. (New York: Alfred A. Knopf, 1988), pp. 235–238.

strong for constitutional revision; a convention met in 1890, for the primary purpose of disfranchising blacks. A suffrage amendment was written that imposed a poll tax of two dollars; excluded voters convicted of bribery, burglary, theft, arson, perjury, murder, or bigamy; and also barred all who could not read any section of the state constitution, or understand it when read, or give a reasonable interpretation of it. Isaiah T. Montgomery, the only Negro delegate to the convention, said that the poll tax and education requirements would disfranchise 123,000 Negroes and only 11,000 whites. He, nevertheless, supported the proposed amendments. Before the convention, Negro delegates from forty counties had met and protested their impending disfranchisement to President Harrison. Doubtless they would have fought ratification, but the Conservatives would run no risk of having their handiwork rejected; after the convention approved the constitution, it was promulgated and declared to be in effect.

South Carolina followed Mississippi by disfranchising blacks in 1895. Ben Tillman had worked toward this goal after he was elected governor in 1890, but he was unable to obtain sufficient support for a constitutional convention until 1894. Tillman was then in the United States Senate, but he returned to the convention to serve as chairman of the Committee on Rights of Suffrage and thus to be certain that the Negro was effectively disfranchised. The clause, when adopted, called for two years' residence, a poll tax of one dollar, the ability to read and write any section of the constitution or to understand it when read aloud, or the owning of property worth three thousand dollars, and the disqualification of convicts.

Negro delegates bitterly denounced this sweeping disfranchisement. In answer to Tillman's charge that Negroes had done nothing to demonstrate their capacity in government, Thomas E. Miller replied that they were largely responsible for "the laws relative to finance, the building of penal and charitable institutions, and, greatest of all, the establishment of the public school system." He declared that numerous reform laws "touching every department of state, county, municipal and town governments . . . stand as living witnesses [on the statute books of South Carolina] of the Negro's fitness to vote and legislate on the rights of mankind." James Wigg of Beaufort County said,

> The Negro . . . has a right to demand that in accordance with his wealth, his intelligence and his services to the state he be accorded an equal and exact share in the government. . . . You charge that the Negro is too ignorant to be trusted with the suffrage. I answer that you have not, nor dare you, make a purely educational test of the right to vote. You say that he is a figurehead, an encumbrance to the state, that he pays little or no taxes. I answer you, you have not, nor dare you make a purely property test of the right to vote. . . . We submit our cause to the judgment of an enlightened public opinion and to the arbitrament of a Christian civilization.

Only two whites joined the six Negroes in voting against the constitution of 1895.

The story was essentially the same in Louisiana in 1898 when a new device, the "grandfather clause," was written into the constitution. This called for an addition to the permanent registration list of the names of all male persons whose fathers and grandfathers were qualified to vote on January 1, 1867. At that time, of course, no Negroes were qualified to vote in Louisiana. If any Negroes were to vote, they would have to comply with educational and property requirements. Booker Washington attempted to prick the conscience of Louisiana Democrats by writing them that he hoped the law would be so clear that "no one clothed with state authority will be tempted to perjure and degrade himself by putting one interpretation upon it for the white man and another for the black man." Negroes led by T. B. Stamps and D. W. Boatner appeared before the suffrage committee and admitted that a qualified suffrage might remedy demoralized conditions; but they pleaded for an honest test, honestly administered.

By 1898 the pattern for the constitutional disfranchisement of blacks had been completely drawn. In subsequent years other states followed the lead of Mississippi, South Carolina, and Louisiana. By 1910 blacks had been effectively disfranchised by constitutional provisions in North Carolina, Alabama, Virginia, Georgia, and Oklahoma. The tension arising from campaigns for white suffrage sometimes flared up into violent race wars. In Wilmington, North Carolina, three white men were wounded, eleven Negroes killed and twenty-five wounded, in a riot in 1898. In Atlanta, there were four days of rioting after an election in 1906 in which disfranchisement was the main issue. Robbery, murder, and brutality were not uncommon during this period.

For the cause of white supremacy the effect was most salutary. In 1896 there were 130,344 Negroes registered in Louisiana, constituting a majority in twenty-six parishes. In 1900, two years after the adoption of the new constitution, only 5,320 Negroes were on the registration books, and in no parish did they make up a majority of voters. Of 181,471 Negro males of voting age in Alabama in 1900, only 3,000 registered after the new constitutional provisions went into effect. On the floor of the Virginia convention Carter Glass had said that the delegates were elected "to discriminate to the very extremity of permissible action under the limitations of the Federal Constitution, with a view to the elimination of every Negro voter who can be gotten rid of, legally, without materially impairing the numerical strength of the white electorate." This was accomplished not only in Virginia, but in every state where such means were resorted to.

The South universally hailed the disfranchisement of the Negro as a constructive act of statesmanship. Afro-Americans were viewed as aliens whose ignorance, poverty, and racial inferiority were incompatible with logical and orderly processes of government. Southern whites said that Negroes had done nothing to warrant suffrage. But as blacks made progress in many walks of life, it became increasingly difficult to allege that they were naturally shiftless and incapable of advancement. The framers of the new suffrage laws, however, were committed to the complete and permanent disfranchisement of blacks regardless of their progress. The Southern white view was summed up by J. K. Vardaman of Mississippi: "I am just as opposed to Booker Washington as a voter, with all his Anglo-Saxon re-enforcements, as I am to the coconut-headed, chocolate-colored, typical little coon, Andy Dotson, who blacks my shoes every morning. Neither is fit to perform the supreme function of citizenship." Southerners would have to depend on the administration of the suffrage laws to keep blacks disfranchised, for there were many who would gradually meet even the most stringent constitutional qualifications. White supremacy would require an abiding belief in racial inequality, reinforced, perhaps, by hatred born of bitter memories.

Once the Negro was disfranchised, everything else necessary for white supremacy could be done. With the emergence of white Democratic primaries, from which all blacks were excluded by rules of the party, whites planned their strategy in caucuses, and the party itself became the government in the South. Whites solemnly resolved to keep the races completely separate, for there could be no normal relationships between them. Laws for racial segregation had made a brief appearance during Reconstruction, only to disappear by 1868. When the Conservatives resumed power, they revived the segregation of the races. Beginning in Tennessee in 1870, white Southerners enacted laws against intermarriage of the races in every Southern state. Five years later, Tennessee adopted the first "Jim Crow" law, and the rest of the South rapidly fell in line. Blacks and whites were separated on trains, in depots, and on wharves. After the Supreme Court in 1883 outlawed the Civil Rights Acts of 1875, the Negro was banned from white hotels, barber shops, restaurants, and theaters. By 1885 most Southern states had laws requiring separate schools. With the adoption of new constitutions the states firmly established the color line by the most stringent segregation of the races; and in 1896 the Supreme Court upheld segregation in its "separate but equal" doctrine set forth in *Plessy v. Ferguson*.

It was a dear price that the whites of the South paid for this color line. Since all other issues were subordinated to the issue of the Negro, it became impossible to have free and open discussion of problems affecting all the people. There could be no two-party system, for the temptation to call upon the Negro to decide between opposing factions would be too great. Interest in politics waned to a point where only professionals, who skillfully deflected the interest from issues to races, were concerned with public life. The expense of maintaining a double system of schools and of other public institutions was high, but not too high for advocates of white supremacy, who kept the races apart in order to maintain things as they were.

Peace had not yet come to the South. The new century opened tragically with 214 lynchings in the first two years. Clashes between the races occurred almost daily, and the atmosphere of tension in which people of both races lived was conducive to little more than a struggle for mere survival, with a feeble groping in the direction of progress. The law, the courts, the schools, and almost every institution in the South favored whites. This was white supremacy.

Jim Crow Narratives

68 | Jim Crow Narratives

Abby Snyder

The life of African Americans under Jim Crow is often told in grim statistics, such as these:

> African Americans came out of the Jim Crow era with an unemployment rate roughly twice as high as the rate for whites; a poverty rate for individuals and intact families more than three times that of whites; and income levels for males and intact families that were only 58.1 percent and 61.4 percent, respectively, of the income levels recorded for their white counterparts. The percentage of African American men and women concentrated in the lowest-paying, least-skilled jobs (primarily private domestic service and farming) was nearly three times as great as the percentage of white men and women holding such jobs. African American men earned only 57.5 percent as much as comparably experienced white men; when both experience and education were taken into account, African American men earned between 60 and 70 percent of the wages paid to white males of similar backgrounds.[1]

Life under government-sanctioned racism and discrimination can be told more vividly through the personal experience of African Americans. One such account involves the infamous Tuskegee Syphilis Experiment.[2]

For forty years, the U.S. Public Health Service engaged in a syphilis experiment on African American men in Tuskegee, Alabama. Approximately four hundred had the disease; two hundred did not, but were kept in the experiment as the control group. The subjects were told they were being treated for "bad blood," but instead of treating them for syphilis, the doctors only observed as the men's conditions worsened in the final stages of the disease. Many subjects died as a direct result of untreated syphilis, and others developed serious health problems related to the disease. One survivor of the experiment gave the following testimony before the Subcommittee on Health of the Committee on Labor and Public Welfare in 1973:

SENATOR KENNEDY: Let's start with you, Mr. Pollard. Would you tell us a little bit about how you heard about this study, how you became involved?

MR. POLLARD: Back in 1932, I was going to school back then and they came around and said they wanted to have a clinic blood testing up there.

SENATOR KENNEDY: How old were you then?

MR. POLLARD: How old was I? Well, I was born in 1906. I had been married—no, I hadn't been married. Anyhow, they came around and give us the blood tests. After they give us the blood tests, all up there in the community, they said we had bad blood. After then they started giving us the shots and give us the shots for a good long time. I don't remember how long it was. But after they got through giving us those shots, they give me a spinal tap. That was along in 1933. They taken me over to John Henry Hospital.

■ ■ ■

So after then they went to seen us once a year. They sent out notices for us to meet at Shiloh School. Sometimes they would just take the blood sample and give us some medicine right there at the school, under the oak tree where we met at Shiloh.

■ ■ ■

SENATOR KENNEDY: What were the shots for, to cure the bad blood?

MR. POLLARD: Bad blood, as far as I know of.

SENATOR KENNEDY: Did you think they were curing bad blood?

MR. POLLARD: I didn't know. I just attended the clinic.

SENATOR KENNEDY: They told you to keep coming back and you did?

MR. POLLARD: When they got through giving the shots, yes. Then they give us that spinal puncture.

SENATOR KENNEDY: Did they tell you why they were giving a spinal puncture?

MR. POLLARD: No.

SENATOR KENNEDY: Do you think it was because they were trying to help you?

MR. POLLARD: To help me, yes.

SENATOR KENNEDY: You wanted some help?

MR. POLLARD: That is right. They said I had bad blood and they was working on it.

■ ■ ■

MR. POLLARD: After that 25 years they gave me $25, a $20 and a $5 bill.

SENATOR KENNEDY: After 25 years?

MR. POLLARD: That is it. They give me a certificate.

SENATOR KENNEDY: They gave you a what?

MR. POLLARD: They gave me a certificate and a picture with six of us on there.

SENATOR KENNEDY: What did the certificate say, do you remember?

MR. POLLARD: This is one of them here in my hand.

SENATOR KENNEDY: It is a certificate of merit, is it?

"U.S. Public Health Service. This certificate is awarded in grateful recognition of 25 years of participation in the Tuskegee Medical Research Study."

■ ■ ■

SENATOR KENNEDY: What do you think the Government ought to do now?

MR. POLLARD: I think the Government ought to do something as they were using us. They ought to give us compensation or something like that, where we can see other doctors and continue our health. That is what I think.[3]

Many African Americans were physically assaulted by the police for engaging in marches and other peaceful demonstrations against racial tyranny. Civil rights leader John Lewis paid a nearly deadly price for protesting the denial of the most basic right of American citizenship—the right to vote.

Bloody Sunday, it was later called, Sunday, March 7, 1965. It started quietly enough. The crowd was large, perhaps six hundred or seven hundred people, almost all of them local. They moved toward the Edmund Pettus Bridge quietly and orderly. But for weeks and months, the two armies had been gathering and now they were finally going to meet in full-scale conflict. If the demonstrators were well organized, then so too were the whites. For Jim Clark had been busy as well; he had issued an order for all white men over the age of twenty-one to meet at the courthouse that day to be deputized as part of his posse. The marchers were aware that the whites had put together an unusually large police force. Selma that day, to John Lewis, who had been through so many confrontations, had felt like a ghost town. There was almost no traffic on the streets, nor were there any pedestrians. Other than the whites who had enlisted in Clark's posse, the white population of Selma seemed to have disappeared, intuitively aware that the best place to be was at home behind closed doors.

■ ■ ■

After Major Cloud gave his command, the state troopers charged the protesters on the bridge, lashing out with their clubs, throwing tear gas at them. The protesters had just started to kneel and pray, and their heads were particularly vulnerable to the sticks. As the troopers began their assault, Lewis saw the protesters tumbling backward at once like a giant row of dominoes. It was a stunningly violent moment: lawmen employed by the state of Alabama striking out with their clubs at the protesters, unrestrained mass violence administered amid clouds of tear gas so thick that suddenly it was almost impossible to see. Lewis was hit hard on his head. The tear gas was terrible, the pain immediate, and he felt himself slipping out of consciousness.

■ ■ ■

That instant, the trooper poised with the club well behind his back after a full windup, marked the exact instant for the second time John Lewis saw his own death. I am going to die, he thought, this is my last demonstration, just let me die here. He thought how odd it was to die in your own country so near to where you were born while exercising your constitutional rights. The last image he had before he blacked out was a terrible one: armed men of the law slashing away with their nightsticks in full fury against defenseless black people, most of them either kneeling in prayer or huddling down, trying to protect themselves.

■　■　■

Lewis was hit so hard that his skull was fractured; he woke up much later in Good Samaritan, the Catholic hospital in Selma. He never knew how he got back to the church and from there to the hospital.[4]

NOTES

1. Roy L. Brooks, *Rethinking the American Race Problem* (Berkeley: University of California Press, 1990), p. 117.

2. See James H. Jones, *Bad Blood: The Tuskegee Syphilis Experiment* (New York: Free Press, 1981).

3. *Quality of Health Care: Human Experimentation, 1973*, Hearings before Subcommittee on Health of the Committee on Labor and Public Welfare, Ninety-Third Congress (Washington, D.C., 1973) III: 1036–1041.

4. David Halberstam, *The Children* (N.Y.: Random House, 1998), pp. 511–14.

Forms of Redress

69 | The United States Has Already Apologized for Racial Discrimination

Bernard H. Siegan

That the adoption by Congress of a resolution apologizing for Jim Crow laws will advance civil rights is highly questionable. To be sure, there are some benefits from any apology. The recipients are gratified and feel morally vindicated. In the case of a congressional apology, its passage may also enhance the moral stature of the civil rights movement, both nationally and internationally.

However, there are two serious problems with such a resolution. First, it is superfluous. This nation has already apologized for Jim Crow laws by adopting in recent years a multitude of statutes and judicial rules outlawing discriminatory policies and practices. Why should Congress spend its valuable time and resources doing something that has already been done?

Moreover, lobbying for an apology may be strategically unwise. It might use up political credits that would not be available for more productive purposes in the future. Advocates of an apology should heed the old political adage about going to the well too often. It may be dry when you need it most.

Second, any proposal for an apology provokes controversy that might impede consideration of other racial issues or even burden the healing process between the races. It is at best uncertain that the benefits of an apology warrant assuming such risks.

For many years now, this nation has engaged in enormous efforts to eliminate racially discriminatory laws. All branches of government have been involved and in the process have expressly or constructively condemned and repudiated racial discrimination as wrongful and unjust. The citizens of this nation accordingly have apologized for the racial misdeeds that once plagued it.

The elimination of racial discrimination was a major objective of the Fourteenth Amendment and has been achieved to the extent that such laws are now considered suspect and presumptively invalid. In recent years the adoption of a host of antidiscriminatory laws and judicial rules has led to extraordinary changes in our country. The southern states have been transformed from a legally segregated society to one where legal segregation no longer exists. The improvement is not confined to the South. Segregation by law is also a matter of the past in the rest of the country. These efforts to eliminate racial segregation laws are an acknowledgment of prior wrongdoing. An apology has indeed been rendered.

The judiciary has actively participated in the struggle against racial discrimination. Consider the changes in education. Prior to the 1954 *Brown* decision,[1] public education in the South was provided by dual school systems, one for white children and the other for black children. When school boards responded to the *Brown* decision by eliminating racial admittance requirements and not much else, the U.S. Supreme Court in the *Green*[2] and *Swann*[3] decisions ruled these responses inadequate. The Constitution demanded the total elimination of racially identifiable schools; the school boards had an affirmative duty to take whatever steps were necessary to demolish the dual system and convert to unitary systems in which racial discrimination was eliminated "root and branch." Not only was this objective mandated for the schools in the South, the Supreme Court required this outcome in schools throughout the nation that were in whole or part intentionally segregated.[4] To be sure, there is still much school segregation in the country; but it is not legally imposed. A tremendous change has occurred peacefully in a fundamental institution of a nation.

The Supreme Court presently applies the most exacting judicial examinations to racial restrictions. Any law that constitutes a limitation on the basis of race is subject to strict scrutiny, the highest standard of judicial review. To pass constitutional muster, a racial restriction must be justified by a compelling state interest, and the means chosen by the state to effectuate this intent must be narrowly tailored to ensure the achievement of that goal. Thus, according to the Supreme Court, the Constitution largely eliminates race as a basis for legally harming or benefiting people.

The modern revival of congressional civil rights activity began with the Civil Rights Act of 1957 and now includes numerous other laws prohibiting discrimination by reason of race, color, or national origin. The civil rights laws not only ban discrimination, they also impose penalties on government officials and private parties guilty of discriminatory practices. I shall briefly discuss some of the most noteworthy antidiscrimination statutes.

In 1965 Congress passed the Voting Rights Act requiring states to alter voting districts when necessary to protect the political representation of minorities, even when the redistricting caused a decrease in voting strength of some ethnic groups. The U.S. Supreme Court case of *United Jewish Organizations v. Carey*[5] concerned a New York redistricting law adopted pursuant to the Voting Rights Act that enhanced black voting strength in order to protect against dilution of the black vote. The redistricting divided the Hasidic Jewish community, which had previously been located in one district, into two districts, each of which had a substantial nonwhite majority. The Supreme Court upheld the redistricting.

To prohibit federal funding of any discriminatory activities, Title VI of the Civil Rights Act of 1964 provides that no person "shall be excluded from participation . . . on the grounds of race, color, or national origin under any program or activity receiving federal financial assistance." In the same year, Congress made it unlawful for employers to discriminate on the basis of race, color, religion, sex, or national origin. It created the Equal Employment Opportunity Commission to prevent discriminatory employment practices. The 1960 Federal Fair Housing Act banned racial discrimination in the rental or sale of housing.

Congress has sought to improve the business opportunities of minorities. In 1977, Congress enacted the Public Works Employment Act, authorizing $4 billion in federal grants to be made by the secretary of commerce to state and local governmental units for use in local public works projects. The legislation included a "minority business enterprise" (MBE) provision requiring that at least 10 percent of any grant be expended for minority business enterprises. An MBE was defined as a business at least 50 percent of which is owned by minority group members. This provision was primarily intended to remedy prior and overcome future discrimination against African Americans in the construction industry.

The Small Business Act of 1981, which provided funding support for small business, declared it to be "the policy of the United States that small business concerns owned and controlled by socially and economically disadvantaged individuals . . . shall have the maximum practicable opportunity to participate in the performance of contracts let by any Federal agency." The Act defines both "socially disadvantaged individuals" and "economically disadvantaged individuals" as those who have been subjected to racial or ethnic prejudices or cultural bias because of their identity as a member of a group without regard to their individual qualities.

The Federal Communications Commission has adopted rules giving preference to minorities. Because it considered racial minorities inadequately represented in the broadcast media, the FCC in 1978 instituted minority preference policies. The policies in question were (1) a program providing an enhancement for minority ownership in comparative proceedings for new licenses and (2) the "minority distress sale" program, which permits a limited category of existing radio and television broadcast stations to be transferred only to minority controlled firms.

Although held to be constitutional when they were litigated, some of the above-described laws would not be sustained as constitutional under the strict scrutiny test the Supreme Court presently applies to all limitations based on race. The Court ruled in the *Adarand* case that the Constitution mandates the same standard of judicial review for racial preferences as for racial deprivations.[6] This ruling has strengthened the principle of racial equality. In the words of former Supreme Court Justice Lewis Powell: "The guarantee of equal protection cannot mean one thing when applied to one individual and something else when applied to a person of another color."[7]

Given this history of governmental activity, why engage in the divisive debate of apologizing for Jim Crow? Why enter this thicket when the American people have loudly and clearly expressed the deepest regret for past racial discrimination in their contemporary legislation and judicial decisions?

NOTES

1. *Brown v. Board of Education of Topeka, Kansas*, 347 U.S. 483 (1954) and 349 U.S. 294 (1955).
2. *Green v. County School Board of New Kent County, Virginia*, 391 U.S. 430 (1968).
3. *Swann v. Charlotte-Mecklenburg Board of Education* 402 U.S. 1 (1971).
4. *Keyes v. School District No. 1*, 413 U.S. 189 (1973).
5. *United Jewish Organizations of Williamsburgh, Inc. v. Carey*, 430 U.S. 144 (1977).
6. *Adarand Constructors, Inc. v. Peña*, 115 S.Ct. 2097 (1995).
7. *Bakke v. Board of Regents*, 438 U.S. 265 (1978).

70 | The Long-Overdue Reparations for African Americans

Necessary for Societal Survival?

Joe R. Feagin and Eileen O'Brien

Many discussions of reparations for African Americans seem to suggest that such compensation is a wild idea well beyond conventional U.S. practice or policy. This is not, however, the case. The principle of individual and group compensation for damages done by others is accepted by the federal government and the larger society in regard to some claims, but only grudgingly and incompletely for others, such as those by African Americans who have been harmed by racial oppression. For example, recent anti-crime legislation, in the form of the Victims of Crime Act, codifies the principle of compensation for victims of crimes. In addition, as a nation, we now expect corporations to compensate the deformed children of mothers who took drugs without knowing their consequences. "A harm to one generation can easily cause foreseeable harm to the next one, and so the law has held."[1] The fact that those who ran the corporation in the initial period of damage are deceased does not relieve the corporation from having to pay compensation to those damaged later on from the earlier actions. Injured children can sue for redress many years later. Clearly, in some cases monetary compensation for past injustices is accepted and expected.

Long after the Nazi party had been out of power and most of its leaders had grown old or died, the U.S. government continued to press the German government to make tens of billions of dollars in reparations to the families of those killed in the Holocaust and to the state of Israel.[2] In recent years, the federal government has grudgingly agreed to (modest) reparations for those Japanese Americans who were interned during World War II. Federal courts have also awarded nearly a billion dollars in compensatory damages to Native American groups whose lands were stolen in violation of treaties. Significantly, however, these slow moves to compensate some victims of racial oppression have not yet been extended, even modestly, to African Americans.

BUILDING WHITE WEALTH AND SABOTAGING BLACK WEALTH

In his 1946 book *The World and Africa,* W. E. B. Du Bois argued that the poverty in Europe's African colonies was "a main cause of wealth and luxury in Europe. The results of this poverty were disease, ignorance, and crime."[3] Du Bois argued that the history of African colonization is omitted from mainstream histories of European development and wealth. A serious understanding of European wealth must *center* on the history of exploitation and oppression in Africa, for the resources of Africans were taken to help create Europe's wealth. To a substantial degree, Europeans were rich because Africans were poor. Africa's economic development—its resources, land, and labor—had been and was being sacrificed to spur European economic progress.

In our view, a similar argument is applicable to the development of the wealth and affluence of the white population in the United States. From its first decades, white-settler colonialism in North America involved the extreme exploitation of enslaved African Americans. European colonists built up much wealth by stealing the labor of African Americans and the land of Native Americans.

Racial oppression carried out by white Americans has lasted for nearly four centuries, and has done great damage to the lives, opportunities, communities, and futures of African Americans. The actions of white Americans over many generations sharply reduced the income of African Americans, and thus their economic and cultural capital. Legal segregation in the South, where most African Americans resided until recent decades, forced black men and women into lower-paying jobs or into unemployment, where they could not earn incomes sufficient to support their families adequately, much less to save. In the 1930s, two-thirds of African Americans still lived in the South, and most were descendants of recently enslaved Americans. They were still firmly entrenched in the semi-slavery of legal segregation, which did not allow the accumulation of wealth. Significant property-holding was not even available as a possibility to a majority of African Americans until the late 1960s.[4]

In addition to state and local governments, the federal government has contributed directly to the build-up of white American wealth. For example, after World War II, new governmental programs such as the Federal Housing Administration, the Veterans Administration housing-loan programs, and the G.I. Bill helped many white families advance into the middle class. These programs were less available to, or unworkable for, the majority of African Americans because of legal or de facto exclusion from virtually all traditional white areas and institutions. Legal segregation not only sharply reduced inherited wealth, it made government programs (even when they were available) of less utility for African Americans seeking to create wealth that could be passed down from generation to generation.

In the 1970s, housing prices tripled and many whites saw their family wealth increase dramatically. Home ownership had become a key component of white wealth. Today, buying a home is the "single most important way of accumulating assets" for Americans. Such assets are ordinarily handed down to one's children and grandchildren in a variety of forms, such as savings or trust accounts, "loans" with no expectation of repayment, help with educational expenses, wedding gifts, and partial or full home down payments. Children who recieve such wealth transfers become the well-off adults of the next generation.[5]

Without wealth, African Americans could not create as many successful businesses as whites, and those they did create were confined to black communities. Melvin Oliver and Thomas Shapiro have shown how difficult it has been for African Americans to build up much family wealth because of legal and de facto segregation. Until the mid-1960s, various forms of government-sanctioned or government-allowed discrimination and segregation kept African Americans from generating the family wealth necessary to compete effectively with whites in the economy.[6]

Some of these older discriminatory practices persist in various forms today. Housing and insurance discrimination are just two examples. Such discrimination continues to seriously limit the capital-formation ability of many black Americans, particularly in building up housing equities that can be used to start a business or help the next generation get a good education.[7]

Black parents often have lacked the economic capital to provide the educational or other "cultural capital" advantages necessary for their children to compete with advantaged whites. When African Americans were locked into a system of legal segregation, they suffered both short-term and long-term consequences. Even though the most brutal forms of oppression have been abolished, they still have major and lingering effects.

For example, today, African American families on average have less than one-tenth the wealth of whites. Even middle-class African Americans, who are thought by many whites to enjoy equal success and opportunity, have only fifteen cents to every middle-class white's dollar. The wealth disparity is even greater for working-class African Americans.[8] Such huge, lingering disparities are a very clear indicator of the long-term costs of governmental and private business policies enforced during the days of de jure discrimination and segregation.

Most whites do not understand the extent to which the racial oppression of the past continues to fuel inequalities in the present. Although affirmative action programs (where they still exist) attempt to redress discrimination by increasing job or educational opportunities for African Americans in a few organizations, such programs do little to address the large-scale wealth inequality between black and white Americans. All the "equal opportunity" programs and policies one could envisage would not touch the assets of whites who long ago reaped the benefits of not being subjected to legal segregation during the United States' most prosperous economic times in the nineteenth and twentieth centuries.

WHITE ARGUMENT: "I NEVER SEGREGATED BLACKS"

A common argument against significant economic reparations for African Americans concedes their suffering and loss under Jim Crow, but points out that most whites who perpetrated such atrocities are either dead or elderly. Furthermore, it is impossible to determine who most of the perpetrators were, how much damage was done, and to whom. Today many whites say such things as "I have never segregated blacks; that was done by my distant ancestors." From this vantage point, reparations are unnecessary because whites today are relatively guiltless; they bear no responsibility for past racial oppression.

This argument obscures reality. In the first place, the claim of innocence is often factually incorrect because many whites still discriminate against African Americans in a variety of blatant, subtle, and covert ways.[9] And even if a particular white person has not or does engage in overt discrimination, most such individuals are the beneficiaries of what their (and others') ancestors did in creating a system of racial oppression that, as we have demonstrated, persists today. Unjust enrichment is another name for contemporary white privileges. Patricia J. Williams has underscored this major principle of law and ethics: "I read a rule somewhere that said if a thief steals so that his children may live in luxury and the law returns his ill-gotten gain to its rightful owner, the children cannot complain that they have been deprived of what they did not own."[10]

Martin Katz has argued forcefully that the harm of past discrimination cannot be "allowed to persist unremedied because its 'cause' cannot be specifically identified." If this is done, "whites will be allowed to retain an advantage which they did not earn, and Blacks will continue to lag behind as a result of acts which, although they may not be amenable to documentation, no one denies were performed in contempt of individuality."[11] Just because many of the specific acts of racial discrimination and exploitation cannot be specifically identified does not exculpate the beneficiaries of racist practice.

For many generations now, white children have inherited ill-gotten gains from the anti-black actions of whites before them. Recognition of this inheritance of privilege is key to understanding arguments for reparations, and key to bringing about reconciliation between blacks and whites.

CONCLUSION

Wealth transmission is a critical factor in the reproduction of racial oppression. Given the nature of whites' disproportionate share of America's wealth and the historical conditions under which it was acquired—often at the expense of African Americans—it is of little significance that legal discrimination and segregation exist today. The argument that "Jim Crow is a thing of the past" misses the point, because the huge racial disparities in wealth today are a *direct* outgrowth of the economic and social privileges one group secured unfairly, if not brutally, at the expense of another group.

Although civil rights laws that attempt to maintain equal opportunity in jobs, education, housing, and voting are necessary and vital to eradicating racial oppression, they alone cannot remedy the continuing inequalities linked to Jim Crow. Redressing the inequality generated by racial oppression will require a major redistribution of white wealth. The ill-gotten privileges and unearned wealth inherited by present-day generations of white Americans must be dismantled and redistributed to those who have inherited the burdens of long-term racial oppression, both past and present. Economic, political, and perhaps other forms of reparations for African Americans are essential if the United States is to begin to approach the equality long ago enunciated in the Declaration of Independence's opening premise: "All men are created equal and are endowed by their creator with certain unalienable rights." Large-scale reparations might be part of the next American revolution.

NOTES

1. Richard Delgado, *The Coming Race War?* (New York: New York University Press, 1996), p. 103.

2. Ibid., p. 104.

3. William E. B. Du Bois, *The World and Africa* (New York: International Publishers, 1965), p. 37.

4. Martin J. Katz, "The Economics of Discrimination: The Three Fallacies of Croson," *Yale Law Journal* 100 (1991): 1033.

5. Melvin L. Oliver and Thomas M. Shapiro, *Black Wealth/White Wealth: A New Perspective on Racial Equality* (New York: Routledge, 1995), p. 8.

6. Ibid., pp. 36–50.

7. Ibid.

8. Oliver and Shapiro, *Black Wealth/White Wealth*, p. 7. See also Katz, "The Economics of Discrimination," pp. 1041–44.

9. For evidence on this, see Joe R. Feagin and Melvin Sikes, *Living with Racism: The Black Middle Class Experience* (Boston: Beacon Press, 1994); Joe R. Feagin, Hernan Vera, and Nikitah Imani, *The Agony of Education: Black Students in White Colleges and Universities* (New York: Routledge, 1996).

10. Patricia J. Williams, *The Alchemy of Race and Rights* (Cambridge: Harvard University Press, 1991), p. 101.

11. Katz, "The Economics of Discrimination," p. 1033.

71 | Reparations
Strategic Considerations for Black Americans

C. J. Munford

The reparations we demand are: Payment for a debt owed; to repair a wrong or injury; to atone for wrongdoings; to make amends; to make one whole again; the payment of damages; to repair a nation; compensation in money or materials payable for damages.

D. B. Lewis

Rumblings and ruminations about reparations reverberate throughout the Black world. As the second millennium turns to the third millennium—as western civilization reckons time—strong voices cry out for compensation, all across the African continent, from Nigeria to the Pan African Movement, headquartered in Kampala, Uganda, to the Organization of African Unity seated in Addis Ababa. In the Caribbean and among Brazil's African millions a Black consciousness stirs, focused on the Black diaspora's just claims for indemnification and remediation. In the United States the National Coalition of Blacks for Reparations in America (N'-COBRA) spearheads the drive.

Supporters of reparations must strive to create an *alternative* discourse within the Black community, one that has the potential to become the dominant discourse. By discourse we mean both formal discussion in writing and open public talk of tactics and strategies, appropriate to Black emancipation and uplift at millennium's end. This must be our conscious purpose, if "honing the weapon of theory" is not to be an empty slogan. We must craft derivative political projects and maneuvers in such a manner as to win the battle of ideas, not merely in the Black academy, but more importantly among our ordinary people, inner city included. Reparations' slogans and buzzwords must become household words across Black America. We must put our issues and topics on every African American lip. Thereby we may hope to regenerate the mass Black liberation movement that has languished in suspended animation since the 1970s.

We must be careful, however. There is a political Waterloo of monumental proportions lurking in this affair. Acceptance of a small symbolical grant, like that doled out to Japanese Americans recently, would end our historical and moral claim to compensation.

REPARATIONS AS AN ATTACK ON CAPITALISM

Black reparations is a claim on the western capitalist socioeconomic system. It is not a claim on socialism, communism, or any other noncapitalist "mode of production" or society. Our unpaid forced labor laid the foundations of the western capitalist order, and no other. Our enslavement alone enabled European civilization to snare the western hemisphere, appropriate its resources, and anchor white wealth and might in the Americas.[1] It is western capitalism that owes us the debt. Hence, despite some of the rhetoric we use at times, the lobbyists for Black reparations are not social revolutionaries in the traditional western, left-wing Marxist sense.[2] We can't afford to be. I will explain why.

Inasmuch as we insist upon reparations, that aim cannot logically encompass the overthrow of the socioeconomic order, since the claim for compensation and indemnification is made specifically against western capitalism—the beneficiary of our ancestors' unpaid labor and the perpetrator of racist atrocities against us. Reparations is addressed precisely to those debts and crimes.

So although many Blacks have no use for capitalism—with good reason—the campaign for reparations, both for Africa and the diaspora, requires western capitalism for the claim to register. Anti-Black racism is deeply rooted among ordinary whites.[3] Ostensibly lower-class whites would provide the main backing for any noncapitalist order—and would be its main beneficiaries. We suspect that under any postcapitalist setup, as under capitalism, the vast majority of whites would continue to look for excuses to deny our just claims. We lay charges against the existing social order. Western capitalism's disappearance *before* the debt is paid is not in the interest of Black people.

REPARATIONS AS A RACE-SPECIFIC MATTER

Historically, Black liberation activism has addressed issues specific to racial discrimination against African Americans. The maximum agenda targeted *white racism*—its theory and practice—and *white supremacy* as a macro-system. In an otherwise fine book, Charles V. Hamilton has sought to prove the contrary.[4] The Black struggle, he asserts, has always given equal time and effort to race-neutral social welfare issues. He is, I think, mistaken. The historical mandate of Black liberation has *always* been Black-race specific, and not merely from the 1950s to 1964. It remains the same today.

Yet the Black agenda is increasingly criticized for failing to widen or shift its focus to "universal" human rights issues, or at least to issues germane to the "mainstream" white, middle-class lobbies. There is pressure on the racial agenda to give way to bones of contention pertinent to ethnic origin, gender, multiculturalism, religion or sexual preference. From the National Association for the Advancement of Colored People (NAACP) to the Southern Christian Leadership Conference (SCLC), the civil rights establishment is browbeaten to switch chiefly to class, poverty-type problems. Martin Luther King III, newly chosen head of the SCLC, has succumbed to this temptation, for instance. The substitute agenda campaigns for reforms designed to better the lot of poor people per se, the absolute majority of whom in the United States and Canada are still said to be *white*. This is an attack on the classical Black rights agenda. The traditional program uttered the demand for freedom, protection, and compensation (the classic "forty acres") on behalf of African-descended persons, enslaved, Jim Crowed, terrorized, and discriminated on the basis of *race*.

The arm twisting comes simultaneously from two opposite political camps—from the right and from the left. Conservatives claim that race-specific advocacy spearheads "racial preferences," quotas, and affirmative action—policies white conservatives hate. The left offers the class analysis that sacrifices Black interests on the altar of "broader," "national" working-class issues. Higher or lower in register, this refrain is rung by all of today's radicals, social democrats, socialists, communists, white trade unionists, and sundry other leftists. They reject "narrow" racial discourse in order to vindicate social reform, class, and socialist agendas, and "unite America's multi-racial working class." They also complain that tax-funded reparations will make African Americans "winners," casting poor whites and ethnics in the role of "losers."

We must not allow the push for reparations to be diverted into any "universalistic" reforms "good for all Americans." History establishes *priorities*. After all, during the Civil War, thousands of white families lost boys, killed or maimed in the Union army, fighting against the pro-slavery army of the Confederacy. In the eyes of those families, they themselves and their lost kin were the "losers," sacrificed to the freedom needs of Blacks, whom many of these northerners despised for racist reasons. Nevertheless, the historical needs of the republic were served.

REPARATIONS AS A DISCOURSE ON RACE

The best way, to my mind, to seize the political initiative and change the timbre of the national discussion of race is to be aggressive in our demands for reparations. Discourse on race is permanent and unavoidable in the United States of America, a constitutive element of life, dictated by the historical centrality of African Americans. Moreover, there are conjunctural political events, such as President Clinton's Race Commission and "national dialogue" on races, times when a critical state of affairs brings issues to a head. This is one of those times. Targeting the mass media, we must make it our priority in the dialogue to obliterate the currently popular anti-Black phraseology, uttered in catchwords such as "racial preferential treatment" and "racial preference." This hateful discourse must be smothered in favor of phrases such as "racist crimes restitution." The nation should be discussing programs of redress. We must get everyone arguing about policies to cancel out the harm done African Americans by slavery, Jim Crow, and current racial discrimination. In other words, we must steer the debate onto favorable grounds. Reframing the race debate must become the historical imperative for the early years of the twenty-first century, just as the abolition of chattel slavery became the historical imperative of the nineteenth century, and just as the removal of Jim Crow laws was the historical imperative of our twentieth century.

We propose this as a frank and militant approach. We advance it in the expectation of long-run political benefits that can never be gained from meekly assuring that African Americans have no wish to "reverse discriminate" against anyone. Avoiding confrontation on matters of principle, compromising a people's fundamental rights, never brings victory. We must forge strategies that go beyond mere lobbying for leverage in the White House, or chasing down liberal legislators in the hope of coaxing enlightened "color-blind" reforms.

CONCLUSION

We should voice our demands for compensation and protection in unmistakable terms, and get on with the historic labor of forming an uncompromising pro-Black coalition with anti-racist whites, comparable to the anti-slavery coalition of Blacks and whites. We should do so with the full understanding that such a coalition would be temporary, not permanent, just as the anti-slavery coalition of the mid-1800s was short-lived—unfortunately.

People do not act *only* according to their own narrow racial, class, religious, or personal interests. At least not everyone, not all the time. A minority of people sometimes take moral stands, a minority of white people included. They stand up for principles they believe will foster the long-range betterment of human society. However, to motivate these sentiments among the minority of whites who are anti-racist, we must proclaim the priority of Black needs bluntly and unambiguously to provide them the opportunity to make a clear moral choice. Only we, African Americans, can activate the relatively few whites (a silent minority) who are anti-racists. Some will accept our leadership and fight unselfishly for Black reparations. A coalition between a Black America *united* for reparations, and an anti-racist white minority rallying in support of Black reparations, can prevail over mass white opposition, just as the coalition between a Black community united in opposition to slavery and white abolitionists—a small minority—helped to bring down chattel slavery 135 years ago. Forging the bloc will not be easy. It will take time, collective effort, sensitivity, and personal sacrifice from all involved, Black and white. But history is patient and bows to determination.

NOTES

1. Clarence J. Munford, *The Black Ordeal of Slavery and Slave Trading in the French West Indies, 1625–1715*, 3 vols. (Lewiston, N.Y.: Edwin Mellen Press, 1991).

2. Robin D. G. Kelley, *Race Rebels, Politics and the Black Working Class* (New York: Free Press, 1994).

3. Jared Taylor, *Paved with Good Intentions: The Failure of Race Relations in Contemporary America* (New York: Carroll and Graf, 1994).

4. Cooper Hamilton, Dona Hamilton, and Charles V. Hamilton, *The Dual Agenda: Race and Social Welfare Policies of Civil Rights Organizations* (New York: Columbia University Press, 1997).

72 | Repatriation as Reparations for Slavery and Jim-Crowism

Robert Johnson, Jr.

Repatriation represents the oldest form of African American nationalist sentiments, traceable to the fifteenth century when the first Africans were taken from the continent. As Africans were ripped from the continent and their cultural and spiritual way of life, most yearned for a return to the homeland. This yearning for reconnection with Africa has never ended. Rather, it has been nurtured and developed over the past four centuries, gaining critical momentum in the nineteenth century in the form of a variety of different colonization efforts and moving closer to an authentic, mass-based model in the twentieth century.

Recently, many scholars and activists such as Clarence Munford, Ronald Daniels, John Hope Franklin, Ronald Walters, U.S. Rep. John Conyers, James Forman, and Rev. Alfred Sharpton have examined and espoused the concept of reparations. Essentially, they articulate the need for African Americans to receive "restitution," "compensation," "indemnity," or "recompense" for centuries of slavery and decades of judicially sanctioned racial subordination. In addition, some of these activists have demanded that White institutions, such as churches, provide monetary compensation. On April 26, 1969, the National Black Economic Development Conference, convened in Detroit, Michigan, issued a *Black Manifesto* that demanded $500 million from the White religious community.[1]

Although some activists, such as Gaidi Obadele and Imari Obadele of the Republic of New Afrika, have argued that African Americans should be granted land within the United States, few have argued that an essential element of the reparations debate should include repatriation to Africa.[2]

Repatriation must be afforded its rightful place within the discourse on reparation ideologies. Drawing upon different Back-to-Africa movements of the nineteenth and twentieth centuries, this chapter argues that it is essential that repatriation take a prominent place in the academic and political discourse on reparations for the twenty-first century.

REPATRIATION IN THE NINETEENTH CENTURY

Repatriation in the nineteenth century occurred through the American Colonization Society, Black nationalist efforts, or Black revolutionary efforts. The latter was best represented by those kidnaped Africans who, under the leadership of the legendary Cinque, not only mutinied but also demanded that they be taken back to Africa. The insurrection occurred in 1839, but the legal battle to allow their return to Africa was not settled until 1841, when the U.S. Supreme Court, in *United States v. Amistad*,[3] decided that they were free to return home. Since the *Amistad* has been the subject of much research, as well as a recent film, this chapter will not discuss repatriation through Black revolutionary efforts.

BLACK NATIONALIST EFFORTS: PAUL CUFFE (1759–1817)

Repatriation in the nineteenth century began with the efforts of Paul Cuffe, as part of the African American independence movement. His voyages were African American conceived, financed, and executed. Cuffe was born to free parents in Westport, Massachusetts, on January 17, 1759. Cuffe Slocum, his father, a native of Ghana, had purchased his freedom in 1728.[4] Beginning in 1775, young Cuffe began to work on whaling ships, and by 1881 he had acquired sufficient maritime skills to construct his own ship and set sail for Sierra Leone. His aim was to engage in commerce and investigate the possibility of repatriating African Americans to Africa. He planned to finance his ventures by selling products acquired in Europe and Africa.

When Cuffe and his crew of nine African American men and one Swede arrived in Sierra Leone on March 1, 1811, they were greeted by the governor of the colony. Even though Cuffe was afforded the best treatment by British colonial officials, he did not fail to meet with traditional rulers and people. He understood that in order for his repatriation plans to succeed, he would need the assistance of the indigenous African people.

After sailing from Sierra Leone to England, Cuffe returned to the United States to garner more support for his repatriation plans. He set sail for Sierra Leone on December 4, 1815, with thirty-eight passengers. On February 3, 1816, he and the repatriates arrived on African soil. These pioneers were from New York City, Philadelphia, and Boston, and had joined Cuffe's voyage because they believed in the importance of reestablishing their ties with Africa. Each of these free African Americans paid for the cost of their passage, which ranged from $100 to $250 per person.[5]

Although Cuffe was aided by White Quaker friends, both in England and America, the entire venture was an African American effort. Among the repatriates and their Quaker supporters, resettlement was seen as a means of righting a wrong that had begun two centuries earlier. For them, as it should be for us, the return to Africa was understood to be a specific, narrowly tailored form of restitution for slavery. It was a most dramatic reparation.

AMERICAN COLONIZATION SOCIETY

For most of the nineteenth century, the American Colonization Society controlled resettlement efforts to Africa. These initiatives were carried out by the U.S. Government, southern plantation owners, northern industrialists, and African Americans who were willing to compromise their nationalist (Black independence, Black self-help) views in order to get to Africa. The results from this unusual partnership were tangible: establishment of the colony of Liberia and the repatriation of a substantial number of African Americans, including John Brown Russwurm (1799–1851), the most illustrious of the early repatriates.

The American Colonization Society was formed in Washington, D.C., one year after Paul Cuffe's Sierra Leone voyage. Its first president was Bushrod Washington, brother of President George Washington. Both Washingtons favored the resettlement of Africans. Henry Clay, the founding secretary of the Society, had this to say about Africans in America: "Can there be a nobler cause than that which, whilst it proposed to rid our country of a useless and pernicious, if not dangerous portion of our population, contemplates the spreading of civilized life, and the possible redemption from ignorance and barbarism of a benighted quarter of the globe."[6]

Clearly the founders of the American Colonization Society did not have the best interests of African Americans at heart. Rather, they saw resettlement as a means of eliminating from the American population free African Americans who could agitate against slavery and for competitive labor. Industrialists and plantation owners, on the other hand, saw the removal of rebellious slaves as a means of securing the plantation system and the southern way of life.

Rarely, if ever, did officials of the American Colonization Society equate colonization with reparations. Nevertheless, they provided substantial financial resources for resettlement. Congress also appropriated a series of large grants (the first being for $100,000) to help fund the Society's resettlement efforts.[7] Although the goals of the Society were designed to advance the interests of Whites, several thousand slaves and free Blacks were able to utilize its considerable support to realize their dream of repatriation.[8]

BISHOP HENRY MCNEAL TURNER (1834–1915)

By 1892, after the American Colonization Society ceased its active involvement with Liberia, the outspoken Bishop Henry McNeal Turner of the African Methodist Episcopal Church (A.M.E.) assumed a leadership role in marshaling support for repatriation. It was Bishop Turner who began, for the first time, to connect the ideas of repatriation and reparations. Bishop Turner was born on February 1,

1834, in Newberry, South Carolina. Like Cuffe, he had been born to free parents. From the end of the Civil War into the twentieth century, Turner was the leading supporter of repatriation.

Despite the promises of a new life after the Civil War, most African Americans found themselves abandoned by the federal government and northern carpetbaggers. As a result, Jim Crow laws restricting the newfound freedom and opportunity of African Americans—enforced by lynching and such hate groups as the Ku Klux Klan—began to emerge. Between 1883 and 1899, 2,500 African Americans were lynched. In the first years of the new century and before the beginning of World War I, 1,100 African Americans met the same fate.[9] It is reported that in 1917, three thousand Whites in Tennessee came out to see what was advertised as the burning of a "live Negro."[10]

The deteriorating socioeconomic and political conditions of African Americans caused Bishop Turner to join a chorus of individuals and groups who supported repatriation to Africa as a necessary component of reparations. Some of the organizations that sprang into existence included the Kansas African Emigration Association (1887) and the Liberian Exodus Company founded by Turner and Martin Delany. The latter organization bought a ship and transported two hundred African Americans to Liberia.[11] Other noteworthy attempts included that of Dr. Alpert Thone, who attempted to transport African Americans to the Belgian Congo in 1915, but failed. From the Gold Coast, Alfred C. Sam raised $100,000 in Kansas and Oklahoma and, in 1915, transported sixty African Americans to Liberia in his ship, *The Liberia*.[12]

In 1891, the Council of Bishops authorized Bishop Turner to take an exploratory trip to Africa. In February 1892, Bishop Turner returned to the United States determined not only to establish missions in Africa, but to repatriate African Americans. His plan was to repatriate 5 million to 10 million African Americans per year. He had hoped that wealthy African Americans would provide support, but few expressed an interest in leaving the United States. Turner believed that the federal government should provide financial assistance as well.[13] The U.S. Government, he argued, owed reparations of about $40 billion for the free service African Americans had provided the United States for two hundred years.

In his appeal to the working-class poor, Turner's philosophy foreshadowed that of Marcus Garvey. The genius of Bishop Turner stemmed from his undying love for African people and his firm belief that in order for Africans to be respected, they must become a nation.

REPATRIATION IN THE TWENTIETH CENTURY

For the most part, nineteenth-century Black nationalist leaders of the repatriation movement came from privileged backgrounds and appealed to a select group of African Americans. The twentieth-century movement, in contrast, was more of a working-class, mass movement. Under his Universal Negro Improvement Association, incorporated in the United States on July 2, 1918, Marcus Garvey sought as his goal "[t]he establishment of a central nation for black people."[14] By 1925 he had established 996 branches in the United States and around the world, with a membership of more than 2 million.[15]

Garvey's movement provided a clear articulation of the need for repatriation. Not only would the return home be a means to escape the hardships of America, but it would also lead to the redemption of Africa. He envisioned 400 million Black people worldwide uniting in a common effort to rid Africa of European control and exploitation. Hence, for Garvey, repatriation served as reparations not only for African Americans, but for Africa as well.

Repatriation efforts were put forth by others, including W. E. B. Du Bois. Ironically, Du Bois led the opposition to Garvey's movement in the 1920s. Eventually, Du Bois repatriated to Ghana, where he died in 1963. His arrival in Africa was significant because he represented the quintessential self-made African American intellectual who, while adopting a Pan-African viewpoint as early as 1919, fundamentally believed himself to be an American.

Between 1971 and 1998 I conducted several interviews with men and women in Africa (East and West) who had left the United States. Many left out of frustration with the racial situation. One man stated as reasons for leaving:

> My ancestors were taken from another land against their will and none of their descendants were ever given the privilege or opportunity to ascertain as to whether or not they wanted to stay or be taken to the land their ancestors came from. Citizenship was forced on my ancestors and they could only live from hand to mouth and could never have the privilege of traveling. . . . The only way I have an opportunity to win is to first constitute the majority. Here in this land my Blackness constitutes the majority and that's why I left there.[16]

Like other Black professionals who have resettled in Africa during the past three decades, this repatriate saw Africa as a way to escape continued racial injustice in the United States. Repatriation was deemed to be a form of reparations effected through self-help rather than governmental policy.

THE STRATEGY FOR THE TWENTY-FIRST CENTURY

What will be the obstacles to raising repatriation as a viable and necessary component of the ongoing reparations debate? Given the history of the past two centuries, factors both within and outside the community will contribute to the creation of obstacles. Internally, most African Americans do not have a realistic understanding of Africa, its people and culture. Scholars can help bridge this educational gap by providing seminars on Africa both on college campuses and in the community.

Another internal hurdle will come from those African Americans who have acquired a "comfortable" place in America (psychologically as well as socioeconomically). They will continue to question the viability and necessity of repatriation as a form of reparations. Even some who view themselves as nationalists (believers in nation-building and self-help) will object to the idea of material resources being provided by government or business to facilitate the exodus of large segments of the African American population. This opposition should not be considered unusual. It is an inevitable reflection of the integration/separation dichotomy that has always been part of the Black experience in America.[17]

Some African American intellectuals will also raise objections. Though involved in the study of African people from a global perspective, many of these scholars have attained the same financial security as the African American middle class and, therefore, would not be willing to leave or to engage in serious scholarly debate on the merits of repatriation. They are driven in their academic pursuits, not by any love for African people and their need for liberation, but by their individual needs for recognition and validation by the very forces, within and outside the academy, that oppress African people.

Some African American politicians will present even more virulent objections. Many will be unwilling to raise the banner of repatriation because such efforts would run counter to their essentially integrationist understanding of the African American political reality. To them, "community" is merely a specific geographic-political district where a loyal constituency of registered and active voters return them to office, election after election. Consequently, a change in their political agenda would directly undermine their hegemony. These politicians would likely be the most vociferous opponents of any plan that might lead to separation.

What forces and factors will most likely advance repatriation as a necessary component of reparations? A prime factor will be the deteriorating socioeconomic conditions of the African American masses. While a significant number of African Americans have entered the middle class over the past three decades, the lives of the vast majority have deteriorated. The nation's leading sociologists and theorists are clear on this point. In his important work, *When Work Disappears*, William Julius Wilson writes:

> For the first time in the twentieth century most adults in many inner-city ghetto neighborhoods are not working in a typical week. The disappearance of work has adversely affected not only individuals, families, and neighborhoods, but the social life of the city at large as well. Inner-city joblessness is a severe problem that is often overlooked or obscured when the focus is placed mainly on poverty and its consequences. Despite increases in the concentration of poverty since 1970, inner cities have always featured high levels of poverty, but the current levels of joblessness in some neighborhoods are unprecedented.[18]

Overall, the median income for an African American family, compared to a White family, has declined over the past twenty years. But most appalling is the fact that African American family income is only 59.8 percent of White family income.[19]

In addition to declining incomes and loss of jobs in the inner city, the massive influx of drugs has destroyed neighborhoods and caused middle-class African Americans to flee from the cities. Manning Marable, professor of history at Columbia

University, sees the federal government as failing to do much to combat the crack cocaine epidemic in the inner cities:

> What else intensifies racism and inequality in the 1990's? Drugs. We are witnessing the complete disintegration of America's inner cities, the home of millions of Latinos and blacks. We see the daily destructive impact of gang violence inside our neighborhoods and communities, which is directly attributable to the fact that for 20 years the federal government has done little to address the crisis of drugs inside the ghetto and the inner city.[20]

CONCLUSION

As socioeconomic conditions continue to deteriorate, African Americans will have more incentive to embrace repatriation as perhaps the only viable and effective form of reparations. But rather than the victims shouldering the burden, repatriation must be implemented like all other forms of reparations. Select African American intellectuals must join with militant community-based leadership to articulate the historical precedent for governmental support for repatriation. They can cite the Marshall Plan and support for Israel, not as paradigms, but as examples for the type of involvement that will be necessary to fully compensate African Americans. Reparations must be seen as a means to make whole a people and their descendants who were stolen from a foreign land and forced to work for centuries without compensation. Scholars must argue that concomitant with the development of America and Europe, there has occurred a corresponding underdevelopment of African Americans and Africans.[21]

In addition, this cadre of enlightened leadership must establish meaningful professional relationships among lawyers, businesspeople, and diplomats to develop a comprehensive plan for locating and procuring a site in Africa for pilot repatriation efforts. The ultimate goal would be to lobby for and obtain congressional commitment to allocate funds for individuals who wish to repatriate. Congress would appear to have this power under both the Thirteenth and Fourteenth Amendments to the Constitution. If not, certainly Congress can draw on the precedent of the financial support it provided to the American Colonization Society in the nineteenth century. Congress has the resources to provide meaningful reparations for racial injustice. The only question is whether it has the will.

NOTES

1. On May 4, 1969, James Forman interrupted services at New York's Riverside Church to present their demands. See Robert S. Lecky and H. Elliott Wright, eds., *The Black Manifesto: Religion, Racism and Reparations* (New York: Sheed and Ward, 1969), p. 3

2. The Republic of New Afrika demanded in March 1968 that the U.S. Government pay $400 billion for the establishment of a Black republic in five southern states. See Clarence J.

Munford, *Race and Reparations: A Black Perspective for the Twenty-First Century* (Trenton, N.J.: Africa World Press, 1996), pp. 418–20.

3. 40 U.S. 518 (1841).

4. Sheldon H. Harris, *Paul Cuffe: Black America and the African Return* (New York: Simon and Schuster, 1972), p. 15.

5. Ibid., p. 192.

6. Robert J. Rotberg, *A Political History of Tropical Africa* (New York: Harcourt, Brace and World, 1965), p. 210.

7. Roy L. Brooks, *Integration or Separation?* (Cambridge: Harvard University Press, 1996), p. 158.

8. Ibid., p. 159.

9. John Hope Franklin, *From Slavery to Freedom: A History of Negro Americans*, 3d ed. (New York: Alfred A. Knopf, 1967), p. 439.

10. Ibid., p. 474.

11. Amy Jacques Garvey, *The Philosophy and Opinions of Marcus Garvey*, 2 vols. (New York: Atheneum Press, 1970).

12. Edwin S. Redkey, *Black Exodus: Black Nationalist and Back to Africa Movements, 1890–1910* (New Haven: Yale University Press, 1969), p. 292.

13. Ibid., p. 251.

14. Tony Martin, *Race First* (Dover: Majority Press, 1976), p. 6.

15. Ibid., p. 15.

16. Author interview of Duke Carter, Dar es Salaam, Tanzania, December 17, 1971.

17. W. E. B. Du Bois has written about this "twoness" in his *Souls of Black Folk* (New York: Vintage Books, 1990), pp. 8–9.

18. William Julius Wilson, *When Work Disappears: The World of the New Urban Poor* (New York: Vintage Books, 1996), p. xiii.

19. James Jennings, *Understanding the Nature of Poverty in Urban America* (Westport, Conn.: Praeger, 1994), p. 68.

20. Manning Marable, *Speaking Truth to Power: Essays on Race, Resistance, and Radicalism* (Boulder, Colo.: Westview, 1996), p. 91.

21. This line of arguments would advance the ideas that have been ably presented by the late historian Walter Rodney in his seminal work *How Europe Underdeveloped Africa* (Boston: South End Press, 1983) and by Manning Marable in his *How Capitalism Underdeveloped Black America* (Washington, D.C.: Howard University Press, 1981).

73 | Rosewood

Kenneth B. Nunn

On April 8, 1994, after two years of political wrangling, the Florida Legislature passed the Rosewood Compensation Act. This was a significant legislative achievement. It marked the first time that any American governmental body had acknowledged its responsibility for an act of racial violence committed against African Americans, in the long history of such acts. The Act was significant also because it was passed by a Southern legislature, in a state controlled by interests that have historically been unsympathetic to African American concerns. Even more remarkable was the fact that the Act was passed during a period of general civil rights retrenchment and white backlash against affirmative action. To understand the content of the Act and the events that led to its passage, it is first important to know something about the town called Rosewood.

Rosewood was a small hamlet of about 350 souls, nestled ten miles or so from the Gulf Coast in the pine scrub of north Florida.[1] By all accounts it was a prosperous town, an African American oasis in a predominately white county. Rosewood had its own school, two general stores, three churches, and a Masonic lodge. Some of the houses in Rosewood compared favorably to the finest houses in the neighboring white town of Sumner. Like the white residents of Sumner, most of the residents of Rosewood earned their living at the nearby sawmill. Others trapped furs or collected turpentine and other naval stores from the surrounding forest.

The trouble in Rosewood began on the morning of New Year's Day, 1923. Believing a white woman had been sexually assaulted by a Black escapee from a county road gang, the area's white citizens engaged in their own version of "ethnic cleansing," bringing to mind contemporary atrocities in Bosnia and Rwanda. As a result of the violence, the village of Rosewood was "obliterated from the map of Florida."[2] At least eight people were killed, dozens were injured, hundreds were forced to flee their homes, and their property was looted and burned. All the while, local and state law enforcers either participated in the destruction or stood idly by while it proceeded.

Notwithstanding its violence, the Rosewood massacre was soon forgotten. Its memory was too embarrassing for the white community, and too painful for the Black community. For sixty years the Rosewood story lay dormant, until fortuitous events brought it to the attention of the public again, and propelled legislation to redress its survivors through the Florida legislature.[3]

The Rosewood Compensation Act signed into law on May 4, 1994, accomplishes several things.[4] First, the State of Florida officially acknowledged that the community of Rosewood was destroyed by white violence, and accepted state responsibility for failing to prevent the destruction. Second, a criminal investigation of these events was required. Third, families were compensated for their real and personal property loss. Each family was eligible for a payment of $20,000, which could be increased up to $100,000 for actual losses shown. Fourth, any African American residents of Rosewood who were "present and affected by the violence that took place" were eligible for an additional payment of up to $150,000. Fifth, a Rosewood Family Scholarship Fund was established that provided individual grants of up to $4,000 to cover tuition and fees for postsecondary education. The twenty-five yearly scholarships were to be made available to "minority persons with preference given to the direct descendants of the Rosewood families." Finally, the state university system was directed to continue research and instruction on the Rosewood incident.

It is important to note that the State of Florida did not approve *reparations* for the victims of the Rosewood massacre, but *compensation*. *Compensation* refers to payments for damages or losses that have been determined through a legal process, such as litigation or a legislative claims act. *Reparations*, on the other hand, is a much broader concept in that it suggests atonement—governmental payments to redress general wrongdoing, such as waging war or human rights violations.[5] During the debates on the Act, this distinction was constantly stressed. While the State of Florida was prepared to compensate the victims of the Rosewood massacre, there was little political support for paying reparations for slavery, or racism generally, in Florida. Additionally, it should be noted that the Rosewood Compensation Act did not include an apology to the residents of Rosewood. The legislature simply acknowledged that the massacre, in fact, occurred and "recognize[d] an equitable obligation to redress the injuries sustained as a result."[6] Finally, although the Act was intended to compensate the victims of the massacre, the amounts actually appropriated were quite modest. Few , if any, of the Rosewood families could repurchase their homesteads or significantly improve their lot in life for the amount of money the state was offering.

Yet, the fact that the Act was passed at all was surprising. The passage of the Act and the redress the Rosewood victims did receive was in no small part due to the precedent set by the passage of the Civil Liberties Act of 1988, which authorized the payment of reparations to Japanese American citizens detained by the government during World War II.[7] Paying reparations to Japanese American citizens made it harder to object to the principle of paying compensation to African Americans. The fact that some of the survivors of the Rosewood massacre were still alive, and could serve as visible reminders of the injustice that was committed, helped garner support for the compensation act. It also helped that the proponents of the Rosewood Compensation Act were successfully able to distinguish Rosewood from other acts of racial violence that occurred during the same era. While, arguably, there is little difference between what happened at Rosewood and what happened in Perry, Florida, Tulsa, Oklahoma, and other American towns and cities,[8] the proponents of the Act argued that Rosewood was a distinctive case, since the violence lasted so long and state authorities had ample time to intervene.

The Rosewood Compensation Act was a modest attempt by a state government to show compassion, dissipate collective guilt, and compensate the victims of an act of unspeakable violence. Yet, modest as it was, the Rosewood Compensation Act was a remarkable first step toward the full recognition of government responsibility for the plight of its African American citizens and the payment of reparations for centuries of racism and slavery.

NOTES

1. For a historical treatment of the Rosewood massacre, see Michael D'Orso, *Like Judgement Day* (New York: Boulevard Books, 1996); "A Documented History of the Incident Which Occurred at Rosewood, Florida, in January 1923," Florida Board of Regents, Tallahassee, Florida (December 22, 1993) (hereinafter cited as "Board of Regents Report").

2. Board of Regents Report, p. 55.

3. The story of the Rosewood massacre's return to the public consciousness and the struggle to pass legislation compensating its victims is told in D'Orso, *Like Judgment Day*, pp. 110–292.

4. Laws of Florida, 1994, c. 94-359.

5. See D'Orso, *Like Judgment Day*, p. 206.

6. Laws of Florida, 1994, c. 94-359.

7. Civil Liberties Act of 1988, 50 U.S.C. § 1989 (1988).

8. See Board of Regents Report, pp. 10–11; William M. Tuttle, Jr., *Race Riot* (New York: Atheneum, 1970), pp. 10–31.

Suggested Readings

Anderson, James D. *The Education of Blacks in the South, 1860–1935*. Chapel Hill: University of North Carolina Press, 1988.

Friedman, Leon, ed. *Argument: The Oral Argument before the Supreme Court in Brown v. Board of Education of Topeka, 1952–55*. New York: Chelsea House, 1969.

Halberstam, David. *The Children*. New York: Random House, 1998.

Jones, James H. *Bad Blood: The Tuskegee Syphilis Experiment*. New York: Free Press, 1993.

King, Martin Luther, Jr. *I Have a Dream*. New York: HarperSanFrancisco, 1993.

———. *I've Been to the Mountaintop*. New York: HarperSanFrancisco, 1994.

———. *Letter from the Birmingham Jail*. New York: HarperSanFrancisco, 1994.

Motley, Constance Baker. *Equal Justice under Law*. New York: Farrar, Straus and Giroux, 1998.

8 | South Africa

Introduction

74 | What Price Reconciliation?

Roy L. Brooks

South Africa, the richest nation in Africa, presents an unprecedented setting for the redress of human injustices. In 1994, after nearly a half century of racial oppression against its black majority, the people of South Africa, in their first nonracial election, chose as their president a black countryman who spent twenty-seven years incarcerated as a political prisoner and who later became head of a once-banned political party, the African National Congress (ANC). Nelson Mandela's election marked the beginning of a period of transition in South Africa. The government's desire to move from a regime of racial oppression and exclusivity to one of racial harmony, national unity, and democratic process is no less overriding today than it was in 1994. This political imperative—what the South Africans call "reconciliation"—underpins the redress movement in South Africa. Reconciliation has produced a unique form of redress—amnesty for the oppressors, the state as well as individuals. The government's Truth and Reconciliation Commission (TRC), which heads the redress movement, has made the difficult and highly controversial judgment that amnesty is the price that must be paid to secure reconciliation.

Part 8 begins with an overview of Apartheid taken from a statement presented to the TRC by the ANC, South Africa's oldest national political organization. A nearly fifty-year regime of racial authoritarianism that has its roots in European colonialism, Apartheid produced racial winners and losers. Where one could live or travel, what one could learn or earn, whether one could vote or hold public office, and even the quality of justice one could expect to receive in the courts depended on the color of one's skin.

A minority of the population could enforce a system of racial oppression on the majority only through the most undemocratic of means—violence and intimidation. The ANC's statement includes a statistical portrait of atrocities committed by the Afrikaners, the Dutch-descended white settlers who ruled the African, Indian, and "Coloured" (a person of mixed-race heritage) citizens of South Africa during Apartheid. Other written and oral testimonies given before the TRC add a human face to the statistics. Of particular note is the testimony of police officer Jeffrey T. Benzien, which follows the ANC's statement. Benzien describes in vivid detail some of the government-directed torture techniques he effectively deployed during his long tenure in law enforcement. In cross-examining Benzien, one of his victims asked the most probing question: What type of person is it who can bring human beings close to death time after time, all the while listening to their pleas for mercy?

Mark Mathabane, the author of *Kaffir Boy*, a memoir of South Africa, poses the following question in a *New York Times* essay: "Is it humanly possible to forgive someone who attaches a power generator to the chained hands and feet of other human beings, calmly turns on the switch and then watches them writhe and foam blood at the mouth and ears as bursts of electricity fry every part of their bodies?" Is it just or morally correct to grant amnesty to the army of scientists who fully confessed to coldly and clinically concocting "poisoned chocolates, plotting to induce brain damage in Nelson Mandela" during his political incarceration, and using germ-warfare agents on black activists, killing many of them? Even retired archbishop Desmond Tutu, who chairs the TRC, found such testimony to be "the most shocking" of the hundreds of testimonies given before the commission since its hearings began in April 1996.

The amnesty question is more difficult to answer than may appear at first glance. Had Apartheid been overturned through armed confrontation, the victors might have sought revenge by trying and punishing the defeated. There would be no search for truth—the trials would take many years and might not uncover the top officials who gave the orders. And there certainly would be no reconciliation; just unconditional surrender and a constant threat of insurgency. Reparations for the perpetrators was the price of a negotiated, peaceful overthrow of Apartheid.

What further complicates the amnesty question is the fact that the record is also replete with atrocities committed by anti-Apartheid forces. In its own statement before the TRC, the ANC confesses to its "adoption of armed struggle on December 16, 1961." Indeed, members of the ANC, including President Mandela's former wife, Winnie, acknowledged their participation in murder and torture while the ANC was a guerrilla group in exile. A court struck down the TRC's grant of amnesty to thirty-seven top ANC officials, including the deputy president of South Africa, Thabo Mbeki, because their testimonies did not sufficiently indicate what each had done.

Other black activist groups also committed atrocities in the fight against Apartheid. One of the most prominent is the African People's Liberation Army (APLA), the military wing of the Pan African Congress (PAC). Benzien's narrative is followed by that of a twenty-one-year-old black man, Bassie Mkhumbuzi, who as an APLA member participated in the bombing of a church, killing eleven and injuring fifty whites and Coloureds. "Attacking the Whites, we knew and we read from the books that they are the ones who took the land from the Africans," Mkhumbuzi told the TRC. The essay by Alexander Boraine, vice chairperson of the TRC, seems to suggest that the existence of black-initiated human rights violations was a significant factor in the structuring of South Africa's peculiar form of reparations.

The primary goal of Boraine's essay, which is taken from one of his speeches, is to chart an authoritative road map through the TRC's statutory purpose and structure. Of particular importance is the position of the Promotion of National Unity and Reconciliation Act (the TRC's enabling legislation) regarding the controversial amnesty provisions. From Parliament's point of view, the "oppressed and oppressors . . . were imprisoned by the chains" of Apartheid. This suggests yet another justification for the amnesty provision, albeit not as strong as the others. The lawmakers, in addition, wanted "to avoid an amnesty which amounted to little more than impunity . . . [and] introduce an amnesty programme which included accountability and disclosure."

But the question remains: Does South Africa's style of total amnesty and the qualifying conditions outlined in Boraine's essay—the most important being that the human rights violation in question must have been guided by broader political objectives—ensure justice? Even though South Africa's highest court has upheld the legality of the amnesty provisions in *Azapo v. President of the Republic of South Africa*, which follows Boraine's chapter, the fairness question is far from decided in South Africa and in the international human rights community.

Two essays here speak to the amnesty question directly. The first, by South African philosophy professor Wilhelm Verwoerd, concedes that the TRC's wider concept of redress—amnesty for perpetrators—presents "an intense conflict" between retributive justice and other moral precepts, such as "truth, reconciliation, peace, [and] the common good," but argues that "in the context of a fragile transition to stable democracy," amnesty combined with "public shaming" and institutional restructuring is the right (meaning moral) thing to do. The essay by Emily McCarthy, an American law student who studied in South Africa, maintains that the TRC's unique concept of redress may in fact be an obstacle to reconciliation and national unity. She points to national opinion polls showing that a majority of South Africans believe the perpetrators should face trial, and notes that "this sentiment is particularly strong among Black South Africans." Hence, "while the Commission is doing a formidable job of uncovering the truth about the apartheid-era crimes," McCarthy argues, "it is having far less success in promoting reconciliation."

The latter point is the focus of the next essay. Eric K. Yamamoto, an American law professor, and Susan K. Serrano, an American law student, analyze the TRC's most recent draft of its final proposals on reconciliation. Reconciliation leading to national unity is the ultimate goal of the redress movement in South Africa. The TRC sees amnesty and reparations (both compensatory and rehabilitative) as the key ingredients of reconciliation. But, as Yamamoto and Serrano observe, "blacks continue to be barred from private establishments" and "whites continue to deny responsibility for the harms of systemic oppression and violence." Indeed, as late as 1998, nearly four years after the reconciliation process began with President Mandela's election, the TRC's chairman was calling on Afrikaners to embrace reconciliation "as their last chance of healing divisions caused by apartheid." Tutu also criticized two Afrikaans-language newspapers, *Die Burger* and *Rapport*, for supporting the TRC's most prominent white antagonist, Apartheid-era president P. W. Botha, who remains as defiant as ever.

Yamamoto and Serrano argue for a different path to reconciliation. While they see value in public confessions ("storytelling"), they believe reconciliation must progress through what they call "the four Rs": recognition, responsibility, reconstruction, and reparations for victims. Without these ingredients, Yamamoto and Serrano doubt South Africa's unprecedented transition to a raceless, democratic society can succeed.

Reparations for victims, along with a formal apology from the government, is indeed part of the TRC's redress structure. The chapter by Hlengiwe Mkhize, chairperson of the TRC's Reparations and Rehabilitation Committee, describes her committee's work. This is followed by the TRC testimony of F. W. de Klerk, South Africa's last president under Apartheid, who extends an official apology to Apartheid's victims.

Part 8 ends with South African professor Linda Human's insightful and well-balanced analysis of the affirmative action question in her homeland. Although jobs have changed hands in the political sphere (to a certain extent), Human argues that little has or is likely to change in the employment arena. This is because Apartheid has given whites a built-in advantage—"patterns of privilege and economic power have become entrenched"—which cannot be eliminated simply by removing discriminatory laws from the books. Reminiscent of the debate that still rages in America, Human maintains that "[w]hat is required is a period of affirmative action before we can even begin to put forth arguments relating to equality of opportunity." Without a narrowly defined, circumscribed program of racial preferences for qualified members of traditionally disadvantaged groups, "not only will the scars of apartheid remain, but also the talents of a broad cross-section of South Africans will remain underutilized to the detriment of the economy and the country."

What makes affirmative action such an "imperfect and complex" form of reparation, to borrow Human's words, is that it is in conflict with the timeless principle of color-blindness. This principle posits that the state must remain neutral as to the race of its citizens. Affirmative action, in contrast, is a timely principle of substantive equality. It is a principle that requires a change in the status quo, not just the formal removal of discriminatory laws. At this point in South Africa's history, "the entrenchment of the status quo would be politically and socially disastrous," Human correctly observes. But the further a nation moves away from ground zero—Apartheid in South Africa, Jim Crow in America—the more untimely, and hence vitiated, timely principles become. Memories of oppression fade, especially among whites, and other factors, such as questions of class, intersect with race to make it more difficult to isolate the cause of present-day inequality. The proliferation of "protected classes" (e.g., the inclusion of women and the disabled in South Africa's affirmative action program) not only adds to the difficulty of pinpointing causation, but can also overload the system. Judges, legislators, and citizens feel the need to curtail "big" affirmative action programs, as has happened in the United States. Finally, there is the natural tendency of a democratic state to gravitate eventually toward timeless principles. That is precisely where the United States is today and may be where South Africa, if its experiment in democratic rule is successful, will be someday. But for the time being, South Africa is perhaps better served by timely rather than timeless principles. This just may be the price South Africans will have to pay for racial reconciliation.

The Apartheid Experience

75 | African National Congress Statement to the Truth and Reconciliation Commission

August 1996

The process of colonial conquest lasted over two centuries, culminating in the formation of the racially exclusive Union of South Africa. In 1948, the National Party (NP) came to power and between 1948 and 1960, legislation was introduced to give material meaning to previous racial segregation and discrimination, to limit civil liberties and to suppress political dissent.

■　■　■

Apartheid was founded on, and represented an intensification of, the colonial system of subjugation of Africans, coloured and Indians.

■　■　■

Apartheid oppression and repression were therefore not an aberration of a well-intentioned undertaking that went horribly wrong. Neither were they, as we were later told, an attempt to stave off the "evil of communism." The ideological underpinning and the programme of apartheid constituted a deliberate and systematic mission of a ruling clique that saw itself as the champion of a "super-race."

■　■　■

During the 1960s the government's transgression of human rights became more blatant. Central to the new authoritarianism were sweeping restrictions on political behaviour; an increase in the powers of the police and further subversion of the independence of the courts; and sweeping provisions for detention without trial that created conditions in which the use of torture during interrogation became widespread.

Formed in 1912, the African National Congress is South Africa's oldest national political organization.

451

From its inception in the early 1960s, the security legislation and its implementation have generated widespread reports of mental and physical abuse of people held in detention. Individual officers abused their powers of interrogation; interrogation became torture; torture became routine.

■　■　■

During the 1960s, concurrent with the new security legislation, the apartheid rulers embarked on radical new forms of social engineering designed to entrench white minority rule. Instances of such "bureaucratic terrorism" included: huge numbers of arrests for contravention of pass laws; large-scale forced removals and resettlements; [and] the redefinition of all Africans as "citizens" ethnic bantustans.

Basic apartheid measures systematically denied black South Africans "first generation" rights like the franchise, civil equality, freedom of movement and freedom of association. The social order underpinned by apartheid also ran roughshod over "second generation" rights, such as the right to education, health care, security and social welfare.

■　■　■

Whole sectors of South African society—the law courts, churches, media, education, business, sports and cultural sectors—both actively and indirectly reinforced apartheid exclusion, discrimination and the violation of human rights.

The South African judicial system was racially and ideologically biased in the interests of the apartheid system. Selected judges were in many cases put in charge of political trials and were responsible for the judicial murder of people fighting against apartheid. In many cases judges allowed evidence that was extracted under torture or duress.

Judicial commissions produced ideologically oriented reports which promoted the goals of the apartheid state. Law societies and bar councils struck from the roll anti-apartheid activists convicted of political crimes.

■　■　■

In the early 1970s, spontaneous and organised mass resistance started to surface for the first time in a decade. The response of the regime was brute force. The actions of the regime in 1976/7 brought out in bold relief the government's intention to deny human rights at all costs.

Notes taken by then Minister of Police Jimmy Kruger illustrate this:

10.8.76 Unrest in Soweto still continues. The children of Soweto are well-trained. The pupils/students have established student councils. The basic danger is growing black consciousness, and the inability to prevent incidents, what with the military precision with which they act. The minister proposed that this movement must be broken and thinks that police should act a bit more drastically and heavy-handedly which will entail more deaths. Approved.

■　■　■

The National Security Management System (NSMS) was instituted in 1979 as an attempt to ensure maximum coordination of practices already in use in line with the government's "Total Strategy."

This period saw the genesis of a trend towards increasingly sophisticated covert operations, continuing into the 1990s, which included illegal methods to suppress and disrupt the resistance movement. In addition to attempts to bolster the discredited bantustan and community councillor systems, there were renewed attempts to find or "create" credible alternatives to the ANC.

▪ ▪ ▪

Repression during this period assumed both a formal and an informal nature. Formal repression included: Successive states of emergency, covering a large number of magisterial districts, were in operation from 1985 to 1989; over 80,000 people were detained without trial, some for periods of up to two and a half years; this number included over 15,000 children and around 10,000 women; over 10,000 detainees were tortured, assaulted or in some way abused; more than 70 detainees died in detention; several newspapers and publications were banned, suspended or restricted; many were sent to jail and others executed; over 100 organisations were banned or restricted; outdoor political meetings were banned, and numerous indoor meetings and funerals were broken up, banned or restricted.

In addition to these overt repressive measures, a whole range of covert activities were conducted by the state or its proxies.

One of the tactics used was that of counter-mobilisation. During 1985 and 1986, a range of front companies were set up in South Africa to orchestrate "black-on-black" violence, foster viable alternative "liberation movements" and spread NP propaganda. No fewer than 23 sub-projects were running in Namibia and South Africa in 1986, some of them with agents in the media.

▪ ▪ ▪

The Human Rights Commission recorded around 100 assassinations and around 200 attempted assassinations of anti-apartheid figures inside and outside the country between 1974 and 1989.

The apartheid regime did not shrink from the use of poison in its attempts to murder its opponents. . . .

The cases of Siphiwo Mthimkulu, Frank Chikane, Thami Zulu, and an attempt to kill Dullah Omar are some of the better known examples of the use of this tactic.

▪ ▪ ▪

Total Strategy included destabilisation in neighbouring countries. In a Commonwealth report of 1989 this destabilisation during the 1980s is described as having reached "holocaust" proportions. The report added that at the time the human cost was 1,500,000 dead through military and economic action, most of them children, while a further four million had been displaced from their homes. The economic cost to the six Frontline states was estimated to exceed 45 billion US dollars, not to mention the destruction of agriculture, industry, education and health care in countries like Mozambique and Angola.

■   ■   ■

The ANC announced its adoption of armed struggle on December 16, 1961. . . .

■   ■   ■

Military struggle was seen as forming only part of, and being guided by, a broader political strategy to ensure that the battle against apartheid was fought on all possible fronts.

■   ■   ■

Apartheid Narratives

76 | Truth and Reconciliation Commission, Amnesty Hearing

Testimony of Jeffrey T. Benzien

July 14, 1997

MR BENZIEN: Chairperson, my . . . date of appointment in the South African Police was the 31st of December 1976. [Description of positions held within the police services through March 1994 omitted.] . . . I am currently employed at the Airwing of the South African Police Service, Cape Town and I was promoted to the rank of Captain with effect from the end of May of this year.

ADV COOK: Chairperson, before we continue, there is something which my client would like to say to the Committee and to all people whom he has harmed. It is an introductory statement that he would like to make before we continue, and I am asking for your time and your patience so that he can read it out to the people.

■ ■ ■

CHAIRPERSON: You may proceed.

MR BENZIEN: Thank you Chairperson. Before I start with reading out of my application, I would like to mention the following: Firstly, I apologise to any person or persons whom I have harmed and I specifically apologise to the families of Ashley Kriel for the death of their son and brother. Although I deny that I killed him unlawfully and wrongfully, he did however die as a result of an action on my part and for that I apologise. Life is precious and judged ex post facto, and based on today's political situation of reconciliation, his death was unnecessary.

Further I also apologise to the people whom I assaulted during interrogation, namely Peter Jacobs, Ashley Forbes, Anwar Dramat, Tony Yengeni, Gary Kruse, Niclo Pedro and Allan Mamba. Director Gary Kruse contacted me last week and we talked about reconciliation. In the position which I am sitting here today, the persons whose names I have now mentioned, have come to me and have shaken my hand and wished me all the best and I think Mrs Forbes, I know her as Mina Pandy, I would like to thank her very much for her attitude. It has strengthened me in this

457

difficult position which I find myself. . . . As Director Kruse mentioned, Jeff, we are all now on the same side. They also told me that they wouldn't oppose my application and I will be eternally grateful to them for that. It is now reconciliation, forgive and forget at its best. . . .

In my application I apply for amnesty for perjury in that I hadn't spoken the truth during the court proceedings and also as a result of the assaults which I have committed on Gary Kruse, Mr Yengeni and the rest, excluded the Ashley Kriel incident. . . . Since Ashley Kriel's death, I stand by my version of the fact that his death was an accident. . . .

■   ■   ■

ADV COOK: Chairperson, I am told that we first have to deal with the assaults and the torture . . . and then we can deal with the incident of Ashley Kriel at a later stage.

■   ■   ■

MR BENZIEN: (Reads) . . . As far as I can remember, the following terrorists who were trained abroad were arrested and questioned by myself of the Investigating team: Peter Jacobs, Ashley Forbes, Anwar Dramat, Tony Yengeni, Gary Kruse, Niclo Pedro and Allan Mamba. . . . The modus operandi of the Unit including myself, was as follows: The Unit received information from a Safety Information System, regarding a member or a liberation movement who was in the Peninsula. I received direct information from my Commanding Officer, Lieutenant, now Superintendent Liebenberg, to trace this person and to arrest him. This had to be done expeditiously to prevent any further act or acts of terror being committed. All those persons arrested by us, had weapons of terror in their possession, or possessed information about acts of terror or gave us information about their hangers-on or sympathisers. Therefore my instructions from my Commanding Officer was that I had to act urgently and to make use of unconventional questioning methods.

This included, inter alia, the wet bag method, whereby a wet bag is placed over the suspect's head to disorientate him and to make him think that he is being suffocated. Very few suspects were assaulted, using an open hand. We did not make use of fists, because we did not want to leave any physical marks. In this way we ensured that no evidence . . . was collected against us. All the abovementioned members of the liberation movement provided us with the necessary information within one session, which never lasted longer than half an hour.

Ashley Forbes was subjected to two sessions. The last case was to extract new information from him. Peter Jacobs is the only one which was subjected to the wet bag method for longer. If I say "longer" here, I mean longer than half an hour. After they gave us the necessary information, the suspects pointed out their hangers-on as well as weaponry. Most of the suspects were arrested within hours after we received the information that they were in the Peninsula.

After the weapons were pointed out to us, or the sympathisers were pointed out to us, they were detained. . . .

The Security Branch then received the docket and took the matter further. . . . [E]xcluding Ashley Forbes, the next occasion which I had any contact with the suspects, was in the courts. There the suspects, then accused, raised the defence that they were assaulted and or tortured which I denied under oath. I then told lies regarding the assaults and the tortures on the orders of the Security Branch.

I questioned Ashley Forbes for plus minus six months. Apart from those two occasions where I questioned him in an unconventional way, we built up an excellent rapport and he provided me with extremely valuable information and I then gave that through to the Security hierarchy.

In conclusion I must add that the pointing-out of weapons indicated that the suspects were terrorists, who wanted to commit acts of terror in the Peninsula. According to my knowledge, only one civilian, a Black man died as a result of an act of terror by the terrorists.

I believed bona fide that due to my expeditious and unorthodox conduct, we made a big difference in the combatting of terror.

■　■　■

The acts which I committed were indeed acts committed with a political objective because as a member of the Security Forces of the State, I within the cause and scope of my duties and within the cause and scope of my express or tacit authority, acted in a bona fide manner with the objective of combatting the ANC, especially the ANC's onslaught against the country and the government and its attempts to make the country ungovernable. . . . The ANC tried to overthrow the government by military means. These terrorists trained abroad and were active in the Peninsula, were instrumental to the objectives of the ANC who tried to make the Peninsula ungovernable by means of acts of terror.

Nobody was however seriously injured or sustained lasting physical or mental harm or damage as far as I know. Ashley Kriel, unfortunately was killed. . . .

The acts were committed on the orders of my immediate Commanding Officer, Lieutenant Liebenberg. . . . The mere fact that the Terrorist Tracing Unit continued to exist for five years until the unbanning of the ANC, in 1990, and I received a medal and a certificate for my service, I believed on reasonable and bona fide grounds that I was acting within the cause and scope of my duties and within the scope of my express or implied authority.

ADV COOK: Mr Benzien, did you benefit in any way financially or otherwise?

MR BENZIEN: No.

ADV COOK: . . . Chairperson, all that now remains is the application in respect of the death of Mr Ashley Kriel. [Description of Kriel's death, the result of a police scuffle, is omitted.] . . .

■　■　■

[Victim Questioning]

MR YENGENI: [Asks Benzien what type of person could repeatedly take people so close to death, all the while listening to their moans and cries for mercy.]

MR BENZIEN: Mr. Yengeni, not only you have asked me that question, I Jeff Benzien, have asked myself that question to such an extent that I voluntarily, and it is not easy for me to say this in a full court with a lot of people who do not know me, approached psychiatrists to have myself evaluated, to find out what type of person am I.

■ ■ ■

MR FORBES: . . . Do you remember saying that you are going to break my nose and then putting both your thumbs into my nostrils and pulling it until the blood came out of my nose?

MR BENZIEN: I know you had a nosebleed [and damage to his eardrum]. I thought it was the result of a smack I gave you.

■ ■ ■

77 Truth and Reconciliation Commission, Amnesty Hearing

Affidavit and Testimony of Bassie Mkhumbuzi

July 9, 1997

AFFIDAVIT: I, the undersigned, Bassie Nzikizi Mkhumbuzi, do hereby make oath and say that I am aged 21 years and I reside at 2023 Unathi, Old Crossroads. I am unmarried and I am the father of three children aged four, one and eleven months.

The facts to which I depose, are true and correct and within my personal knowledge, unless the context otherwise indicates.

I grew up in Cape Town and went to school in Cape Town and reached standard 8, at Vuyiseka High School in Woodstock.

I am currently facing eleven charges of murder, charges of attempted murder and three of unlawful possession of arms and ammunition.

I am out on bail at the moment and I am currently stationed at 3 SYI Infantry Battalion in Kimberley doing my basic military training. I will shortly be transferred to the Northern Cape Command on a permanent basis.

The charges which I face, relate to the events at the St James Church in 3rd Avenue, Kenilworth in the District of Wynberg, on Sunday, the 25th of July, 1993. At the time, I was 17 years old.

I have submitted an application for amnesty in terms of Section 18 of the Act in respect of the charges which I face. I have been a member of the Pan African Congress since 1989 and a member of the African People's Liberation Army since November 1992.

Before that, as an organiser of the PAC Youth League, AZANYO, I had actively supported members of APLA by providing assistance when called upon to do so.

I was a member of an APLA Unit of which Makoma was a trainer, that is one of the other applicants. We held regular weekly meetings where we allocated each other various tasks.

We would always report back at the weekly meetings whether or not the tasks we were given at the previous meeting, was carried out. As a member of APLA I was

461

trained by APLA Operators and Commanders in various aspects of conducting guerilla warfare.

The training I received included physical training, attending political classes and receiving instructions on how to use and operate weapons, ammunition, arms and handgrenades.

I was also taught how to make petrol bombs referred to as Molotov Cocktails. Approximately a week before the St James incident took place, Makoma told me that an operation was going to take place and that we were to prepare ourselves.

He did not tell me when or where or what operation would take place or what the target or targets would be. He instructed me to prepare myself by getting into top physical condition and more importantly, I was instructed to get weapons and ammunition in Umtata, Transkei from comrades at the APLA High Command.

I cannot recall the names of these persons, I was given their code names and I cannot remember them any longer. I went to the Transkei on the Monday before the incident and returned on the Thursday. I went alone on a bus, I went to the address I was instructed to go to and there met some APLA comrades and they gave me two R4 rifles, 365 rounds of R4 ammunition, 3 M26 handgrenades plus [a sum of money]. . . .

At this point I was not told why I had to collect the arms and ammunition, or for what purpose it would be used. I knew, however, from my training, that it would be used for some or other operation. On my return to Cape Town, on the Thursday, I took the bag containing these arms and ammunition to a house in Khayelitsha.

After I left the arms and ammunition at the house, I was instructed to inform Sichomiso Nonxuba, now deceased where the house was where I stored the arms and ammunition.

I did as I was told and took Nonxuba to the house, left him there and I don't know what happened to the arms and ammunition after that. I did however, see the same bag on the Sunday when the operation took place and while we were at the Langa taxi rank. I assumed that the same military hardware was in the bag.

On that Thursday when I left Nonxuba at the house in Khayelitsha he told me that we would meet again on the Saturday, the 24th of July, 1993 at approximately three o'clock at the Iona shopping centre in Guguletu.

When I arrived there the Saturday afternoon I saw Nonxuba and Mlambisa there for the first time. Nonxuba introduced Mlambisa to me as Aubrey and he told me that Aubrey was going to work with us.

Nonxuba instructed me to prepare four petrol bombs on the Saturday and that I had to have it ready for the operation on the Sunday. At this point, all that Nonxuba told me and Aubrey, that there would be an operation the following day, the Sunday.

On that Saturday I prepared the petrol bombs. On Sunday, 25 July 1993, we met at the Uluntu community centre in Guguletu. This time Makoma was also with us. We met between eleven and twelve noon.

At this point Nonxuba told me that I was going to be part of the operation. He still had not told me what the nature of the operation was, what the target would be or what time it would take place.

We were told to meet again at 6 pm at the Langa taxi rank. I was ordered to bring along the petrol bombs. When I got to the Langa taxi rank before 6 pm Nonxuba was already there and I noticed that he had brought the bag which I had brought from the Transkei.

A little later Mlambisa and Makoma arrived in a Datsun motor vehicle. When I got into the car, the Commander of the operation, Nonxuba, said that we were going to the target. He still did not reveal any details of what the target was going to be.

I was told that I would be the security, Mlambisa the driver. I was sitting in front with Mlambisa. Nonxuba and Makoma were going inside.

After they came out of the building I was to use the petrol bombs to throw them inside. As Mlambisa drove, Nonxuba was giving him directions as to how to drive and where to drive. It is only when we got to the place which was identified by Nonxuba as the target did I realise that it was the St James church.

We had circled the church about three times. There were many cars and it appeared as if there were many people inside the church. Mlambisa drove into the parking area at the church and parked approximately 10 metres from the entrance to the church.

Mlambisa reversed the car so that the back was facing the entrance. Nonxuba and Makoma got out, each one armed with a rifle and a grenade. They then entered the church. I heard a grenade and gunshots and then saw a red car stopping in front of us, apparently to block us.

I got out of the car and threw a petrol bomb at the car and Mlambisa got out and shot at the car, causing the car to speed away. Then Nonxuba and Makoma came out of the church, jumped into the car and we immediately sped away.

I did not do what I was supposed to do, that is to throw the petrol bombs inside the church. I do not know what happened inside the church, but I am fully aware that with the arms and ammunition carried by Makoma and Nonxuba, that people would be killed or injured. [Eleven people were killed and fifty were injured.]

■　■　■

I stayed in Umtata in a safe house. I was arrested in February 1996 in connection with the St James case. . . .

I deeply regret the loss of life which occurred as a result of the operation of which I was a part on Sunday the 25th of July 1993.

At the time I was 17 years old and I followed the orders that I was given without questioning it. I was very impressionable then and regarded the older APLA operators such as Nonxuba as heroes.

I wish to ask the family, relatives and friends of the deceased and other victims who were injured, for forgiveness.

I respectfully submit that my application complies with the requirements of the Act, that the offences which I committed and associated myself with, were offences associated with the political objective, committed in the course of the conflicts of the past and that it accords with the provisions of Section 22 and 23 of the Act and that I have made full disclosure of all the relevant facts relating to the St James incident, which is within my personal knowledge.

Accordingly, I respectfully request that I be granted amnesty in respect of those offences relating to the St James incident.

Signed: Bassie Nzikizi Mkhumbuzi. Date: 7th of July 1997.

■ ■ ■

CROSS-EXAMINATION BY ADV BEMBRIDGE: . . . Mr. Mkhumbuzi, can you tell me . . . [h]ow did your training with APLA begin?

MR. MKHUMBUZI: I can say that I was a member of the Task Force. I was working for the Task Force. From there there were known contacts who were known to the leaders of the Task Force. From there you would be a member of APLA.

■ ■ ■

ADV BEMBRIDGE: [The Task Force] was there to protect the members against as it states, attacks by members of rival political organisations? Is that correct?

■ ■ ■

MR. MKHUMBUZI: Please explain your question how?

■ ■ ■

ADV BEMBRIDGE: Did you see or did you consider the members of the congregation at the St James church as people who would, who were a rival political organisation to the PAC and who may attack the members or leaders of the PAC?

■ ■ ■

MS KHAMPEPE: May I interpose Mr. Bembridge? I think what Mr. Mkhumbuzi has said is that he was a member of the Task Force which was formed to protect and defend members of the PAC. The evidence that has been admitted through the affidavit indicates that the church was attacked by him whilst he was a member of APLA. . . .

■ ■ ■

ADV BEMBRIDGE: What is your attitude to the fact that it was not only White people in the church?

MR. MKHUMBUZI: The only thing that I can say is that I sympathise with those who were non-White in the church, I apologise to them, even to the Whites, but they could also understand how was the situation during that time and how quick things could happen, so we couldn't differentiate that these were White and these were Coloureds.

ADV BEMBRIDGE: Why was it necessary to attack a church?

MR. MKHUMBUZI: As I've said that I did not know that we were going to attack a church. I didn't know that the target was the church.

But I felt as I've said before, the Whites were also using churches to oppress the Blacks. They took our country using churches and Bibles as we are reading the history. We as the oppressed ones.

CROSS-EXAMINATION BY ADV DE JAGER: Do I understand you correct, even if you've known that it was a church, you would have attacked the people in the church?

MR. MKHUMBUZI: Yes.

ADV DE JAGER: If it was a church for Black people and there were only Black people, would you have attacked the church then?

MR. MKHUMBUZI: No, we couldn't have done that.

ADV DE JAGER: So you attacked the church and you would have attacked it even if you knew it was a church and there were White people in the church?

MR. MKHUMBUZI: Can you please come again with the question.

ADV DE JAGER: You would have attacked in any event, if you had known it is a church and if you knew beforehand that there was White people in that church?

MR. MKHUMBUZI: Yes, we would have continued with the attack.

■   ■   ■

ADV DE JAGER: Why did you want to attack the White people?

MR. MKHUMBUZI: By doing so, attacking the Whites, we knew and we read from the books that they are the ones who took the land from the Africans.

That was the main reason for us to attack the Whites.

CHAIRMAN: Any further questions?

ADV BEMBRIDGE: May I just ask, do you ever go to church yourself, have you ever been to church yourself?

MR. MKHUMBUZI: Yes, I do go to church.

ADV BEMBRIDGE: So you know that people go there to pray and to pray for peace amongst other things?

MR. MKHUMBUZI: Yes, I know that.

■   ■   ■

CROSS-EXAMINATION BY MR. BRINK: . . . So you were fighting and you decided to fight unarmed, defenceless, peaceful people who were at prayer in the house of God?

MR. MKHUMBUZI: Can you please repeat your question because I don't clearly understand.

MR. BRINK: No, I don't want to put it again Mr. Chairperson. I will read to you a copy of a letter I received from one of the victims in fairness, because the Committee has it and I indicate that this gentleman who is not present, opposes the application.

I want to read his letter to you and you may comment on it if you wish. I, Dimitri Makogon, will be out of Cape Town on July the 9th and 10th, 1997 and do wish to make known my opinion regarding the amnesty application by those responsible for the St James massacre in which I lost both legs and my right arm.

The aim of the TRC is to establish the truth, the truth is that on July the 25th, 1993, the three applicants killed 11 and injured more than 50 civilians, gathered in a church, unarmed and defenceless.

Would you like to comment on that?

■   ■   ■

MR. MKHUMBUZI: . . . I would like to meet him and apologise to him. Maybe he would understand because what we did was not right, we do regret that, but I wish we could meet with him, maybe he would like to listen when we try to apologise. . . .

■   ■   ■

The Redress Movement

78 | Alternatives and Adjuncts to Criminal Prosecutions

Brussels, Belgium, July 20–21, 1996

Dr. Alexander Boraine, Vice Chairperson, South African Truth and Reconciliation Commission

In order to understand the nature and implications of the Truth and Reconciliation Commission in South Africa it is important to see the Commission both in the national and international contexts.

South Africa, oppressed and oppressors together, were imprisoned by the chains with which one group sought to bind the other for many generations. . . .

■ ■ ■

. . . [A]partheid was a system of minority domination of statutorily defined colour groups on a territorial, residential, political, social and economic basis.

It was a system which was entrenched for almost 50 years. Although the cards seemed to be stacked against South Africa achieving a relatively peaceful and relatively democratic election, the transition from oppression, exclusivity and resistance to a new negotiated, democratic order in 1994 has been realised. The chains which bound the majority of her people in what appeared to be perpetual servitude have been shattered. Many people, both within South Africa and beyond its borders, have described this transition as nothing short of a miracle.

However, because of the social and economic legacy there remains unfinished business which has to be tackled otherwise it will be impossible to sustain the miracle, consolidate democracy and ensure a peaceful future for all South Africa.

Therefore any serious attempt at dealing with the legacy of the past will include at least a strong commitment to transformation in the economic and social life of the majority of South Africa's citizens.

There is also a compelling need to restore the moral order which was put in jeopardy by the abdication of the rule of law and gross violations of fundamental human rights.

One of the ways in which to start the healing process in South Africa is an honest assessment and diagnosis of the sickness within our society in an attempt to give people, both perpetrators and victims, an opportunity to face the past and its consequences and to start afresh. The Truth and Reconciliation Commission is an opportunity to make a contribution in order to deal finally with the past without dwelling in it and to help create the conditions for a truly new South Africa.

Whilst it is true that South Africa's Commission has been shaped very much by its own history and the circumstances and the nature of its particular and peculiar transition, there are many similarities to the experiences in eastern Europe and South America which impinge upon the nature of the Commission in South Africa. These can be listed briefly as follows:

A shift from totalitarianism to a form of democracy;
A negotiated settlement—not a revolutionary process;
A legacy of oppression and serious violations of human rights;
A fragile democracy and a precarious unity;
A commitment to the attainment of a culture of human rights and a respect for the rule of law;
A determination that the work of the Commission will help to make it impossible for the gross violations of human rights of the past to happen again.

South Africa, in company with many other countries, has had to face up to three critical questions. Firstly, how do emerging democracies deal with past violations of human rights? Secondly, how do new democratic governments deal with leaders and individuals who were responsible for disappearances, death squads, psychological and physical torture and other violations of human rights? Thirdly, how does a new democracy deal with the fact that some of the perpetrators remain part of the new government and/or security forces or hold important positions in public life? . . .

■   ■   ■

There are, however, some unique features to the South African model. . . .

The process by which South Africa arrived at its Commission is quite different from any other that I know of. It was essentially democratic and gave as many people as possible an opportunity to participate in the formation of the Commission.

The idea of a truth commission came first from the African National Congress prior to the election in 1994 [South Africa's first nonracial election, in which Nelson Mandela was elected president]. Ironically, that is seen against the background of widespread human rights violations committed by the South African state over many decades, the ANC was accused of perpetrating human rights violations in some of its camps whilst in exile. The response of the ANC was to appoint an internal commission of inquiry. A report was published but there was considerable criticism in that it lacked impartiality. A second independent commission was appointed. Its findings were made known to the national executive of the ANC and their decision was that there were grounds for criticism but that these should be seen against the overall human rights violations which gripped South Africa over a very long period, and the way to resolve this was the appointment of a truth commission.

Two major conferences were held under the auspices of civil society in South Africa. The first was simply entitled "Dealing with the Past" and a number of leading scholars and human rights practitioners from eastern Europe, central Europe and South America were invited to share their experiences with a group of South Africans. A book was published under the same title of the conference which was distributed very widely throughout South Africa and thus the debate was joined.

A second conference was held some months later entitled "Truth and Reconciliation." The majority of participants were from South Africa but there were key participants from Chile and Argentina as well. The Minister of Justice, who had been appointed soon after the election, was the keynote speaker and he developed the idea of a commission which he had already announced in Parliament. A second book was published under the title of "The Healing of a Nation?" which was also widely read and a number of workshops and conferences were held throughout South Africa, looking at the concept of a truth and reconciliation commission and considerable input was gained from participants from a wide spectrum of society.

This input was sent to the parliamentary standing committee on justice who were charged with the finalisation of the Parliamentary bill. Public hearings were held and this was followed by the debate in Parliament itself where the Promotion of National Unity and Reconciliation Bill was finally passed by an overwhelming majority.

One further contribution to the democratic process was President Mandela's decision to appoint a small representative committee who drew up a list of 25 names from which he would appoint the final 17 commissioners, which the Act required. People from all walks of life were encouraged to apply and 299 names were received. After a process which involved public hearings, 25 names were sent to President Mandela and he then, in consultation with his cabinet, appointed the 17 commissioners, who now form the heart of the Truth and Reconciliation Commission.

■　　■　　■

I have already referred to the Act of Parliament which brought the Truth and Reconciliation Commission into being. . . .

■　　■　　■

[The] . . . 17 commissioners . . . serve full-time. The Commission has to complete its work in 2 years (an additional 3 months is allowed in order for the final report to be completed).

The Act also provides for three separate committees: a Human Rights Violations Committee which conducts public hearings for victims/survivors; a Reparation and

Rehabilitation Committee which works on policies and recommendations arising from those hearings; and an Amnesty Committee which hears applications for amnesty.

In addition to the 17 commissioners, a number of Committee Members are allowed for, plus a professional and administrative staff and an Investigative Unit.

A critical decision was made relating to the hearings of the Committees, both in terms of human rights violations and the stories of victims, as well as the amnesty hearings. Despite the risk and the additional complications, it was decided that these hearings should be open to the media and to the general public. This has placed an enormous burden on the commissioners who travel throughout South Africa conducting hearings because they haven't the benefit of working quietly and in private, but are constantly under the scrutiny of the media and of the public. On the other hand, there is the enormous advantage of the nation participating in the hearings and the work of the Commission from the very beginning through radio, television and the print media and the right of anyone to attend any of the hearings. This enables transparency and also a strong educative opportunity so that healing and reconciliation is not confined to a small group but is available to all.

A further departure from the norm was the decision to publish the names not only of the victims and some details of the human rights violations suffered by them, but also the publication of the names of perpetrators. A major problem was the need to ensure due process and a fairly elaborate system has been worked out so that people who are going to be named by victims are alerted ahead of time and are invited to make either written representation or, if desired, may appear at a subsequent hearing. . . .

A further difference from most commissions is the powers which are vested in the Commission. The Commission has powers of subpoena and of search and seizure. This enables the Commission to firstly invite alleged perpetrators or those who may have critical information to come to the Commission and share that information with the Commission. If that invitation is spurned, it can proceed to subpoena those concerned. It also means that the Commission can secure files and documents which have been secreted away by the previous government and its agents. This has resulted in agreements made by political parties and military and security institutions to make public submissions to the Commission.

There is also a major difference in the approach of South Africa's Commission to amnesty. . . .

. . . It is clear that for most people in South America the only experience of amnesty was what could be termed a "general" or a "blanket" amnesty which, in most instances, was devised and imposed by the very regime which was responsible for the violations of human rights. It is understandable, therefore, that general amnesty is looked upon by human rights organisations and human rights lawyers as a betrayal of those who suffered those violations and is something to be avoided at all costs.

It was in order to avoid an amnesty which amounted to little more than impunity that we attempted to introduce an amnesty programme which included accountability and disclosure.

■　　■　　■

South Africa has attempted to avoid the problem of a general amnesty in the following ways. Firstly, amnesty has to be applied for on an individual basis—there is no blanket amnesty. Secondly, applicants for amnesty must complete a prescribed form which is published in the Government Gazette and which calls for very detailed information relating to specific human rights violations. Thirdly, applicants must make a "full disclosure" of their human rights violations in order to qualify for amnesty. Fourthly, in most instances applicants will appear before the Amnesty Committee and these hearings will be open to the public. Fifthly, there is a time limit set in terms of the Act. Only those gross human rights violations committed between the period of 1960 to 1993 will be considered for amnesty. [Also,] . . . there is a 12 month period during which amnesty applications may be made, from the time of the promulgation of the Act, which was in December 1995, and a cut-off point on 15 December 1996. Finally, there is a list of criteria laid down in the Act which will determine whether or not the applicant for amnesty will be successful [the most important being that the particular act or omission under consideration must have been associated with a political objective].

■　　■　　■

A further point is that the Truth and Reconciliation Commission is not a substitute for criminal justice. The fact that 17 former military generals (including the former Minister of Defence) are on trial for murder illustrates this fact. Only last week warrants for the arrest of five persons in the former security force were issued. Three of the persons who will appear in court in two weeks' time have already applied for amnesty! The combination of judicial stick and TRC carrot may emerge as a potent force in flushing out former operatives who have adopted a "wait-and-see" approach.

Nevertheless, there are problems relating to the amnesty provisions as laid down in the Act. There are those in South Africa, some organisations and individual families, who have suffered very grievously from human rights violations who believe that there ought to be no amnesty provisions whatsoever. They want nothing more and nothing less than trials, prosecutions and punishment. More especially they are concerned that in terms of the Act those who apply for amnesty and are successful will never again be liable, either criminally or civilly. Some are even prepared to accept that if one has to pursue the way of amnesty as a price for peace and stability in South Africa there still ought to be an opportunity to bring civil action against either the organisation, the state or the individual. There are those who feel so strongly about this that they have brought a case against the Act before the Constitutional Court, which is the highest court in the land and even has sovereignty over

Parliament. We are awaiting the result of that court application. [The case has been decided and is discussed in chapter 79.]

The dilemma is that if people are encouraged to apply for amnesty but are then still liable in a criminal court or in a civil court, what is the incentive for their coming forward?

Many of us believe very strongly that if reconciliation is to become a reality in South Africa then both victim and perpetrator must be encouraged to participate in the life and work of the Truth and Reconciliation Commission.

■   ■   ■

Forms of Redress

79 Summary of Anti-Amnesty Case

Azanian Peoples Organization (AZAPO) and Others v. The President of the Republic of South Africa

CCT 17/96 Constitutional Court, July 25, 1996

This summary of the decision was prepared by members of the Witwaterstrand Law School faculty in South Africa.

The applicants applied for direct access to the Constitutional Court and for an order declaring § 20(7) of the Promotion of National Unity and Reconciliation Act 34 of 1995 unconstitutional. Section 20(7), read with other sections of the Act, permits the Committee on Amnesty established by the Act to grant amnesty to a perpetrator of an unlawful act associated with a political objective and committed prior to 6 December 1993. As a result of the grant of amnesty, the perpetrator cannot be criminally or civilly liable in respect of that act. Equally, the state or any other body, organization or person that would ordinarily have been vicariously liable for such act, cannot be liable in law.

The Court upheld the constitutionality of the section. It acknowledged that the section limited the applicants' right in terms of § 22 of the interim Constitution to "have justiciable disputes settled by a court of law, or . . . other independent or impartial forum." However, in terms of § 33(2) of the Constitution, violations of rights are permissible either if sanctioned by the Constitution or if justified in terms of § 33(1) of the Constitution (the limitation section). The Court held that the epilogue ("National Unity and Reconciliation") to the Constitution sanctioned the limitation on the right of access to court.

The Court held that amnesty for criminal liability was permitted by the epilogue because without it there would be no incentive for offenders to disclose the truth about past atrocities. The truth might unfold with such an amnesty, assisting in the process of reconciliation and reconstruction. Further, the Court noted that such an

From http://www.law.wits.ac.za/judgements/azaposum.html

amnesty was a crucial component of the negotiated settlement itself, without which the Constitution would not have come into being. It found that the amnesty provisions were not inconsistent with international norms and did not breach any of the country's obligations in terms of public international law instruments.

The Court held that the amnesty for civil liability was also permitted by the epilogue, again because the absence of such an amnesty would constitute a disincentive for the disclosure of the truth.

The Court held that the epilogue permitted the granting of amnesty to the state for any civil liability. The Court said that Parliament was entitled to adopt a wide concept of reparations. This would allow the state to decide on proper reparations for victims of past abuses having regard to the resources of the state and the competing demands thereon. Further, Parliament was authorized to provide for individualized and nuanced reparations taking into account the claims of all the victims, rather than preserving state liability for provable and unprescribed delictual claims only.

The Court held that the epilogue authorized the granting of amnesty to bodies, organizations or other persons which would otherwise have been vicariously liable for acts committed in the past. The truth might not be told if these organizations or individuals were not given amnesty. Indeed, according to the Court, the Constitution itself might not have been negotiated had this amnesty not been provided for.

The judgment of the Court was delivered by Mahomed DP and was concurred in by the other members of the Court. Didcott J delivered a separate concurring judgment.

80 | Justice after Apartheid?
Reflections on the South African TRC

Wilhelm Verwoerd

■ ■ ■

The primary purpose of this paper is to help "answer" . . . [certain] "justice"-driven criticisms, which threaten to undermine the legitimacy and, therefore, the efficacy of the TRC process. I want to defend the claim that, in principle, for South Africa, the TRC is the most appropriate protest against and response to a specific kind of wrongdoing, namely large scale politically motivated crimes within a transitional context. Furthermore, as far as the rectification of the more wide-ranging Apartheid injustices are concerned, I want to argue that the TRC's contribution to "reconstruction and development" is vital, though limited.

To do this I will be distinguishing between two approaches to the relationship between justice and the TRC, namely one which highlights the conflicts between the (criminal) justice system and the TRC and another which, in various ways, tries to hold on to justice within an institution like the TRC.

JUSTICE VERSUS THE TRC

Let us . . . look at the kind of criticism which demands: "No amnesty, no amnesia, just justice." For many people the TRC, through its different committees, seems to be sending out conflicting, confusing messages. On the one hand it is constantly

Department of Philosophy, University of Stellenbosch and Researcher, TRC, Cape Town. Mr. Verwoerd took a two-year leave from the University to join the Research Department of the South African Truth and Reconciliation Commission in April 1996. This chapter is an excerpt from a paper delivered at the Fifth International Conference on Ethics and Development, "Globalization, Self-Determination and Justice in Development," Madras, India, 2–9 January 1997.

emphasized that the TRC is a victim-driven process. A central goal is also the strengthening of the rule of law and a culture of human rights in post-Apartheid South Africa. On the other hand, perpetrators can apply for amnesty, violators of human rights are apparently not being punished (at least not in proportion to their crimes).

This can easily create the impression that with the right hand the TRC is trying to contribute to the healing of wounds, but with the left hand it is actually (unintentionally) rubbing salt into wounds. When perpetrators of gross human rights violations are pardoned instead of being punished, when they are even allowed to occupy (privileged) positions of power, it can be seen as a form of re-victimization, as an insult added to grievous injuries.

■ ■ ■

Perhaps the best response to this deeply felt opposition to an aspect of the TRC's work is, firstly, to accept the common definition of (criminal) justice [justice defined as retributive punishment, such as incarceration and fines] and acknowledge openly that amnesty is unjust. This acknowledgement should also involve a recognition of the reality and legitimacy of the feelings of anger and frustration, the deep sense of injustice at stake.

However, this is not the end of the story. It can then be made clear, in the second place, that this kind of criticism is misdirected: the Truth and Reconciliation Commission is not trying to achieve justice. Guaranteeing amnesty is the price we, unfortunately, have to pay for peace, for the common good, for a negotiated settlement in 1994 which led to a democratic South Africa.

Underlying this response is the assumption that justice does not encompass the whole of morality, which would've meant that to talk about what is just and unjust simply would've been another way to talk about what is right and wrong. Taking justice to be a part of morality enables one to establish that something is just or unjust and still intelligibly inquire whether it is right or wrong. Many people, for example, think that capital punishment is right even though it inevitably kills a certain number of innocent people, something which is clearly unjust.[1] In a similar vein one might enquire whether (criminal) justice in the case of perpetrators of gross human rights violations is necessarily the right course of action to take. It is clearly unjust to let these people off the hook, but does that mean it is always wrong to grant (qualified) amnesty?

In other words, we might have to accept that there is indeed a moral conflict between justice, as embodied in the justice system, and values such as truth, reconciliation, peace, the common good underlying this kind of Commission. The important point is, however, that (criminal) justice is not the only social goal, nor always the ultimate value. And sometimes one will be faced with difficult choices between these values, sometimes one must make judgements about their relative importance. In the context of a fragile transition to a stable democracy, for example, political compromises, such as amnesty, might be justified for the sake of, say, the common good and peace.

■ ■ ■

This kind of response helps one to understand the difficult experience, high-lighted by the apparently conflicting activities of the Human Rights Violations and Amnesty Committees, of being confronted with an intense conflict between moral values. This understanding helps to clear at least some of the confusion, though it doesn't take away the conflict. It also makes it easier to work within the TRC with the price of political compromises and still retain one's sense of moral integrity: It is easier to learn to live with a moral conflict than a moral compromise, than being branded a sell-out to the cause of justice.[2]

■ ■ ■

JUSTICE AND THE TRC

The truth emerging as a result of the amnesty process—with full disclosures of mis-deeds a precondition for receiving amnesty—can be seen as a response to wrongdo-ing which remains to some extent true to the spirit of justice, which fulfills to some extent the repudiating function of criminal prosecution. Though amnesty prevents human courts from properly punishing those perpetrators who qualify, injustices are at least named out loud (in the final report and through the publication of the names and offences of those who receive amnesty). This naming can be seen as some punishment in the form of public shaming,[3] though it certainly is not a pun-ishment which is in proportion to the gravity of the gross human rights violations being pardoned. Through the work of the Reparation and Rehabilitation Commit-tee there is also at least some recognition of victims' right to compensation.

It is also important to emphasize that perpetrators not only have to meet certain criteria before they qualify for amnesty (i.e., it is not just a matter of filling in a few forms), they also may apply only until 15 December 1996. This means that those who do not qualify or do not apply leave themselves open for prosecution. In this sense the truth emerging through the amnesty process might actually aid/comple-ment, instead of impede, the justice system.

Political crimes not only present problems as far as the prosecution and punish-ment of elusive offenders are concerned. What about the rehabilitation of these of-fenders, which, at least in theory, is another important goal of punishment?

According to Jorge Correa, who served as executive secretary of the Chilean TRC, it is generally accepted that sending human rights violators to jail is not a very effective device, because the political motivation ("ideological fanaticism") leading to the crimes cannot be rehabilitated through special treatments. He be-lieves that most of these people, once they have recovered political power, are likely to violate human rights again.[4]

However, the issue is not only the rehabilitation of individual malefactors. When one is dealing with political crimes the real question is: "who/what must be rehabil-

itated?" Only concentrating on individual or a few prominent human rights violators—as was the case during the Nuremberg and Tokyo war tribunals, largely following the procedures of the conventional criminal justice system—only deals with
the tip of the iceberg. How does one rehabilitate and transform the institutions, say
the different branches of the security establishment, which to a large extent made
the commitment of many gross human rights violations possible? This shift in emphasis from individual to social and institutional reparation prepares the way for a
discussion of the TRC's contribution towards greater social justice in [South
Africa].

■   ■   ■

We have referred a number of times to the "transitional context" within which
the relationships between amnesty, justice and the TRC must be understood. It now
becomes important to describe this transition itself in the language of justice.

Rawls' notion of a "nearly just society"—which he defines as a society with legitimately established democratic government that is "well-ordered for the most part
but in which some serious violations of justice nevertheless do occur"[5]—provides a
useful point of departure. This notion draws our attention to the fact that the government, as the main agent for the distribution of benefits and burdens, of rights
and duties should be a legitimate one, i.e., the final adjudicator, enforcer, and protector of justice in a society, should itself be justly constituted. If this foundation on
which the central task of rendering justice is missing, if there is no legitimately constituted democratic government we have what can be called a "radically unjust society."[6]

This means that though amnesty may amount to a lack of justice on an individual
level, it helped to lay the foundation for a more just social order in [South Africa];
i.e., as a precondition for the negotiated settlement, which allowed a relatively
peaceful transition from a white minority regime to a legitimately established democratic goverment, amnesty was a key stepping stone from a "radically unjust" to a
"nearly just" society.[7]

■   ■   ■

One of the objectives of the TRC as set out in the Promotion of National Unity
and Reconciliation Act is "restoring the human and civil dignity of victims by
granting them an opportunity to relate their own accounts of the violations of
which they are the victims."[8]

This restoration of human and civil dignity is a crucial part of the consolidation
of the legitimacy of the main agent of justice beyond the founding democratic elections. Given the dehumanisation of most South Africans by the Apartheid state,
given the ways in which people were treated as subjects and "migrant labour"
under the previous governments, there is not only a great need for reconciliation
between the formerly privileged white citizens and the majority of "new" citizens,
but also between the first truly democratic government and all her citizens.

■ ■ ■

Justice at the level of the social order is not only about laying the foundation and consolidating the legitimacy of the "final adjudicator, enforcer and protector of justice,"[9] it is also a demand for rectification for wrongs done by the previous illegitimate state and other institutions. It can be argued that the justice system, with its primary focus on individual legal responsibility, is less suited to deal with this level of reparation than a Truth Commission—trying to get "as complete a picture as possible of the nature, causes and extent" of gross human rights violations, placing the more wide-ranging moral responsibility of institutions like the state, the judiciary, the (security) police in the centre of the picture.

The TRC is not only trying to bring to light dark deeds of individual perpetrators, [but], even though it cannot impose penal sanctions, it is [also] attempting to highlight the responsibility of various institutions—through acts of commission and acts of omission—for injustices in the form of gross human rights violations. Chains of command beyond the actions of "foot soldiers" are investigated, submissions are requested/received from church groupings, the media, different sectors within the health profession and the judiciary. These hearings and investigations are also accompanied by a consultative process of preparing detailed recommendations to prevent similar violations in the future.

This public protest against wrongdoing, which includes but also goes beyond the individual level, is, therefore, not intended as a witch-hunt exercise. It is based "on the need to restore a national moral conscience [because] the future will remain elusive unless we seriously start to work towards a society based on respect for human rights and human dignity."[10] It is done for the sake of democracy:

> We must encourage the revival of moral conscience to fuel a democratic, caring future . . . we must appreciate that true reconciliation is more meaningful than merely asserting that new structures have been put in place, like this Parliament, or the Constitutional Court, or the Human Rights Commission. We must assert not only the structures, but also the new value system which overcomes the old master-servant, overlord-victim assumptions.[11]

■ ■ ■

The abovementioned (potential) links between the TRC and democratisation are not sufficient to address the basic needs, the very real material concerns of those victims who want more than symbolic acknowledgement/reparation, who want to extend the scope of the TRC's work and/or those critics questioning the distribution of very scarce resources to the TRC. . . .

■ ■ ■

In response to this deeply troubling type of criticism one could start by making it clearer, for example to the millions of people who have been forcefully removed,[12] what the TRC cannot do. [In other words,] . . . one could appeal to a necessary division of labour between the TRC and the Land Claims Court. . . . After all, the TRC is only a stepping stone towards "reconciliation and the reconstruction of society."[13] However, it remains very difficult to "exclude" people from the TRC process in this way—victims who fall outside the TRC's definition of "gross human rights violations" may indeed feel that the TRC (which is certainly, at the moment, the most visible of the available stepping stones) regards their violation as not "gross" enough. Thus the TRC may unintentionally be adding insult to their injuries.[14]

On the other hand, [it is important] . . . to draw out the painful implications of what might be termed a tension between individual and social/national reparation underlying the work of the TRC. This tension is highlighted by the limited reparation and rehabilitation on offer to those victims of gross human rights violations clearly falling within the TRC's mandate as a result of a comprehensive amnesty, which not only precludes the criminal prosecution of (certain) individual wrongdoers, but also deprives victims and their families from their right to seek civil redress through the courts and the right to require the State to make good the losses which had been suffered in consequence of the crimes and delicts of the employees of the State.

These consequences of amnesty have recently been challenged as an impermissible, unconstitutional infringement of victims' rights in the case of *Azanian People's Organisation and Others v. President of the Republic of South Africa*.[15] [This case was discussed in chapter 79.]

■ ■ ■

Faced with the "agonising problem" of competing demands between victims as defined by the TRC and those victims of the "crass inhumanity of Apartheid which so many had to endure for so long," between the "formidable delictual claims of those who had suffered from acts of murder, torture or assault perpetrated by servants of the State" and the desperate need to correct massive wrongs in the crucial areas of education, housing and health care, the makers of the Constitution were, therefore, entitled to favour "the reconstruction of society." This "hard choice" in favour of "a wider concept of 'reparation'" [would] allow the State to take into account the competing claims on its resources but, at the same time, to have regard to the "untold suffering" of individuals and families whose fundamental human rights have been invaded during the conflict of the past."

This "perhaps even more imaginative and fundamental route to the 'reconstruction of society' . . . appears to have been chosen by Parliament through the mechanism of amnesty and nuanced and individualised reparations in the [Promotion of National Unity and Reconciliation] Act."[16]

However, this route does not remove the tension between "narrow" and "wide" reparation, because victims of "gross human rights violations" no longer have an enforceable right to reparation, and, furthermore, the prioritization of the intense demands of present and future generations on very scarce resources will unfortunately limit the funds eventually allocated by Parliament for the individualized scholarships, medical interventions, training, housing subsidies etc. provided to victims of past political conflicts.[17]

■ ■ ■

NOTES

1. R. L. Holmes, *Basic Moral Philosophy* (Belmont, Calif.: Wadsworth, 1993), pp. 176–177.

2. See in this regard M. A. Garreton's conceptualization of a conflict between an "ethical-symbolic" logic and "political-state" logic in "Human Rights in Processes of Democratization," *Journal of Latin American Studies* 26 (1994): 221–234.

3. P. A. French, *Collective and Corporate Responsibility* (New York: Columbia University Press, 1984).

4. J. Correa, "Dealing with Past Human Rights Violations: The Chilean Case after Dictatorship," in *Transitional Justice*, ed. Neil J. Kritz, vol. 2 (Washington, D.C.: United States Institute of Peace Press, 1995), p. 487.

5. John Rawls, *The Theory of Justice* (Cambridge: Harvard University Press, 1971), p. 363.

6. H. P. P. Lötter, *Justice for an Unjust Society* (Amsterdam: Rodopi, 1993), pp. 3–4.

7. This link between legitimacy, democracy, justice, and the amnesty part of the TRC's work can also be applied to the TRC as a whole when one notices the uniquely democratic process whereby the TRC itself was constituted: the formulation of the objectives and the specific procedures of the TRC, and the appointment of the Commissioners have been characterized by an unprecedented process of public debate and scrutiny.

8. *Promotion of National Unity and Reconciliation Act*, Number 34, Section 3(c), (1996).

9. Lötter, *Justice for an Unjust Society*, p. 3.

10. Hansard, *Debates of the National Assembly*, Second session, First Parliament (Capetown: The Government Printer, May 16–18, 1995), p. 1347 (quoting Minister of Justice Dullah Omar).

11. Ibid., p. 1381 (quoting Min. Kadar Asmal). See also P. DuPreez, *Genocide: The Psychology of Mass Murder* (London: Bowerdean Publishing Co., 1994) on the prevention of genocide. This need for moral (and political) "re-skilling" seems to go much further than past authoritarian developing countries. For an interesting argument about the sources of alienation between state and citizens in modern liberal democracies and the resulting need for a radicalization of democracy to improve the quality of citizens' participation in public life, see C. Offe and U. K. Preuss, "Democratic Institutions and Moral Resources," in *Political Theory Today*, ed. David Held (Cambridge: Polity Press, 1991).

12. The Surplus People's Project has estimated that about 3.5 million have suffered under this aspect of the institutional violence of Apartheid. See African National Congress, *Statement to the TRC* (Marshalltown: DIP, 1996).

13. Statement by Minister of Justice Dullah Omar.

14. See in this regard Fraser's argument that justice today requires both redistribution and recognition. N. Fraser, "From Redistribution to Recognition? Dilemmas of Justice in a 'Post-Socialist' Age," *New Left Review* 212 (1995): 68-93.

15. Cf. Sen's arguments for "capabilities" as the most defensible normative foundation for

development and Nussbaum's "thick, but vague theory of the good." A. Sen, *Commodities and Capabilities* (Amsterdam: North Holland, 1985); A. Sen, "Justice: Means vs. Freedoms," *Philosophy and Public Affairs* (1990): 111–121. See also D. A. Crocker, "Toward Development Ethics," in *Ethical Principles for Development: Needs, Capacities or Rights*, ed. K. Aman (Upper Montclair, N.J.: Institute for Critical Thinking, Montclair State, 1991), pp. 5, 19, 457–483.

16. *Promotion of National Unity and Reconciliation Act*, pp. 1038–1039, paragraphs 42–46, (1996).

17. Ibid., paragraph 45. The rather vivid image of "collective vomiting" is used to make this point. See in this regard Bremner's argument for the potential complementarity between needs-based development theory and practice, such as HSD, and conflict resolution theory and practice. D. Bremner, "Development's Catch-22: No Development without Peace, No Peace without Development," *Track Two, Constructive Approaches to Community and Political Conflict* 3 (1994): 1–4. See also Kraybill's argument that the successful implementation of the RDP requires the urgent development of widespread conflict resolution skills. By framing the TRC as part of this process to resolve conflicts (in this case from the past), then the relevance for the RDP becomes very clear.

81 Will the Amnesty Process Foster Reconciliation among South Africans?

Emily H. McCarthy

■   ■   ■

The amnesty process is predicated on the belief that uncovering the "truth" about the apartheid past will pave the way toward reconciliation among the diverse ethnic and political groups in South Africa. As one journalist aptly described the Truth Commission and the amnesty process:

> The effort assumes that truth is a balm, and that recording the horrors of the past will by itself help diminish the chance they will be repeated in the future. Not everyone agrees that recording the horrors is enough. The truth commission itself is the result of a compromise embodied in its guarantee of amnesty to those who confess. One side favored unrelenting punishment for political criminals. . . . The other wanted to wash its hands of apartheid, without even paying the price of humiliation through exposure.[1]

Archbishop Tutu, the champion and chairman of the Truth Commission, concedes that "[t]he commission remains a risky and delicate business," but insists that "it remains the only alternative to Nuremberg on the one hand and amnesia on the other."[2] In an appeal to political leaders and potential amnesty applicants to come forward, Archbishop Tutu said:

> There is no instrument in the country with the same potential as this process for ending the accusations and counter-accusations about the past, the recriminations and the political bickering which will plague this country's life for generations to come if you do not seize the opportunity of using properly the Commission which you created.[3]

From Emily H. McCarthy, "South Africa's Amnesty Process: A Viable Route Toward Truth and Reconciliation?" *Michigan Journal of Race and Law* 3 (1997): 248–253.

Despite Archbishop Tutu's conviction that the Truth Commission and the amnesty process provide the only path toward reconciliation and national unity in South Africa's deeply divided society, many South Africans seriously question the value of the Truth Commission's work.

Public criticism of the Truth Commission suggests the amnesty process has been much better at establishing the truth than at promoting reconciliation. Many of the attacks have come from White conservatives who claim the Commission is a one-sided organization, intent on discrediting the Afrikaners and glorifying the ANC [African National Congress]. For example, one editorial complains that

> [t]he commission is obviously being used to present a bad image of the previous government and put the Afrikaans people in a bad light. . . . The object is evidently to show to the world that apartheid was the greatest evil in South Africa. The terrorists were all pure, innocent people who never put a foot wrong but were unjustly persecuted.[4]

Another conservative editorial called the Truth Commission hearings a "judicial charade, with histrionics, fables, uncorroborated evidence, and [a] lack of cross examination" and accused the "biased" Commission of "bring[ing] itself and everyone connected with it into disrepute."[5] De Klerk has repeatedly criticized the Commission as "uneven-handed" and "biased" against the former government.[6] Even Archbishop Tutu has chastised Commission members for making statements during hearings that could be characterized as biased.[7] According to national surveys, a third of Whites interviewed perceive the Commission to be favoring Black over White South Africans[8] and many Whites scornfully refer to the Commission as the "Kleenex Commission"[9] because of all the tears it has generated.

These observations ignore the reality of the Amnesty Committee hearings. Thus far, the decisions handed down by the Amnesty Committee have demonstrated considerable leniency toward conservative Whites. For example, in December 1996, the Committee not only granted Brian Mitchell amnesty, but also granted amnesty to four Afrikaner men belonging to right-wing groups who planted bombs in Black schools after Mandela began negotiating with de Klerk.[10] Most of the amnesty hearings before March 1997 involved supporters of the apartheid regime, and the Mitchell precedent virtually assures that these applicants will receive amnesty provided they do not conceal relevant facts and did not commit their crimes for explicitly personal reasons. Additionally, White conservatives have the Truth Commission to thank for the extension of the cut-off date until May 10, 1994, which has allowed several White conservatives who set off bombs at polling stations in April 1994 to come forward.[11] Without the Commission's pressure, President Mandela would likely have remained opposed to a time extension.[12]

Although the majority of South Africans interviewed in national surveys endorse the work of the Commission, many oppose the granting of amnesty to grave human rights violators and more than half believe the "perpetrators" testifying before the Commission should face trial.[13] This sentiment is particularly strong among Black South Africans. As one editorial explained, "Many black activists resent that police and others who brutalized members of the country's black majority may go unpunished, literally getting away with murder."[14] On the whole, Black South Africans have been extraordinarily tolerant of an amnesty process that has operated to benefit many White applicants at the expense of primarily Black victims. However, sometimes the decisions of the Amnesty Committee may go too far. Decisions like those granting amnesty to Brian Mitchell[15] and to the Afrikaners convicted of blowing up Black schools, and the pressure put on Mandela to extend the cut-off date primarily to cover right-wing bomb attacks against Blacks in early 1994[16] have many Black South Africans wondering if these attempts to buy "truth" have come at too costly [a price].[17]

Official reactions from predominantly Black parties were mixed. The ANC party publicly endorsed the extension of the cut-off date and the application deadline, as well as the Mitchell decision.[18] The ANC found Mitchell's testimony extremely valuable because it identified the apartheid security network as being primarily responsible for the "Black on Black" violence and implicated senior level IFP [Inkatha Freedom Party] members in major attacks on the ANC.[19] The PAC [Pan African Congress] denounced the Committee's decisions of December 1996 as "naked injustice for these victims of apartheid crime."[20] Leaders of the PAC's military wing complained that many of its anti-apartheid activists were "rotting" in jail while apartheid criminals were walking around free.[21]

The IFP, a predominantly Black party, has publicly opposed the Truth and Reconciliation Commission [TRC] from its inception and discourages IFP members from applying for amnesty.[22] As a result, very few IFP members have applied for amnesty.[23] The IFP continues to attack the TRC as "a monster which is not only failing to heal the old wounds but, indeed, is opening new ones" and to accuse Archbishop Tutu of infecting the TRC with his own pro-ANC and anti-IFP "bias."[24] In May 1997, the IFP issued a statement reiterating these criticisms: "As currently constituted the Truth Commission is not promoting reconciliation and nation building. The [pro–] African National Congress sympathies of the commission are patent. All other parties are treated in a second-class manner bordering on contempt."[25] Given that violent clashes between the IFP and the ANC are one of the most pressing problems facing South Africa today,[26] the IFP's response to the Truth Commission suggests that reconciliation between these two groups is unlikely.

In August 1997, AZAPO [Azanian Peoples Organization], a mostly Black anti-apartheid movement, seriously questioned the Committee's decision to grant amnesty to Dirk Coetzee, a former police hit squad commander, and his police operatives, Almond Mofomela and David Tshikilange, for the highly publicized murder of human rights lawyer Griffiths Mxenge in 1981.[27] The three men had been convicted of Mxenge's murder on May 15, 1997, in the Durban High Court.[28] A spokesperson for AZAPO said the Amnesty Committee's decision confirms that the truth and reconciliation process has "nothing to do with justice . . . [or] reconciliation," but rather "has everything to do with political expediency of the government."[29] The spokesperson went on to explain how the amnesty process affects victims and their families: "[I]t is like turning the knife after the initial blow to the heart. It causes more pain and reveals the futility of saying the families can always oppose the granting of amnesty."[30]

South Africans across the political and racial spectrum have been voicing doubt about the Commission's ability to foster reconciliation and national unity. At the same time that members of the Black community are finding their sense of justice sorely tested by the seemingly indiscriminate grants of amnesty to White applicants, much of the White and conservative populations in South Africa are accusing the Commission of "bias" against Whites.[31] While the Commission is doing a formidable job of uncovering the truth about the apartheid-era crimes, it is having far less success in promoting reconciliation. Although there is logic in the argument that the ANC government "must temper its reaction to the past, given how it came to power and the continuing importance of the white population to the economy and in the security forces,"[32] the Truth Commission must pay heed to the complaints from the much larger Black population in South Africa if the Commission is serious about promoting reconciliation in the vast majority of South Africans. For the amnesty process to succeed, the Commission must focus more of its attention on fostering reconciliation and less of its attention on exposing the painful "truth" at the expense of justice.

■ ■ ■

NOTES

1. Jerelyn Eddings, "The Shield of Truth," *U.S. News and World Report*, February 10, 1997, p. 13.

2. Ibid.

3. *An Open Appeal to Political Leaders and Potential Amnesty Applicants*, Truth and Reconciliation Commission Press Release, December 9, 1996, available at <http://www.truth .org.za/pr/p961209a.htm>

4. C. M. J. van Rensburg, "ANC Campaign of Violence," *Citizen,* October 30, 1996, p. 21.

5. Cassandra Verfontein, "EL Truth Hearings Show Utter Bias," *Citizen*, November 21, 1996, p. 25.

6. *De Klerk's Attack on TRC Deplorable: LHR*, Reports from SAPA, March 27, 1997, available at <http://www.truth.org.za/sapa9703/s970327a.htm>

7. Robert Brand, "Tutu Lashes TRC Members for Their Bias," *Star*, November 26, 1996, p. 1.

8. Richard Carmel, "Fierce Emotions as South Africa Seeks Peace," *National Catholic Reporter*, January 10, 1997.

9. See *Sixty Minutes: Profile: Forgive But Not Forget; Commission Set Up in South Africa to Hear War Atrocities; Criminals Given Amnesty* (CBS television broadcast, February 16, 1997).

10. See "Apartheid Commission Pardons Seven as Amnesty Appeals Flow In," *Agence*

France Presse, December 12, 1996, available in LEXIS, World Library, AFP File; "South Africa Acts on Amnesty Petitions," *Chicago Tribune*, December 13, 1996, p. 13.

11. Suzanne Daley, "Mandela Broadens Limits for Apartheid-Era Amnesty," *New York Times*, December 14, 1996, p. A6.

12. See Robert Brand, "TRC Worried as Deadline for Amnesty Nears," *Star*, December 3, 1996, p. 3.

13. See Carmel, "Fierce Emotions as South Africa Seeks Peace."

14. "A Struggle with Many Truths," *Chicago Tribune*, February 15, 1997, p. 24.

15. See "Healing South Africa's Wounds," *Fresno Bee*, December 16, 1996, p. B4.

16. Daley, "Mandela Broadens Limits for Apartheid-Era Amnesty," p. A6.

17. Hugh Dellios, "Pardons for Apartheid Crimes Angering Many Blacks," *The Record*, December 22, 1996, p. A27.

18. *PAC Condemns Mitchell's Release*, Reports from SAPA, December 11, 1996, available at <http://www.truth.org.za/sapa9612/s961211e.htm>

19. Ibid.

20. Ibid.

21. Ibid. See also *PAC Accuses TRC of Bias Against APLA Cadres*, Reports from SAPA, February 14, 1997, available at <http://www.truth.org.za/sapa9702/s970214a.htm> (noting the PAC's accusation that the TRC is unfairly prioritizing cases of people like Dirk Coetzee and Brian Mitchell over hundreds of applications from imprisoned APLA cadres).

22. In August 1997, IFP leader Mangosuthu Buthelezi ran a half-page advertisement in newspapers that called on IFP's members to boycott all TRC activity. See *TRC Concern over Buthelezi's Advertisement*, Reports from SAPA, August 14, 1997, available at <http://www.truth.org.za/sapa9708/s979814f.htm>

23. See Brand, "TRC Worried as Deadline for Anmesty Nears," p. 3. At the close of the first deadline for applications in December 1996, only a few IFP members had applied as individuals, but the IFP had not applied as a group. "South Africa; Jailbirds Rush for Amnesty," *Africa News*, December 20, 1996, available in LEXIS, World Library, AFRNWS File.

24. *TRC Is a Circus Led by a Clown and Should Be Shut Down: IFP*, Reports from SAPA, May 22, 1997, available at <http://www.truth.org.za/sapa9705/s970522e.htm>

25. *NP Withdrawal from TRC Not Surprising: IFP*, Reports from SAPA, May 19, 1997, available at <http://www.truth.org.za/sapa9705/s970519a.htm>

26. See "Inkatha Leaders Blamed for 1994 Massacre," *Agence France Presse*, July 7, 1996, available in LEXIS, World Library, AFP File. ("Nearly 20,000 people have died during 11 years of violence between ANC and IFP supporters.")

27. See *Granting Amnesty to Coetzee a Bitter Reality to Many: AZAPO*, Reports from SAPA, August 5, 1997, available at <http://www.truth.org.za/sapa9708/s970805b.htm> [hereinafter *Bitter Reality*].

28. *Coetzee Gets Amnesty, But Mxenge Murder Masterminds Still Free*, Reports from SAPA, August 4, 1997, available at <http://www.truth.org.za/sapa9708/s970804g.htm>

29. See *Bitter Reality*.

30. Ibid.

31. Jeffrey Herbst, "Truth May Do More Than Hurt as Apartheid Crimes Are Told," *Los Angeles Times*, February 9, 1997, p. M2 (noting that "[t]he protracted transition [from apartheid to democracy] afforded [the apartheid officials] plenty of time to destroy the paper trails leading to the brutality and bungling that were once so common").

32. Ibid., p. M6.

82 | Healing Racial Wounds?

The Final Report of South Africa's Truth and Reconciliation Commission

Eric K. Yamamoto and Susan K. Serrano

Lukas Baba Sikwepere described the last time he saw the world. At a regional hearing of South Africa's Truth and Reconciliation Commission, he told of his escape in 1985 from a political conflict near Cape Town. After police fired shots into a group of South African blacks, Sikwepere attempted to flee. "[W]hen I arrived at the place when I thought now I am safe, I felt something hitting my cheek . . . I felt my eyes itching . . . I was scratching my eyes, I wasn't quite sure what happened to my eyes." Sikwepere also told the Commission of later beatings by police with electric ropes, of suffocation, and of being forced into an empty grave. And he expressed relief in finally recounting those traumatic events: "I feel that what has been making me sick all the time is the fact that I couldn't tell my story. But now—it feels like I got my sight back by coming here and telling you the story."[1]

"Telling the story" is an important step in the Truth and Reconciliation Commission's ongoing efforts at racial reconciliation. Storytelling by both victims and perpetrators, the Commission hopes, will be therapeutic. It will build a new "truth" upon which relationships central to the nation's health can be reforged. At the same time, the Commission acknowledges that storytelling is only the beginning of a long and difficult healing process. To move the country toward reconciliation, white and black South Africans need to acknowledge appropriate responsibility for past wrongs, both as individuals and as group agents. Indeed, the Commission's draft Final Report suggests that meaningful reconciliation is possible only with full participation and engagement by both victims and perpetrators.

In this essay, we describe Chapter 5 ("Reconciliation") of the Commission's draft Final Report. That chapter articulates principles of national racial reconciliation and sketches both observations and criticisms of the Commission's reconciliation efforts. We also briefly describe the Commission's recent reparations proposals as a component of its overall racial healing process. Finally, we offer a preliminary assessment of the Commission's approach to reconciliation in light of its work to date.

THE TRUTH AND RECONCILIATION COMMISSION

Following the fall of Apartheid in South Africa, Nelson Mandela joined hands with F. W. de Klerk and declared, "Let's forget the past! What's done is done!" Mandela, head of South Africa's new government and former prisoner of de Klerk's white National Party regime, sent a clear message: reconciliation between whites and blacks is a fundamental first step toward healing historic wounds and rebuilding the nation. Since this optimistic proclamation, the process of interracial healing has moved forward in fits and starts.[2]

Among his first presidential acts, Nelson Mandela signed the Promotion of National Unity and Reconciliation Bill that established the Truth and Reconciliation Commission. Headed by Nobel Peace laureate Archbishop Desmond Tutu, the seventeen-member Commission is composed of three committees with distinct but related functions: (1) to investigate gross violations of human rights; (2) to consider amnesty for those who confess to political crimes; and (3) to recommend reparations and rehabilitation for victims.

The Commission embarked on its mission in 1995. The Commission's regional hearings provided victims of human rights abuses a public forum both for denouncing the specific atrocities of Apartheid and for initiating healing processes. The Commission also asked perpetrators to confess in the interest of healing—the payoff for which might be indemnity from prosecution and civil liability.[3]

In June 1996, the Commission's Reparation and Rehabilitation Committee recognized the pressing need for interim reparations and adopted a *Policy Framework for Urgent Interim Reparations Measures* that focused on the socioeconomic reordering of society. This framework made recommendations for substantial governmental (but not private) reparations, including payments for medical, emotional, and educational services for those in "urgent need."

The Commission issued its Final Report in October 1998. Yet controversy surrounding the Commission continues. Has the Commission been biased in favor of the African National Congress? What if prominent white South Africans, such as former president P. W. Botha, refuse to participate in the process? Should perpetrators of human rights abuses be granted amnesty? Is saying "sorry" enough? Are the proposed reparations salutary or illusory?

In light of the stunning breakthroughs and continuing controversies, the prognosis for the Commission's work toward long-term racial reconciliation is split between the potential for extraordinary success or dispiriting failure. As the draft Final Report suggests, some whites have stepped forward to "acknowledge collective responsibility for acquiescence in constructing and maintaining a wretched system of discrimination, exclusion and repression." At the same time, however, some victims observe that many wrongdoers "are not coming to tell what they have done so that at least [we] can forgive them." Whether the Commission's work, including a planned program of reparations, will ultimately generate a collective sense of "justice done" and foster genuine racial healing is a question open to speculation.

THE COMMISSION'S FINAL REPORT (DRAFT)

RECONCILIATION

Chapter 5 of the Commission's draft Final Report, entitled "Reconciliation," outlines a process of national reconciliation. To illuminate the Commission's racial healing work, the chapter delineates four interconnected steps toward reconciliation: (1) restoring the dignity of victims and survivors; (2) acknowledgment of guilt and apology; (3) forgiveness; and (4) reparations or restitution. The chapter describes each step through selected examples of testimony by those suffering and those who inflicted the harm.

The Commission's detailed description of its truth hearings in the black township of Duduza are most revealing. Like many townships, Duduza experienced police violence in the 1970s and 1980s. White police in the township repeatedly detained, tortured, and killed people in attempts to suppress political protests. Black and white victims in Duduza and other townships told these stories of violence. Some felt "relieved," others "freed from prison." It was "almost as if the silence is ending," said one, "as if we are waking up from a long bad nightmare."

While many participating in the hearings felt similarly satisfied, others expressed concern that perpetrators and collaborators had not come forward to recognize the hurts they inflicted. "[The perpetrators'] conscience will tell them that if they want forgiveness, they should come and expose themselves so that they can also get the healing that the victims are getting. . . . The people we want to make peace with are not coming to tell us what they have done so that at least [we] can forgive them."

Still others worried about empty apologies and hollow reconciliation. Some felt both "offended" and increasingly "despondent" when they were not asked to testify. Some suspected that the African National Congress and the National Party councilors in charge of community organizing deliberately attempted to suppress stories that might implicate them. Others felt misled when they learned that the Commission's goal was to verify victims' statements and uncover higher official involvement but not to bring the guilty to legal justice. The testimonies quoted in Chapter 5 reflect catharsis and hope as well as deep skepticism.

The draft of Chapter 5 also highlights the effect of minimal white participation in the process. Some whites recognized that "only through the process of truthful disclosure and reconciliation [will we] finally be freed from the burden of [the] baggage of [past wrongs]." On the whole, however, whites rarely attended Commission hearings, many proclaiming that "we did not know—how can you blame us" and "let us rather forget about the past."[4]

Perhaps most important, Chapter 5 offers six broad observations about racial healing—observations akin to principles of reconciliation. First, reconciliation is a long process. "Reconciliation is not an event. People cannot simply one day decide that they want to forgive and forget." Forgiveness for many requires that perpetrators demonstrate remorse and alter long-term behavior. Second, reconciliation is "multi-dimensional." People respond to oppression in varying ways and therefore have differing social and economic needs. Third, reconciliation cannot treat racial conflict as a static past event; historical conflicts, unless resolved, evolve into present-day controversies. Genuine reconciliation links past conflicts with current racial dynamics. Fourth, reconciliation must be "built from the bottom up." The unique histories and needs of each community are integral to relational healing. Fifth, reconciliation requires "truth, empowerment," and a "vision of a new society." Individuals need to "know who to forgive and what they are forgiving them for." Sixth, reconciliation requires direct engagement. Victims need to tell their suffering to perpetrators and demand explanations. Perpetrators need to respond affirmatively.

The chapter closes on a cautionary note. The reconciliation process has begun, and profound steps toward racial healing have been taken. Yet much remains to be done. Although the South African government formally abolished the institution of Apartheid, blacks continue to be barred from private establishments, and all-white Afrikaans schools are commonplace. Many whites continue to deny responsibility for the harms of systemic oppression and violence.

The entire reconciliation process is ongoing. It requires "a platform for storytelling, revealing of the truth, holding the perpetrator accountable, reparations, remorse, and forgiveness. These are steps in a process that people now understand, and that they accept as legitimate." The truth hearings so far, the chapter concludes, "at the least forced people to examine their own understanding of what reconciliation and forgiveness means to them and their community."

REPARATIONS PROPOSALS AND RECONCILIATION

For the Commission, reparations for victims of human rights abuses are an essential part of the reconciliation process. The Commission's Reparations and Rehabilitation Committee talked with those injured, community organizations, social service professionals, faith communities, and government officials. In doing so, the Committee came face-to-face with two dissonant realities: many perpetrators had received amnesty for their crimes; yet the victims of those and similar crimes might realize few if any "tangible gains" from the Commission's work. For that reason, in an April 1997 draft proposal, the Committee emphasized its commitment to reparations. The Committee deemed urgent interim reparations a "moral imperative" and final reparations integral to societal healing.[5]

In October 1997, the Committee outlined five components of its forthcoming reparations proposal: (1) urgent interim reparation; (2) individual reparation grants; (3) symbolic reparation/legal and administrative measures; (4) community rehabilitation programs; and (5) institutional reform. The proposal's central principle is that "reparation should be development-centered to empower individuals and communities to take control of their own lives."[6]

More specifically, the proposal first targets those in urgent need and recommends interim reparations for emotional, medical, educational, and material needs.[7] The proposal then suggests final Individual Reparations Grants of between 17,000 and 23,000 rand a year (the median household income in South Africa) for six years.[8] The planned source for these reparations payments is a "President's Fund" financed by the South African government, individuals, corporations, and the international community.[9]

Individual reparation payments are deemed necessary to "acknowledge the suffering caused by the gross violations of human rights." Reparations are also essential to meet the social and economic needs of victims and to ease communities' "psycho-social burdens." Reparations "will offer South African society as a whole a systematic way of re-visiting and dealing with the memories of the apartheid years, and of entrenching a human rights culture."

A BRIEF ASSESSMENT

How are victims and perpetrators of human rights abuses to think of the Commission's work? What are justice advocates and government officials to make of the Commission's reconciliation efforts and plans? Four dimensions of "interracial justice" provide an approach for inquiring into, ruminating on, and fashioning paths for acting upon intergroup tensions marked both by conflict and distrust and by a desire for peaceable and productive relations.[10] These dimensions are characterized by the "four Rs": recognition, responsibility, reconstruction, and reparations. *Recognition* asks racial group members to recognize and empathize with the anger and hope of those wounded; to acknowledge disabling social constraints imposed by one group upon another and the resulting group wounds; to identify justice grievances often underlying present-day group conflict; and to examine critically stock stories of racial group attributes and interracial relations ostensibly legitimating those constraints and grievances.

Responsibility suggests that amid struggles over identity and power, racial groups can be simultaneously subordinated in some relationships and subordinating in others. In a given situation, group power is both enlivened and constrained by specific social and economic conditions and political alignments. Responsibility therefore asks racial groups to assess carefully the dynamics of group agency for the imposition of disabling constraints upon others and, where appropriate, to accept group responsibility for healing resulting wounds.

Reconstruction entails active steps toward healing the social and psychological wounds resulting from disabling group constraints. These acts might encompass apologies by aggressors; where appropriate, forgiveness by those injured; and a joint reframing of stories of group identities and intergroup relations.

The fourth dimension, closely related to the third, is *Reparation*. It addresses repairing damage to the material conditions of racial group life to attenuate one group's power over the other. This means material changes in the structure of the relationship (social, economic, political) to guard against "cheap reconciliation," where healing efforts are "just talk."

In short, interracial justice entails "a hard acknowledgment of ways in which racial groups harm one another, along with affirmative efforts to redress grievances with present-day effects."[11] For groups seeking to live together peaceably and work together politically, interracial justice often serves as a bridge between presently felt racial wounds and workable intergroup relations. In this section we employ the four broad dimensions of the interracial justice framework to offer a preliminary assessment of the Commission's Final Report draft chapter on Reconciliation within the context of the Commission's overall work.

The Final Report, although still in draft form, reveals the problems and promise of racial reconciliation in South Africa. Overall, the Commission has taken great strides in one important aspect of reconciliation—the first "R," the need for "recognition" through storytelling. For many, the telling of stories was the beginning of a "process of overcoming . . . psychological barriers that they have been living with, often for many years."

Some South Africans worry, however, that storytelling and apology without meaningful reparations will lead to "cheap reconciliation." The Commission's report observes that many victims felt discouraged when, after the "initial outpouring," apologies and reparations did not follow. Others bemoaned the fact that many white South Africans did not take responsibility for the imposition of disabling social and economic constraints upon others. Nor did wrongdoers accept responsibility for acting affirmatively to heal resulting wounds.

Chapter 5 of the Final Report highlights the importance of this second "R." White and black South Africans need to acknowledge appropriate "responsibility" for hurts. As a white doctor testified, "The challenge has nothing to do with self-flagellation or wallowing in guilt, it has everything to do with accepting responsibility for our actions and our lack of action."

The Commission's draft report also recognizes that reconciliation is a complex, ongoing, multidimensional process; those involved cannot simply "forgive and forget." While these observations are salutary, the chapter provides little concrete guidance about the third "R," "reconstruction." How are the Commission's aspirations of reconstructing damaged lives and institutions to be carried out? For some South Africans, national reconciliation requires building just social and economic institutions. For them, the unlocking of painful bonds and the mutual liberation of all South Africans will likely require more than survivor storytelling, confessions without contrition, and weak apologies. As one white South African observed, an institutional apology "was a necessary step along the road we are travelling, but was only a step. Our wholehearted participation in the work of this Commission is yet another step on this road, but again only a step. It will only be through the process of truthful disclosure and reconciliation that we will finally be freed from the burden of this baggage [of past wrongs]."[12]

For still others, reparation—the fourth "R"—is essential to any structural and attitudinal transformation of the society. The Reparations and Rehabilitation Committee's recommendations aspire to the type of material structural change likely to foster a willingness to forgive—to reconcile. Its reparations proposals aim to rebuild intergroup relations through institutional reordering and the rebuilding of shattered lives.

The Committee's articulated principles and goals are valuable. Implementation, however, will require huge financial resources and the creation of bureaucratic structures. The key question for many is whether the new South African government is able to act fully on the proposal.

The government's 1998–1999 allocation of 100 million rand ($20 million U.S.) appears to be a significant start, one that extends beyond the merely symbolic.[13] Material changes in the lives of those who suffered human rights abuses may be in the offing. In light of financial and other realpolitik limitations (such as political backlash against blacks by resentful white South Africans), however, the Commission's ambitious overall reparations and rehabilitation plan could prove illusory if the commitment to full funding wanes. This could lead to what Dietrich Bonhoefer calls "cheap grace," or false reconciliation.

These varied prospects raise the question, Will the Commission's approach to reconciliation ultimately lead to repair, or will it instead prolong victimization and aggravate intergroup racial wounds?

An apology and some form of reparation are often necessary for reconciliation. Yet, they may not be enough to foster psychic healing. As Archbishop Desmond Tutu emphasized, the proposed payments alone are not compensation for suffering: "None of us labours under any delusions—you cannot put a monetary value to a person's suffering."[14] Nevertheless, as the Reparations and Rehabilitation Committee recognized, "while such [reparations] measures can never bring back the dead, nor adequately compensate for pain and suffering, they can and must improve the quality of [victims'] lives."[15] When victims and survivors see reconstruction of socioeconomic conditions and institutional structure—in addition to recognition and acceptance of responsibility—then those long disenfranchised in South Africa may sense a kind of justice that liberates, that contributes to intergroup healing.

CONCLUSION

Taken together, Chapter 5 of the draft Final Report and the Committee's reparation proposals illuminate the promise of meaningful reconciliation for South Africans. Whether the Commission's work over time will in reality engender a restorative justice that leads to reconciliation is an open question. What is clear from the report is that the often wrenching reconciliatory process thus far has fostered healing for some but not others, that some groups have grasped the opportunity for beginning rapprochement and others have not. In terms of prospects for long-term transformation, amid the successes and failures, collective reframing has yet to occur concerning "what happened," "who is responsible" and "how we are to get on with the new South Africa." The Commission, indeed much of South Africa, is struggling to craft a new societal narrative that both acknowledges the past and transcends it. Whether new collective memories will lead to collective forgiveness and a release of the "baggage of past wrongs"—repair—is the question of South Africa's future.

NOTES

1. Truth and Reconciliation Commission, *Reconciliation*, Chapter 5, Final Report, pp. 2–3 (draft on file with authors; hereinafter cited as *Final Report*).

2. Eric K. Yamamoto, "Race Apologies," *Journal of Gender, Race and Justice* 1 (1997): 47, 55.

3. Ibid., pp. 55–56.

4. Truth and Reconciliation Commission, *Final Report*, pp. 2, 10, 26, 29.

5. Truth and Reconciliation Commission, *Proposed Policy for UIR and Final Reparation Discussion Document*, April 2, 1997, pp. 5, 9 (hereinafter cited as *Discussion Document*).

6. "Truth Commission Announces Reparation Plan," *Africa News Service*, October 24, 1997 (statement by Hlengiwe Mkhize, Chairperson, Reparation and Rehabilitation Committee of the Truth and Reconciliation Commission).

7. According to Archbishop Desmond Tutu, the payments are designed to provide initial access to services while the South African government makes its final decisions on reparations. "Message from Archbishop Desmond Tutu," TRC Special Report, SABC Television, March 29, 1998. The remaining South Africans likely to be officially declared victims of gross human rights abuses may have to wait a few months beyond the submission of the Commission's final report for the first of their reparations payments. John Yeld, "Relief Soon for Victims of Rights Abuses," *Africa News Service*, October 24, 1997. The Committee estimates that 20 percent of deponents will qualify for Urgent Interim Reparations. Truth and Reconciliation Commission, *Discussion Document*, p. 18.

8. "Tutu Welcomes Government Reparations Allocations: Statement by Archbishop Desmond Tutu on Allocation for Reparations in the Minister of Finance's Budget," *Africa News Service*, March 11, 1998. Only "primary" victims who suffered a gross violation of human rights would be eligible for individual reparations payments. Relatives or dependents of victims would receive payments only if granted by the primary victim or if the primary victim is deceased or dies. Truth and Reconciliation Commission, *Discussion Document*, p. 11.

9. Truth and Reconciliation Commission, *Discussion Document*, p. 23. In addition to individual grants, the Committee deemed symbolic reparation necessary to commemorate as a national community "the pain and victories of the past." By symbolic reparations, the Committee contemplates building memorials and monuments, renaming streets, and establishing a national day of remembrance and reconciliation. On an individual level, symbolic reparation entails assistance to survivors in acquiring death certificates, clearing their names from

criminal records, having relatives exhumed and reburied, and providing headstones or tombstones. See "Truth Commission Announces Reparation Plan."

10. Eric K. Yamamoto, *Interracial Justice: Conflict and Reconciliation in Post–Civil Rights America* (New York: New York University Press, forthcoming). The four dimensions listed in the text below are taken more or less verbatim from *Interracial Justice*.

11. Ibid.

12. Truth and Reconciliation Commission, *Final Report*, p. 17.

13. The reparations allocation is scheduled to increase to 200 million rand in 1999–2000 and 300 million rand in 2000–2001. See "Tutu Welcomes Government Reparations Allocations."

14. Yeld, "Relief Soon for Victims of Rights Abuses."

15. Truth and Reconciliation Commission, *Discussion Document*, p. 4.

83 Introductory Notes to the Presentation of the Truth and Reconciliation Commission's Proposed Reparation and Rehabilitation Policies

23 October 1997

Hlengiwe Mkhize, Chairperson, Reparation and Rehabilitation Committee of the TRC

The Truth and Reconciliation Commission is today pleased to announce its proposed reparation and rehabilitation policies.

The proposals have been discussed with the Government but they nevertheless remain proposals at this stage. They will be considered fully by Government and Parliament when the Commission's final report is presented next year.

The Commission is not empowered to implement recommendations on a final reparations policy, so final decisions on our recommendations are in the hands of the Government.

WHY REPARATIONS?

But before I sketch to you an outline of the policies, . . . I would like to deal first with the question of why there should be reparations at all. The reason for reparations can be summarised as follows: The conflicts of the past in our country produced many casualties, as a result of which there are a range of needs:

- Health needs;
- Mental health needs;
- Psycho-social burdens for communities and society at large; and
- Education and training needs.

Reparation and rehabilitation measures are necessary to counter-balance the amnesty process; R&R measures and services will offer South African society as a

501

whole a systematic way of re-visiting and dealing with the memories of the apartheid years, and of entrenching a human rights culture.

Remembering suffering is important to ensure that the mistakes of the past are not forgotten. To take a Christian paradigm, Jesus, when he had supper with his disciples, warned them not to forget his suffering but rather to remember it with the aim of striving towards perfection, lest they cause somebody else to suffer. Our own political leaders have challenged future generations not to forget the pain and suffering of those who liberated South Africans.

There is also a legal basis for reparations: the Preamble to the Act which gives us our mandate says one of our objectives is to provide for the "taking of measures aimed at the granting of reparation to, and the rehabilitation and the restoration of the human and civil dignity of, victims of violations of human rights."

POLICY DEVELOPMENT

In formulating the policy and recommendations, the Reparation and Rehabilitation Committee of the Commission was guided by a number of processes:

- Witnesses' statements: We took into account the aspirations of those who suffered by listening to their testimony;
- The TRC database: We analysed the needs and expectations of victims and survivors as extracted from their written statements and recorded on our database;
- An intensive consultative process: We conducted monthly regional workshops in each regional office, including representatives of Non-Governmental Organisations, Community-based Organisations, faith communities, academic institutions, government departments and youth structures. We presented our ideas to significant bodies such as the American Psychiatric Association, the British Medical Association, the United Nations and the World Health Organisation.

IMPLEMENTATION OF PROPOSALS AND PRINCIPLES OF POLICY

How should the policy proposals be implemented? What should be the guiding philosophy?

Accountability should be in the President's Office. [Also,] implementation strategy should allow for active community participation. To ensure that the process is driven from the grassroots, we propose the following pillars upon which each service should be founded:

- It should be development-centred;
- It should be simple and efficient;
- Measures should be culturally appropriate;

- Services should be community based;
- Measures should aim at building capacity; and
- They should promote healing the reconciliation.

STRUCTURE OF POLICY

What does the structure of the proposed policy look like? The proposed reparation and rehabilitation policy has five components:

- *Urgent Interim Reparation (UIR)*
  UIR is assistance for people in urgent need to access appropriate services and facilities. Limited financial resources will be made available to facilitate this access. . . .
- *Individual Reparation Grants (IRG)*
  It is proposed that individual reparation should take the form of a scheme under which victims or survivors of gross human rights violations will receive individual, annual financial grants for a period of six years. Most of the value of the grant would acknowledge the suffering caused by the gross violation of human rights. However, people living in rural areas, where it is more difficult to access services such as health care, and those with many dependents, could receive higher grants. Past compensation granted as a direct result of the violation would be deducted.

  The minimum payment will be about R17,000 a year for six years. However, the annual payment may be topped up for those who have many dependents or those who live in rural areas. The maximum "top-up" would take the annual payment to an amount of R23,000 a year for six years.
- *Symbolic Reparation/Legal and Administrative Measures*
  Symbolic reparation encompasses measures to facilitate the communal process of commemorating the pain and victories of the past. Amongst other measures, symbolic reparation will entail identifying a national day of remembrance and reconciliation [plus] erection of memorials and monuments. On a more individual level, symbolic reparation could also mean assistance to individuals in obtaining death certificates and finalising outstanding legal matters, or clearing their names from criminal records. Victims may be eligible to have relatives exhumed and reburied, or in some cases to receive a headstone or tombstone.

  The Commission has further recommended that streets and community facilities should be renamed to reflect and honour individuals or events in communities. It identified a need for culturally appropriate ceremonies in certain communities, which could in some instances include cleansing ceremonies. We believe local and provincial authorities should arrange such ceremonies in close co-operation with faith communities and cultural and community organisations.

- *Community Rehabilitation Programmes*

  These are proposals for the establishment of community based services and activities, aimed at promoting the healing and recovery of individuals and communities which have been affected by human rights violations.

  Community Rehabilitation Programmes hinge on the main policy principle that reparation should be development centred, to empower individuals and communities to take control of their own lives. It therefore implies the provision of sufficient knowledge and information about available resources to victims through a participatory process.

  The Commission states clearly in its proposal that providing individuals with resources to access services is not enough as these services are in many cases "unavailable, inaccessible or inappropriate." It also notes that entire communities have been subjected to systematic abuse, and may suffer from post-traumatic stress symptoms. The proposals make provision for rehabilitation programmes at community and national levels.

  Among the categories of community rehabilitation recommended are health care, mental health care, education and housing. A programme to demilitarise the youth who have come to accept violence as a way of resolving conflict is included under emotional health care, as is a multi-disciplinary programme involving all ministries and departments to resettle the thousands of "internal" refugees driven from their homes due to political conflict. The Commission further proposes mental health interventions on a community level, as well as specialised trauma counselling services and family-based therapy. It calls for housing projects in communities where gross violations of human rights led to mass destruction of property and/or displacement. All these programmes would make provision for the establishment of services and activities in the community, aimed at promoting the healing and recovery of individuals and communities affected by violations.

- *Institutional Reform*

  These proposals include legal, administrative and institutional measures designed to prevent the recurrence of human rights abuse. Institutional reform overlaps with the broader aims of the Commission, including measures designed to prevent the recurrence of human rights abuses, for implementation in a wide range of sectors such as the judiciary, media, security forces and business. Recommendations of a legal, administrative and institutional nature, to ensure the development of a human rights culture in South Africa, will be included in the Final Report of the TRC.

84 | Truth and Reconciliation Commission Hearing Testimony of Former President F. W. de Klerk

May 14, 1997

■ ■ ■

Chairperson . . . I shall limit my opening remarks. . . . [A] number of commentators as well as my political opponents continue to claim that I have not apologised for apartheid. This is simply not true. Clearly they have not listened or they don't care to listen to the numerous statements I have made on the subject over the years. They fail to take note of my unqualified apology on the 30th of April 1993. They have studied neither my first nor second submission to the Truth and Reconciliation Commission. They equate the efforts that I made, and may I say at the Commission's request, to try to explain in context the circumstances which gave rise to apartheid with some or other attempt to defend or justify the policies of the past. The latter has never been my intention.

Let me place once and for all a renewed apology on record. Apartheid was wrong. I apologise in my capacity as leader of the National Party to the millions of South Africans who suffered the wrenching disruption of forced removals in respect of their homes, businesses and land. Who over the years suffered the shame of being arrested for pass law offences. Who over the decades and indeed centuries suffered the indignities and humiliation of racial discrimination. Who for a long time were prevented from exercising their full democratic rights in the land of their birth. Who were unable to achieve their full potential because of job reservation. And who in any other way suffered as a result of discriminatory legislation and policies. This renewed apology is offered in a spirit of true repentance, in full knowledge of the tremendous harm that apartheid has done to millions of South Africans.

■ ■ ■

85 | Affirmative Action as Reparation for Past Employment Discrimination in South Africa

Imperfect and Complex

Linda Human

The last six years have seen a great deal of debate in South Africa about concepts such as affirmative action and employment equity. Many people, however, rely on newspapers for their understanding of what affirmative action is and how it will affect their lives. More interesting (or alarming) is how such reports are taken at face value, particularly if they tell us about how affirmative action has failed in other countries, such as the United States. This negative reporting obviously affects the attitudes of blacks and whites toward affirmative action. Because of the association made between affirmative action and tokenism, "quotas," and window-dressing, many competent black people argue that they want to be judged according to the same criteria as whites. In other words, affirmative action is seen as an affront to their competence and dignity rather than as reparation for past unfair discrimination. In contrast, others, especially blacks, would argue that the suggested employment equity and affirmative action measures do not go far enough. Given the inequalities wreaked by apartheid, they argue, the government has a responsibility to implement a quota system to ensure that blacks are given back what is justly theirs.

In South Africa, these debates have recently been given some shape by the various drafts of the Employment Equity Bill, a postapartheid legislative act that is designed to promote fair employment practices.[1] The message at last is slowly being driven home: affirmative action is not just another term for societal transformation; rather, it is a limited and imperfect intervention that affects only those employed by organisations above a certain size. Clarification is also taking place in terms of what employment equity and affirmative action are and how they should be implemented.

For example, contrary to popular opinion in the early 1990s, employment equity guidelines have generally viewed affirmative action as a means of overcoming barriers to equal employment opportunity rather than as a means of unfairly "advantaging" the interests of various groups at the expense of others. In other words, affirmative action has been conceived generally as a process to eliminate discrimination rather than as a process whereby one form of discrimination is replaced by another. This is the view taken in the United States by the government agency charged with administering that country's employment discrimination laws. The Equal Employment Opportunity Commission (EEOC) has issued paradigmatic guidelines that define affirmative as "actions appropriate to overcome the effects of past or present practices, policies, or other barriers to equal employment opportunity."[2]

Other general aspects that most affirmative action programme guidelines appear to share include the following. Affirmative action should seek to increase employment opportunities for ethnic, racial, gender, and other groups traditionally excluded from mainstream societal institutions. This goal should be achieved without recourse to tokenism, in the sense of bringing in "unqualified" persons, and without "unnecessarily trammeling" the expectations of white males. Affirmative action programmes should be temporary interventions that will cease as soon as equal employment opportunity has been achieved.[3]

In South Africa, a government document called the "White Paper on Affirmative Action in the Public Service," launched in March 1998, defines affirmative action "as the additional, corrective steps which must be taken in order that those who have been historically disadvantaged by unfair discrimination are able to derive full benefit from an equitable employment environment."[4] This definition is similar in spirit to that of the EEOC. In addition, it builds on the framework and requirements of the Employment Equity Bill.

The Employment Equity Bill, which will soon become law in South Africa, involves both eliminating discrimination and establishing specific measures to accelerate the advancement of "blacks" (by which is meant black Africans, Coloureds, and Asians collectively), women, and the disabled. One of the measures being used to accelerate the advancement of these groups is affirmative action. Under affirmative action, these historically disadvantaged groups are to be given preferential treatment in appointments and promotions. In this way, affirmative action is intended to be part of a broader range of activities designed to promote employment equity.

What the Employment Equity Bill attempts to do, then, is to use affirmative action in a limited fashion—namely, to proactively eradicate the effects of past unfair discrimination without resorting to reverse discrimination. This is an extremely complex process, and one which proponents of equality of opportunity would oppose, arguing that formal equality and the removal of discriminatory legislation are sufficient. Proponents of the equality of outcome perspective would disagree with this contention by stating that we have to work toward substantive equality; in other words, they would argue that we cannot talk about equality in circumstances where, historically, some groups have been unfairly disadvantaged. What is required is a period of affirmative action before we can even begin to put forward arguments relating to equality of opportunity.

The latter view is essentially correct. Although the end result of any employment equity program theoretically should be the removal of any form of consideration of race and gender in hiring and promotion decisions, the consequence of doing this in the short-term would be the entrenchment of the status quo. In South Africa, the entrenchment of the status quo would be politically and socially disastrous. Any society with South Africa's demographics and inequalities would be unstable in a situation where nothing changes. And little will change if we accept the principles of so-called "equal opportunity" in the absence of affirmative action. In South Africa, as in all societies, patterns of privilege and economic power have become entrenched. This means that, over generations, the vast majority of the poor remain poor and the vast majority of the rich stay rich.

The classical sociological perspective of the social reproduction of existing relations of power suggests that elites in the majority of countries of the Western world have tended to maintain power across generations. By a process of "social closure" that involves the use of two main exclusionary devices—property and credentials—groups attempt to optimize their own rewards by restricting access to resources and opportunities to a limited number of people whom they regard as "eligible."[5] The ability of the few to govern the many—both economically and politically—depends heavily on the process of "exclusionary closure," by means of which property ownership and the (interlinked) possession of educational qualifications result in internal cohesion or group hegemony. Research suggests that the sons of fathers working at the top of the job hierarchy have substantial advantages in terms of life chances over those born to fathers working in blue-collar jobs.[6] Of particular relevance appears to be the ability of the more privileged to provide educational opportunities for their children; such opportunities, in turn, often provide access to higher level jobs.

Although the political scene has transformed dramatically in South Africa in recent years, the workplace is still scarred by the ravages of apartheid. Discriminatory legislation against blacks and gender discrimination have created a situation where white males generally occupy the top half of the occupational hierarchy, and blacks and women the lower level jobs. Indeed, the overall occupational structure remains one in which whites dominate the upper categories of employment out of all proportion to their participation in the labor force, and the disadvantaged groups, in particular black Africans, are overrepresented in the lower categories of employment.

According to the Employment Equity Bill of 1997, the bottom fifth of income-earners in South Africa earn 1.5 percent of national income while the wealthiest 10 percent of households capture 50 percent of national income. On top of this, 95 percent of the poor are black African, and two-thirds of black Africans are poor. Among black Africans, unemployment is approximately 41 percent, among Coloureds 23 percent, Asians 17 percent, and whites 6.4 percent. More women are unemployed than men. Moreover, a white male is five thousand times more likely than a black African woman to be in a top management position. A survey of some 107 organisations by the *Breakwater Monitor* in 1996 indicated that, in the top managerial ranks of companies (Paterson F Grade), 3 percent were black Africans, 0.5 percent Coloureds, 0.2 percent Asians, and 96 percent whites.

These statistics indicate that race, gender, and class intersect in many different ways and that, because of built-in privilege, little is likely to change on its own. Although, to a certain extent, jobs have changed hands in the political sphere, the extent to which educational opportunity is affected by family circumstances will continue to influence patterns of privilege and reward in the absence of affirmative action measures.

Such measures, however, are up against the consequences of a sedimented social structure within which whites will naturally do all that they can to retain their positions and to educate their children. They are also up against traditional attitudes toward blacks, women, and the disabled, plus cynicism about employment equity on the part of many of those impacted by it. Even so, employment equity and affirmative action measures are necessary to eradicate historical and present-day discrimination. As a process of reparation, they are both imperfect and complex. However, without them, not only will the scars of apartheid remain, but also the talents of a broad cross-section of South Africans will remain underutilized, to the detriment of the economy and the country.[7]

NOTES

1. *Employment Equity Bill* (Pretoria: Department of Labour, 1997, 1998).

2. Roy L. Brooks, *Integration or Separation? A Strategy for Racial Equality* (Cambridge: Harvard University Press, 1996), p. 73.

3. See, e.g., *United Steelworkers v. Weber*, 443 U.S. 193, 208 (1979); Roy L. Brooks, "The Affirmative Action Issue: Law, Policy, and Morality," *Connecticut Law Review* 22 (1990): 323, 341; Alfred W. Blumrosen, *Improving Equal Employment Opportunities: Lessons from the United States Experience* (paper prepared for Royal Commission on Employment Opportunity of the Government of Canada), pp. 423–440.

4. "White Paper on Affirmative Action in the Public Service," Notice 564 of 1998 (Pretoria: Department of Public Service and Administration, 1998), p. 4.

5. Frank Parkin, *Marxism and Class Theory: A Bourgeois Critique* (London: Tavistock, 1979).

6. Anthony Heath, *Social Mobility* (Glasgow: Fontana, 1981).

7. See Linda Human, "Discrimination and Equality in the Workplace: Defining Affirmative Action and Its Role and Limitations," *International Journal of Discrimination and the Law* 2 (1996): 23–37.

Suggested Readings

Biko, Steven. *I Write What I Like*. New York: Harper and Row, 1978.

Gordimer, Nadine. *July's People*. New York: Viking Press, 1981.

Langston, Lundy R. "Affirmative Action, A Look at South Africa and the United States: A Question of Pigmentation or Leveling the Playing Field?" *American University Law Review* 13 (1997): 333.

Mallaby, Sebastian. *Nelson Mandela*. New York: St. Martin's Press, 1998.

Meredith, Martin. *Nelson Mandela: A Biography*. New York: St. Martin's Press, 1998.

Paton, Alan. *Cry, the Beloved Country*. New York: Charles Scribner's Sons, 1948.

"Symposium: Constitution-Making in South Africa," *Michigan Journal of Race and Law* 3 (1997): 1–306.

Appendix

Selected List of Other Human Injustices

Brazilian Slave Trade (1500–1888). Brazil imported more black slaves than any other nation in the Western hemisphere. The president of Brazil drafted policies aimed at compensating Afro-Brazilians in 1996.

Removal of Aboriginal Children from Their Original Families by the Australian Government and the Catholic Church (1850–1967). Australian state and federal policies encouraged the removal of as many as one hundred thousand Aboriginal children from their families. The Catholic Church's assimilation policy was aimed at eliminating the spiritual and cultural identities of Aborigines. Children were placed in "welfare" camps or church-run orphanages. While under government care, many of the children were physically and sexually abused or forced to work as unpaid laborers. The Catholic Church issued an apology in 1996.

New Zealand Race Wars (1863). British-initiated bloody race wars stripped New Zealand's Maoris of their tribal lands. Queen Elizabeth issued a formal apology and reparations in 1993. New Zealand issued an apology and reparations in 1996.

Overthrow of the Sovereign Kingdom of Hawaii (1893). The United States aided in the illegal overthrow of the sovereign Kingdom of Hawaii. An apology was issued in 1993.

Turkish Genocide of Armenians (1914–1915). At least 1 million Armenians were driven into the desert, beaten, starved to death, or forced into labor camps following official orders of the central government of Turkey.

Armistrar Massacre (1919). British soldiers opened fire on a crowd of unarmed Indians protesting the extension of World War I detention laws. Between four hundred and one thousand were killed. Queen Elizabeth paid her respects at the scene of the massacre in 1997.

Soviet Massacre of Polish Officers (1935–1945). During World War II the Soviet secret police massacred fifteen thousand Polish officers. Boris Yeltsin issued an apology in 1993.

My Lai Massacre (1968). United States troops massacred 504 unarmed Vietnamese women, children, and old men at a hamlet called My Lai, located in central Vietnam.

Chilean Dictatorship (1973–1990). Thousands of Chileans were tortured, murdered, or exiled by General Augusto Pinochet after he seized power and declared himself President of Chile.

Khmer Rouge's Reign of Terror (1975–1979). An estimated 2 million Cambodians were starved, worked to death, or executed by communist leader Pol Pot. This extermination effort was later termed "the killing fields."

Argentine Persecution of Suspected Leftist Dissidents in the "Dirty War" (1976–1983). At least nine thousand suspected leftist dissidents were arrested, tortured, and possibly murdered by Argentine naval officials during what was called the "Dirty War."

Gendarmerie Terrorization in Senegal (1983–Present). Gendarmerie, an armed opposition group, is responsible for the arbitrary arrest, brutal mutilation, and torture of Casamance citizens. Crimes include forced confessions from suspects, torture in front of family members, unlawful executions, and possible mass graves. Since 1990, they have also killed villagers who refuse to give the group food or money.

Tienanmen Square Massacre (1989). Hundreds of lives were lost in a bloodbath in Beijing, China, when the People's Liberation Army (PLA) killed protesters who blocked their path. Many of the protesters were unarmed students and workers who were killed as they were pinned under road blocks and military equipment.

Indian Oppression of Kashmiris (1989–Present). Thousands of Kashmir people have been raped, tortured, and murdered by Indian forces who occupy the country of Kashmir.

Taliban Oppression in Afghanistan (1992–Present). Taliban leaders and militia have tortured and killed thousands of civilians in Afghanistan during their struggle for power.

Rwandan Genocide (1994). In Rwanda the extremist Hutu government killed more than five hundred thousand Tutsis and moderate Hutus in a mass extermination effort.

Croatian Army's Forced Serbian Exile (1995). Approximately 150,000 Serbs who lived in the Krajina region were forced to flee their homes to Bosnia and Serbia by the Croatian Army.

Massacre in Bosnia (1995). Bosnian Serbs killed as many as 7,000 Muslims in a rural area outside Srebrenica in what has been called the worst war crime in Bosnian history. The United Nations has indicted two Bosnian Serb leaders for genocide.

Shan State Atrocities in Myanmar (1996–1998). Hundreds of the Shan ethnic minority have been tortured and killed by the Burmese army. Approximately three hundred thousand were also forced to leave their homes.

Rebel Killings in Sierra Leone (1996–Present). Hundreds of unarmed civilians are being brutally killed and mutilated by members of the Armed Forces Revolutionary Council (AFRC) and the Revolutionary United Front (RUF). The war of terror waged by the rebel alliance against Sierra Leone citizens has also resulted in the amputations, rapes, enslavement, and abduction of civilians.

Ethnic Riots in Indonesia (1998). Brutal riots resulted in the death of at least one thousand people in Jakarta alone. In addition, approximately 150 women, mostly of the Chinese minority, were raped and thousands of shops and vehicles were set on fire.

Contributors

AMERICAN HORSE, a leader among the Sioux Indians, lived in the nineteenth century.

KARL R. BENDETSEN, former Undersecretary of the Army and Special Assistant to the Secretary of State during World War II, died in 1989.

JEFFREY T. BENZIEN is a former official in the South African Police.

HAIRY BEAR, a member of the Ponca Indians, lived in the nineteenth century.

BORIS I. BITTKER is Sterling Professor of Law Emeritus at Yale University and the author of several books and numerous articles in the areas of federal taxation and political and civil rights.

DR. ALEXANDER BORAINE is the Vice Chairperson of the South African Truth and Reconciliation Commission.

ROY L. BROOKS is Warren Distinguished Professor of Law at the University of San Diego and the author of twelve books and numerous articles in several areas, including human and civil rights.

IRIS CHANG is a full-time author living in California. She is the recipient of the John T. and Catherine D. MacArthur Foundation's Program on Peace and International Cooperation award, as well as major grants from the National Science Foundation, the Pacific Cultural Foundation, and the Harry Truman Library.

JENNIFER F. CHEW received her J.D. from the University of California Hastings College of the Law in 1994.

JOHN CONYERS is a Democratic congressman from Michigan.

RADHIKA COOMARASWAMY, a lawyer, is the Special Rapporteur on Violence Against Women to the U.N. Commission on Human Rights. Pursuant to her mandate, Ms. Coomaraswamy is investigating the causes and consequences of violence against women around the world, focusing on prevention, punishment for perpetrators, and the provision of remedies for victims. She also directs the International Center for Ethnic Studies in Colombo, Sri Lanka, and is a founder of the Asia Pacific Forum on Women, Law and Development.

ROGER DANIELS served in the armed forces during World War II and the Korean War. He has published widely, but is especially known for his works on Japanese Americans. Daniels has worked as a consultant to the Commission on Wartime Relocation and Internment of Civilians (CWRIC) and has participated in making a number of historical films for television. He is Professor of History at the University of Cincinnati.

ALAN DAVIES is Professor of Religion at the University of Toronto. A native of Montreal, Canada, he is the author or editor of several books dealing with the subjects of religion and anti-Semitism.

FREDERICK WILLEM DE KLERK succeeded P. W. Botha as president of South Africa in 1989 and began the process of ending state-sanctioned apartheid by freeing Nelson Mandela from prison and legalizing the previously banned African National Congress. This ultimately led to South Africa's transition to black majority rule. In 1993, de Klerk shared the Nobel Peace Prize with Nelson Mandela, his presidential successor.

JOE R. FEAGIN, Graduate Research Professor of Sociology at the University of Florida, has done extensive research on racism and sexism issues. His research can be seen in three dozen books. He has served as a scholar-in-residence at the United States Commission on Civil Rights (1974–1975), and is currently a nominee for president of the American Sociological Association.

JENNIFER FLEISCHNER is Associate Professor of English at University of Albany, State University of New York. The author or editor of several books, she is currently writing a book about Elizabeth Keckley and Mary Lincoln.

GERALD R. FORD, the thirty-eighth president of the United States, served in the Congress for twenty-five years, including a stint as House Minority Leader. He was the first vice president chosen under the terms of the Twenty-fifth Amendment and, in the aftermath of the Watergate scandal, succeeded the first president ever to resign, Richard M. Nixon.

JOHN HOPE FRANKLIN is James B. Duke Professor of History Emeritus and for seven years was Professor of Legal History at Duke University Law School. His numerous publications have instructed generations of students about the African American ethos. In addition, he is a recipient of the Presidential Medal of Freedom as well as more than one hundred honorary degrees. He served as Chair for President Clinton's Initiative on Race Advisory Board.

HOWARD W. FRENCH is an award-winning writer for the *New York Times* specializing in African affairs.

LAURENCE ARMAND FRENCH has a Ph.D. in sociology and in psychological and cultural studies. He is the author of dozens of articles and seven books on Native American issues. French is a Professor of Psychology and the Chair of the Department of Social Sciences at Western New Mexico University.

THOMAS GEOGHEGAN is a labor lawyer and author.

JAMES GRAHAME, Esq., a British citizen who lived in the nineteenth century, received his LL.D. from Harvard University.

TONY P. HALL is a Democratic congressman from Ohio.

The Honorable IAN HANCOCK is Professor of English, Linguistics, and Asian Studies at the University of Texas at Austin. He is the Roma representative to the United Nations and to UNICEF, Praesidium Head of the International Romani Union, and was appointed to the United States Holocaust Memorial Council by President Clinton in 1997. He was 1997 winner of the Rafto International Human Rights Prize (Norway) and 1998 recipient of the Gamaliel Chair in Peace and Justice. He has authored nearly three hundred articles and books.

LESLIE T. HATAMIYA is the daughter of former Japanese American internees and a graduate of Stanford Law School. She has served as Special Assistant to former U.S. Senator Bill Bradley of New Jersey and as a law clerk to Judge David Tatel of the United States Court of Appeals for the D.C. Circuit.

GEORGE HICKS is a professional writer who lives in Singapore and is a leading scholar on Japan's war crimes.

A. LEON HIGGINBOTHAM, JR., was Public Service Professor of Jurisprudence at the John F. Kennedy School of Government, Harvard University, and of counsel to Paul, Weiss, Rifkind, Wharton & Garrison. He also served as Chief Judge on the United States Court of Appeals for the Third Circuit, was a recipient of the Presidential Medal of Freedom, and was one of the most respected scholarly jurists in America.

RICK HILL is a member of the faculty in the American Studies Department at University of Buffalo, State University of New York. He is a member of the Tuscarora Nation, an activist scholar, and a museum professional.

LINDA HUMAN is a professor at the University of Stellenbosh School of Business in South Africa.

TETSUO ITO was the Director of the Legal Affairs Division, Treaties Bureau, Ministry of Foreign Affairs of Japan. He is currently Counselor for the Japanese Embassy in London.

JUDITH JAEGERMANN (née Pinczovsky) is a Holocaust survivor who has devoted her life to teaching about the Holocaust.

ROBERT JOHNSON, JR., is a playwright, attorney, and Professor of Africana Studies at the University of Massachusetts, Boston.

HUBERT KIM is a law student at the University of San Diego School of Law, Class of 1999.

RUTH LEVOR is Associate Director of the Legal Research Center of the University of San Diego School of Law.

LITTLE HILL, chief of the Winnebago Indians, lived in the nineteenth century.

EMILY H. McCARTHY is Law Clerk to the Honorable Norma Holloway Johnson, Chief Judge, United States District Court for the District of Columbia. She received her J.D. from the University of Michigan Law School in 1997.

JOHN J. McCLOY, former Assistant Secretary of War during World War II, and Wall Street lawyer, died in 1989.

ROBERT S. McELVAINE is Elizabeth Chisholm Professor of Arts and Letters and Chair of the Department of History at Millsaps College in Jackson, Mississippi. He is the author of several books.

NAOMI MEZEY is Associate Professor of Law at Georgetown Law Center.

NORMAN Y. MINETA is a former Democratic congressman from California.

HLENGIWE MKHIZE is Chairperson of the Reparation and Rehabilitation Committee of the Truth and Reconciliation Commission in South Africa.

BASSIE MKHUMBUZI is a member of the Pan African Congress and African People's Liberation Army.

ALFRED A. MOSS, JR., is Associate Professor of History at the University of Maryland, College Park.

C. J. MUNFORD is Professor of Black Studies and History at the University of Guelph, Ontario, Canada. He has taught in Nigeria, Europe, and the United States. He is an award-winning author of numerous scholarly books on the black experience worldwide.

NELL JESSUP NEWTON is Dean and Professor of Law at the University of Denver College of Law in Denver, Colorado, and a leading scholar on Native American law.

KENNETH B. NUNN is Professor of Law at the University of Florida. He is Cooperating Attorney for the NAACP Legal Defense Fund and a member of the Executive Committee of the National Association for Public Interest Law.

EILEEN O'BRIEN is a doctoral candidate in sociology at the University of Florida, specializing in race and ethnic relations. Her current research is on white antiracist activities in the United States. She has contributed to two edited volumes and is completing her dissertation on this topic.

OTTO OHLENDORF was Nazi SS Group Leader, Lieutenant General of Police, and Director of the Reich Security Main Office.

CAMILLE PAGLIA is Professor of Humanities at the University of the Arts in Philadelphia. She is a best-selling author and public intellectual.

PALANEAPOPE, a member of the Sioux Indians, lived in the nineteenth century.

KAREN PARKER received her J.D. from the University of San Francisco in 1983; Diplome (International and Comparative Law of Human Rights), Strasbourg. She practices in the fields of international human rights and humanitarian (armed conflict) law and is the chief representative to the United Nations of International Educational Development, Inc. In 1989, she coauthored the Jandel-Parker Report to the Commission on Human Rights on Substitute Prisons in Japan.

ANTHONY R. PICO is Chairman of the Viejas Band of Kumeyaay Indians in California.

WANDA POLTAWSKA is a Holocaust survivor and an author.

DARRELL L. PUGH is Professor of Public Administration and Urban Studies and Director of the Graduate Program in Public Administration at San Diego State University.

FRANKLIN DELANO ROOSEVELT (1882–1945), the thirty-second president of the United States and architect of the New Deal, led the United States through the turmoil of the Great Depression and World War II. Earlier in his career, Roosevelt served as a New York state senator, assistant secretary of the Navy, and two terms as the governor of New York. He was the only American president to be elected to four terms.

SUSAN K. SERRANO received her J.D. from the University of Hawaii School of Law in 1998 and is Law Clerk to Justice Robert Klein of the Hawaii Supreme Court.

WILLIAM TECUMSEH SHERMAN (1820–1891) was one of the more controversial figures of the American Civil War. As a general in the Union army, he was best known for the scorched-earth tactics he employed during the military campaign in Georgia, culminating in the burning of Atlanta and his infamous March to the Sea. Prior to the war, Sherman was superintendent of the Louisiana State Seminary and Military Academy, which later became Louisiana State University.

BERNARD H. SIEGAN is Distinguished Professor of Law at the University of San Diego School of Law.

MARY E. SMITH is a law student at the University of California at Berkeley, Boalt Hall, Class of 2000.

ABBY SNYDER is a law student at the University of San Diego School of Law, Class of 1999.

SANDRA TAYLOR is Professor of History at the University of Utah. She has published many books and articles in American diplomatic history. Her special interests lie in American–East Asian relations and the history of Japanese Americans.

TURNING HAWK, a leader among the Sioux Indians, lived in the nineteenth century.

WILHELM VERWOERD teaches in the Department of Philosophy at the University of Stellenbosch and was a researcher for the Truth and Reconciliation Commission in Cape Town, South Africa.

ROBERT A. WILLIAMS, JR., is Professor of Law and American Indian Studies at the University of Arizona. He is a member of the Lumbee Indian Tribe of North Carolina and a leading scholar in Native American law.

PETE WILSON is the former governor of California and a Republican.

ERIC K. YAMAMOTO is Professor of Law at the University of Hawaii. He has served as an advisor to the Native Hawaiian Advocacy Council and is a member of the Board of Directors for the Advocates for Public Interest Law.

Permissions

The editor and publisher wish to thank the following for permission to use copyright material.

Hippocrene Books, Inc., for: "The Human 'Guinea Pigs' of Ravensbruck," *And I Am Afraid of My Dreams* (New York: Hippocrene Books, 1989).

The New York Times Company for: Howard W. French, "The Atlantic Slave Trade: On Both Sides, Reasons for Remorse," *New York Times*, April 5, 1998, sec. 4 (Week in Review), p. 1. © 1998 by The New York Times Company. Reprinted by permission.

Oxford University Press for: *In the Matter of Color: Race and the American Legal Process: The Colonial Period* by A. Leon Higginbotham, Jr., © 1978 by Oxford University Press, Inc. Used by permission of Oxford University Press, Inc.

Random House, Inc., for: *From Slavery to Freedom*, 6th edition, by John Hope Franklin. © 1987 by Alfred A. Knopf, Inc. Reprinted by permission of the publisher.

Salon Magazine for: Camille Paglia, "Ask Camille" column, July 8, 1997, *Salon* Magazine at http://www.salonmagazine.com.

Smithsonian Institution for: Tamara L. Bray and Thomas W. Killion, eds., *Reckoning with the Dead*, © 1994; published by the Smithsonian Institution.

Stanford Law Review for: Naomi Mezey, "The Distribution of Wealth, Sovereignty, and Culture through Indian Gaming," *Stanford Law Review* 48 (1996): 711–716, 736–737. © 1996 by the Board of Trustees of the Leland Stanford Junior University.

University of California, Hastings College of the Law, for: "Compensation for Japan's World War II War-Rape Victims," *Hastings International and Comparative Law Review*, Vol. 17, No. 3, pp. 498–510, 536–541. © 1994 by University of California, Hastings College of the Law.

University of Michigan for: Emily H. McCarthy, "South Africa's Amnesty Process: A Viable Route toward Truth and Reconciliation?" *Michigan Journal of Race and Law* 3 (1997): 248–253.

University of Washington Press for: Roger Daniels, et al., *Japanese Americans: From Relocation to Redress,* pp. 3–5, 8, 213–216, 219–221. © 1991 by the University of Washington Press.

Index

Except when Anglicized, Asian names have not been inverted in honor of the Asian tradition.

About the Editor

Roy L. Brooks is Warren Distinguished Professor of Law at the University of San Diego. He received his J.D. from Yale University where he served as Senior Editor of the *Yale Law Journal*. After law school, he served as a law clerk to the Honorable Clifford Scott Green, United States District Court Judge for the Eastern District of Pennsylvania. He then practiced corporate and securities law at the New York law firm of Cravath, Swaine & Moore.

Professor Brooks began his teaching career in 1979 at the University of San Diego. He has taught courses in civil procedure, civil rights, jurisprudence, corporate finance, corporations, employment discrimination law, and public law litigation at San Diego, the University of Minnesota Law School (where he was tenured from 1990–92), the University of Florida Law School (serving as the Stephen C. O'Connell Visiting Professor of Law, spring 1992), and the University of California at San Diego (appointed as Distinguished Visiting Professor in the Ethnic Studies Department, fall 1993). His appointment as Warren Distinguished Professor came in 1995. Professor Brooks has written twelve books including *Integration or Separation? A Strategy for Racial Equality* (Harvard University Press, 1996) and *Rethinking the American Race Problem* (University of California Press, 1990), both of which received the Meyer Center Outstanding Book Award. He also has written dozens of articles, given several nationally distinguished lectures including the Virgil Hawkins Address and the Carter G. Woodson Lecture, and presented over two dozen scholarly papers at Harvard Law School, Yale Law School, Michigan Law School, Bowdoin College, and other law schools, colleges, and universities. He is a member of the American Law Institute, the Author's Guild, and the Authors League of America.